Improving Outcomes with Clinical Decision Support: An Implementer's Guide

Second Edition

Jerome A. Osheroff, MD, FACP, FACMI
Jonathan M. Teich, MD, PhD, FACMI, FHIMSS
Donald Levick, MD, MBA, FHIMSS
Luis Saldana, MD, MBA, FACEP
Ferdinand T. Velasco, MD
Dean F. Sittig, PhD, FACMI, FHIMSS
Kendall M. Rogers, MD, CPE, FACP, SFHM
Robert A. Jenders, MD, MS, FACP, FACMI

CRC Press is an imprint of the
Taylor & Francis Group, an **informa** business

Sponsor
Agency for Healthcare Research and Quality

CRC Press
Taylor & Francis Group
6000 Broken Sound Parkway NW, Suite 300
Boca Raton, FL 33487-2742

© 2012 by Taylor & Francis Group, LLC
CRC Press is an imprint of Taylor & Francis Group, an Informa business

Visit the Taylor & Francis Web site at
http://www.taylorandfrancis.com

and the CRC Press Web site at
http://www.crcpress.com

Contents

Authors and Project Leadership

Jerome A. Osheroff, MD, FACP, FACMI
Principal
TMIT Consulting, LLC
Cherry Hill, NJ
Strategic Advisor*
Thomson Reuters
Adjunct Associate Professor of Medicine
University of Pennsylvania
Philadelphia, PA

Jonathan M. Teich, MD, PhD, FACMI, FHIMSS
Chief Medical Informatics Officer
Elsevier Health Sciences
Philadelphia, PA
Assistant Professor of Medicine
Harvard University
Department of Emergency Medicine
Brigham and Women's Hospital
Boston, MA

Donald Levick, MD, MBA, FHIMSS
Chief Medical Information Officer
Lehigh Valley Health Network
Allentown, PA

Luis Saldana, MD, MBA, FACEP
Associate Chief Medical Information Officer
Texas Health Resources
Arlington, TX

Ferdinand T. Velasco, MD
Chief Medical Information Officer
Texas Health Resources
Arlington, TX

Dean F. Sittig, PhD, FACMI, FHIMSS
Professor
University of Texas School of Biomedical Informatics
    at Houston
UT-Memorial Hermann Center for Healthcare
    Quality and Safety
National Center for Cognitive Informatics and
    Decision Making
Houston, TX

Kendall M. Rogers, MD, CPE, FACP, SFHM
Associate Professor of Medicine
Chief of Hospital Medicine
University of New Mexico Health Sciences Center
Albuquerque, NM

Robert A. Jenders, MD, MS, FACP, FACMI
Staff Scientist
National Library of Medicine
U.S. National Institutes of Health
Bethesda, MD
Professor of Medicine
Georgetown University
Washington, DC

---

* During development of this book, Dr. Osheroff was Chief Clinical Informatics Officer for Thomson Reuters.

Acknowledgments

Associate Editors

Dylan R. Sherry
Researcher
Partners HealthCare System
Boston, MA

Chuck Appleby
Principal
Appleby Ink Strategic Communications
Benicia, CA

Major Reviewers/Contributors

These individuals reviewed the entire manuscript
and provided substantial input.

Raymond Trenor Williams, MD
CEO
Clinovations
Washington, DC

Adam Wright, PhD
Assistant Professor of Medicine
Harvard Medical School
Research Scientist
Division of General Medicine
Brigham and Women's Hospital
Boston, MA

Major Component Reviewers/ Contributors

These individuals reviewed components of the book
and provided substantial input.

Anne M. Bobb, RPh
Director, Informatics Quality
Children's Memorial Hospital
Chicago, IL

Joseph Fortuna, MD
CEO
PRISM
Troy, MI

James L. Holly, MD
CEO
Southeast Texas Medical Associates
Beaumont, TX

Robert J. Jackson, MD, MMM
President and Medical Director
Accountable Healthcare Alliance
Allen Park, MI

LuAnn Kimker, RN, MSN
Principal Consultant
Arcadia Solutions
Burlington, MA

Paul Kleeberg, MD, FAAFP, FHIMSS
Medical Director, Clinical Decision Support
HealthEast Care System
Saint Paul, MN

Eboni Price-Haywood, MD, MPH
Co-Executive Director
Tulane Community Health Centers
Chief Medical Officer
Tulane University Office of Community Affairs and
    Health Policy
New Orleans, LA

Jacob Reider, MD
Albany Medical College
Albany, NY

ONC and ACDS Contributors
ONC Contributors

These staff members from the U.S. Department of Health and Human Services, Office of the National Coordinator for Health Information Technology (ONC), provided helpful input on components of the Guide, facilitated the collaboration with the Advancing Clinical Decision Support (ACDS) project outlined below or the ONC Regional Extension Centers, or facilitated content development in other ways.

Parmeeth Atwal, JD, MPH
Health Communications Specialist

Melinda Beeuwkes Buntin, PhD
Director of the Office of Economic Analysis, Evaluation and Modeling

Matthew F. Burke, MPA
Policy Analyst

Charles Friedman, PhD
Chief Scientific Officer

Geoffrey Gerhardt
Senior Policy Advisor to the National Coordinator

Leah Marcotte
Policy Analyst, Meaningful Use Team
MD Candidate, University of Pennsylvania School of Medicine

Aaron McKethan
Director of the Beacon Community Program

CDR Alicia Morton, DNP, RN-BC
Senior Analyst

Farzad Mostashari, MD, ScM
National Coordinator for Health Information Technology

Kyle E. Nicholls
Project Officer, Meaningful Use

Kristen Ratcliff
Special Assistant to the National Coordinator

Allen Traylor, MPH, MBA
Policy Analyst, Meaningful Use

Keviar Warner
Executive Assistant to the National Coordinator

ACDS Contributors

These individuals contributed via a collaboration between HIMSS and ONC's ACDS project. Members of the respective teams collaborated on developing closely related content around CDS implementation lessons, as required for selected ACDS deliverables and this HIMSS guidebook update. The resulting material was then adapted for each distribution channel.

Douglas S. Bell, MD, PhD
Principal Investigator of the ACDS Project
Research Scientist
RAND Corporation
Los Angeles, CA

Colene Byrne, PhD
Senior Study Director
Westat, Inc.
Cambridge, MA

Doug Johnston, MTS
Senior Study Director
Westat, Inc.
Cambridge, MA

Lauren Mercincavage, MHS
Research Associate
Westat, Inc.
Cambridge, MA

Blackford Middleton, MD
Co-Principal Investigator of the ACDS Project
Director for Clinical Informatics Research and
    Development
Partners HealthCare System, Inc.
Boston, MA

Eric Pan, MD
Senior Study Director
Westat, Inc.
San Diego, CA

Gordon Schiff, MD
Associate Director
Center for Patient Safety Research and Practice
Brigham and Women's Hospital
Boston, MA

Dylan R. Sherry
Researcher
Partners HealthCare System, Inc.
Boston, MA

Other Reviewers/Contributors

These individuals provided helpful feedback and input to specific components of the book such as the Tasks, Considerations for Hospitals/Health Systems and Small Practices, HIT Software Providers, Case Studies, and other elements.

Vinod Aggarwal, MD, MSHI
Physician IT Adoption Expert
McKesson Provider Technologies
Houston, TX

Adele Allison
National Director
Government Affairs
SuccessEHS Inc.
Birmingham, AL

Joan Ash, PhD, MLS, MS, MBA
Professor and Vice Chair
Department of Medical Informatics and Clinical
    Epidemiology
Oregon Health & Science University
Portland, OR

David W. Baker, MD, MPH
Michael A. Gertz Professor in Medicine
Chief, Division of General Internal Medicine
Feinberg School of Medicine, Northwestern
    University
Chicago, IL

Eytan Behiri, MD
Director, CIS EBM and Order Sets
North Shore-Long Island Jewish Health System
New York, NY

Elisabeth Belmont, Esq.
Corporate Counsel
MaineHealth
Portland, ME

Eta S. Berner, EdD
Professor, Health Informatics
Department of Health Services Administration
University of Alabama at Birmingham
Birmingham, AL

Keith W. Boone
Standards Architect
GE Healthcare
Boston, MA

William F. Bria, MD, FCCP, FHIMSS
CMIO
Shriners Hospital for Children
Board President
Association of Medical Directors of Information
    Systems (AMDIS)
Tampa, FL

Jane Brokel, PhD, RN
Assistant Professor
University of Iowa
Iowa City, IA

James Bulger
Manager, Library Services
Allina Hospitals & Clinics
Minneapolis, MN

John Chuo, MD, MS
Neonatal Quality Informatics Officer
Children's Hospital of Philadelphia
Assistant Professor of Pediatrics
University of Pennsylvania
Philadelphia, PA

David C. Classen, MD, MS
Associate Professor of Medicine
University of Utah
Salt Lake City, UT

Beverly Collins, RN, PhD-C
Clinical Decision Support Senior Analyst
Allina Hospitals & Clinics
Minneapolis, MN

David A. Collins, MHA, CPHQ, CPHIMS, FHIMSS
Senior Director
Professional Development
HIMSS
Chicago, IL

Steven Davidson, MD, MBA, FACEP, FACPE
CMIO
Maimonides Medical Center
Brooklyn, NY

Richard (Dick) H. Esham, MD, FACP
Medical Director
CPSI
Mobile, AL

Raymond Fabius, MD
Chief Medical Officer
Thomson Reuters
Philadelphia, PA

Robert Greenes, MD, PhD
Ira A. Fulton Chair and Professor
Department of Biomedical Informatics
Arizona State University
Scottsdale, AZ

Tonya Hongsermeier, MD, MBA
Principal Informatician
Partners HealthCare
Boston, MA

Ginger Hook, RN, MSN
Director Clinical Informatics
Saint Joseph Regional Medical Center
Mishawaka, IN
Clinical Informatics Steering Team
Trinity Health
Novi, MI

Shadaab Kanwal, MBA, MISM
Director, Clinical Informatics
UCLA Hospital System
Los Angeles, CA

Kensaku Kawamoto, MD, PhD
Director of Knowledge Management and
   Mobilization
University of Utah Health Care
Assistant Professor
University of Utah Department of Biomedical
   Informatics
Salt Lake City, UT

Geralyn Keane, RN, BSN, MSS, ELS
Manager Clinical Terminology
Thomson Reuters
Greenwood Village, CO

Maxine Ketcham, RN, MBA, CPHQ
Clinical Decision Support Analyst: CareConnect
Texas Health Resources
Arlington, TX

Michael Krall, MD, MS
Family Practice Physician
Northwest Permanente, PC
Portland, OR

Mary Lambert, MBA, RHIA
Director, Clinical Decision Support and
    Optimization
Allina Hospitals & Clinics
Minneapolis, MN

David F. Lobach, MD, PhD, MS, FACMI
Associate Professor and Chief
Division of Clinical Informatics
Department of Community and Family Medicine
Duke University School of Medicine
Durham, NC

Farah Magrabi, PhD
Senior Research Fellow
Centre for Health Informatics
Australian Institute of Health Innovation
University of New South Wales
Sydney, Australia

Rick Mansour, MD
CMIO, Allscripts
Associate Professor of Medicine
Feist-Weiller Cancer Center
Shreveport, LA

Greg Maynard, MD, MS
Clinical Professor of Medicine and Chief
Division of Hospital Medicine
University of California San Diego Medical Center
La Jolla, CA

Mike McGregory, PharmD, MBA, BCPS
Manager, Inpatient Pharmacy
Indiana University Health Methodist Hospital
Indianapolis, IN

Edward R. Melnick, MD
Assistant Professor
Dept. of Emergency Medicine
Yale University School of Medicine
New Haven, CT

Robert E. Murphy, MD
Chief Medical Informatics Officer
Memorial Hermann Healthcare System
Adjunct Associate Professor
University of Texas School of Biomedical Informatics
Houston, TX

Jeff Nielson, MD, MS
Director of Informatics
Dept. of Emergency Medicine
Summa Akron City and St. Thomas Hospitals
Akron, OH

Ken Ong, MD, MPH
Chief Medical Informatics Officer
New York Hospital Queens
Adjunct Assistant Professor
Columbia University School of Medicine and
    Mailman School of Public Health
New York, NY

Judy Ozbolt, PhD, RN, FAAN, FACMI, FAIMBE
Consultant in Health and Biomedical Informatics
Asheville, NC

Larry Ozeran, MD
President
Clinical Informatics, Inc.
Associate Clinical Professor
University of California Davis Health Informatics
    Program
Sacramento, CA

Thomas Payne, MD, FACP
Clinical Associate Professor, Health Services
Clinical Associate Professor, Medical Education &
    Biomedical Informatics
Clinical Associate Professor, Medicine
University of Washington
Seattle, WA

Stephen Persell, MD, MPH
Assistant Professor
Department of Medicine, Division of General
    Internal Medicine
Feinberg School of Medicine, Northwestern
    University
Chicago, IL

J. Rush Pierce, Jr., MD, MPH
Associate Professor
University of New Mexico
Albuquerque, NM

Eric Pifer, MD
Chief Medical Officer
El Camino Hospital
Mountain View, CA

Melissa Portz, RHIT
Senior Analyst - Clinical Decision Support
Allina Hospitals & Clinics
Minneapolis, MN

Gordon Schiff, MD
Associate Director
Center for Patient Safety Research and Practice
Brigham and Women's Hospital
Boston, MA

Richard Schreiber, MD, FACP
Chief Medical Informatics Officer
Holy Spirit Hospital
Camp Hill, PA

Dorian Seamster, MPH
Director of Quality Improvement Services
California Health Information Partnership and
    Services Organization (CalHIPSO)
Oakland, CA

Richard Shiffman, MD, MCIS
Associate Director for Education, Professor of
    Pediatrics
Center for Medical Informatics
Yale University School of Medicine
New Haven, CT

Joel Shoolin, DO, FAAFP, MBA
VP, Clinical Informatics
Advocate Health Care
Oak Brook, IL

Edward H. Shortliffe, MD, PhD, FACMI
President and Chief Executive Officer
AMIA
Bethesda, MD

Michael Shrift, MD
VP/CMIO
Allina Hospitals & Clinics
Minneapolis, MN

Steven R. Simon, MD, MPH, FACP
Chief, Section of General Internal Medicine
Veterans Affairs
Boston Healthcare System
Boston, MA

Elise Singer, MD, MBA
Chief Medical Officer
California Health Information Partnership and
    Services Organization (CalHIPSO)
Oakland, CA

Craig A. Umscheid, MD, MSCE
Assistant Professor of Medicine and Epidemiology
Director, Center for Evidence-based Practice
University of Pennsylvania
Philadelphia, PA

Mark Van Kooy, MD
Director of Medical Informatics
Aspen Advisors
Pittsburgh, PA

James M. Walker, MD, FACP
Chief Health Information Officer
Geisinger Health System
Danville, PA

P. Jon White, MD
Director, Health Information Technology
Agency for Healthcare Research and Quality
Rockville, MD

Andrew M. Wiesenthal, MD, SM
Director
Delioitte Consulting, LLP
San Francisco, CA

Administrative and Technical Support
The following individuals provided substantial technical and logistical support to the development of this book's content.

Raghav Srinivasan
Student, Drexel University/Intern, Thomson Reuters
Philadelphia, PA

Tisha Clinkenbeard
Clinical Information Systems Professional
Powderly, TX

Desiree Wilson
Executive Assistant
Thomson Reuters
Philadelphia, PA

Sponsor
The Agency for Healthcare Research and Quality (www.ahrq.gov) provided funding to support content development for this update under its Structuring Care Recommendations for Clinical Decision Support (eRecommendations) project.

Co-publishers

The other co-publishers of this book listed next supported HIMSS in this publishing effort by endorsing the work product, facilitating broad access to their membership for participation in content development (e.g., through organizational listserves), and assisting with dissemination of the material to their constituencies.

The following are brief statements by HIMSS and co-publisher executives about the relevance of this publication to their organization and membership.

Healthcare Information and Management Systems Society (HIMSS)
Patricia Wise, RN, MS, MA, FHIMSS,
Vice President, Healthcare Information Systems
As the healthcare industry's membership organization focused on providing global leadership for the optimal use of healthcare information technology and management systems for the betterment of healthcare, HIMSS is keenly interested in promoting clinical decision support as a highly effective method to improve patient safety and outcomes at the point of care and throughout the continuum of care. We were proud to publish the first edition in 2005 as a book designed to assist healthcare organizations in using CDS to measurably improve outcomes. That edition has become a landmark resource, used extensively by clinicians across the globe to help implement and fully leverage CDS, and it has become HIMSS' best-selling book of all time.

This new edition has been developed by an impressive group of authors, led again by Jerry Osheroff, who graciously gave their time and considerable expertise to significantly revise, expand, and enrich this Guide. This book is a groundbreaking collaboration of individuals and organizations, as evidenced by the diverse and highly experienced contributors and esteemed co-publishers. This new edition has substantial input from ONC and its

grantees, with explicit coverage in each chapter of considerations for small practices (in addition to a strong focus on hospitals and health systems). The book also includes input from—and detailed guidance for—health IT software vendors.

Together, all have contributed to this practical Guide that will surely assist CDS implementers in selecting, customizing, and implementing CDS to improve outcomes in their organizations.

Scottsdale Institute (SI)
Shelli Williamson, Executive Director, and
Stan Nelson, Chairman
The challenge of implementing and managing CDS systems, technologies, and governance will continue to be of critical importance to Scottsdale Institute members, many of whom are leaders in the development and use of these systems. SI member organizations are at the forefront of next-generation approaches to improving care quality, safety, and efficiency and in making sophisticated use of CDS to achieve these goals. As a forum for sharing IT-enabled best practices, the SI community has helped set the stage for major changes in care delivery that lead to better performance.

SI community members have both contributed to and benefited from other books in this series aimed at synthesizing and disseminating best practices for improving outcomes with CDS. Likewise, SI as an organization has played an important role by convening the collaborative that led to the 2009 book on CDS in medication management—and co-sponsoring and co-publishing that book. Co-publishing this book is a logical next step on this collaborative journey because it means bringing the knowledge and experience of many CDS leaders to the industry and thus supports our 501c3 mission: sharing best practices and lessons learned, which is at the heart of our purpose. Ultimately, we believe this virtual way of working together across organizations and industries will be expected and demanded for all those engaged in operations and quality improvement: both knowledge and its workers are becoming increasingly decentralized. We are proud to co-publish this important work and are confident that its use and impact will be ongoing and widespread.

American Medical Informatics Association (AMIA)

Edward H. Shortliffe, MD, PhD, FACMI, President and Chief Executive Officer

AMIA is the professional home for investigators and practitioners who are transforming healthcare through trusted science, education, and practice in biomedical and health informatics. AMIA members—4,000 informatics professionals from more than 65 countries—belong to a rigorous informatics community in which they actively share best practices and research for the advancement of the field. The organization and its members direct substantial attention to clinical decision support (CDS) and believe that such capabilities are central to realizing benefit from clinical systems. In 2006, an AMIA steering group worked with a wide range of collaborators to create a robust National Roadmap for Clinical Decision Support that identified key steps for progress with respect to knowledge management (KM) and CDS in the United States. This new edition again contributes to a realization of that Roadmap. AMIA is involved in many CDS-related efforts—an AMIA CDS workgroup now complements groups on clinical information systems (CISs) and clinical research, and new decision-support systems and methods are routinely presented at our scientific meetings.

AMIA is committed to continued leadership and collaboration on pivotal biomedical informatics challenges, such as CDS, that will shape the future of healthcare. Although these challenges are complex and significant, the potential for improvement and progress to date justify our commitment.

Association of Medical Directors of Information Systems (AMDIS)

William F. Bria, MD, FCCP, FHIMSS, Board President and Richard L. Rydell, CEO

The Association of Medical Directors of Information Systems is a 2,000-member organization of clinicians with formal responsibility for healthcare information technology leadership. In particular, AMDIS is dedicated to the education and networking of Chief Medical Information Officers (CMIOs). In the last decade, the CMIO role has evolved to become the central architect of the implementation of computerized CDS in healthcare. The evolution of applied medical informatics has transitioned from implementation and pure technology focus to integration and relevance to the point-of-care application of medical knowledge in service of improved safety and quality of care. CDS has now become the instrument by which the traditions of clinical practice, information technology, and medical research meet, fueling a new quality cycle. Going forward, CDS systems will be essential to education, practice, and refinement of healthcare delivery. AMDIS is proud to be a co-publisher of this work as we continue to champion the integration of informatics and patient care.

Society of Hospital Medicine (SHM)

Joseph Ming Wah Li, MD, SFHM, FACP, President, and Larry Wellikson, MD, SFHM, CEO

SHM is a professional organization representing over 30,000 hospitalists practicing in the U.S. Hospitalists are hospital-based physicians whose primary professional focus is the general medical care of hospitalized patients. Hospitalists care for more hospitalized patients than any other physician group, and we are uniquely positioned to lead the system-level changes and quality improvement efforts that are essential to the successful performance of hospitals and the healthcare systems. The niche of hospital medicine is in process and quality improvement, and our members are becoming leaders throughout the industry. SHM is dedicated to promoting the highest quality of care and quality of service for all patients.

SHM is committed to supporting technology that promotes improved quality and patient safety and recognizes clinical decision support as a critical tool to be utilized in achieving these goals. However, this science appears to be in its infancy and the exist-ing IT systems that hospitalists use on a daily basis are limited. Enhancing the development of this field needs to be a priority, given the potential that clinical decision support tools have to reduce harm and ensure the provision of optimal care to patients. It is our hope that this Guide will educate our hospitalist members about this critical resource, as well as drive the field forward in developing the tools that our front-line clinicians need to provide the highest quality of care.

Foreword

By Farzad Mostashari, MD, ScM
National Coordinator for Health Information Technology
Office of the National Coordinator for Health Information Technology
U.S. Department of Health and Human Services

In the 13 years since the Institute of Medicine published its report "To Err is Human," much has occurred, including passage in the U.S. of the most significant healthcare reform legislation since Medicare became law in the 1960s. These events have punctuated and accelerated a transformation of U.S. healthcare—resonant with related changes occurring around the globe—that is dizzying in its implications. Notwithstanding modern healthcare delivery's unfolding nature, an unbreakable thread runs through this transformation: the drive for better care quality, safety, efficiency and cost-effectiveness, and ultimately, better health.

Information technology, especially clinical IT, has become the critical enabler for these performance improvement imperatives. While a core of clinical IT is the electronic health record (EHR) incorporating computerized practitioner order entry (CPOE), the brains are clinical decision support or CDS. Simply put, CDS involves making sure that all those engaged in care processes—patients, nurses, physicians, pharmacists, and many others—have the information they need to make good decisions and take appropriate action that will lead to desirable outcomes. Straightforward to say, not so easy to do.

We know there are gaps in care delivery and opportunities for better healthcare processes and results. We also know that making an impact requires multiple factors occurring simultaneously: achieving widespread and successful clinical IT use, applying proven performance improvement techniques from healthcare and other industries, engaging patients in new ways of care, and (in the U.S. and elsewhere) reforming the payment system to support wellness, prevention, and efficient condition management.

Countries around the globe are pushing hard to fill those gaps and seize those opportunities, and CDS is a powerful improvement engine. In the U.S., for example, CDS plays a key role in Meaningful Use and is therefore an important component in the work of Regional Extension Centers (RECs), Beacon Communities and related public and private initiatives. As accountable care organizations (ACOs), the patient-centered medical home, health information exchanges and pay-for-performance drive new models of care and payment, effective clinical decision support will become an increasingly central component of these efforts as well.

As a domain within health informatics, we know that successful CDS implementation requires a balance of work with (1) people (who must drive the needed changes, the most difficult part), (2) process (what are we doing and why, at several different levels), and (3) technology (which we must leverage in context of the first two to drive better outcomes). In the current hyperdynamic healthcare environment, attributes of each dimension are undergoing substantial change. This further complicates the challenge of "getting CDS right."

CDS is a powerful tool for measurably improving care: getting the *right information* to the *right person* at the *right point in workflow* in the *right intervention format* through the *right channel*. This approach can be applied across the continuum of care, whether an acute-care hospital, physician's office, community clinic, patient's home—or anywhere in between. I have seen it in action.

I often reflect on my own experience with the Primary Care Information Project. Our mission was to improve health through the appropriate use of health IT, and we strove to provide the tools, incentives, and support for physicians in New York City to transition from paper to electronic records. I saw firsthand the critical role that CDS, when done right, can play in determining whether the EHR is simply an electronic "filing cabinet" or an indispensable tool by which to deliver better health. When we worked with EHR vendors to improve the usability and applicability of alerts, order sets, registries, and other tools in EHRs and showed physicians how to use these tools to measurably improve their quality of care, we watched as physicians who had previously been wary of technology quickly became its champions. Over a relatively short period, those who had previously been skeptics now couldn't imagine practicing medicine any other way. Indeed, ensuring the right information is available to the right person at the right time makes all the difference in the world.

Addressing pressing challenges in healthcare is literally a matter of life, death, and well-being for individuals and organizations around the world. Time is of the essence and resources are limited. Clinical decision support is a proven and powerful—yet complex—part of the solution, and we are a long way from realizing its full value. Much more work is needed to define, disseminate and apply best practices for improving care processes and outcomes by ensuring that all participants have the critical information they need, when, where, and how they need it. Collaborative efforts such as this Guide will be a key part of that effort.

Preface

This is more than a book—it's part of an important movement. Think of this Guide less as a book than as a dynamic roadmap for the journey to transform healthcare quality, safety, and efficiency. Members of the global healthcare community contributed to these best practices for improving care delivery with *clinical decision support* (CDS). You have an opportunity to be more than just a passive consumer of this material by contributing to this growing body of essential guidance. For example, Scottsdale Institute, the Society of Hospital Medicine, HIMSS, and others are beginning to develop a CDS collaborative to help implementers apply and enhance the concepts in this book as they address high-priority healthcare improvement targets. More about this in the Epilogue.

In almost all of the landmark studies of the last few decades that demonstrate the ability of health information technology (HIT) to prevent errors, reduce adverse events, and improve the quality of care, the gains came directly from applying CDS interventions—reminders, alerts, constrained choices, tailored forms, just-in-time references and others—to care processes. The seminal Institute of Medicine (IOM) reports beginning with "To Err is Human" endorsed CDS as one of the most powerful tools available in the national quest toward improved patient safety and healthcare quality.

CDS is all about intelligence: clinical knowledge and data intelligently applied at the point where healthcare decisions are made. A good CDS program provides the wellspring from which valuable CDS interventions that enhance care processes and outcomes emerge. Good CDS interventions, in turn, help make sure that information about the best way to treat an individual person with a specific condition is readily available, and consistently applied as appropriate. While CDS may find its most powerful incarnation in robust clinical IT platforms—electronic health records (EHRs), personal health records (PHRs), and many other complex and sophisticated systems—we approach CDS broadly in this Guide to include settings where these systems are not yet fully available. A warning sticker on a patient's paper chart can potentially save a life, and such low-tech approaches to decision support shouldn't be overlooked when they are the best that is available.

To have a positive impact and change the way care is delivered, the intelligent application of clinical knowledge requires a pragmatic approach that accounts for real-world opportunities and limitations. This is an implementer's Guide, not an academic tract—our aim is to provide practical advice useful for advancing CDS efforts in all types of care settings. Our history reflects this emphasis. This Guide is the culmination of the collective intelligence of scores of individuals, healthcare delivery organizations, professional societies, vendors and others who work every day to apply CDS to patient care in 'real world' settings.

CDS knowledge is advancing quickly as this movement gains momentum. This Guide is the fourth in the HIMSS CDS Guidebook series. The first collaborative effort in 2004 led to the online PDF publication, *The CDS Implementers Workbook*. This was downloaded thousands of times in the first few months it was published and was shortly followed in 2005 by the expanded volume developed with broader feedback, *Improving Outcome with Clinical Decision Support: An Implementer's Guide*, which this Guide updates. Used widely by CMIOs, IT staff, and quality leaders around the globe, this has become HIMSS' best-selling book ever—testifying to the strong and growing hunger of implementers and others for guidance on this subject that is such a critical component of healthcare performance improvement. That was followed in 2009 by *Improving Medication Use and Outcomes with Clinical Decision Support: A Step-by-Step Guide*, also published by HIMSS, which addressed implementers' expressed need for more detailed guidance on CDS strategies for improving specific high-priority objectives, starting with better use of medications. This book was developed by a broad collaboration of pertinent societies and individuals, and co-sponsored by a federal agency (AHRQ) and three clinical information systems vendors, and it too has become an award-winning bestseller.

This current Guide update contains highly vetted and practical guidance for addressing a central challenge in HIT-mediated performance improvement: getting CDS right. It is a very substantial update from the 2005 edition. All material was carefully reviewed and updated, with input from a broad array of knowledgeable stakeholders (see previous acknowledgments). Other major enhancements include dividing the content into separate parts that cover CDS programs and interventions and adding sections to each chapter on considerations for hospitals and health systems, small practices, and HIT suppliers. Also new are synthesized threaded case studies of the Guide's recommendations in action in a small practice and a community hospital.

The challenge of improving healthcare has never been primarily due to a lack of innovation, but in failing to implement, evaluate, and disseminate the myriad promising innovations awaiting our attention. That is true in CDS, for which low industry-wide adoption of effective approaches limits the value CDS interventions actually deliver. In many ways, the collaborative process embodied in this book and the broader HIMSS Guidebook series is just getting started. We remain committed until the job is done and hope you will join is in this quest.

Jerome A. Osheroff, MD, FACP, FACMI
Jonathan M. Teich, MD, PhD, FACMI, FHIMSS
Donald Levick, MD, MBA, FHIMSS
Luis Saldana, MD, MBA, FACEP
Ferdinand T. Velasco, MD
Dean F. Sittig, PhD, FACMI, FHIMSS
Kendall M. Rogers, MD, CPE, FACP, SFHM
Robert A. Jenders, MD, MS, FACP, FACMI

Introduction

SCOPE OF THE BOOK

The purpose of this Guide is to help drive measurable CDS-enabled improvements in care quality, patient safety, and efficiency. We hope to achieve this goal by providing practical, widely useful guidance on implementing CDS to information system implementers and developers, as well as other key participants in the care process.

Our overarching objective is to help the audience develop and implement a successful, sustainable CDS program. Under that programmatic umbrella, we want to help readers build their skills and success in selecting, prioritizing, configuring, testing and deploying, monitoring and enhancing CDS interventions that ultimately have high acceptance and positive impact.

We define CDS broadly and aim to provide a comprehensive CDS strategy that will be valuable for supporting care processes across the spectrum, from solo practices to large health systems in the U.S. and abroad.

AUDIENCE

The primary audience for whom this Guide is intended is CDS implementers:

- Hospitals and health systems, through CMIOs and their teams; medical, quality and safety officers interested in understanding the capabilities of HIT and CDS as arrows in their performance improvement quiver; clinicians engaged in supporting CDS programs;
- Physician office practices and those who support them, such as consultants, HIT Regional Extension Centers (RECs); and
- Others using clinical information systems in care delivery processes to achieve strategic and tactical goals.

This Guide is also aimed at the suppliers of EHRs, CDS interventions, and other HIT applications to help them build and integrate effective CDS tools into systems—tools that satisfy purchaser, implementer, and end-user needs and objectives and ultimately support better population health and healthcare delivery. We believe that there is significant opportunity to accelerate CDS-mediated performance improvement through better shared understanding of CDS goals, strategies and tools between HIT suppliers and implementers. We've designed this book—for example, by adding a section on Considerations for HIT Software Suppliers to each chapter—to help promote such improved collaboration.

Others will benefit from the Guide as a resource for building their understanding of the broad issues and nuances related to improving care processes and outcomes with CDS:

- Informatics and medical students;
- Healthcare and HIT policy makers;
- Public health staff;
- Hospital/practice administrative leaders;
- Informatics researchers;
- Payers interested in CDS as a tool for improving care quality, safety, and efficiency.

Potential CDS Guide users sometimes ask, "At what stage in the evolution of our [care delivery organization's] underlying technology infrastructure is it appropriate to start applying this guidance?" Our assumption is that every person and organization delivering care is somewhere on the journey to more sophisticated HIT use and that this Guide should provide value in optimizing that transition regardless of starting point. In that vein, this Guide should not only help those in settings with mature clinical IT infrastructure such as EHR with CPOE, but also should be valuable for those earlier in the journey—including those organizations on the trailing edge of achieving Meaningful Use in the United States or in otherwise resource-constrained environments in the U.S. or abroad.

HOW TO USE THIS BOOK

This book is about helping you do two things: **Part I** (Chapters 1 through 4) helps you set up (or refine) a successful CDS program in a hospital, health system, or physician practice; and **Part II** (Chapters 5 through 9) helps you configure and launch specific CDS interventions that recipients appreciate and that measurably improve targeted outcomes. At the beginning of each part, we provide a summary diagram to illustrate how the chapter topics flow, an overview of the key tasks discussed in the chapters, and two case studies that illustrate what it looks like when the recommended processes work well for hospitals and small physician practices, respectively.

The case studies are synthesized stories based on real-world experiences that illustrate how a "real-life" CDS program—and specific CDS interventions—might evolve in (1) a hypothetical community hospital, and (2) a hypothetical small physician practice. The hospital example is set in a 200-bed community hospital and explores reducing hospital-acquired blood clots (venous thromboembolism, or VTE), a common, severe and potentially preventable inpatient complication. The ambulatory example is set in a practice with five internal medicine physicians and explores improving diabetic patient management. These clinical conditions have global importance, and also feature prominently in Meaningful Use requirements in the U.S. These case studies can be helpful as an introduction to the key themes discussed in the chapters in each part. They can also be useful for reviewing key success factors and strategies, and communicating to others in your organization a picture of successful CDS activities.

After the last main chapter, the Epilogue provides information about ongoing collaborations to leverage CDS in improving outcomes, and the Appendix explores some medico-legal considerations that CDS implementers face.

We designed this Guide to be a broad and integrated roadmap for success with CDS but also modular to quickly address specific needs. Students and CDS implementers with limited CDS experience may wish to read this Guide linearly from the beginning through the end. If you are a CDS implementer, HIT vendor or other CDS stakeholder already familiar with CDS, and facing a specific need for guidance related to your CDS program or interventions, you may wish to jump directly to that section. The tasks and key lessons at the beginning of each chapter, as well as the many tables and worksheets throughout the book, may be particularly valuable for providing quick support on a particular issue without having to read the entire book.

CHAPTER STRUCTURE

Each of the nine chapters in this Guide follows a standard format with highly interdependent sections to guide you—whether implementer, HIT vendor, student or other CDS stakeholder—toward understanding and applying the chapter's guidance. These sections are:

Tasks
- An overview of what you must do in order to address the goals outlined in the chapter.

Key Lessons
- What you should know to address the tasks and achieve the chapter's objectives.

General Approach
- Main in-depth discussion of the chapter's key lessons and strategies.

Considerations for Hospitals/Health Systems
- Bulleted guidance on applying the General Approach in hospitals and health systems.

Considerations for Small Practices
- Bulleted guidance on applying the General Approach in small physician practices.

Considerations for Health IT Software Providers
- Bulleted guidance on the chapter's topic for HIT-solutions suppliers to help them and those who purchase and use their systems collaborate successfully on improving care delivery and outcomes with CDS.

Worksheets

- Forms to help you document and use information needed for your CDS program or interventions, as outlined in the chapter. The worksheets are populated with sample data to illustrate their use. These worksheets can generally be adapted for use in hospitals, health systems, large and small ambulatory practices and other settings.

References

- Resources that document, support and enhance the information presented in that chapter.

Part I

Building a Strong Conceptual Foundation and CDS Program

A poor farmer produces weeds.
A good farmer produces crops.
A wise farmer produces soil.

—Zen saying

The primary purpose for your clinical decision support activities is to provide CDS interventions into care delivery in a manner that improves care processes and outcomes. There is important organizational context in which these CDS interventions are selected, configured, deployed and produce results—whether in a solo physician practice or a large integrated delivery network. As we will define in more detail in Chapter 1, these contextual components together comprise the "CDS Program." When the program includes effective mechanisms for achieving clarity and alignment around CDS goals and strategies—and other core capabilities related to executing interventions—it is more likely that individual CDS initiatives will achieve desired results.

Using the metaphor in the quote at the beginning of this section, many attempts at CDS have produced weeds. Those organizations that can repeatedly leverage CDS to significantly and measurably improve targeted outcomes have cultivated effective and fruitful CDS programs.

Chapters 1 through 4 that follow provide guidance on developing (or refining) CDS programs so that they contain the necessary ingredients to reliably produce valuable CDS interventions. Figure PI-1 illustrates these building blocks and how they are addressed in the Part I chapters. Note

that knowledge management is an ongoing process that draws from and feeds back into CDS program management.

As described in the "How to Use This Book" section of the front matter, the introduction to each part contains two case studies—one in a community hospital and one in a small office practice. These hypothetical examples (based on synthesized real-world experiences) illustrate what it might look like to follow portions of the guidance presented in the chapters that follow.

You can examine the example(s) most pertinent to your setting before you dive into the chapter details, refer back to them as you review the chapter, and perhaps share the material with others on your team to help them understand the relevant processes and desired outcomes. In both case studies, each text section is introduced by a "Task" that relates to the material presented in the chapters. These headings help make explicit the key points that are being illustrated.

CASE STUDY FOR HOSPITALS: REDUCING POTENTIALLY PREVENTABLE INPATIENT VTE INCIDENCE

Establish a strong, shared foundation of knowledge for yourself and your team around basic

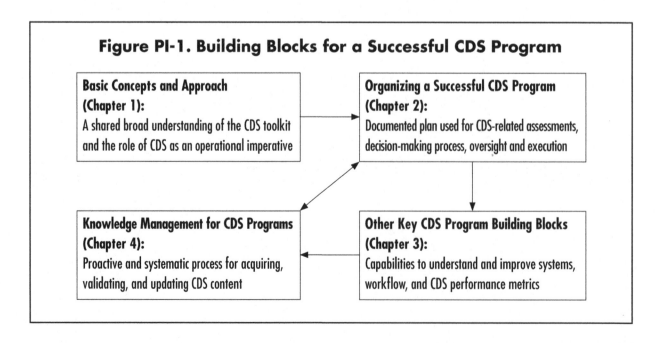

Figure PI-1. Building Blocks for a Successful CDS Program

Basic Concepts and Approach (Chapter 1):
A shared broad understanding of the CDS toolkit and the role of CDS as an operational imperative

Organizing a Successful CDS Program (Chapter 2):
Documented plan used for CDS-related assessments, decision-making process, oversight and execution

Knowledge Management for CDS Programs (Chapter 4):
Proactive and systematic process for acquiring, validating, and updating CDS content

Other Key CDS Program Building Blocks (Chapter 3):
Capabilities to understand and improve systems, workflow, and CDS performance metrics

concepts such as the broad CDS definition and toolkit, and CDS's role as a strategic tool for driving measurable performance improvement. Use this foundation to underpin your efforts to develop successful CDS programs and interventions.

At Grandview Hospital, Mrs. Sadie Adler, a 75-year-old postoperative hip fracture patient, developed a potentially preventable venous thromboembolism (VTE) and then died suddenly as a result. A review of her case at Grandview's Morbidity and Mortality Conference identified that she had not received interventions (broadly referred to as "VTE prophylaxis") that might have prevented this condition and tragic outcome.

Hospitalist Dr. Glenda Goldsmith had performed Mrs. Adler's pre-op evaluation, and after the Morbidity and Mortality Conference, she chose to champion this process improvement (PI) project for the hospital. Dr. Goldsmith understood the challenge was daunting but was fortunate to quickly enlist Grandview CEO Albert LaSalle's support after presenting this case to the Medical Executive Committee. CEO LaSalle noted that the hospital chose VTE as a quality measure in its contract with Alpha Health Plan and that addressing this issue effectively could also result in a bonus payment to the hospital. In addition, the Joint Commission had just requested that the hospital begin reporting its incidence rate of potentially preventable VTE.

These forces made it logical for Grandview and the Medical Executive Committee to select the improvement of VTE prophylaxis as a key performance goal for the next year. They created a financial incentive program to help ensure adequate attention—among myriad other priorities—to this initiative by pertinent stakeholders.

At the time of this tragic event, Grandview had strong nursing leadership and a physician champion for its electronic health record (EHR) efforts, but the remaining physicians were hesitant to change. The hospital was also fortunate to have IT and quality departments that were engaged and responsive. While Grandview had implemented computerized practitioner order entry (CPOE), at the time of this

event it had no house-wide VTE prophylaxis order sets—and the ones it had were scattered among admission and postoperative orders. Standardized risk assessment and prophylaxis selection were virtually nonexistent and clinical care varied widely. Among hospital employees, there was little awareness of VTE as a significant issue, and it was mostly up to individual physicians to order prophylaxis. Also, there were no checks for prophylaxis by nursing or pharmacy, and no regular auditing of VTE rates.

PI leader Goldsmith had been intrigued over the past few years by the promise of clinical decision support (CDS) to improve care processes and outcomes and spent time learning about this subject from journal articles, sessions at medical conferences, and books devoted to the topic. She had been a physician liaison for the CPOE implementation, and in light of Mrs. Adler's potentially preventable death, saw that there was tremendous opportunity to enhance Grandview's use of CDS to address VTE prophylaxis and other high-priority conditions. Her CDS studies had convinced her that for Grandview to be successful, it would need to build a robust CDS program that would provide fertile soil for CDS interventions focused on VTE prophylaxis and other key conditions could be developed and maintained over the long term. This would require the sustained effort and collaboration of many stakeholders and new organizational structures and processes. Potentially daunting, but …

Determine and document the who, why, what, how and when of your CDS approach and activities.

Fortunately, Grandview had a strong complement of leaders who shared a vision of quality care and patient safety. These included physician champions in medicine and surgery, a chief nursing officer and nursing executive champion, and a chief financial officer (CFO) who could appreciate the nuanced link between Grandview's financial health and its core healing mission. Other key quality advocates included the director of pharmacy, and the chief information officer (CIO) and his IT staff. Grandview had recently hired an internist on staff,

Dr. Fred Jones, as part-time director of clinical informatics. He had some formal informatics training and was initially engaged to support the hospital's EHR and CPOE efforts, but he would soon step up to a more central role in Grandview's improvement efforts.

The recent tragic events—and the attention they drew in various Grandview forums—galvanized recognition in these leaders that they must work together to more effectively leverage their information system to provide better care—not just for VTE prophylaxis, but for the increasing number of clinical goals and quality measures that were becoming important to the organization. They needed a new, but strong and effective, CDS program. The leaders committed early on to engaging the entire hospital on this journey. A key ingredient was to gain commitment from each clinical unit to measure and improve targeted outcomes and to engage in the full lifecycle of CDS interventions to drive this change.

Realizing that clinical, operational and financial outcomes were all-important and inter-related, they made sure that leaders with accountability for all these dimensions were engaged in developing the CDS program and that this effort would likewise be coordinated with other related organizational activities such as committees related to quality and operational improvement.

The CDS Committee was formally established with the support of senior administration. Clinical Informatics Director Jones was the natural choice to chair this committee, and he and Grandview agreed to increase his time devoted to this role (and corresponding compensation) to accommodate the additional important responsibilities. The CDS Committee included members who sat on existing relevant committees within the hospital. Members from the P&T Committee, the EHR Committee, the Patient Quality and Safety Committee and nursing unit directors, as well as senior leadership were represented. Leadership recognized the importance of "cross-pollinating" the committee so that the CDS Committee could both be influenced by and understand the committee's effect on other aspects of the

hospital's practices and culture. While the committee established its CDS charter and processes/procedures, VTE prophylaxis would be the first focus for the group. It was recognized, however, that this committee could not drive quality improvement (QI) projects itself, so they recommended the formation of a VTE QI Team with whom they would work closely on the specifics related to this condition.

Hospitalist Goldsmith, who had been inspired to become the physician leader in this effort, agreed to lead the VTE QI Team with a nursing unit director as co-chair. Leadership ensured that the team had adequate representation including two floor nurses, a pharmacist, an IT representative, a surgeon, the physician champion, nursing director and a quality consultant. Dr. Goldsmith would report and work directly with CDS Committee Chair Jones and the rest of the CDS Team to develop the tools recommended by the QI Team.

They began by evaluating the current state of VTE prophylaxis utilization: the hospital had open admitting and considered itself ahead of the game with a fully functional EHR and CPOE in place for three years. The QI Team quickly realized that the VTE-related death was not an isolated event. While difficult to monitor, Grandview floor nurses often reported patients not being placed on VTE prophylaxis. The surgeon on the QI Team reported not having any order sets or guidelines to help prompt him to remember to start VTE prophylaxis, and he was unaware as to how well his colleagues were doing in their prophylaxis efforts. He knew some doctors had added this to post-op orders, but there was no standardization. No one seemed to recognize the significant gap between the hospital's current approach to VTE prophylaxis and best practices.

At their first joint meeting, the QI Team and CDS Committee identified the committees with which they needed to interact in order to improve care processes and workflows. They noted that VTE prophylaxis is a part of national quality organization recommendations and aligned with hospital efforts to reduce non-reimbursed complications—so they would need to collaborate with all hospital groups focusing on those issues. Although an initial focus for the joint efforts was VTE prophylaxis, the CDS Committee participants recognized that that it would be important to use this particular improvement effort as a scalable model for approaching other PI projects. For example, they needed to determine who would take ownership of defining patient selection criteria, intervention standards of care and related protocols for best practice VTE prophylaxis—and would need to likewise achieve local consensus on best patient care practices as a central component of other CDS projects as well.

Understand and cultivate key CDS building blocks including your deployed information technology, documentation of clinical workflows and capacity to measure intervention effects.

Chair Jones and other CDS Committee members were aware that some EHR systems and CDS vendors had pre-configured CDS interventions that addressed VTE prophylaxis through risk assessment forms, order sets for appropriate therapy, and other tools. However, they didn't have any readily available documentation or shared sense of the information system capabilities and content, patient data availability and other key elements that would underpin their VTE CDS interventions. A first order of business was therefore to appoint a subgroup to gather this needed information.

From consultation with the QI Team, the CDS Committee realized the hospital had only anecdotal knowledge of its VTE prophylaxis performance—that is, how often it was actually received by patients for whom it was indicated. They realized that to measurably improve quality and safety, they needed reliable baseline and post-intervention data on key outcomes, as well as processes that contributed to those outcomes. For the VTE project, the CDS Committee and VTE QI Team decided that the outcome measure would be preventable VTE (how often patients developed a clinically evident VTE while in the hospital); the care process measures would be rate of 'any' prophylaxis and rate of 'appropriate' prophylaxis validated by a risk-assessment

tool. The team then devised a 'dashboard' for these measures with run graphs so they could see if the interventions had any impact over time. In addition, they agreed that as they selected specific CDS interventions to improve these measures, they would need additional metrics to shed light on whether and how these interventions were being used.

The QI Team's rough estimate was that approximately 75 percent of patients were on appropriate prophylaxis. However, when they tried to gather data from the EHR, it required time-consuming chart reviews because, at the time, reporting mechanisms with the level of detail needed couldn't be readily obtained from the system. Team members strongly agreed that going forward, they would ensure that reporting and measurement would be automated to the greatest extent practical in any intervention they designed. Still, they launched a chart review that revealed only 45 percent of patients were on any type of VTE prophylaxis—including just mechanical prophylaxis—and the rate of *appropriate* prophylaxis was a dismal 25 percent. The QI Team developed as an "aim statement" for their VTE prophylaxis project that they would strive toward an appropriate VTE prophylaxis rate of greater than 90 percent.

Confronted with the unacceptable current rates, the team began discussions to identify processes in place for assessing patient VTE risk and ordering prophylaxis. Despite the fact the team had wide representation from hospital services, members realized they lacked adequate "on-the-floor" knowledge. So they engaged the hospital's quality department to observe front-line workers and develop an accurate process map for how VTE prophylaxis is handled for admissions and transfers.

As the team assessed workflows, it considered all the staff involved in managing patients at risk for VTE. The team established that the workflow—risk-assessment, initiation of prophylaxis, and monitoring of patients for signs and symptoms of VTE—was best handled as a shared responsibility of the care team. They knew that it was critical to distinguish VTE present on admission from that acquired during hospitalization because of the different implications for performance improvement efforts and reimbursement. This evaluation and mapping exercise revealed many 'weak links in the chain' of ensuring that all patients for whom it was indicated received VTE prophylaxis in the appropriate manner.

Examining current VTE prophylaxis-related work processes also provided an opportunity to understand more deeply how the IT infrastructure at Grandview supported these processes and how it might be leveraged more fully. For example, the QI Team noted inconsistent ways that clinicians documented the presence of a VTE during or prior to the admission. This observation spawned a dialog with the CDS Committee and other pertinent Grandview committees about revisiting policies for problem list documentation to create a more reliable foundation for CDS interventions to address VTE, and other improvement imperatives as well.

Directly witnessing these information flow weak links and decision support opportunities in both workflow and underlying systems triggered many ideas among the QI Team observers and their CDS Committee colleagues. They considered ways to strengthen key processes by ensuring that the individuals taking these steps had the information-based tools they need to support the appropriate decisions and actions. These insights from the VTE exercise spawned follow-up conversations between the QI and CDS Teams about how they could further build upon and apply these analysis and problem-solving approaches in other joint projects. The effort to catalog EHR and other system capabilities pertinent to VTE prophylaxis also triggered a productive dialog with Grandview's EHR vendor about optimally leveraging those tools for VTE and related projects.

Establish knowledge management policies along with tools and processes to enforce these policies.

After gaining a better understanding of current practices and rates of VTE prophylaxis at Grandview Hospital and after establishing their initial 'dashboard,' the QI Team began to research the evidence base and related best practices for assessing VTE risk and providing appropriate prophylaxis. They

uncovered a variety of approaches that other hospitals used with good results, ranging from physician-led assessment tools within admission order sets, to pharmacist-driven monitoring and nursing-driven risk assessments.

The CDS Committee recognized that identifying, tracking and applying best care practices at Grandview as clinical evidence evolved would be a complex process for VTE—let alone the other topics they would address over time. After lengthy discussions with hospital staff and the Medical Executive Committee, the CDS Committee helped establish a sister group—the Knowledge Management (KM) Committee—to plan for and handle the acquisition, validation and updating of CDS content used at Grandview. The new committee created subcommittees to conduct evidence reviews, define best practices and perform gap analyses—which would identify the variance between the proposed new process and current processes.

As its first project, the KM Committee identified authoritative sources of VTE guidance to be the American College of Chest Physicians (ACCP), the American College of Physicians (ACP), and the American Academy of Family Physicians (AAFP), among others. They discussed when and how these national guidelines might be modified for needs, infrastructure and the specific patient populations at Grandview. Work began to develop a guideline policy and the processes required to ensure adherence to these clinical recommendations.

Focusing on the process of ordering appropriate VTE prophylaxis, the team broke the process into three parts based on the evidence they found: (1) assessment of VTE risk and evaluation of potential contraindications to prophylaxis; (2) ordering of appropriate mechanical or pharmacologic agents or documentation of exceptions for not ordering; and (3) ongoing monitoring and assessment during hospitalization.

The team initially endorsed a complicated scoring system for VTE-risk assessment; however, the time to complete it was found to be overly burdensome. More research led to agreement on a very simple 'three bucket' approach to risk assessment: patients would be identified (according to evidence-based criteria) as low, medium/high and very high risk for VTE on initial hospital presentation. These risk levels were presented in a simple table format to allow for rapid patient evaluation and categorization—especially when incorporated into CDS interventions later on in the process.

Working with the KM Committee, the QI Team developed a brief written guideline policy for hospital approval that outlined their agreed-upon risk-assessment levels, relative and absolute contraindications for prophylaxis, recommended prophylaxis interventions for each risk level, and expectations for order-related documentation and timing for physicians and nursing staff. They agreed that having this written consensus document would serve as a resource now and in the future while working on tools to ensure compliance. The KM Committee recognized that evidence is always changing and so dated their current guideline and decided on a six-month review to ensure it was up-to-date.

At this point, the VTE Prophylaxis QI Team—in collaboration with the KM Committee—had gained an understanding of current practice, developed written and approved clinical care guidelines, and established the beginnings of a quality dashboard. The CDS Committee reflected on this good work and considered its implications for the Committee's own responsibilities, for example, emphasizing the importance of close collaboration with other Grandview bodies to help it understand and align its work with organizational improvement priorities, evidence-based care protocols and the realities of care delivery workflow at Grandview.

CASE STUDY FOR SMALL PRACTICES: IMPROVING DIABETES CONTROL IN THE OUTPATIENT SETTING

Establish a strong, shared foundation of knowledge for yourself and your team around basic concepts such as the broad CDS definition and tool-kit, and CDS's role as a strategic tool for driving measurable performance improvement. Use this foundation to underpin your efforts to develop successful CDS programs and interventions.

Having recently implemented a new certified EHR* and gained some experience in quality measurement, a five-physician, community-based, primary-care internal medicine practice began to consider the next steps to improve the practice's clinical and business performance. Key participants in this process at Elm Heights Internal Medicine included Dr. Myrna Franks as the performance improvement (PI) leader; Tom Beck, the practice's only RN; and Paula Matthews, the practice manager (PM).

During one of their weekly business meetings, the five physicians began discussing possible quality performance improvement initiatives. PI leader Franks suggested that implementing additional EHR functionality beyond the core documentation, ordering and data review functions they were finally becoming comfortable with might help to improve quality measures. Practice manager Matthews noted that implementing this functionality would also support the practice's efforts to address Meaningful Use incentive requirements and, depending on the focus of their initiatives, for potential participation in pay for performance (P4P) initiatives. The other members of the practice agreed with these ideas and suggested that Beck, Matthews and Franks coordinate the initiative for the practice.

By discussing the importance of building a continuous quality improvement program with everyone in the office, PI leader Franks and practice manager Matthews explored with the practice how they could leverage their EHR to help achieve better clinical and operational outcomes. They understood that many tools they wanted to incorporate into their EHR would fall under the category of clinical decision support (CDS). They considered questions about what resources the enhanced CDS activities would require (see Chapter 2 for personnel and organizational requirements) and what rewards it could bring (see Chapter 1 for discussion of the Promise

---

* See ONC's Certified Health IT Product List: http://onc-chpl.force.com/ehrcert.

of CDS). They also noted that the different practice members expressed various concerns and priorities for the program. The team recognized they needed to articulate a shared vision of the "why, what and how" of the effort. They also had to be able to identify the "what's in it for me?" from the program for the physicians, and for everyone else in the practice (including the patients).

The last thing that PI leader Franks, nurse Beck, and practice manager Matthews (who had dubbed themselves "The CDS Team") wanted was to get off on the wrong foot by making the CDS program and intervention activities appear as yet another cost or burden that would impact productivity. In her role as practice manager, Matthews researched the return on investment (ROI) from an intensified practice focus on CDS (see Figure 1-3 in Chapter 1) and shared his assessment with the group. If done well, the program would be well worth the time and money invested, and considering the costs and other challenges up front would help ensure everyone's expectations were in line with reality.

The CDS Team also discussed the importance of considering patient and practice management workflow implications associated with an intensified focus on CDS. For example, routinely using CDS interventions as part of their quality improvement initiatives would require an important fundamental shift in how the practice viewed its information generation and use; that is, it would need to handle information and medical knowledge in an even more systematic and goal-directed fashion than was required in the initial EHR install.

They decided to create an Elm Heights Vision to document their CDS-enhanced quality improvement program's basic principles and essential operating procedures. That would help the practice develop an explicit plan for how they would more efficiently and effectively record, manage and leverage patient data in their information systems—and the best available clinical evidence and care practices—to improve their patient care process and outcomes. The payoff was optimizing their performance on key clinical quality and safety measures and ensuring

optimal health for their patients. In addition, they anticipated increased patient and staff satisfaction and other related benefits to the practice and its members. The vision document would be incorporated into the Elm Heights Internal Medicine Business Plan when it was revised in the coming year.

The CDS Team expected that a stronger "culture of care value" would emerge from the intensified practice focus on leveraging patient data, clinical knowledge and care processes more effectively for the benefit of all. They agreed that care value could be summarized by the following equation, where efficiency and costs are pertinent to both the practice *and* the patient.

$$\text{Care Value} = \frac{\text{Quality of Care X Efficiency of Care}}{\text{Costs Incurred}}$$

Their integrated, CDS-enhanced approach to optimizing this equation was expected to increase patient, physician and staff satisfaction, as well as patient and practice health and well-being.

Determine and document the who, why, what, how and when of your CDS approach and activities.

PI leader Franks, nurse Beck and practice manager Matthews understood that care delivery is best when everyone appreciates and appropriately engages all other care team members (including the patients). Similarly, they recognized that such a team-based approach is imperative for this next step in their quality improvement efforts to more fully leverage CDS. Without an actively engaged team working together with a purpose, these efforts can turn into an annoyance (for example, through unwelcome and unhelpful CDS interventions) and become an impediment to quality care (by distracting people from more productive practice- and patient-management activities). They have learned that unless there is teamwork present at every level—from improvement target selection through intervention execution and follow-up—the result will be inefficiency, increased cost, potential for errors and an undermining of the practice's vitality. Part of this learning came from another practice's CDS horror story resulting from their failure to work together to carefully define role responsibilities and workflows for responding to automated reminders about critical overdue testing.

In thinking broadly about whom they might involve in their CDS efforts, the CDS Team agreed that in addition to closely involving everyone in the practice, they had to also look outside for collaboration and support. The CDS Team agreed that participating in their EHR vendor's user group and leveraging support from their local HIT Regional Extension Center (REC)* could help them network with other practices on a similar path and share tools and ideas, so they wouldn't have to "reinvent the wheel."

Even before reaching out to others, the CDS Team recognized that the efforts required by practice members to achieve new CDS-enabled advances— planning, implementation, monitoring and maintenance—had to be carefully balanced against the other demands for running the practice. Ideally, the responsibilities of each person working on (or receiving) CDS would not appreciably slow down other normal operations. They knew that their CDS/PI plan should help each member to work smarter, not harder, to achieve the practice's CDS-enabled quality and efficiency vision. Thinking ahead, they recognized that careful attention to understanding clinical workflows and practice management activities—and improving them in the context of the practice culture and goals—would be key to success.

Elm Heights Internal Medicine had always taken pride in their ability to manage patients with complex chronic conditions. As they were acclimating to the EHR, each of the five physicians began to notice opportunities for the system to provide better workflow and decision support to further improve the care and outcomes for their many patients with diabetes, asthma, depression, heart disease and other chronic conditions. The new Elm Heights Vision

and plan provided them with the foundation to turn this promise into reality.

The CDS Team immediately recognized that care for these chronic conditions was the focus of many payer P4P programs and a critical component in national ambulatory quality initiatives such as those used by the Physician Quality Reporting System (PQRS) and National Committee for Quality Assurance (NCQA) and also part of Meaningful Use clinical quality measures. PI leader Franks also noted that the performance measures in these programs could be used to drive the design of CDS interventions to improve care assessed by these measures. For example, in the case of diabetes, that measures for hemoglobin A1c (HbA1c) testing and values, completion of diabetic foot and eye exams and LDL cholesterol testing and values could be used to inform CDS interventions that support appropriate attention to and management of these care needs.

Having considered themselves and discussed with others the key ingredients of their new CDS efforts, the CDS Team drafted a plan for cultivating and leveraging CDS capabilities—which will be used in deploying specific CDS interventions—to measurably enhance the practice's care value. They discussed this plan with everyone in the office during formal practice meetings, and informally as well. Based on the thoughtful input and helpful feedback they received from all who conducted or were affected by care activities, they produced a few iterations until they had a version everyone was excited about making happen.

The plan reinforced that the program had to enhance provider and patient decisions, actions and results—and track each to the extent practical. It identified changes to current roles and new activities that were required for the program to be successful. The Elm Heights physicians and staff were well-prepared to accept these enhancements, since the plan identified how the new way of working would benefit them. For example, proactive support that highlighted information needed for decision making

---

* See ONC website on RECs at: http://healthit.hhs.gov/portal/server.pt/community/healthit_hhs_gov__rec_program/1495. Accessed October 21, 2011.

and 'makes the right thing the easy thing to do' for common and important care processes would save everyone time and improve efficiency. Diagnosis-based order sets that facilitated fast and accurate ordering of tests, patient education materials and follow-up appointments were one of many examples.

Understand and cultivate key CDS building blocks including your deployed information technology, documentation of clinical workflows and capacity to measure intervention effects.

The practice's certified EHR provided part of the foundation for their new generation of CDS interventions, but the CDS Team knew they would need to expand how they viewed and used other key systems, such as the practice management system. They would have to consider how to optimize these systems' role in supporting workflow and decision making, and providing more analytical information about care processes and the outcomes they produce.

As a first step, the CDS Team assessed in detail the capabilities of the office EHR system. When selecting their EHR, Elm Heights Internal Medicine decided to use a certified EHR so that they would be poised to take advantage of government programs such as the one that provides incentive payments for Meaningful Use of EHRs. Although the EHR had been in place for a little over a year, the CDS Team knew that the practice had not yet exploited the software's full capabilities. For example, they had not fully implemented the secure patient messaging module, health maintenance alerts were only partially implemented, and the e-prescribing module did not flag high-cost medications.

To begin analyzing how the EHR and practice management systems were currently used to support care processes in the practice, PI leader Franks guided the group through a preliminary evaluation of current patient management workflows pertinent to the chronic conditions on which they would be focusing their CDS efforts. This set the stage for—and began triggering ideas about—next-generation CDS interventions that could enhance processes and outcomes.

Since they did not yet have a lab interface, they quickly recognized that they would need to analyze the workflows associated with the lab results that are received by fax. This would require accelerating the effort to deploy an interface from the lab system, or an interim change in workflow to include manually entering the results into the system as structured data elements. Better lab value management through an electronic lab interface would help with their medical home efforts and would be critical to providing discreet data needed to trigger the many disease management CDS interventions that depended on this information—not to mention increased staff efficiencies and decreased opportunity for errors and omissions compared to manually handling lab data.

This workflow analysis highlighted that practice physicians typically document that lab results have been reviewed and communicated to the patient in an office note narrative, despite the presence of a specific checkbox for these activities on one of the EHR templates. Use of the template would both standardize the documentation and potentially improve data entry for these important activities. They realized that to link additional decision support and reporting to these results review and communications functions, the corresponding workflows would need to be standardized. In addition, they realized that there was an opportunity to better utilize current care team members to simplify and improve these processes, for example, using in-office messaging through the EHR could facilitate communication between the physicians and nurse Beck about lab result handling.

The CDS Team realized from the workflow analysis that issue of "structured data" (such as the check being present or absent in the lab handling EHR template field) as opposed to unstructured "free text" (such as the narrative patient progress notes) was an important and recurring issue. Structured data are important for documentation, reporting and decision support—and could therefore lead to higher reimbursement. On the other hand, free text is more comfortable to the practice physicians, and several considered it more appropriate to capture important clinical nuances. It would take careful thought and work with the entire practice—and the EHR vendor—for the CDS Team to strike an appropriate balance between capturing and using structured and unstructured data in their CDS efforts.

To help with next steps in understanding and leveraging the practice's EHR, PI leader Franks contacted the vendor and arranged for a Web meeting to include practice manager Matthews and nurse Beck. The meeting's goal was to discuss their CDS goals with the vendor and to fully understand how to optimize the systems capabilities—including ordering tools, alerting functionality, relevant data display, documentation tools, and others—in supporting their performance improvement efforts.

The meeting with the vendor revealed many useful insights about this system, for example, that it does have helpful capabilities for alerting about interventions required for chronic disease management, such as HbA1c testing in diabetic patients. The CDS Team learned how they could create an alert for patients with overdue HbA1c tests. They also learned about better approaches for fine-tuning alert specificity planned for a forthcoming EHR release. The vendor also provided tips from other clients about how to optimize the use of templates for capturing structured data.

The meeting results were discussed with the full practice, which agreed to revisit documentation-related workflows and roles, and consider changes in the documentation process to capture important CDS-related information in a structured format: for example, they would establish where and how to document in a structured way eye exams, foot exams and retinopathy diagnoses. They would also establish policies and procedures to automatically add diabetes as a chronic problem when it was used in documenting a patient assessment. The physicians also agreed that an upgrade to the system to acquire new CDS capabilities may be appropriate, especially if gains in office efficiency and financial reimbursement for quality reporting were to offset the upgrade cost. In any case, the practice re-confirmed that any

contemplated system and workflow changes had to be determined by the group to have an appropriate benefit/cost ratio before being implemented.

The system and workflow review highlighted other changes that would likely be required for the practice to realize full benefits from their next-generation CDS efforts. For example, physicians would need to encode office visit diagnoses using a standard dictionary (such as ICD-9 / ICD-10) to support quality reporting and the creation of disease registries.

Since these new CDS efforts were focused on driving *measurable* improvements in performance, it was clear to the CDS Team that developing stronger capabilities around measurement and reporting would be foundational. Key metrics would include performance against improvement targets—such as how many diabetic patients have their HbA1c measured at the recommended frequency and have achieved desirable levels—both before and after new CDS interventions for these targets were implemented. Looking ahead, they realized that broader outcome measures—such as how often diabetic patients were hospitalized, had heart attacks, suffered kidney problems and the like—would become increasingly important.

Likewise, they would need to be able to accurately assess clinician use of, satisfaction with, and actions based on all CDS interventions they would implement. This included the hoped for positive effects, as well as any unintended consequences (both negative and positive) from the interventions. Without such measurements, the practice wouldn't know where they needed to improve or where and how they have improved, or created, new problems. These measurement-related needs triggered another round of meetings with the EHR vendor and the full practice, as well as reaching out to the vendor's User Group and REC. Based on this input, the CDS Team drafted notes on an overall CDS-related measurement plan to underpin their approach to the specific target-focused CDS interventions they would soon be deploying.

Establish knowledge management policies along with tools and processes to enforce these policies.

PI leader Franks had shouldered the responsibility to acquire, update and validate the new CDS interventions that would underpin the practice's enhanced "Care Value." She emphasized the importance of this task with the other practice clinicians and staff and secured their commitment to help as needed. In addition, she searched for help outside of the practice.

She reached out to the practice's EHR vendor, other vendor clients within their users group (who might share success strategies and specific CDS intervention samples), and their local REC. She found each of these resources helpful in various ways that kept her from having to 'reinvent the wheel.' Nonetheless, she recognized that the practice had to maintain responsibility for vetting any CDS content they received from outside sources.

She had also found—following tips from colleagues in other practices and the REC—helpful CDS content sources from commercial suppliers, as well as authoritative and trustworthy public websites. This all helped, but PI leader Franks appreciated that keeping this content up-to-date was a constant challenge. She intended to explore mechanisms whereby the EHR might notify practice staff at specified times about the need to re-evaluate the applicability and currency of their deployed CDS interventions (such as yearly in the case of specific health maintenance alerts). If there were no feasible options for automated processes, however, she planned to use a more automated tracking method such as spreadsheets and/or automated reminders in a computer-based calendar.

She discussed with the CDS Team who exactly should be responsible for the intervention tracking system. They understood some parts of the monitoring function—such as calling attention to which interventions need review when—wouldn't have to be filled by a physician. However, they did plan to assign a practice physician to conduct periodic literature reviews—and share results formally with whole practice—to ensure that the CDS interventions on a particular topic remained timely and accurate. They agreed that by sharing responsibility for this review across all the practice, physicians would reinforce their ownership and investment in these important performance improvement ingredients. In addition, each physician and nurse Beck agreed to immediately bring to the CDS Team's attention any information they gleaned from their reading and continuing education activities that might suggest the need to modify any of their deployed CDS interventions.

These explorations helped the CDS Team—in consultation with the full practice—to develop and document their CDS-related knowledge management processes. These include CDS content and intervention acquisition; vetting the material to ensure consistency with practice patterns (and sorting things out when there's a difference); maintaining the content and interventions so they remain consistent with evolving clinical knowledge, evidence-based guidelines and practice policy; and making, executing and documenting decisions about content and interventions and related practice policies. After it was approved by the practice, this knowledge management plan became a component of their CDS/PI plan.

Chapter 1

Basic Concepts and Approach

Tasks

- Establish a strong, shared foundation for yourself and your team around basic concepts such as the broad CDS definition and toolkit and the 'CDS Five Rights' framework. Use this foundation to underpin your efforts to develop a successful CDS program and target-focused CDS interventions. (Worksheet 2-2)
- Begin to build a shared vision among all those who will be touched by your CDS efforts about the role of CDS efforts in enhancing clinical, operational and financial performance.
- Consider critical goals—driven by internal and external forces—that can inform strategic victories to be pursued and claimed as a centerpiece of your CDS program. Recognize that these drivers increasingly require measurable performance improvement, so include measurement (such as before and after CDS interventions) as a foundational element in your CDS approach. (Worksheet 2-1)
- Become familiar with resources for information about CDS literature and best practices such as those provided by ONC, AHRQ and HIMSS.

KEY LESSONS

- Clinical Decision Support is a process for ensuring that health-related decisions and actions are informed by pertinent patient information and clinical knowledge to enhance health and healthcare delivery.
- CDS should be used as a strategic tool for achieving priority care delivery objectives. These objectives are driven by external forces such as payment models and regulations related to improving care quality, safety and costs, as well as internal needs for better efficiency and other performance enhancements.
- Think of CDS broadly, not narrowly—CDS can involve different kinds of information provided to different care delivery participants in a variety of formats through different channels into various points in workflow. Addressing these collective information delivery dimensions appropriately to drive targeted improvements is referred to as the 'CDS Five Rights.'

KEY LESSONS *continued*

- Be aware of situations where CDS has been shown to be of value such as improving appropriate medication dosing, enhancing process measures related to preventive care, and decreasing mortality by increasing deep vein thrombosis prophylaxis.
- Appreciate the limits of evidence about when and how CDS is most useful, and supplement this with best practices and insights from your peers.
- Be familiar with known and sometimes unanticipated CDS pitfalls such as failure to adequately address change management issues and 'alert fatigue' from excessive or inappropriate alerting.

GENERAL APPROACH

When pilots fly airplanes they are constantly receiving guidance. When financial advisors invest money they do so with the assistance of software programs that use evidence and predictive modeling on investment options. Those involved in patient care delivery—where the stakes involve well-being, life and death—also should be robustly supported. Clinical decision support (CDS) is about helping all those involved in delivering healthcare, and the recipients of that care, make clinical decisions and take actions in a manner fully informed by pertinent information, so that desirable outcomes are achieved. As we'll outline shortly, there are many important ways that care delivery can and should be better—ways that CDS can help. This is true across all care settings (e.g., inpatient, outpatient, and patient homes) and around the globe. Strong forces—especially from those who pay for and oversee healthcare delivery—are increasingly demanding better outcomes. Because you are reading this book, you likely appreciate that 'doing CDS better' is a foundational component in rising to this challenge.

An important initial step on the journey to highly valuable and well-received CDS in any setting is to build a shared understanding among all who will be affected by basic CDS-related concepts and approaches. This includes what clinical decision support is (and is not), what CDS can (and can't)

accomplish, what tools are included in the CDS toolkit and frameworks for how these tools can be applied to improve outcomes. The following sections in this chapter start laying out these themes, beginning with key definitions.

CDS and Related Key Definitions

CDS has been defined in different ways by different people—with some focusing quite narrowly on alerts and reminders.[1] The first edition of this CDS guide[2] provided the following definition for clinical decision support:

> CDS refers broadly to providing clinicians or patients with clinical knowledge and patient-related information, intelligently filtered, or presented at appropriate times, to enhance patient care. Clinical knowledge of interest could include simple facts and relationships, established best practices for managing patients with specific disease states, new medical knowledge from clinical research, and many other types of information.

This definition informed how CDS was defined in "A Roadmap for National Action on Clinical Decision Support."[3] This whitepaper was commissioned by the U.S. Office of the National Coordinator for Health Information Technology (ONC) in 2005 and has influenced federal action on CDS since then, including the CDS definition noted in the Meaningful Use Final Rule:[4]

> In the proposed rule, we described clinical decision support as HIT functionality that builds upon the foundation of an electronic health record (EHR) to provide persons involved in care processes with general and person-specific information, intelligently filtered and organized, at appropriate times, to enhance health and health care.

In this Guide update, we retain the intent of our original broad CDS definition and add some modifications guided by the Meaningful Use Final Rule. Further enhancements to sharpen key points leads to the following definition:

> Clinical Decision Support is a process for enhancing health-related decisions and actions with pertinent, organized clinical knowledge and patient information to improve health and healthcare delivery. Information recipients can include patients, clinicians and others involved in patient care delivery; information delivered can include general clinical knowledge and guidance, intelligently processed patient data, or a mixture of both; and information delivery formats can be drawn from a rich palette of options that includes data and order entry facilitators, filtered data displays, reference information, alerts and others.

In this definition, we have purposefully omitted the qualifiers "HIT functionality that builds upon the foundation of an EHR" from the Meaningful Use definition in order to accommodate non-EHR and even non-computer-based channels for delivering CDS interventions. We certainly agree with the desirability in most, if not all, cases of using more robust information delivery tools but also recognize that in many settings across the U.S. and abroad, these tools may not be readily available. Our goal is to provide a framework and an approach for optimizing CDS that does not rule out using paper-based and other infrastructures for CDS when these are the best that are available.

Other key terms used in this Guide include:

CDS-related Terms

DS Program: The people, processes and technologies used by a care delivery organization to support care team decisions in a manner that improves care delivery and outcomes. The CDS program includes the improvement targets and the CDS interventions deployed to address those goals. It defines the processes used to select and prioritize the CDS targets and interventions and to implement the interventions and evaluate and improve their results. An overview of these processes is presented as a diagram in Figure PI-1 in the Introduction to Part I, and Chapters 1–4 provide detailed guidance on setting up a successful CDS program.

CDS Intervention: Providing information to enhance decisions and actions related to health and healthcare delivery. Intervention components may include a trigger, logic, notification, data presentation and action items. Key information delivery dimensions include the answers to these questions about the intervention: *what* (information), *who* (recipient), *how* (intervention type), *where* (information delivery channel), and *when* (in workflow).

CDS Intervention Package: A collection of one or more CDS interventions directed toward a particular *objective* (see definition below).

CDS Five Rights: A framework for approaching and configuring CDS interventions. This framework asserts that successfully applying CDS to improve a targeted objective requires that the *right* information be delivered to the *right* person in the *right* intervention format through the *right* channel at the *right* point in workflow. Chapter 5 contains a detailed taxonomy of CDS intervention types (see Figure 5-5) and further discusses these dimensions.

Knowledge Management: A comprehensive process for acquiring, adapting and monitoring information for use in clinical decision support that keeps it up to date with current clinical evidence, expert consensus and local conditions including pertinent health information system implementation(s) (see Chapter 4).

Target-related Terms

Goals: Strategic or overarching improvement targets. Examples include optimizing patient safety or clinical performance across a range of measures required for public reporting and/or reimbursement and improving the speed and quality with which the care team makes and executes clinical decisions (see Chapter 2).

Objective: More specific and measurable components of goals, such as increasing the percentage of patients who receive testing indicated to assess control of their diabetes or hospitalized patients who receive therapy to prevent blood clots as indicated (discussed later in Chapter 1 and in Chapter 2). In many cases, a family of objectives will have to improve to achieve a goal. For example, to improve morbidity in diabetic patients (a goal), many objectives related to monitoring and managing biological parameters, and others, must be addressed.

Outcomes [of care delivery]: Care delivery results that are important to stakeholders such as clinicians, administrators, payers and especially patients. These results may include the patient's health, wellness or mortality; costs associated with care delivery (e.g., costs to patient, payer or provider); the time or efficiency with which clinicians or patients complete care tasks; clinician and patient satisfaction with the care process; and others. **Outcome measures** quantify these results.

Care Processes: Activities that occur during care delivery and that contribute to care outcomes; for example, whether drugs or tests were used in specific patients for whom they were indicated. **Process measures** quantify these activities.

Meaningful Use: Escalating requirements for deploying health information technology that hospitals and professionals must meet to quality for incentive payments (till 2015) and avoid penalties (thereafter). These requirements are framed in the 2009 U.S. HITECH (Health Information Technology for Economic and Clinical Health) Act and are further defined by federal regulation. The requirements are currently divided into three stages, focusing in turn on improving EHR deployment, care processes, and finally, outcomes.[5]

Delivery Channel-related* Terms

Health Information Technology (HIT): A broad range of electronic (typically computer-based) systems through which CDS interventions can be delivered.

Clinical Information System (CIS): HIT deployed in hospitals, office practices and other care delivery settings to manage patient data and related information.

Electronic Health Record (EHR): A type of CIS for creating and managing a computer-based record of health-related information for individual patients.

CDS Is a Means to an End

In this Guide, we advocate approaching CDS as a foundational strategy and toolset for achieving high-priority improvements in care processes and outcomes. As we'll describe in Chapter 2 and elsewhere, this approach takes strongest root when the provider culture and leadership are focused on efficiency and effectiveness. When these facilitators are *not* in place, a more tactical approach has typically prevailed when CDS interventions are undertaken. This may include simply 'checking off' specific CDS functionality from a 'punch list' *without* focusing sharply on driving measurable improvements in important clinical and cost targets.

These narrow 'check box' items may include drug-drug interaction checking or CDS rules deployed as part of an EHR rollout, or efforts to address regulatory requirements such as those related to Stage 1 Meaningful Use in the U.S. While these targets are important, they are only interim steps to

---

* The definitions provided here are pragmatic guides to term usage in this Guide. There are not currently widely adopted definitions; for example, see a 2008 report for ONC on definitions for key terms available online at http://healthit.hhs.gov/portal/server.pt/gateway/PTARGS_0_10741_848133_0_0_18/10_2_hit_terms.pdf and a somewhat different definition of EHR provided by vendors of these systems: http://www.himssehra.org/docs/EHRVA_application.pdf. Both available online. Accessed October 23, 2011.

more fundamental goals—namely, reducing adverse drug events and broadly improving care outcomes. Failing to keep the ultimate destination in mind when applying CDS to intermediate steps substantially increases the risk that you won't achieve essential outcomes.

Given the global pressures on providers to deliver better healthcare—and the purchaser imperative to do it more efficiently—such a less-than-strategic approach to applying CDS to performance improvement is increasingly untenable. It means not fully leveraging substantial technology investments to address these growing pressures and not harnessing the substantial power of well-executed CDS to drive improvement across a broad range of targets (see Figure 1-1 for examples of business benefits from CDS). Before too long, it just will not be possible to survive as a healthcare provider without well-

executed CDS programs and target-focused interventions. The evolution of the CDS-related U.S. Meaningful Use requirements—from demonstrating CDS-related capabilities in Stage 1 to demonstrating CDS-enabled outcome improvements in Stage 3—is but one national example of this strong tide.[6] The shift of the U.S. Medicare system to value-based purchasing and the UK's Quality and Outcomes Framework for pay-for-performance programs are other examples. These are outlined further in the CDS Goals section later in this chapter, and in Chapter 2, Strategic Context.

A well-run CDS program provides the processes whereby the practice or other care delivery organization determines and achieves consensus on what priority improvement targets it will address with CDS and how it will address them. The other chapters in Part I of this book describe the target prioritization

---

Figure 1-1: Types of Business Benefits That Can Accrue from CDS Programs

- Reduced resource waste due to redundant and inefficient activities to support clinicians' decision making;

- Reduced costs of care (e.g., via more appropriate testing, cheaper and more appropriately utilized medications and therapies, reduced staff rework, and better care delivery coordination);

- Reduced costs associated with medical errors (e.g., from legal liability and averted safety problems, and additional work, tests and therapies to remediate them);

- Reduced liability insurance premiums based on demonstrably improved safety;

- Increased revenue (e.g., from pay-for-performance incentives);

- Increased market share (e.g., from more engaged and satisfied patients and demonstration of high-quality process and outcomes);

- Improved staff retention (e.g., by providing a high-quality professional knowledge management and decision support environment);

- Improved staff utilization (e.g., redeploy Quality Assurance nurse from chart reviews to CDS implementation);

- Enhanced leverage to improve outcomes from investments (and data) in CIS;

- Enhanced quality of healthcare professional education provided by the organization;

- Improved health services research capabilities and ability to attract grants.

process and other key CDS program development components in more detail. Part II describes how these capabilities can be applied to select, configure, launch and monitor CDS interventions that drive targeted outcome improvements.

The CDS Five Rights: A Framework for Achieving Desired Ends

When deploying CDS interventions, you must address key questions about the intervention configuration, including what information will be delivered, to whom and in which format, through which channel, and at what point in workflow. If the targeted objective is the 'why' for the CDS effort, then these five questions reflect the "what, who, how, where and when" for the CDS intervention(s) focused on this target.

The 2009 CDS guide in this series[7] introduced the 'CDS Five Rights' framework, which asserts that to successfully improve outcomes, CDS implementers (and developers) must configure CDS interventions to appropriately address each of these five questions. The CDS Five Rights section in Chapter 5 outlines this framework in more detail. For now, you can peek ahead—and keep these dimensions in mind as you work through the rest of the guidance in Part I, since the material on setting up a CDS program helps you build capacity to address these dimensions.

For example, the CDS Five Rights framework will help you interpret and apply the CDS literature we will discuss shortly and will be useful as you consider with your colleagues how CDS might be helpful in addressing priority improvement goals. A shared understanding about a systematic and goal-oriented approach to realizing value from CDS will provide a strong foundation for your CDS program and intervention activities as outlined in the remainder of this Guide.

Likewise, it is important for your team to have a shared understanding of the rich toolkit of CDS intervention types from which the answers to the 'how' questions are drawn. You can peek ahead to Chapter 5, Figure 5-5, to get a sense of these before you work through the rest of this Part I material.

Embedding questions about the 'right' configuration for the various CDS dimensions (what, who, how, where and when) into your CDS program activities helps broaden everyone's mindset for improving outcomes beyond the traditional narrow focus (e.g., relying excessively on interruptive alerts delivered to physicians to inform care delivery). This narrow approach to CDS has been highly problematic in the many instances when it has been over-emphasized. Our belief—reinforced by anecdotal experience—is that well-accepted CDS interventions that produce valuable results require careful attention to optimizing the CDS Five Rights' dimensions. That is, delivering the right information to the right individuals in the right formats through the right channels at the right points in workflow.

CDS Promise and Pitfalls— A Peek at the Literature

The introductions to Part I and Part II of this book contain synthesized case studies to illustrate what it can look like when things go right in setting up CDS programs and outcome-improving interventions, respectively. In addition to keeping exemplars like this in mind, it is important for you to consider what is (and is not) known from research studies about where and how CDS can be successfully applied, as well as where it has been problematic.

Evidence Base for CDS Value

Mirroring the push for evidence-based patient care, the evidence base for CDS intervention effectiveness and value should ideally help guide you where and how this technology can be most fruitfully applied. This subset of the process-improvement knowledge base answers the question "what effects do information management and delivery processes (i.e., CDS) have on health and patient care?" These insights complement the related literature that characterizes the effects that other clinical interventions, such as treatments and tests, have on care processes and outcomes.

This Guide is intended to be highly practical and not an academic treatise; we provide the following details about these studies to help you with specific tasks. These include establishing credibility with others on your team based on your grasp of documented CDS strengths and limitations, and enabling you to build your own efforts on top of this knowledge foundation.

CDS intervention effects on care delivery have been studied for decades; a landmark article in a high-profile medical journal about computer-based reminders, the quality of care, and the non-perfectibility of man is an important early example.[8] The global push to improve healthcare quality and efficiency using health IT intensifies this need to build, collate and apply the CDS evidence base. As we'll describe next, CDS intervention effects on care process and outcomes are increasingly studied through federal and private funding, and periodic reviews examine and collate these findings.

Various CDS literature reviews—both systematic and non-systematic—have attempted to analyze evidence on CDS implementation and effects and draw conclusions about what we know and have yet to learn about this important topic. We briefly outline results from four recent literature analyses, focusing on their implications for CDS implementers. These reviews include an AHRQ (Agency for Healthcare Research and Quality)-commissioned white paper by Berner published in 2009;[9] a systematic CDS literature review in 2011 by Lobach and colleagues from the AHRQ Evidence-based Practice Center at Duke University;[10] a deliverable report by Byrne and colleagues entitled "Key Lessons in Clinical Decision Support Implementation" published in 2010 under the ONC contract on Advancing CDS (ACDS);[11] and a 2011 *Health Affairs* article by Buntin and colleagues.[12]

An overview of the scope and finding highlights from these analyses follows. Your CDS efforts unfold against this backdrop.

Berner 2009 Whitepaper:

- Research identified on the effects of CDS was largely limited to academic medical centers using systems developed internally. Little systematic research on outcomes or implementation strategies of commercial CDS in community settings was noted. It was concluded that CDS in ambulatory settings needs more attention.

- Meta-analyses examining studies of alerts and reminders have shown fairly consistently that they can alter clinician decision-making and actions, reduce medication errors, and promote preventive screening and use of evidence-based recommendations for medication prescriptions. The data on how those decisions affect clinical outcomes are more limited, but some studies have shown positive effects. Overall, the studies indicate that CDS has the potential to improve care quality.

Byrne et al. ACDS 2010 Report:

- Reviewed current literature and exemplary CDS implementations, and discussed CDS implementation with subject matter experts to discover and synthesize useful practices and key lessons. Many of the lessons contained in previous books in the HIMSS CDS Guidebook series were reinforced and expanded upon in their report, with examples of real CDS experiences tailored to specific practice settings.

- "Successful implementation is a complex combination of art and science. As a result, the great majority of recommendations, lessons learned and useful practices [presented in this report] are based on mostly anecdotal and not empirical assessments by the literature authors or subject matter experts."

Lobach et al. 2011 AHRQ Evidence-based Practice Center Systematic Literature Review:

- Screened 15,176 abstracts and manuscripts dating from 1976 through 2010: a total of 311 comparative studies were identified, 148 of which were randomized controlled trials (RCTs).

- CDS effects were examined in three categories: process outcomes, clinical outcomes (such as morbidity, mortality, length of hospital stay, health-related quality of life, and adverse events), and economic outcomes (such as cost). Only 29 RCTs assessed the impact of CDS systems (CDSSs) on clinical outcomes, 22 assessed costs, and three assessed knowledge management system (KMS) effects on any outcomes. Overall, many more studies addressed process measures than clinical or economic effects.

- There was limited evidence showing CDS effects on clinical workload and efficiency.
- The effect on process outcomes showed the strongest level of evidence. These processes included:
  - Recommended preventative care service ordered/completed
  - Recommended clinical study ordered/completed
  - Recommended treatment ordered/prescribed
  - Impact on user knowledge
- The review concluded: "Strong evidence now shows that CDSSs are effective in improving process measures across diverse academic and nonacademic settings using both commercially and locally developed systems. Evidence for the effectiveness of CDSSs on clinical outcomes and costs and KMSs on any outcomes is minimal, and more studies are needed in these areas."

Buntin et al. 2011 HIT Review in Health Affairs:

- Examined 154 studies conducted between July 2007 and February 2010 that addressed 278 individual outcome measures. Forty-four studies assessed clinical decision support systems, 30 of which assessed the effects of clinical decision support systems on care quality and/or efficiency.
- Sixty-two percent of the studies overall were positive (health IT was associated with improvement in one care aspect without noted detriment to other aspects), and 92 percent were either positive or mixed-positive (indicating authors' overall conclusion was positive despite noted detriments). Ten studies reported overall negative findings such as increased errors and workflow impediments.
- Non-published analysis from the study found that articles assessing the effects of CDS were no more or less likely to reach positive overall conclusions than articles that did not assess CDS. However, articles evaluating the effects of CDS were more likely (45 percent versus 19 percent of articles, p<0.001) to include a positive or mixed-positive effect on care quality compared to those that did not.

These literature syntheses provide reassurance that CDS can favorably affect care processes. Further, this evidence is expanding from its historical confines in academic centers to cover systems and settings more broadly. The report by Byrne et al. draws on systematic and non-systematic evidence to suggest useful practices for the implementation and use of CDS. Nonetheless, there is much more work to be done to systematically define which CDS approaches work best to drive better clinical, operational, and financial outcomes.

EVIDENCE HIGHLIGHTS—A DEEPER SAMPLING

There are a few key areas where there is good evidence that CDS can improve a particular type of care process. You should keep these strong evidence signals in mind as you and your team consider where your CDS efforts might be most fruitfully applied. Figure 1-2 summarizes some of this information, followed by additional details.

Keep in mind that the CDS evidence base is growing continuously, as suggested by the differing states of evidence about settings and systems in the two years between the Berner and Lobach reviews. Don't conclude that there isn't a strong evidence signal on a CDS topic of interest just because it hasn't been identified by the studies discussed here. AHRQ and ONC have funded these particular reviews, and the CDS portions of their websites[13] are among the sources you can check to keep current on CDS literature syntheses. HIMSS[14] and other organizations also maintain CDS Web pages that can be helpful in keeping current on literature and best practices.

In Lobach et al., the Summary of Key Findings also outlines topic areas where the evidence for CDS benefit was not as strong. These are highlighted next based on how the review describes CDSS effects on the different outcomes. Again, readers should keep in mind that the CDS literature is evolving. Lack of strong effects in these areas to date does not mean that additional approaches and studies won't reveal significant CDS benefits in these domains. As with the findings in Figure 1-2, this information gives you

Figure 1-2: Literature Sampling Demonstrating That CDS Improves Care Process and Outcomes*

Targeted Improvement	Level of Evidence	CDS Effects	Evidence for Effect *Identified as highly relevant studies by Lobach et al.*
		Process Outcomes	
Recommended treatment ordered/prescribed	High Relative Risk/Odds Ratio: 1.57 Confidence Interval: 95%, 1.28 to 1.89	"There is strong evidence from the academic, community, and VA inpatient and ambulatory settings that locally and commercially developed CDSSs integrated in CPOE or EHR systems that automatically delivered system-initiated (push) recommendations to providers synchronously at the point of care and did not require a mandatory clinician response were effective at improving appropriate treatment ordering/prescribing."	Inpatient Setting:[15] *McGregor (2006):* Pharmacology *Paul (2006):* Diagnosis, Pharmacology *Rood (2005):* Chronic disease management *Rothschild (2007):* Other — Transfusion ordering *Tamblyn (2003):* Pharmacology *Vanwyk (2008):* Diagnosis, Preventative, Other — Screening and treatment of dyslipidemia *Zannetti (2003):* Pharmacology Outpatient Setting:[16] *Ansari (2003):* Pharmacology, Chronic disease management ***Bell (2010): Chronic disease management*** ***Field (2009): Pharmacology*** ***Fortuna (2009): Pharmacology*** ***Hicks (2008): Chronic disease management*** *Linder (2009):* Diagnosis, Pharmacology, Chronic disease management *Martens (2007):* Pharmacology
Recommended preventative care service ordered/completed	High Relative Risk/Odds Ratio: 1.42 Confidence Interval: 95%, 1.27 to 1.58	"There is strong evidence from studies conducted in the academic, VA (Veterans Administration), and community inpatient and ambulatory settings that locally and commercially developed CDSSs that automatically delivered system-initiated (push) recommendations to providers synchronously at the point of care and did not require a mandatory clinician response were effective at improving the appropriate ordering of preventive care procedures."	Inpatient Setting:[17] *Dexter (2001):* Immunization, Pharmacology *Dexter (2004):* Immunization *Kucher (2005):* Preventative Outpatient Setting:[18] *Demakis (2000):* Immunization, Chronic disease management, Preventative *Kenealy (2005):* Preventative *Peterson (2008):* Chronic disease management

continued on next page

Figure 1-2 *continued*

Targeted Improvement	Level of Evidence	CDS Effects	Evidence for Effect * *Identified as highly relevant studies by Lobach et al.*
Recommended clinical study ordered/completed	Moderate Relative Risk/Odds Ratio: 1.72 Confidence Interval: 95%, 1.47 to 2.00	"There is modest evidence from studies conducted in the academic and community inpatient and ambulatory settings that CDSSs integrated in CPOE or EHR systems and locally and commercially developed CDSSs that automatically delivered system-initiated (push) recommendations to providers synchronously at the point of care and did not require a mandatory clinician response were effective at improving the appropriate ordering of clinical studies."	<u>Outpatient Setting:</u>[19] *Bell (2010):* Chronic disease management ***Lo (2009):* Lab test ordering** *Raebel (2006):* Lab test ordering *Roukema (2008):* Diagnosis, Lab test ordering ***Sundaram (2009):* Lab test ordering**
Clinical Outcomes			
Morbidity	Moderate Relative Risk/Odds Ratio: 0.88 Confidence Interval: 95%, 0.80 to .96	"There is modest evidence from the academic and community inpatient and ambulatory settings that locally developed CDSSs that automatically delivered system-initiated (push) recommendations to providers synchronously at the point of care were effective or demonstrated a trend toward reducing patient morbidity."	<u>Outpatient:</u>[20] *Ansari (2003):* Pharmacology, Chronic disease management ***Cleveringa (2008):* Chronic disease management** *Heindrich (2007):* Pharmacology <u>Inpatient:</u>[21] *Graumlich (2009):* Other — Discharge planning *Kucher (2005):* Preventative *Paul (2006):* Diagnosis, Pharmacology

* This figure is adapted with permission from Table 12: Summary of Key Findings, Appendix D: Evidence Table, and Appendix H: Summary Tables for Key Question 3, in Lobach et al., 2011. The studies cited in the Evidence for Effect column in Figure 1-2 are only a small sampling of the pertinent studies presented in the report. Studies provided here were all described in the review as being of "Good" quality and were published later than 2000. Furthermore, we highlighted studies from both inpatient and outpatient settings and with different clinical objectives (as defined in the review). The bolded studies with asterisks above were noted in the review as being "high quality, recently published papers in which the CDSS interventions were thoroughly described." Appendix D in the review details the setting, duration of the study, description of the system, and applicability of the study, among many other factors.

a feeling for the research foundation underpinning some important targets in your CDS efforts.

Process Outcomes

Impact on User Knowledge: CDSS impact on user knowledge was limited. The study cites a few examples in which providers reported that their knowledge improved by using CDSS. A diabetes care reminder,[22] a cancer-risk assessment tool,[23] and a tool for managing hyperlipidemia[24] were the examples cited. The review concludes, however, that the evidence is limited to make any broad conclusions about CDS effects on user knowledge.

Clinical Outcomes

Mortality: In the meta-analysis of CDSS effects on mortality, patients in the intervention group were 90 percent as likely to die as those in the control. Although a few studies show a trend toward decreasing mortality,[25] none of these achieved statistical significance.

Length of Stay: Lobach et al. conclude that the evidence is limited for the positive CDSS effects on hospital length of stay. There were only four studies in which the number of patients studied was greater than 2,000[26] and only one study in which the study duration was greater than one year.[27] These studies showed that there is limited evidence that CDSSs that automatically delivered system-initiated (push) recommendations to providers were effective at reducing length of stay or demonstrated a trend toward reducing length of stay.

Health-Related Quality of Life: There is limited evidence for CDSS improving the health-related quality of life of patients in ambulatory settings.[28] Most of the studies only evaluated between 500 and 1,000 patients, with four of the studies lasting for more than one year.[29]

Adverse Events: From the meta-analysis of CDSS effects on adverse events, the intervention group was equally as likely to experience an adverse event as the control group. One paper, described as of high quality,[30] concluded that the decrease from CDS in prescriptions implicated in

adverse interactions was statistically significant. Overall, there is limited evidence from the academic setting that CDSSs that delivered recommendations to providers synchronously at the point of care demonstrated an effect on reducing or preventing adverse events.

Economic Outcomes

Cost: Lobach et al. report great variability in the savings incurred by using CDSS. One study showed savings of $6,000 with an intervention offering recommendations for abdominal radiograph orders; another study showed savings of $84,194 when using an intervention for providing recommendations for appropriate antimicrobial ordering. The review concludes that there is modest evidence for cost savings from CDS in that CDSS demonstrated a trend toward lower treatment costs, total costs, and greater cost-savings than did the control groups and other non-CDSS intervention groups.

Cost-Effectiveness: The evidence for the cost-effectiveness of using CDSS is conflicted. Lobach et al. point out that there are studies that suggest cost-effectiveness,[31] but one high-quality and recently published group of studies[32] suggests otherwise. The authors note that in studies with greater than 2,000 patients and studies lasting longer than one year, CDSS are shown to be more cost-effective than usual care. These studies, however, were all published earlier than 2008.

Specific Clinical Topics

In addition to evidence about the role of CDS in addressing broad outcome categories such as those previously listed, it would be helpful for implementers to have evidence-based guidance on applying CDS in more specific circumstances. This important research base—and syntheses thereof—is still developing.

Reviews previously mentioned and others, as well as further searching on your own, can provide deeper details as needed. For example, the Berner 2009 whitepaper outlines the state of a few key areas at that time, including medication errors, DVT (deep vein thrombosis) prophylaxis, diabetes care management, and diagnostic errors:

> Although the studies showing the ability of CDS to prevent medication errors (incorrect decisions) have been consistently positive, the results of research studies on the ability of CDS to avert adverse drug events (harm to the patient) have tended to be mixed. Few of the studies examining the impact on health outcomes were RCTs, many studies were poorly designed, and not all studies showed statistically significant effects.[33] In terms of other outcomes, in one recent randomized controlled trial of the impact of CDS on use of DVT prophylaxis, mortality was improved with CDS[34]; however, well-designed studies of diabetes outcomes do not consistently show positive effects.[35] CDS studies that focus on providing diagnostic decision support have also shown mixed results, and fewer of these systems have been evaluated in practice settings.[36] However, studies comparing CDS diagnostic suggestions with expert clinicians' analyses of challenging clinical cases have shown that the diagnostic CDS can remind even expert physicians of potentially important diagnoses they did not initially consider.[37]

In particular, improving medication use and outcomes is a frequent and important focus for CDS efforts, and the 2009 HIMSS guide on this topic cited earlier in this chapter[7] presents a sampling of the pertinent research demonstrating the proven value of CDS in this domain. Since that guide was published, a meta-analysis looking specifically at prompting and alerting interventions for medication prescribing (e.g., drug allergy and interaction warnings, age and renal function dosing guidance) concluded that "most empiric studies evaluating the effects of computerized prompts and alerts on prescribing behavior [23 out of 27] show positive, and often substantial, effects."[38] For example, these benefits included correct dose adjustment of medications in patients with renal impairment and reduced lengths of stay. As discussed later under CDS pitfalls, however, alerts can be associated with significant adverse effects themselves, so careful attention to their proper use is required.

Figure 1-2, previously shown, and the evidence-base practice center (EPC) review on which it is based, point to additional studies that shed light on the evidence base for applying CDS to specific target areas. Increasing interest in reinforcing the evidence base for "knowing what works in healthcare"[39] offers promise that research to guide CDS implementers in selecting specific interventions to address priority outcomes will increase over time.[40]

Evidence for Effective CDS Intervention Features

In their extensive literature review discussed earlier, Lobach et al. identified nine CDS system features (cited verbatim) correlated to success:

- Automatic provision for decision support as part of clinician workflow
- Provision of decision support at time and location of decision making
- Provision of a recommendation, not just an assessment
- Integrating with charting or order entry system to support workflow integration
- No need for additional clinician data entry
- Promotion of action rather than inaction
- Justification of decision support via provision of research evidence
- Local user involvement in development process
- Provision of decision support results to patients as well as providers

This review found these features in CDS implementations within diverse venues (including community care settings) using both commercial and homegrown systems. They found strong evidence that including these CDS features positively affected care processes including prescribing treatments, facilitating preventive care services, and ordering clinical studies. These features help define what 'right' means for many of the CDS Five Rights dimensions, and echo many of the "Ten Commandments" for CDS implementations distilled from one pioneering organization's experiences.[41] CDS developers and implementers should keep these evidence-based design features in mind.

Unfortunately, the Lobach et al. review was not able to identify equally strong evidence to support more detailed guidance on critical deployment features related to the content and nature of effective CDS interventions, the appropriate recipients for that support, how the CDS can best be integrated into workflow, and other issues related to widespread and successful CDS use. That's where resources such as this book come in; they attempt to extract and synthesize CDS best practices based on experiences and the expertise of a broad cross section of stakeholders. The CDS Five Rights framework introduced earlier is a tool for considering such key "what, how, who, where and when" CDS configuration elements. Of note, there are preliminary explorations underway into more systematically capturing and sharing CDS configuration experience and results in a manner conducive to further developing evidence-based best practices for CDS interventions.[42]

Evidence Highlighting CDS Pitfalls

Efforts to improve outcomes with CDS can 'go wrong' in a variety of ways, with major categories including failing to deliver expected benefits, and creating new unintended problems. It is most important to stress that the stakes are higher when CDS tools misguide. Instead of individual clinicians and patients making wrong decisions, CDS tools that reach many healthcare decision makers can just as easily lead to poor choices as better ones. Sampling the literature about these pitfalls underscores cautionary notes for CDS implementers and supports recommendation themes presented throughout this Guide.

EVIDENCE ABOUT HIT AND CDS FAILING TO DELIVER RESULTS

Reviews are published periodically showing that EHRs and their CDS components do not deliver broadly on the anticipated improvements in quality and costs. For example, a systematic review entitled "The Impact of eHealth on the Quality and Safety of Health Care" published online in PLOS Medicine[43] in early 2011 examined CDS as one of three components of "eHealth." The authors concluded, "There is a large gap between the postulated and empirically demonstrated benefits of eHealth technologies."

Another study looked at physician survey data from ambulatory visits and correlated it with quality measure data.[44] The authors concluded, "Our findings indicate no consistent association between EHRs and CDS and better quality. These results raise concerns about the ability of health information technology to fundamentally alter outpatient care quality." This study raised quite a stir given its coincidence in the U.S. with unprecedented investments and attention to widespread use of EHRs and CDS as components of Meaningful Use. Many commentators[45] pointed out reasons for optimism despite these negative findings, including the fact that the EHRs and CDS approaches reported in this study were not mature, for example, preceding EHR certification requirements associated with Meaningful Use. Furthermore, commentators suggest that because the data used to draw the negative conclusion were generated for a different purpose, they do not necessarily indicate that a relationship between EHRs and CDS does not exist.[46]

The literature cited earlier that documents CDS value provides reassurance that under appropriate circumstances CDS interventions can be beneficial. Negative articles such as those just noted reinforce that measurable benefits on a broad scale still can't be taken for granted. An explicit goal of this CDS Guide edition is to foster further dialog among CDS system developers and implementers. For example, we hope that the subsection in each chapter on "Considerations for HIT Software Providers" and other content in this update will promote collaborations and advances that produce both better systems and more valuable implementation of those systems.

EVIDENCE ABOUT UNINTENDED CONSEQUENCES FROM CDS

Of greatest concern is when HIT and CDS implementations themselves cause patient harm. A 2005 article published in *Pediatrics*[47] entitled "Unexpected increased mortality after implementation of a commercially sold computerized physician order entry system" loudly sounded this alarm. This article reported a 3.3-fold increase in the mortality rate for children transferred in for specialty care when it first implemented a computerized practitioner order entry (CPOE) system.

Although commentators noted methodological problems affecting conclusions that can be drawn from this report, this troubling account highlights important lessons for CDS and HIT implementers. Some of these are summarized in a commentary[48] to the article published in a subsequent *Pediatrics* issue. The lessons—echoing core messages in this Guide—include meticulous attention to workflow and policy changes introduced by new implementations, multidisciplinary stakeholder engagement and communication, and providing the 'right information' as part of the deployment (such as appropriate order sets to enhance system-based workflow), among others. Furthermore, other studies following sound implementation practices did not find such negative effects.[49]

Some reports focus specifically on unintended consequences from HIT deployment and use. For example, in December 2008 The Joint Commission—which accredits healthcare organizations around the world—issued a Sentinel Event Alert[50] entitled "Safely Implementing Health Information and Converging Technologies." This alert mentions CDS specifically as a cause of technology-related adverse events. Contributing factors include alert fatigue, failure to keep knowledge bases current, poor workflows and the like.

Corrective actions outlined in the Alert mirror suggestions in this book (e.g., careful attention to workflow, testing, training, and communication, as well as end user engagement throughout the process of planning, selecting, designing, and evaluating and improving technology solutions). There have also been reviews that have specifically examined unintended consequences from CDS.[51]

The literature reviews citing positive CDS effects also highlight important negative and unintended consequences from CDS interventions. The Byrne et al. ACDS deliverable "Key Lessons in CDS Implementation" cited earlier describes some of these pitfalls, including those related to the alert intervention type:

> Over-alerting and high rates of alert overrides have been widely acknowledged as a deterrent to CDS acceptance and appropriate use. (8-13)[52]

Similarly, from the Berner 2009 whitepaper:

> This issue of ignoring the advice of the CDS has been shown for a variety of types of CDS including those that provide diagnostic suggestions[53] evidence-based treatment recommendations[54] or alerts for potentially dangerous drug interactions.[55] The problem of overriding drug interaction alerts, in particular, has been shown in inpatient, long-term care, and outpatient settings.[56] Until there is a better understanding of why clinicians either do not access, or choose to ignore, the CDS recommendations, assessing the effect of CDS on quality will be very difficult. Because clinician decision-making influences care processes, it is important to examine the literature on why clinicians fail to utilize CDS suggestions.

The review then outlines literature related to several major categories of reasons why these suggestions are not followed:

- Match of CDS to users' intentions
- User control, disruptiveness and risk
- Integration of CDS into work processes.

These issues are addressed in detail in the following chapters.

Avoiding CDS Pitfalls

The literature sampling on CDS pitfalls outlined earlier echoes anecdotal experience in highlighting two major inter-related contributors to CDS deployment problems. Most obvious are problems related to specific **CDS interventions** themselves. They may fail to deliver expected benefits, or be perceived as unhelpful or worse by recipients. Following is a brief overview of some common pitfalls:

- Poor user intervention adoption resulting from failure to adequately consider user needs and workflow;
- Over-reliance on interruptive alerting leading to high over-ride rates, alert fatigue and user frustration;
- Failing to prepare end users appropriately for intervention rollout;
- Overwhelming end users by rolling out too many interventions at once;
- Reinforcing sub-optimal care due to out-of-date intervention content;
- Failing to achieve intended improvement objectives because the interventions are not linked tightly enough to goals, and key stakeholders have not been engaged in CDS efforts to close the gaps.

Part II of this Guide lays out a step-by-step approach to selecting, configuring, and launching CDS interventions to avoid these and other problems.

Of perhaps greater importance for your long-term success with CDS though, are more fundamental and overarching components of how you approach CDS. These include issues such as performance-improvement priorities, culture and approach to managing change, approaches to decision making and communication, use of underlying technology infrastructure, ability to examine and enhance workflows, and capacity to evaluate interventions. These and other important dimen-

sions comprise your **CDS Program**. Here are some examples of these CDS Program pitfalls:

- Failing to have decision making and governance processes that tightly link CDS activities to improvement imperatives and business processes for addressing these goals;
- Approaching CDS in general as something that is done *to* recipients and others as opposed to something that is done *with* them;
- Not devoting appropriate emphasis and resources to measuring intended and unintended intervention results;
- Not having an adequate, proactive approach to keeping interventions current and appropriate over time;
- Not using CDS tools within the greater context of a culture of patient safety and quality improvement.

The remaining chapters in Part I provide a step-by-step approach to avoiding these and other pitfalls as you establish or refine your CDS program.

Getting Everyone Focused and On the Same Page

Whether you work in a solo physician practice or a large heath system—or with an HIT supplier, a consultancy or in some other setting—it is important to have a shared framework for what you are trying to accomplish with CDS and how you are going to achieve the shared goals. An important component of these conversations and explorations is building a picture of the costs (including monetary, time, and others) and benefits (related to patient care, finances, efficiency) you might expect from your CDS efforts. Figure 1-3 outlines a few sample costs and benefits to seed your thinking and discussions about this CDS return on investment (ROI). Consider also the CDS business benefits outlined in Figure 1-1, shown earlier.

In Chapters 2 and 5 we'll delve more deeply into selecting and prioritizing specific goals to address with CDS. At this foundational stage of discussing CDS programs, it's useful to begin considering the

Figure 1-3: Some Factors to Consider Regarding CDS Program ROI

Costs and Revenue Reductions	Explanation
Additional staffing costs	Additional staff and/or work hours may be required to handle increased responsibilities related to CDS program and interventions
Required software upgrades and additional CDS content acquisition	If current EHR system is not certified for Meaningful Use or does not have required functionality or content
Additional hardware requirements	More devices may be required for data collection/analysis and adequate availability to users at point of need
Decrease in physician and staff productivity	Related to potential additional documentation and other workflow changes associated with major new interventions and managing the CDS program

Cost & Revenue Enhancements/Other Benefits	Explanation
Access additional revenue from P4P programs	May be possible from 'value-based purchasing' programs from Medicare and other payers
Avoid potential penalties for not meeting quality targets	HITECH legislation calls for such penalties after period of financial incentives; other payers considering likewise
Attract additional patients to the practice/hospital based on strong quality program	Patients are increasingly encouraged—in some case with financial incentives—to seek care from high-quality providers
Better use of clinician time and practice resources	Efficiencies can result from better CDS-enabled decision making and workflows

types of internal and external performance improvement drivers for which your focused CDS efforts will yield the most valuable returns. An important theme is that these goals should be *measurable and measured*. That is, important enough so that it really matters if your CDS interventions focused on them are making a difference, so much so that it will be imperative that you find the time, resources and expertise needed to do this measurement right. If not, then all the CDS steps that follow (particularly those outlined in Part II) are on shaky ground.

High-level CDS Goal Types
There are many different dimensions for categorizing strategic targets to address with your CDS

program and interventions. For example, you will want to consider external drivers such as regulatory, payment, and accreditation requirements. Many of these may be focused on specific clinical conditions, identified nationally for their high avoidable costs and/or improvement opportunities.

There is a natural set of driver activities unfolding, each component of which presents opportunities to leverage CDS. Although the examples in Figure 1-4 are drawn largely from the U.S., the movement to address these drivers and the corresponding CDS opportunities are global in nature.

Forces resulting from drivers of this sort will motivate the goals you address in your CDS program. Identifying and prioritizing goals and

Figure 1-4: Sample Drivers and Related CDS Opportunities

Driver Type	Driver Example	Sample CDS Opportunity
Promote performance measurement and transparency through incentives for reporting care process and outcomes measures	CMS/Joint Commission core measures reported via CMS Hospital Compare[57] and Physician Compare websites. Includes process (e.g., rates of appropriate test and medication use), outcome (e.g., mortality and readmission rates) and patient satisfaction measures (e.g., HCAHPS* scores). The U.S. National Quality Strategy[58] points toward a measurement trajectory	Support gathering data at the point of care needed for measurement; improve performance on publicly reported measures
Provide incentives for those who deploy specific CDS interventions or capabilities	Stage 1 Meaningful Use[4]	Leverage good CDS practices to ensure that the selected intervention delivers optimal value
Penalize for avoidable complications caused by care delivery	Avoidable medication errors,[59] infections, and other Healthcare Associated Conditions (HACs) that are not reimbursed	Monitor care delivery via CDS rules and notify when precursors suggest increased risk for HACs
Define increasing threshold for better patient-focused outcomes	Stage 3 Meaningful Use,[4] public and private Value-based Purchasing programs[60]	Improve outcomes by helping ensure that best clinical practices are reliably used
Promote more cost-effective care	Financial incentives to decrease hospital readmissions	Support more cost-effective decisions by stakeholders within care delivery process
Coordinate care across delivery settings	Incentives for forming 'Accountable Care Organizations'[61]	Promote context-specific data access and outcome-improving information delivery across the care continuum
Local improvement needs and imperatives	Improvement imperatives identified by internal quality assurance efforts or externally generated performance analytics (e.g., from payers)	Ensure that CDS efforts simultaneously address priority improvement opportunities evident from local care processes, as well as external drivers.

* HCAHPS = Hospital Consumer Assessment of Healthcare Providers and Systems.

related objectives are explored in more detail in Chapter 2 (see Figures 2-2 and 2-3 and related discussions).

Essential Ingredients for Successful CDS Programs and Interventions

There are many key steps to implementing a CDS Program, and valuable CDS interventions within that program. If you want an overview of these steps before continuing, you can review the process flow diagrams and case studies in the Introductions to Part I and Part II. For a deeper dive, you can scan the Tasks and Key Lessons listed at the beginning of each chapter.

CONSIDERATIONS FOR HOSPITALS/HEALTH SYSTEMS

The size and complexity of hospitals and large care delivery organizations have important implications for all facets of CDS programs and interventions. For example, there are many individuals with competing needs and priorities, which can dramatically amplify communication, political, cultural and other challenges that can be problematic enough in smaller care delivery settings. Under this 'Considerations' subheading in each chapter, we outline issues that those working in hospitals and health systems can consider in applying the guidance outlined in the 'General Approach' section to accomplishing the tasks outlined at the beginning of the chapter. These considerations are presented in bullet format in each, except for Chapter 2 where there is more detailed information in prose format. The material is organized around activity categories that are central to CDS efforts.

The Case Study for Hospitals presented in the Introductions to Part I and Part II of this Guide illustrates how these issues may play out in a synthesized scenario covering CDS program and intervention development, respectively. The Considerations for HIT Software Providers section in each chapter provides recommendations for these software suppliers, including opportunities for deepening collaborations with their implementer clients.

People (Stakeholder Involvement)

- Number of stakeholders is large; need to consider who they are, and how best to get everyone on the same page regarding basic concepts (more on this in later chapters).
- There will be much emphasis and attention by many stakeholders—e.g., Chief Medical Informatics Officers (CMIOs), Chief Information Officers (CIOs), their teams and others—on getting clinical information systems deployed and used. Remain constantly vigilant in your approach and interactions with stakeholders to ensure that these system strategies and deployments are delivering on the intended improvements, which depend critically on getting CDS right.
  - For example, a CDS-related study report title emphasizes this point: "High Rates of Adverse Drug Events in a Highly Computerized Hospital."[62] This deployment had sophisticated systems with CDS, but the CDS was not optimally focused on the adverse event causes.

Planning (Tasks)

- Even when there is a clear organizational focus on a specific goal, CDS success in a hospital or health system requires a strong CDS program (as outlined in Part I of this Guide) and careful attention to the specific tasks related to intervention configuration and launch outlined in Part II.
  - A failed project in a community hospital within a health system that attempted to apply CDS to improve performance on congestive heart failure care illustrates this point. Study authors reported: "Overall, the pilot implementation of the CDSS to improve compliance with CHF core measures performed poorly, leading to its withdrawal."[63] They attributed some of the problem to difficulties in identifying congestive heart failure patients with appropriate sensitivity and positive predictive value. They also noted other problems related to intervention selection and user interface, as well as physician engagement. This

conclusion by the study authors resonates with an important theme of this Guide: "Ultimately, we learned that CDSSs may succeed better if they avoid alerts aimed at physicians and develop a methodology that fits better in the existing workflow." This reinforces the call for a shared understanding of the CDS Five Rights approach among all pertinent stakeholders as a foundational component for CDS programs.

Capabilities

- The powerful movements (especially in the inpatient setting) toward 'value-based purchasing' and non-payment for 'never events' are strong drivers and important opportunities to add organizational value by aligning your CDS efforts with these initiatives. Following is a sampling of specific objectives of particular interest in the inpatient setting:
  - CMS withholds additional payment to cover the cost of treating preventable care complications that occur during a patient's hospitalization.[64] CDS can play an important role in decreasing how often several of these conditions occur. Figure 1-5 provides several examples, along with their CDS implications.
  - The Medicare value-based purchasing program builds on performance measures anchoring 'pay for reporting' initiatives by associating payments with performance on the measures.[65] This amplifies the importance of applying CDS to improve performance in inpatient areas addressed by reporting initiatives, including management of pneumonia, myocardial infarction, congestive heart failure, surgical care and patient satisfaction. Once again, CDS can play a key role in ensuring that the condition monitoring, management and patient education required in these measures[66] reliably occurs in hospitalized patients; for one of many examples, the Hospital Consumer Assessment of Healthcare Providers and Systems (HCAHPS)[67] patient survey results that are posted to Hospital Compare and used in Medicare's value-based purchasing program. One of the survey questions—"How often did your caregivers inform you about medicines you were given in the hospital"—is clearly an opportunity for you to leverage CDS to bring this information into clinical workflow and optimize performance on this measure.

Figure 1-5: Hospital-acquired Conditions Not Reimbursed by CMS, and Example CDS Approaches

Hospital-acquired Condition	Example CDS Approaches
Vascular catheter-associated infections such as central line–associated bloodstream infections (CLABSI), catheter-associated urinary tract infection (CAUTI)	CDS can help ensure catheters aren't left in unnecessarily, and thereby reduce infection risk
Venous thromboembolism (VTE) following surgical procedures	CDS can help ensure appropriate preventive therapies are administered
Falls	CDS can help reduce risk for falls, e.g., by identifying patients at high risk who can benefit from additional intervention, and by helping decrease inappropriate use of medications that increase fall risk
Poor glycemic control	CDS can facilitate appropriate blood sugar monitoring and management

CONSIDERATIONS FOR SMALL PRACTICES

In a small practice, fewer people than in larger settings need to be engaged, but there are also fewer hands and resources to get things done. Think about the 'most important things' to accomplish with the CDS program (i.e., how the information presented in the 'General Approach' section of this and other chapters apply to your practice). The process for starting or enhancing a CDS program, and implementing effective CDS interventions, will be adapted based on the resources, available personnel, and clinical objectives unique to a small practice.

Under this 'Considerations' subheading in each chapter, we outline issues that those working in small practices can consider in applying the guidance outlined in the 'General Approach' section to accomplishing the tasks outlined at the beginning of the chapter. These considerations are presented in bullet format in each chapter and are organized around activity categories central to CDS efforts. These recommendations were vetted with clinicians in small practices who have successfully used CDS—and consultants who help enable these successes.

The Case Study for Small Practices presented in the Introductions to Part I and Part II of this Guide illustrates how these issues may play out in a synthesized scenario covering CDS program and intervention development, respectively. The Considerations for HIT Software Providers section in each chapter provides recommendations for these software suppliers, including opportunities for deepening collaborations with their implementer clients.

People

- Even though there may only be a few people involved, make sure you develop a shared understanding and full 'buy in' among *all* key participants (including physicians, nurses, implementers, practice managers, office staff and patients as appropriate) about the role of CDS in enhancing the practice's clinical, operational, and financial performance.

- Each practice participant should be able to satisfactorily answer the question, "What's in it for me?" CDS effort leaders should articulate and discuss clinical and financial risks and benefits from the CDS activities (see Figures 1-1 and 1-3). This will help ensure that everyone in the practice is engaged and enthusiastic about this work. The literature summary previously outlined can help inform this conversation.

Planning (Processes)

- Begin building a shared, broad perspective on the CDS toolkit—for example, the many potential content and intervention types, recipients, delivery channels and workflow opportunities (that is, the CDS Five Rights approach for improving outcomes with CDS configurations that optimize these dimensions).

- In order to understand CDS's role in enhancing practice workflows, the CDS effort leaders must know the reality of how the practice operates. How one *thinks* the practice operates is not always the same as the *reality*.

Capabilities

- For small practices, the EHR functionality can be a limiting factor for CDS. It is helpful to ensure that the CDS lead—and ideally the full practice—understands well the EHR's CDS-related functionality. The system supplier can be helpful here. For example, when feasible, attend EHR vendor conferences to discover new functionality. Request a demo from the vendor so that you can see how a new product version, or the addition of a new product, could improve your workflow and outcomes.

- Since small practices will be heavily dependent on their HIT suppliers for needed CDS functionality and related support, you should invest the time and effort needed to establish a close working relationship focused on optimizing this functionality and support.

- Although you should fully leverage your available clinical information systems as the channel for

CDS intervention delivery, consider other channels—including paper—for CDS delivery when you don't have more robust tools. For example, paper-based care flows, flowsheets and documentation forms (addressing chronic conditions and preventive care), and other 'low tech' CDS approaches can still be valuable and appropriate when paper is the best channel available for a particular intervention needed to improve decisions and workflow.

Communication

- Leverage the formal and informal practice communication channels with *everyone* in the group to elicit performance improvement needs and opportunities where CDS might be of value.
- Use your knowledge of CDS and the practice, together with personal relationships, to plant seeds with individuals in the practice for how CDS could actually help address these. Vet and refine these ideas (using the CDS Five Rights framework) as outlined in subsequent chapters.
- It is particularly important that CDS become part of the quality improvement initiatives in a practice. In order to be most successful, the program should be "bottom-up," since a "top-down" approach might be perceived as an unwelcome mandate rather than a team initiative toward shared goals.
- To complement the bottom-up approach, the practice's CDS initiative leader should continuously cultivate and reinforce the value proposition for the CDS activities. Modeling effective engagement in—and benefits from—the CDS efforts helps create a fertile culture for CDS value to flourish.

Planning (Goal Selection)

- Begin outlining, or refining, a set of initial strategic victories to be pursued and claimed.
- Make sure these goals are reasonable and scaled to the resources that the practice has available. Starting with something manageable and useful is important to building confidence. The

process requires patience and the celebration of small victories.
- Pay careful attention to care processes and outcomes tied to reimbursement or accreditation, which may heighten interest in CDS approaches and provide incentives and tools for measuring their effects.

CONSIDERATIONS FOR HIT SOFTWARE PROVIDERS

Meaningful Use requirements in the U.S.—and many other global imperatives for enhancing healthcare quality, safety, efficiency and costs—make it increasingly urgent for healthcare providers to deploy health IT systems that help improve clinical decisions, actions and outcomes. Each chapter in this Guide includes a section aimed at suppliers of these systems—e.g., clinical information and decision-support vendors—and their interactions with their healthcare provider clients that deploy these systems. This material is intended to help you with the following functions related to the goal of outcome-improving CDS that are shared between suppliers and implementers:

- HIT supplier organizational capabilities;
- HIT supplier system functionality;
- HIT supplier support services to providers;
- Implementer expectations of their HIT suppliers;
- Implementer-HIT supplier dialog and collaboration throughout the system procurement and deployment lifecycle.

Broadly successful HIT supplier-implementer collaborations of the sort we hope to foster with this material are early in their development, so we view these 'HIT Software Provider Consideration' sections as a starting point—rather than the final word—on optimizing these joint efforts. The HIT Software Provider Considerations are intentionally ambitious in an effort to help accelerate much needed progress. As with the Hospital/Health System and Small Practice Considerations sections in each chapter, the bullets in this section in each chapter are organized by key CDS activity categories.

Capabilities

- Think broadly about CDS intervention types and the channels through which they are delivered because these are often largely under the supplier's control. Consider also the other components of the CDS Five Rights, since they are the context in which the resources you supply are used. Cultivate an internal business culture focused on a shared, solid understanding of how these can best be leveraged to help clients achieve their business and clinical goals.

- Collaborate with healthcare provider clients on developing and applying a shared, broad perspective on the CDS toolkit—that is, considering the many potential CDS content and intervention types, recipients, delivery channels and workflow opportunities.

- To ensure that you are responsive to providers' care-improvement imperatives, track (or preferably, participate in) the national effort to improve healthcare performance—for example, efforts related to defining improvement priorities (such as the National Priorities Partnership[68] in the U.S.), standards related to CDS (e.g. HL7[69], national standards and certification standards efforts[70]), and the like. Small practices, and even large healthcare systems, will increasingly rely on their CIS (clinical information systems) and CDS suppliers to help them digest and address these drivers.

- Understand imminent regulatory and payer requirements that put an increased emphasis on both CDS and quality measurement; these requirements are dynamic, and you will need to track and address them over time.

- Base your CDS-related strategy not just on single targets and techniques, but consider broader drivers as recommended to providers earlier in this chapter. For example, make sure you are offering solutions that measurably enhance management of particular clinical conditions (to support care quality), as well as broader processes such as medication management (to support care

safety). Consider also how your all CDS offerings can measurably improve care delivery costs and efficiency.

Communication

- Just as CDS implementers must cultivate a shared vision within their organizations that CDS is a strategic tool, you should nurture a shared vision between your HIT supplier team and your clients. This should address the strategic role that these systems play and how your tools and capabilities can support clients in meeting care delivery imperatives. This may include having your representatives participate in your clients' strategic planning and execution, and vice versa.

- Because you and your clients depend on each other for success, you should provide—and your clients will increasingly expect—a strong and mutually beneficial relationship. This provides a valuable foundation for successful CDS implementation, adoption and value realization. It provides a context for reconciling the technology capabilities with business and clinical goals, in light of required workflows and other clinician and patient needs.

WORKSHEETS

In chapters that follow, we present more detailed guidance on building successful CDS programs and interventions. As noted earlier, much of the guidance is organized around important tasks for you as implementers (and those who support you) that anchor each chapter. In addition, each of the remaining chapters in this book provides worksheets to help document and address these action items. Below are items to consider at the introductory stage covered by this chapter, together with pointers forward to worksheets where these items are explored in more detail.

❑ Begin (or enhance) conversations with other key individuals toward a shared understanding of CDS goals, objectives and approaches (see Worksheets 2-1 and 2-2).

❑ Create (or review) a draft list of your promising targets for CDS efforts (see Worksheets 2-1, 5-1 and 5-2).

❑ Scan the CDS Five Rights discussion (Chapter 5), and consider its implications for ways to enhance how CDS can be applied to enhancing care in your environment (see Worksheets 6-1, 6-2 and 6-3).

❑ List strategies for how you would know (or know better) how your CDS interventions are positively and negatively affecting important care dimensions (see Worksheets 9-1, 9-2 and 9-3).

REFERENCES

1   Richardson JE, et al. Multiple Perspectives on the Meaning of Clinical Decision Support. AMIA Annu Symp Proc. 2010; 2010: 672–676. http://www.ncbi.nlm.nih.gov/pmc/articles/PMC3041408/. Accessed June 15, 2011.

2   Osheroff JA, Pifer EA, Teich JM, Sittitg DF, Jenders RA. *Improving Outcomes with Clinical Decision Support: An Implementer's Guide.* Chicago: HIMSS; 2005.

3   Osheroff JA, Teich JM, Middleton B, et al. A roadmap for national action on clinical decision support. *JAMIA.* 2007;14:141-145.

4   See Federal Register, Wednesday July 28, 2010. Part II. Department of Health and Human Services. Center for Medicare and Medicaid Services. 42 CFR Parts 412, 413, 422, et al. Medicare and Medicaid Programs; Electronic Health Record Incentive Program; Final rule. Page 44350. Available online at: http://edocket.access.gpo.gov/2010/pdf/2010-17207.pdf. Accessed June 15, 2011.

5   CMS EHR Meaningful Use Overview. Centers for Medicare and Medicaid Services website. Available online at: https://www.cms.gov/EHRIncentivePrograms/30_Meaningful_Use.asp. Accessed June 15, 2011.

6   See discussion in HIMSS editorial on 'meaningful meaningful use': Available online at: http://www.himss.org/ASP/ContentRedirector.asp?ContentId=72799&type=HIMSSNewsItem. Accessed June 15, 2011.

7   Osheroff JA. Improving Medication Use and Outcomes with CDS: A Step-by-Step Guide. Chicago: HIMSS; 2009.

8   McDonald CJ. Protocol-based computer reminders, the quality of care and the non-perfectability of man. *N Engl J Med.* 1976; 295(24):1351-1355. Available online at: http://www.nejm.org/doi/full/10.1056/NEJM197612092952405. Accessed June 16, 2011.

9   Berner ES. Clinical Decision Support: State of the Art. AHRQ Publication No. 09-0069-EF. Rockville, Maryland: Agency for Healthcare Research and Quality. June, 2009. Available online at: http://healthit.ahrq.gov/images/jun09cdsreview/09_0069_ef.html. Accessed June 15, 2011.

10 Lobach DF, Sanders GD, Bright TJ, et al. Enabling Health Care Decisionmaking through Clinical Decision Support and Knowledge Management. Evidence Report No. #TBD. (Prepared by the Duke Evidence-based Practice Center under Contract No. 290-2007-10066-I.) AHRQ Publication No. #TBD. Rockville, MD. Agency for Healthcare Research and Quality. In Press. Available online at: http://www.effectivehealthcare.ahrq.gov/ehc/products/278/607/Decision%20Support_Draft%20Report%2012-06-2010.pdf . Accessed October 23, 2011.

11 Byrne C, Sherry D, Mercincavage L, et al. Key Lessons in Clinical Decision Support Implementation. Prepared for: Department of Health and Human Services Contract # HHSP23320095649WC, Task order HHSP23337009T, Office of the National Coordinator ARRA Contract entitled "Advancing Clinical Decision Support." March 6, 2011. Available online at: http://www.westat.com/Westat/expertise/health_and_medical/health_it.cfm. Accessed November 15, 2011.

12 Buntin MB, et al. The benefits of health information technology: A review of the recent literature shows predominantly positive results. Available online at: http://content.healthaffairs.org/content/30/3/464.abstract. Accessed June 15, 2011.

    A brief interview with article co-author and former U.S. National Coordinator for Health IT is available online from *CMIO*: http://www.cmio.net/index.php?option=com_articles&view=article&id=26676:blumenthal-feature-health-it-improves-outcomes-patient-satisfaction-is-next&division=cmio. Accessed June 15, 2011.

13 Clinical decision support. Agency for Healthcare Research and Quality website: http://healthit.ahrq.gov/portal/server.pt?open=514&objID=5554&mode=2&holderDisplayURL=http://wci-pubcontent/publish/communities/k_o/knowledge_library/key_topics__backup/health_briefing_01242006122700/clinical_decision_support.html. Accessed June 15, 2011.

Clinical Decision Support. Office of the National Coordinator for Health Information Technology website: http://healthit.hhs.gov/portal/server.pt/community/healthit_hhs_gov__cds/1218. Accessed June 15, 2011.

14 Clinical decision support. Healthcare Information Management and Systems Society website: http://www.himss.org/ASP/topics_clinicalDecision.asp. Accessed June 15, 2011.

15 McGregor JC, Weekes E, Forrest GN, et al. Impact of a computerized clinical decision support system on reducing inappropriate antimicrobial use: a randomized controlled trial. *J Am Med Inform Assoc.* 2006; 13(4):378-384.

Paul M, Andreassen S, Tacconelli E, et al. Improving empirical antibiotic treatment using TREAT, a computerized decision support system: cluster randomized trial. *J Antimicrob Chemother.* 2006; 58(6):1238-1245.

Rood E, Bosman RJ, van der Spoel JI, et al. Use of a computerized guideline for glucose regulation in the intensive care unit improved both guideline adherence and glucose regulation. *J Am Med Inform Assoc.* 2005; 12(2):172-180.

Rothschild JM, McGurk S, Honour M, et al. Assessment of education and computerized decision support interventions for improving transfusion practice. *Transfusion.* (Paris) 2007; 47(2):228-239.

Tamblyn R, Huang A, Perreault R, et al. The medical office of the 21st century (MOXXI): effectiveness of computerized decision-making support in reducing inappropriate prescribing in primary care. *CMAJ.* 2003; 169(6):549-556.

van Wyk JT, van Wijk MA, Sturkenboom MC, et al. Electronic alerts versus on-demand decision support to improve dyslipidemia treatment: a cluster randomized controlled trial. *Circulation.* 2008; 117(3):371-378.

Zanetti G, Flanagan HL, Jr., Cohn LH, et al. Improvement of intraoperative antibiotic prophylaxis in prolonged cardiac surgery by automated alerts in the operating room. *Infect Control Hosp Epidemiol.* 2003; 24(1):13-16.

16 Ansari M, Shlipak MG, Heidenreich PA, et al. Improving guideline adherence: a randomized trial evaluating strategies to increase beta-blocker use in heart failure. *Circulation.* 2003; 107(22):2799-2804.

Bell LM, Grundmeier R, Localio R, et al. Electronic health record-based decision support to improve asthma care: A cluster-randomized trial. *Pediatrics.* 2010; 125(4): E770-E777.

Field TS, Rochon P, Lee M, et al. Computerized clinical decision support during medication ordering for long-term care residents with renal insufficiency. *J Am Med Inform Assoc.* 2009; 16(4):480-285.

Fortuna RJ, Zhang F, Ross-Degnan D, et al. Reducing the prescribing of heavily marketed medications: a randomized controlled trial. *J Gen Intern Med.* 2009; 24(8):897-903.

Hicks LS, Sequist TD, Ayanian JZ, et al. Impact of computerized decision support on blood pressure management and control: a randomized controlled trial. *J Gen Intern Med.* 2008; 23(4):429-441.

Linder JA, Rigotti NA, Schneider LI, et al. An electronic health record-based intervention to improve tobacco treatment in primary care: a cluster-randomized controlled trial. *Arch Intern Med.* 2009; 169(8):781-787.

Martens JD, van der Weijden T, Severens JL, et al. The effect of computer reminders on GPs' prescribing behaviour: a cluster-randomised trial. *Int J Med Inform.* 2007; 76 (suppl 3):S403-S416.

17 Dexter PR, Perkins S, Overhage JM, et al. A computerized reminder system to increase the use of preventive care for hospitalized patients. *N Engl J Med.* 2001; 345(13):965-970.

Dexter PR, Perkins SM, Maharry KS, et al. Inpatient computer-based standing orders vs. physician reminders to increase influenza and pneumococcal vaccination rates: a randomized trial. *JAMA.* 2004; 292(19):2366-71.

Kucher N, Koo S, Quiroz R, et al. Electronic alerts to prevent venous thromboembolism among hospitalized patients. *N Engl J Med.* 2005; 352(10):969-977.

18 Demakis JG, Beauchamp C, Cull WL, et al. Improving residents' compliance with standards of ambulatory care: results from the VA Cooperative Study on Computerized Reminders. *JAMA.* 2000; 284(11):1411-1416.

Kenealy T, Arroll B, Petrie KJ. Patients and computers as reminders to screen for diabetes in family practice. Randomized-controlled trial. *J Gen Intern Med.* 2005; 20(10):916-921.

Peterson KA, Radosevich DM, O'Connor PJ, et al. Improving diabetes care in practice: findings from the TRANSLATE trial. *Diabetes Care.* 2008; 31(12):2238-2243.

19 Bell LM, Grundmeier R, Localio R, et al. Electronic health record-based decision support to improve asthma care: A cluster-randomized rrial. *Pediatrics.* 2010; 125(4): E770-E777.

Lo HG, Matheny ME, Seger DL, et al. Impact of non-interruptive medication laboratory monitoring alerts in ambulatory care. *J Am Med Inform Assoc.* 2009; 16(1):66-71.

Raebel MA, Chester EA, Newsom EE, et al. Randomized trial to improve laboratory safety monitoring of ongoing drug therapy in ambulatory patients. *Pharmacotherapy.* 2006; 26(5):619-626.

Roukema J, Steyerberg EW, van der Lei J, et al. Randomized trial of a clinical decision support system: impact on the management of children with fever without apparent source. *J Am Med Inform Assoc.* 2008; 15(1):107-113.

Sundaram V, Lazzeroni LC, Douglass LR, et al. A randomized trial of computer-based reminders and audit and feedback to improve HIV screening in a primary care setting. *Int J STD AIDS.* 2009; 20(8):527-533.

20 Ansari M, Shlipak MG, Heidenreich PA, et al. Improving guideline adherence: a randomized trial evaluating strategies to increase beta-blocker use in heart failure. *Circulation.* 2003; 107(22):2799-2804.

Cleveringa FG, Gorter KJ, van den Donk M, et al. Combined task delegation, computerized decision support, and feedback improve cardiovascular risk for type 2 diabetic patients: a cluster randomized trial in primary care. *Diabetes Care.* 2008; 31(12):2273-2275.

Heidenreich PA, Gholami P, Sahay A, et al. Clinical reminders attached to echocardiography reports of patients with reduced left ventricular ejection fraction increase use of beta-blockers: a randomized trial. *Circulation.* 2007; 115(22):2829-2834.

21 Graumlich JF, Novotny NL, Stephen Nace G, et al. Patient readmissions, emergency visits, and adverse events after software-assisted discharge from hospital: cluster randomized trial. *J Hosp Med.* 2009; 4(7):E11-E9.

Kucher N, Koo S, Quiroz R, et al. Electronic alerts to prevent venous thromboembolism among hospitalized patients. *N Engl J Med.* 2005; 352(10):969-977.

Paul M, Andreassen S, Tacconelli E, et al. Improving empirical antibiotic treatment using TREAT, a computerized decision support system: cluster randomized trial. *J Antimicrob Chemother.* 2006; 58(6):1238-1245.

22 Del Fiol G, Haug PJ, Cimino JJ, et al. Effectiveness of topic-specific infobuttons: a randomized controlled trial. *J Am Med Inform Assoc.* 2008; 15(6):752-9.

23 Emery J, Morris H, Goodchild R, et al. The GRAIDS Trial: a cluster randomized controlled trial of computer decision support for the management of familial cancer risk in primary care. *Br J Cancer.* 2007; 97(4):486-493.

24 Hobbs FD, Delaney BC, Carson A, et al. A prospective controlled trial of computerized decision support for lipid management in primary care. *Fam Pract.* 1996; 13(2):133-137.

25 Paul M, Andreassen S, Tacconelli E, et al. Improving empirical antibiotic treatment using TREAT, a computerized decision support system: cluster randomized trial. *J Antimicrob Chemother.* 2006; 58(6):1238-1245.

Roumie CL, Elasy TA, Greevy R, et al. Improving blood pressure control through provider education, provider alerts, and patient education: a cluster randomized trial. *Ann Intern Med.* 2006; 145(3):165-175.

Kuperman GJ, Teich JM, Tanasijevic MJ, et al. Improving response to critical laboratory results with automation: results of a randomized controlled trial. *J Am Med Inform Assoc.* 1999; 6(6):512-522.

26 McGregor JC, Weekes E, Forrest GN, et al. Impact of a computerized clinical decision support system on reducing inappropriate antimicrobial use: a randomized controlled trial. *J Am Med Inform Assoc.* 2006; 13(4):378-384.

Paul M, Andreassen S, Tacconelli E, et al. Improving empirical antibiotic treatment using TREAT, a computerized decision support system: cluster randomized trial. *J Antimicrob Chemother.* 2006; 58(6):1238-1245.

Overhage JM, Tierney WM, Zhou XH, et al. A randomized trial of "corollary orders" to prevent errors of omission. *J Am Med Inform Assoc.* 1997; 4(5):364-375.

Kline JA, Zeitouni RA, Hernandez-Nino J, et al. Randomized trial of computerized quantitative pretest probability in low-risk chest pain patients: effect on safety and resource use. *Ann Emerg Med.* 2009; 53(6):727-735.

27 Kline JA, Zeitouni RA, Hernandez-Nino J, et al. Randomized trial of computerized quantitative pretest probability in low-risk chest pain patients: effect on safety and resource use. *Ann Emerg Med.* 2009; 53(6):727-735.

28 Tierney WM, Overhage JM, Murray MD, et al. Effects of computerized guidelines for managing heart disease in primary care. *J Gen Intern Med.* 2003; 18(12):967-976.

Tierney WM, Overhage JM, Murray MD, et al. Can computer-generated evidence-based care suggestions enhance evidence-based management of asthma and chronic obstructive pulmonary disease? A randomized, controlled trial. *Health Serv Res.* 2005; 40(2):477-497.

Murray MD, Harris LE, Overhage JM, et al. Failure of computerized treatment suggestions to improve health outcomes of outpatients with uncomplicated hypertension: results of a randomized controlled trial. *Pharmacotherapy.* 2004; 24(3):324-337.

Subramanian U, Fihn SD, Weinberger M, et al. A controlled trial of including symptom data in computer-based care suggestions for managing patients with chronic heart failure. *Am J Med.* 2004; 116 (6):375-384.

Thomas HV, Lewis G, Watson M, et al. Computerised patient-specific guidelines for management of common mental disorders in primary care: a randomised controlled trial. *Br J Gen Pract.* 2004; 54(508):832-837.

29 These include the studies noted in reference 28, except for Thomas et al. 2004.

30 Terrell KM, Perkins AJ, Dexter PR, et al. Computerized decision support to reduce potentially inappropriate prescribing to older emergency department patients: a randomized, controlled trial. *J Am Geriatr Soc.* 2009; 57(8):1388-1394.

31 Fretheim A, Aaserud M, Oxman AD. Rational prescribing in primary care (RaPP): economic evaluation of an intervention to improve professional practice. *PLoS Med.* 2006; 3(6):e216.

Fretheim A, Oxman AD, Havelsrud K, et al. Rational prescribing in primary care (RaPP): a cluster randomized trial of a tailored intervention. *PLoS Med.* 2006; 3(6):e134.

McDowell I, Newell C, Rosser W. A randomized trial of computerized reminders for blood pressure screening in primary care. *Med Care.* 1989; 27(3):297-305.

Rosser WW, Hutchison BG, McDowell I, et al. Use of reminders to increase compliance with tetanus booster vaccination. *CMAJ.* 1992; 146(6):911-917.

32 Cleveringa FG, Gorter KJ, van den Donk M, et al. Combined task delegation, computerized decision support, and feedback improve cardiovascular risk for type 2 diabetic patients: a cluster randomized trial in primary care. *Diabetes Care.* 2008; 31(12):2273-2275.

Cleveringa FG, Welsing PM, van den Donk M, et al. Cost-effectiveness of the diabetes care protocol, a multifaceted computerized decision support diabetes management intervention that reduces cardiovascular risk. *Diabetes Care.* 2010; 33(2):258-263.

33 Eslami S, bu-Hanna A, de Keizer NF. Evaluation of outpatient computerized physician medication order entry systems: a systematic review. *J Am Med Inform Assoc.* 2007 Jul; 14(4):400-406.

Ammenwerth E, Schnell-Inderst P, Machan C, et al. The effect of electronic prescribing on medication errors and adverse drug events: a systematic review. *J Am Med Inform Assoc.* 2008 Sep; 15(5):585-600.

Wolfstadt J, Gurwitz J, Field T, et al. The effect of computerized physician order entry with clinical decision support on the rates of adverse drug events: a systematic review. *J Gen Intern Med.* 2008 Apr; 23(4):451-458.

34 Kucher N, Koo S, Quiroz R, et al. Electronic alerts to prevent venous thromboembolism among hospitalized patients. *N Engl J Med.* 2005; 352(10):969-977.

35 Love TE, Cebul RD, Einstadter D, et al. Electronic medical record-assisted design of a cluster-randomized trial to improve diabetes care and outcomes. *J Gen Intern Med.* 2008; 23(4):383-391.

Meigs JB, Cagliero E, Dubey A, et al. A controlled trial of web-based diabetes disease management: the MGH diabetes primary care improvement project. *Diabetes Care.* 2003; 26(3):750-757.

36 Miller RA. Medical diagnostic decision support systems—past, present, and future: a threaded bibliography and brief commentary. *J Am Med Inform Assoc.* 1994; 1(1):8-27.

Garg AX, Adhikari NKJ, McDonald H, et al. Effects of computerized clinical decision support systems on practitioner performance and patient outcomes. *JAMA.* 2005; 293(10):1223-1238.

Berner ES. Testing system accuracy. In: Berner ES, ed. Clinical Decision Support Systems: Theory and Practice. New York: Springer-Verlag New York, Inc.; 1999. p. 61-74.

Ramnarayan P, Kapoor RR, Coren M, et al. Measuring the impact of diagnostic decision support on the quality of clinical decision making: development of a reliable and valid composite score. *J Am Med Inform Assoc.* 2003 Nov; 10(6):563-572.

Ramnarayan P, Winrow A, Coren M, et al. Diagnostic omission errors in acute paediatric practice: impact of a reminder system on decision-making. *BMC Med Inform Decis Mak.* 2006; 6:37.

Ramnarayan P, Roberts GC, Coren M, et al. Assessment of the potential impact of a reminder system on the reduction of diagnostic errors: a quasi-experimental study. *BMC Med Inform Decis Mak.* 2006; 6:22.

37 Ramnarayan P, Kapoor RR, Coren M, et al. Measuring the impact of diagnostic decision support on the quality of clinical decision making: development of a reliable and valid composite score. *J Am Med Inform Assoc.* 2003; 10(6):563-572.

Berner ES, Webster GD, Shugerman AA, et al. Performance of four computer-based diagnostic systems. *N Engl J Med.* 1994; 330(25):1792-1796.

Apkon M, Mattera JA, Lin Z, et al. A randomized outpatient trial of a decision-support information technology tool. *Arch Intern Med.* 2005; 165(20):2388-2394.

38 Schedlbauer A, Prasad V, Mulvaney C, et al. What evidence supports the use of computerized alerts and prompts to improve clinicians' prescribing behavior? *J Am Med Inform Assoc.* 2009 Jul-Aug; 16(4):531-538.

39 See, for example, the Institute of Medicine Report: "Knowing what works in healthcare: a roadmap for the nation." Available online at: http://www.iom.edu/ Reports/2008/Knowing-What-Works-in-Health-Care-A-Roadmap-for-the-Nation.aspx. Accessed June 15, 2011.

40 For example, the Patient-centered Outcomes Research Institute formed in 2011 by U.S. federal law will help generate evidence from studies "that compare drugs, medical devices, tests, surgeries or ways to deliver health care." See About Us page on PCORI website: http://www.pcori. org/aboutus.html. Accessed June 15, 2011.

41 Bates DW, Kuperman GJ, Wang S, et al. Ten commandments for effective clinical decision support: Making the practice of evidence-based medicine a reality. *J Am Med Inform Assoc.* 2003 Nov–Dec; 10(6): 523–530. doi: 10.1197/jamia.M1370. Available online at: http:// www.ncbi.nlm.nih.gov/pmc/articles/PMC264429/. Accessed June 15, 2011.

42 See the Epilogue in this book for more details.

43 Black AD, Car J, Pagliari C, et al. The impact of eHealth on the quality and safety of health care: A systematic overview. Available online at: http://www.plosmedicine.org/article/ info%3Adoi%2F10.1371%2Fjournal.pmed.1000387. Accessed June 15, 2011.

44 Electronic health records and clinical decision support systems impact on national ambulatory care quality. Max J. Romano, BA; Randall S. Stafford, MD, PhD. *Arch Intern Med.* Published online January 24, 2011. doi:10.1001/ archinternmed.2010.527. http://archinte.ama-assn.org/cgi/ content/abstract/archinternmed.2010.527v1. Accessed June 15, 2011.

45 See for example, this one by Basch in the *Journal Health Affairs'* blog: http://healthaffairs.org/blog/2011/02/11/the-case-for-meaningful-use-strengthened-not-weakened/ and this one by Hersh: http://informaticsprofessor.blogspot. com/2011/01/electronic-health-records-do-not-impact. html. Both accessed June 15, 2011.

46 Mohan V, Hersh WR. EHRs and health care quality: Correlation with out-of-date, differently purposed data does not equate with causality. *Arch Intern Med.* 2011 May 23; 171(10):952-953.

47 Han YY, Carcillo JA, Venkataraman ST, et al. Unexpected increased mortality after implementation of a commercially sold computerized physician order entry system. *Pediatrics.* 2005; 116(6):1506–1512.

48 Sittig et al. Lessons from "Unexpected increased mortality after implementation of a commercially sold computerized physician order entry system." Available online at: http:// pediatrics.aappublications.org/cgi/content/full/118/2/797. Accessed June 15, 2011.

49 Del Beccaro MA, Jeffries HE, Eisenberg MA, et al. Computerized provider order entry implementation: no association with increased mortality rates in an intensive care unit. *Pediatrics.* 2006 Jul; 118(1):290-295.

50 Safely implementing health information and converging technologies. Joint Commission. Issue #42. 2008 Dec 11. Available online at: http://www.jointcommission.org/ assets/1/18/SEA_42.PDF. Accessed June 15, 2011.

51 Ash JS, Sittig DF, Campbell EM, et al. Some unintended consequences of clinical decision support systems. AMIA Annu Symp Proc. 2007 Oct 11:26-30.

52 Strom BL, Schinnar R, Aberra F, et al. Unintended effects of a computerized physician order entry nearly hard-stop alert to prevent a drug interaction: A randomized controlled trial. *Arch Intern Med.* 2010 Sep 27; 170(17):1578-1583.

Isaac T, Weissman JS, Davis RB, et al. Overrides of medication alerts in ambulatory care. *Arch Intern Med.* 2009 Feb 9; 69(3):305-311.

van der Sijs H, Aarts J, van Gelder T, et al. Turning off frequently overridden drug alerts: Limited opportunities for doing it safely. *J Am Med Inform Assoc.* 2008; 15(4):439-448.

Ko Y, Ararca J, Malone DC, et al. Practitioners' views on computerized drug-drug interaction alerts in the VA system. *J Am Med Inform Assoc.* 2007 Jan-Feb; 14(1):56-64.

Shah NR, Seger AC, Seger DL, et al. Improving acceptance of computerized prescribing alerts in ambulatory care. *J Am Med Inform Assoc.* 2006 Jan-Feb; 13(1):5-11.

Payne TH, Nichol WP, Hoey P, et al. Characteristics and override rates of order checks in a practitioner order entry system. Proc AMIA Symp. 2002; 602-606.

53 Berner ES, Maisiak RS, Heudebert GR, et al. Clinician performance and prominence of diagnoses displayed by a clinical diagnostic decision support system. AMIA Annu Symp Proc. 2003; 76-80.

Goodacre S, Webster A, Morris F. Do computer generated ECG reports improve interpretation by accident and emergency senior house officers? *Postgrad Med J.* 2001 Jul; 77(909):455-457.

54 Love TE, Cebul RD, Einstadter D, et al. Electronic medical record-assisted design of a cluster-randomized trial to improve diabetes care and outcomes. *J Gen Intern Med.* 2008 Apr; 23(4):383-391.

Tierney WM, Overhage JM, Murray MD, et al. Effects of computerized guidelines for managing heart disease in primary care. *J Gen Intern Med.* 2003 Dec; 18(12):967-976.

Tierney WM, Overhage JM, Murray MD, et al. Can computer-generated evidence-based care suggestions enhance evidence-based management of asthma and chronic obstructive pulmonary disease? A randomized, controlled trial. *Health Serv Res.* 2005 Apr; 40(2):477-497.

55 Isaac T, Weissman JS, Davis RB, et al. Overrides of medication alerts in ambulatory care. *Arch Intern Med.* 2009 Feb; 169(3):305-311.

Weingart SN, Toth M, Sands DZ, et al. Physicians' decisions to override computerized drug alerts in primary care. *Arch Intern Med.* 2003 Nov; 163(21):2625-2631.

Tamblyn R, Huang A, Taylor L, et al. A randomized trial of the effectiveness of on-demand versus computer-triggered drug decision support in primary care. *J Am Med Inform Assoc.* 2008 Jul; 15(4):430-438.

56 Eslami S, bu-Hanna A, de Keizer NF. Evaluation of outpatient computerized physician medication order entry systems: a systematic review. *J Am Med Inform Assoc.* 2007 Jul; 14(4):400-406.

Isaac T, Weissman JS, Davis RB, et al. Overrides of medication alerts in ambulatory care. *Arch Intern Med.* 2009 Feb; 169(3):305-311.

Weingart SN, Toth M, Sands DZ, et al. Physicians' decisions to override computerized drug alerts in primary care. *Arch Intern Med.* 2003 Nov; 163(21):2625-2631.

Tamblyn R, Huang A, Taylor L, et al. A randomized trial of the effectiveness of on-demand versus computer-triggered drug decision support in primary care. *J Am Med Inform Assoc.* 2008 Jul; 15(4):430-438.

Teich JM, Merchia PR, Schmiz JL, et al. Effects of computerized physician order entry on prescribing practices. *Arch Intern Med.* 2000 Oct; 160(18):2741-2747.

Glassman PA, Belperio PP, Simon BM, et al. Exposure to automated drug alerts over time: effects on clinicians' knowledge and perceptions. *Med Care.* 2006 Mar; 44(3):250-256.

Matheny ME, Sequist TD, Seger AC, et al. A randomized trial of electronic clinical reminders to improve medication laboratory monitoring. *J Am Med Inform Assoc.* 2008 Jul; 15(4):424-429.

Gurwitz JH, Field TS, Rochon P, et al. Effect of computerized provider order entry with clinical decision support on adverse drug events in the long-term care setting. *J Am Geriatr Soc.* 2008 Dec; 56(12):2225-2233.

57 Explanation of core measures reported on the CMS Hospital compare website: (www.hospitalcompare.hhs.gov/) can be found here: http://www.hospitalcompare.hhs.gov/ Hospital/Static/ConsumerInformation_tabset.asp?active Tab=2&Language=English&version=default&subTab=4. Accessed October 23, 2011.

58 Report to Congress: National strategy for quality improvement in health care. Healthcare.gov web site: http:// www.healthcare.gov/center/reports/quality03212011a.html. Accessed June 15, 2011.

59 There are international organizations devoted this issue. See, for example, IMSN (International Medication Safety Network) and this quote on their website: "…medication errors are an important system-based public health issue, and an integral component of the patient safety agenda." About IMSN: http://www.intmedsafe.net/contents/ AboutIMSN.aspx. Accessed June 16, 2011.

60 For example, private health insurer, WellPoint, announced such a move in 2011 (see FierceHealth's report online at: http://www.fiercehealthcare.com/story/wellpoint- reimbursement-increases-now-tied-quality-indicators/2011- 05-16. Accessed July 20, 2011). The U.S. Medicare Value- based Purchasing program for hospitals is referenced in the next section.

61 See, for example, report in the *New England Journal of Medicine* about \ the proposed rule for Medicare Shared Savings Program for accountable care organizations (ACOs): http://healthpolicyandreform.nejm.org/ ?p=14106&query=OF. Accessed June 15, 2011. The quality performance standards outlined correspond to targets for which CDS can be fruitfully applied, e.g., improved preventive care and monitoring and management of at-risk populations.

62 Nebeker JR, Hoffman JM, Weir CR, et al. High rates of adverse drug events in a highly computerized hospital." *Arch Intern Med.* 2005; 165:1111-1116.

63 Wadhwa R, Fridsma DB, Saul MI, et al. Analysis of a failed clinical decision support system for management of congestive heart failure. AMIA Annu Symp Proc. 2008: 773-7. Available online at: http://www.ncbi.nlm.nih.gov/ pmc/articles/PMC2655961. Accessed June 15, 2011.

64 CMS Hospital-Acquired Conditions (Present on Admission Indicator) Overview. Centers for Medicare and Medicaid Services website: http://www.cms.gov/ HospitalAcqCond/06_Hospital-Acquired_Conditions. asp#TopOfPage. Accessed June 15, 2011.

65 See Fact Sheet "Administration Implements New Health Reform Provision to Improve Care Quality, Lower Costs" online at healthcare.gov: http://www.healthcare.gov/news/factsheets/valuebasedpurchasing04292011a.html, Accessed June 15, 2011; and article from the Society of Hospital Medicine's *The Hospitalist* publication entitled, Value-based purchasing: raising the stakes. May 2011. Available online at: http://www.the-hospitalist.org/details/article/1056049/Value-Based_Purchasing_Raises_the_Stakes.html. Accessed June 15, 2011.

66 Measures covered under the Medicare Value-based purchasing program are those posted online at: http://hospitalcompare.hhs.gov/. This page has links to more detailed measure specifications, as well as information about potential future value-based purchasing measures. Accessed June 15, 2011.

67 See the HCAHPS home page at: http://www.hcahpsonline.org. The survey instruments can be viewed by clicking the "Survey Instruments" tab in the left hand navigation bar on this web page. Accessed June 15, 2011.

68 See the National Priorities Partnership home page at: http://www.nationalprioritiespartnership.org/. Accessed June 15, 2011.

69 Health Level 7. Health Level 7 International Home Page at: http://www.hl7.org/. Accessed June 15, 2011.

70 See, for example, the home page for the ONC's HIT Standards Committee, http://healthit.hhs.gov/portal/server.pt/community/healthit_hhs_gov__health_it_standards_committee/1271. Accessed June 15, 2011.

Chapter 2

Organizing a Successful CDS Program

Tasks

- Determine and document the CDS program approach and activities, addressing key dimensions including why, what, how, who and when. (Worksheets 2-1, 2-2)
- Integrate the CDS program with overall operations governance, and especially with quality and HIT planning and execution.
- Document a plan for prioritizing CDS-mediated improvement goals, based on internal/external drivers (e.g., Meaningful Use, Patient Centered Medical Home Certification, clinical quality measures, value-based purchasing). (Worksheets 2-1, 5-1)
- Establish CDS Team, including clinical champion(s), technical resources, and administrative support. Ensure availability of staff, consultants, and/or vendor personnel to fill essential roles needed for CDS program success, including those related to program governance, as well as intervention design, development, implementation and evaluation.
- Approach CDS as a shared effort *with* intervention recipients as part of a collaborative improvement culture. Engage all key stakeholders in the CDS program in a way that each recognizes personal advantages from the CDS activities.
- Establish oversight and communications mechanisms for key strategic and tactical decisions and activities, such as initiating, deploying and monitoring CDS interventions to achieve priority goals and objectives. (Worksheet 2-2)
- Identify primary champions representing "a collection of respected figures in various positions, such that everyone else will listen to at least one of them" and richly engage them in processes related to CDS program and intervention development.
- Consider how you will measure and report CDS program results, and address these issues in your CDS program charter as appropriate.

KEY LESSONS

A comprehensive CDS Program should include all of the following to ensure success:

- Support for the program comes from all levels of the organization.
- Key stakeholders are involved.
- A clinically oriented leader guides the effort and is able to form an effective bridge between improvement requirements and system and organizational capabilities.
- A multidisciplinary CDS committee includes supporters and potential resistors because CDS is a "team sport" regardless of organization size or type.
- CDS program goals are aligned with strategic goals of the organization.
- There's an ongoing commitment to bi-directional communication about the CDS efforts with all levels of the organization.
- The target audience for CDS interventions and other stakeholders are involved and engaged: do CDS *with* them and not *to* them.
- There are staff and mechanisms in place to ensure strong support and rapid problem resolution before, and especially during, early intervention implementation.
- There is emphasis on measuring CDS program effects in an ongoing fashion from the earliest stages of program development; this is necessary to make the program's value clear and compelling to stakeholders and to enhance this value over time.

GENERAL APPROACH
Setting the Stage: Foundations for Successful CDS Programs

A successful CDS program requires many parts, all working together toward measurable improvements in priority outcomes. The Key Lessons presented earlier outline these components.

The most critical element is that your organization is committed to improving care quality and efficiency. Once that commitment is made, you must connect your CDS efforts to your organization's strategic goals—whether your organization is a solo practice or a large integrated delivery network (IDN)—by tightly integrating the processes for managing the CDS program with processes for

running the healthcare delivery business. You can do this by assigning an influential operations group as explicit "owner" of CDS activities, or having the operations group oversee them via a subcommittee. Either will help ensure the CDS program goals and investments align with and support strategic targets, such as improved medication safety and improved care efficiency and cost-effectiveness. The entire framework outlined in this book emphasizes maintaining a tight link between organizational priorities and the CDS program's interventions and results.

CDS interventions represent one piece of a complex approach to these organizational goals. Many businesses use management systems that link high-level goals to specific performance objectives and process outcomes.[1] These approaches will likely find wider application in patient care delivery as reimbursement is increasingly tied to clinical performance. Your CDS program goals—discussed shortly—will emerge from the interplay of external drivers (such as regulatory changes and pay-for-performance programs) and internal priorities and needs.

The CDS Team

Your CDS Team is a critical component of your CDS program. At the minimum, the Team should consist of a clinical leader, an administrative or nursing leader, and a technical expert (within your organization or your EHR vendor's) who can operationalize desired CDS interventions. Team size grows with organizational size; individual roles become more specialized and overlapping in larger and more complex organizations. The CDS Team should meet regularly to develop and refine CDS strategy, guide execution, monitor progress and results, and address challenges that arise (see Figure 2-1 for a sampling of CDS Team activities and corresponding roles).

As you are forming the CDS Team—or if you haven't done it previously—you should explicitly document the key program dimensions. These include the CDS Program's 'why, what, how, who and when.' This adds discipline to the group pro-

cesses and helps with communication about the program to other stakeholders. Discussions that follow in this chapter can help fill in this documentation, for example, through sample CDS program governance diagrams (Figure 2-4), a roles and responsibilities chart (Figure 2-6), and sample CDS Program charters (see sidebar, pages 61–63). Literature is emerging that identifies useful CDS governance practices based on systematic analysis in small practices and larger organizations.[2] Key lessons have been incorporated into this Guide, but the fuller details can also provide useful input for setting up or refining your CDS program governance.

HIT suppliers such as EHR and CDS vendors will play an important role in your CDS efforts and should work closely with—if not be represented on—the CDS Team. The Considerations for HIT Software Providers section in this chapter (and in all the other chapters) includes issues to keep in mind as you build these collaborations.

Later in this chapter, we'll say more about engaging stakeholders in CDS Team efforts, and Part II describes in greater depth CDS Teamwork that pertains to specific interventions.

Leadership and Support

Major change initiatives require support from all organizational levels, and CDS programs and

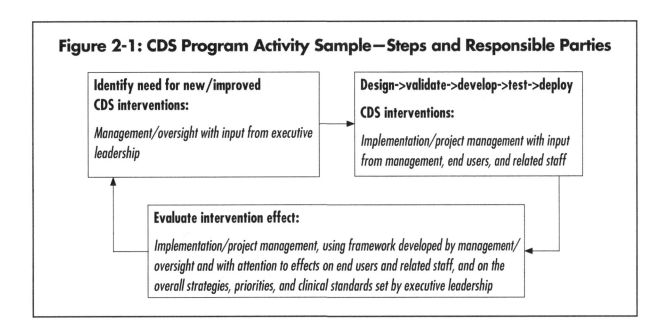

Figure 2-1: CDS Program Activity Sample—Steps and Responsible Parties

Identify need for new/improved CDS interventions:

Management/oversight with input from executive leadership

Design->validate->develop->test->deploy CDS interventions:

Implementation/project management with input from management, end users, and related staff

Evaluate intervention effect:

Implementation/project management, using framework developed by management/ oversight and with attention to effects on end users and related staff, and on the overall strategies, priorities, and clinical standards set by executive leadership

interventions are no exception. Administrative and clinical leadership backing—whether from the same person in a solo practice or a multi-stakeholder executive committee in a large integrated system—is critical to demonstrate commitment to goals, whether they be high-level such as "We will reduce preventable medication errors by 20 percent," or a more CDS-specific goal such as "We will comply with all CDS-related requirements for Meaningful Use in a manner that is appreciated by our clinicians."

Similarly, clinical leaders and medical informatics team leads should support, through words and actions, more detailed objectives and intervention tactics. In a small practice, these people might include a lead physician and practice manager, while in a health system they would typically include heads of nursing, pharmacy and clinical departments together with a CMIO. This group plays an important role in gaining staff input to, and engagement with, the overall CDS program and target-focused efforts.

Strategies for making this executive support meaningful include involving these leaders in the feedback loop around launch time and demonstrating the CDS Team's responsiveness to major concerns that surface. As emphasized repeatedly throughout this Guide, you should "bake" the monitoring of CDS intervention benefits and unintended consequences into the program from the outset. This can involve the physician lead/CMIO, super-users or various direct, paper and electronic channels (such as surveys, bulletin boards, mailboxes for the support team), CDS Team walk rounds and others. In any case, interest demonstrated by the clinical/quality and other leaders in this feedback can reinforce for end users that CDS and performance improvement are a collaborative effort. Your CMIO/physician lead should remain in close contact with other clinical leaders and staff, always available for feedback.

Perhaps even more important than "support from above," however, is that your champions—the targeted users' peers—strongly engage end users and model desired interactions with the CDS program

and interventions.[3] Some additional detail on this important role follows.

Champions

Champions play a critical role in CDS program and intervention success. These individuals are respected members of the constituencies who will receive the CDS (for example, nurses, pharmacists, patients, administration staff and physicians) who fully understand and support the CDS efforts, goals and strategies and can serve as ambassadors for successful use by their peers.

You should engage these champions from the earliest stage of the CDS program and intervention development, and work closely with them throughout the lifecycle of each. They serve as a rich, bi-directional information conduit between their peers and the CDS Team. At launch, they will be enthusiastic intervention consumers and a wellspring of encouraging anecdotes that stimulate similar successes by their colleagues. These anecdotes should include anticipated benefits, such as time saved, errors avoided, increased professional satisfaction through better access to information for answering questions and guiding decisions, and the like.

Champions are an important role for all organizational sizes and types. Ideally, clinical champions should:

- Be effective communicators—perhaps the most important role requirement.
- Be influential and highly regarded among their end user peers, so they can successfully represent and support their colleagues.[4]
- "Lead the charge" and act as a "Change Agent" for the CDS intervention and as the liaison between the end users and the technical staff.
- Not necessarily be "technical people," but have a basic understanding of the available information system capabilities and limitations. They should also understand the healthcare environment and be able to articulate the organizational goals and priorities, as well as why and how CDS is being used to address them.

- Be clinically active if clinical champions—this will contribute to credibility with intervention recipients in patient care roles. The clinical champion's specialty is less important than his or her having good clinical rapport and credibility with the target audience.
- Have dedicated time to be successful in champion-related activities, including working with the technical team and/or vendor, learning about and then communicating with staff about the CDS program and individual interventions before, during and after their launch, and helping to refine interventions (in collaboration with the technical team) after implementation.

End users respect champions as peers and consider them to be spokespersons for their needs and constraints. These champions can therefore serve as liaisons between your development team and end users, helping to ensure that both groups' needs and constraints are addressed. The champion role in the intervention lifecycle is described in more detail in Part II.

Strategic Context for CDS
Organizational Goals

As outlined in Chapter 1, your CDS program must design and implement CDS interventions in the context of your organization's goals and strategic initiatives. These will revolve around improvement drivers such as those outlined in Figure 1-4 and typically include disease management measures, quality and safety initiatives, regulatory requirements, and external HIT programs (including pay-for-performance and other reimbursement-based programs).[5] These improvement imperatives create opportunities to apply CDS to generate required enhancements to care processes and outcomes. The CDS efforts must focus on specific objectives, and Figure 2-2 presents examples of how such objectives flow from higher-level goals.

Strategic Prioritization

After your CDS Team and organizational leadership have a clear, shared sense of the strategic focus areas for your CDS efforts, the next step is to prioritize the more specific goals—such as those in the middle column of Figure 2-2—for which you will use CDS interventions. Figure 5-2 describes factors that affect the desirability of even more specific CDS objectives (such as those in the third column of Figure 2-2), and those factors can also be useful in prioritizing broader goals.

To summarize these factors, ideal targets for CDS interventions include:
- Patient management issues that occur frequently;
- Activities that are associated with a significant gap in performance or a missed opportunity to optimize care;
- Care events in which the performance shortfall substantially boosts clinical costs or lowers quality and safety; and
- Activities in which performance can be improved through better access to improved communication or heightened attention to important clinical data.

Building on Figures 1-4 and 2-2, Figure 2-3, following, provides additional information to help you identify, select, and prioritize target areas for your CDS efforts. Worksheet 2-1 can help you document discussions with stakeholders about these targets.

The prioritization process builds on your CDS Team's dialog with the medical and administrative leadership and sets up ongoing collaborations among these groups throughout the CDS Program lifecycle. Leadership is responsible for ensuring that the CDS Team is "working on the right things" and delivering desired results through valuable CDS interventions, while the CDS Team is responsible for the work to deliver those results. Figure 2-6, later in this chapter, outlines interlocking CDS Program roles and responsibilities in larger organizations, and it can be adapted for smaller settings as well.

Strategic CDS "Don't Dos"

As your CDS Team and organizational leadership consider where CDS can be fruitfully applied, it is important to keep in mind where CDS (or a particular intervention) is *not* an appropriate tool. Because

Figure 2-2: Examples of Organizational Goals and Corresponding Clinical Goals and Objectives

Organizational Goal	Typical Clinical Goal	Typical Clinical Objective
Develop disease management/ condition-specific initiatives to improve outcomes for particular complaints, diagnoses, or procedures (e.g., diabetes)[6]	• Decrease complications associated with target diagnoses (e.g., diabetic cardiovascular disease)	• Increase number of diabetics who receive screening for blood pressure and abnormal cholesterol
Improve overall care safety	• Minimize adverse drug events • Optimize critical information transfer among clinicians within hospitals, inpatient and outpatient clinicians, generalist and specialist clinicians	• Decrease occurrence of severe drug interactions • Decrease inadequate follow-up of critical test results, such as abnormal biopsies, radiological studies, and laboratory tests
Optimize reimbursement for care	• Increase percent of patients with target conditions who meet pay-for-performance criteria • Improve billing levels and appropriateness	• Increase percent of eligible patients with heart attack given beta blockers on arrival at the hospital • Improve coding levels from ambulatory encounters
Optimize cost-effectiveness of care	• Improve referral appropriateness • Reduce unnecessary or duplicative tests • Safely reduce inpatient length of stay	• Reduce unnecessary referrals for Pap smears • Reduce overly-frequent x-ray studies or inappropriate lab test ordering
Enhance patient education and empowerment	• Optimize patient adherence with indicated screening tests for preventive care	• Increase percentage of eligible women who receive screening mammography
Foster compliance with evidence-based clinical guidance[7] (see also Figure 2-3) and reporting and regulatory requirements[8]	• Optimize performance on specific quality measures	• Increase percentage of stroke patients who are discharged from the hospital on aspirin
Address clinicians' recognized and unrecognized information needs	• Provide "just-in-time" relevant treatment information for a disease/condition, within clinical workflow	• Address the majority of questions clinicians pose to computer-based resources at the point of care with condition-specific, context-sensitive information
Enhance clinician satisfaction	• Provide tools that save clinician time or increase their efficiency	• Seamlessly introduce into clinical workflow drug-prescribing calculations, such as weight-based dosing

Figure 2-3: Some Target Categories and Sources for Related Clinical Goals and Objectives

Target	Examples/references
• Value-based purchasing and transparency initiatives at national and state levels	• U.S. Medicare and other national value-based purchasing programs[9,10,11] • U.S. state-based quality reporting[12] • Physician Quality Reporting Systems (PQRS)[13] • CMS Hospital Quality Initiative[14] • Leapfrog Group; Rewarding Results[15] • National Committee for Quality Assurance (NCQA) Accreditation[16]
• CDS interventions addressed in CIS certification programs and government-supported CIS initiatives	• Meaningful Use Regulations from CMS[17] • ONC-Authorized Testing and Certification Body (ONC-ATCB) certification[18] • e-prescribing covered under Medicare Modernization Act[19]
• Improved accountability for organizations that are assuming financial risk in providing care services	• Accountable Care Organizations[20] • Bundled payments[21]
• Improved care through better care coordination and improved technology use	• CMS Patient Centered Medical Home Demonstration Project[22]
• Clinical interventions for which trials have demonstrated that CDS approaches are or might be effective in improving healthcare processes and outcomes[23]	• Practices supported by evidence[24] • Practitioner performance[25] • Medication safety[26] • Disease management[27] • Chronic care management[28]
• Clinical errors or quality problems identified in systematic analyses	• U.S. Pharmacopeia (USP) MedMarx database[29] • Health and Human Services (HHS) patient safety reporting systems[30] • McGlynn et al., The Quality of Health Care Delivered to Adults in the United States[31] • NCQA State of Health Care Quality report[32] • Preventable adverse drug events[33] • Common medical error types[34]
• Improved care efficiency and costs while maintaining or improving quality	• Formulary compliance • Converting medications from intravenous to oral route when appropriate • Cost-effective diagnostic and therapeutic approaches for high volume and cost conditions

CDS can influence important care processes (such as ordering drugs and tests, and many other activities) so broadly and deeply, some may find it tempting to look for CDS interventions to solve challenges outside the appropriate scope. This can be especially true when CDS has been successfully implemented in one area, such as an alert to prevent a particular medication error. This approach (e.g., alerting) might then be viewed as "the big hammer," and all the organization's challenges appear as "nails" that can be handled with alerts.

For example, in one study report a "hard-stop" (i.e., workflow interrupting) alert was found to be "extremely effective" in changing prescribing practices, but the study was stopped early when it was found that the alert was associated with clinically important treatment delays.[35] In Part II we discuss in detail when and how to use alerts in the context of other intervention types. The point for now is that the CDS Team may have to educate colleagues about when and how CDS can best be applied, especially when they have (inappropriate) preconceptions that the primary tool for addressing quality and safety issues is always workflow-interrupting alerts to physicians.

As another example, you shouldn't use CDS to make or enforce clinical policy; instead, CDS should *make it easier to comply with previously agreed-upon policies*. Many organizations are wrestling with core measures compliance. Successful compliance requires a multidisciplinary approach and potentially significant changes in workflow.[36] Although standard order sets and clinical rules can be employed to support compliance, clinicians are responsible for the pertinent actions. If they don't agree with the action addressed in the measures, or feel they don't apply in a specific circumstance, then *dialog and education* are called for, instead of CDS intervention. Intrusive CDS (such as alerts that interrupt workflow) for these clinicians will only cause irritation. Worse yet, poorly targeted alerts that appear when the patient's care is guideline compliant will punish and irritate those already doing the right thing and contribute to 'alert fatigue' (discussed in Part II).

A final example on boundaries for applying CDS broadly includes supporting documentation in the EHR. This documentation typically includes both structured and unstructured text, although automated quality measurement and reporting (such as for compliance with smoking cessation counseling recommendations) requires structured data entry. CDS can help ensure that clinicians enter the information into the appropriate EHR fields in the proper structured manner, but there must first be a shared understanding about necessary workflow modifications between the CDS Team providing these interventions and those who will use them. The documentation intervention alone may either generate resistance (if it is forced and not understood or accepted) or 'workarounds' that negate the intervention's intent.

Part II describes in detail how to select, configure, deploy and evaluate specific CDS interventions that are well received and achieve desired results. The lesson here is that the CDS Team needs to have effective governance mechanisms in place to ensure that CDS approaches are only considered and used in a strategically appropriate manner and with careful and collaborative planning and evaluation.

Engaging Stakeholders

A core CDS Team with solid governance processes, and a shared sense with leadership and other key stakeholders about the broad CDS program direction, provide the foundation for engaging others needed to refine goals and deliver priority outcome improvements.

Do CDS with Affected Stakeholders, Not to Them

Foundational work for a CDS program includes building a shared appreciation among pertinent stakeholders about the critical challenges adversely affecting care delivery, conducting a detailed analysis of pertinent end-user workflow, and building capacity to deliver CDS interventions that address targeted improvement opportunities. Launching of individual CDS interventions shouldn't be the first time your CDS Team has reached out to end users and other stakeholders. Rather, the launch phase should be more like the tip of an iceberg, with extensive collaborative work as described in this and subsequent chapters.

The people affected by the CDS program should always be engaged at some level as partners and contributors in program activities to the greatest extent possible. These people should never feel like unwilling "targets" of the CDS program and that changes are being forced upon them. We therefore repeatedly emphasize throughout this book that it is essential to identify and involve CDS intervention end users and other key stakeholders during all phases of the CDS program and intervention lifecycle. Your success depends on building the perception in these individuals and groups—based on reality—that you are "doing" CDS *with* them and not *to* them. Keeping this in mind from the very beginning of the CDS program development process will contribute to building a shared appreciation for CDS opportunities and challenges—and fully leveraging available talent and resources to address them. As noted in Chapter 1, evidence to support this approach can be found in the studies examined by Lobach and colleagues in their AHRQ Evidence-based Practice Center report on the CDS literature.[37]

As you build capacity to launch valuable CDS interventions, consider the full spectrum of intervention end users and others affected, as well as the workflows that will be involved; for example, those who supply information upstream (such patient weights or other data) needed for intervention success or those who provide downstream services or supplies (such as mammogram testing, or vaccines and staff to inject them) needed to carry out the intervention's ultimate intent. Champions, discussed earlier, can help you identify and communicate with these other stakeholders. As you build (or enhance) your CDS Team, consider people and mechanisms necessary to fully understand and support care delivery activities that underpin and integrate the work these people do. Workflow analysis is covered in more detail in Chapter 3.

Stakeholder Communications

Once you have identified all the people who will be essential for successful CDS efforts, you need to build channels to support communications with them to ensure good program processes and results. These communications may start with informal dialog as the CDS program foundation is being established but will then evolve into more formal meetings (with minutes recorded) and other mechanisms. Even in a solo physician practice, the CDS Team's work will always generate information that this group should communicate with others (such as other staff and the EHR vendor) and important input that the team needs.

You should begin these communications early in CDS program development; for example, to build awareness for the CDS program goals and how they support organizational (and individual) priorities and related initiatives. This awareness is a prerequisite for constructive stakeholder participation in CDS-related efforts to achieve important results. Early communications from the CDS Team set the tone for these ongoing collaborations, and they should come from all the various team members and convey a consistent message; for example, that the CDS work is based on a collaborative approach to driving measurable improvements in important areas.

Appropriate communication channels and approaches will vary based on organizational size and other factors, and in any case, multiple channels should be used. These might include informal conversations, email updates, discussions in pertinent organizational meetings, posters with important information and other channels, to provide periodic updates about CDS program development and progress toward goals.

Keep in mind that communications must flow richly both *from* and *to* the CDS Team. Robust opportunities for CDS intervention end users and other stakeholders to give input and feedback about the CDS program are a critical requirement for launching and maintaining CDS programs. The CDS Team must continually answer questions, address concerns and receive feedback on CDS program activities. Positive and negative feedback about these activities, as well as input about CDS-related needs, challenges and opportunities, is essential to the continuous improvement process that underlies all CDS efforts. This constructive dialog can help even a wide group of stakeholders feel connected to the CDS program work, and this engagement and trust are further strengthened when stakeholders see the CDS Team responding to specific concerns and feedback.

Chapter 8 provides suggestions about stakeholder communications and feedback related to specific CDS interventions, and those approaches can be adapted to communications about the CDS program as well. For example, Worksheet 8-2 presents outgoing communication examples, and Worksheet 8-6 is an example of an intervention feedback documentation form.

Building Support

Having stakeholders understand the CDS program goals and work—and how these support broader organizational priorities—is an important building block for effective collaboration. Engagement is strengthened when this understanding underpins meaningful contributions that stakeholders make to the program's activities. In order for busy individuals to devote additional time and energy to CDS-related work, however, there must be some personal justification.

In some cases, "It's your job" may be adequate. However, the more the CDS Team can leverage stakeholder's "WIFM" (What's in It For Me) perspective, the more it can tap into substantially greater support including their time, energy, creativity, enthusiasm and even financial and human resources they can allocate to CDS efforts. For example, physicians, nurses, pharmacists and other clinical staff may find improving care quality and safety to be a compelling reason for supporting the CDS program and projects, but if the CDS activities make their work easier or faster, they likely will be much more engaged. Such CDS interventions

with direct benefit to physicians include those that reduce callbacks for clarification or to supply missing information in orders, or automatically provide them with data that would otherwise have to be calculated manually.[38]

Overcoming Resistance

As you build the CDS Team and its network of interactions, remember to include unofficial opinion leaders, including those who both support and those who may be a source of resistance. Many stakeholders will not be as positive about the CDS program and interventions as the champions. Thoughtful individuals might be neutral, or be "resistors" who push back, or "detractors" who actively work against the CDS-related efforts.[39] Keep in mind that these individuals may be those whose work is affected in some way by new CDS-enabled processes, as well as those who are intended CDS recipients. Their concerns might include liability fears (see Appendix: Medico-legal Considerations), alert fatigue, user interface complexity, extra time requirements and reduced clinician autonomy.

It is essential for you to engage resistors and detractors in active dialogue—they can be a critical source of feedback about the program and play an important role in its success or failure. You should do this early in the development and implementation process to reduce problems later that could potentially derail the CDS program or specific interventions. Inviting potential detractors to participate in work related to the broader CDS program or specific interventions may convert them to champions, and former skeptics can be the best evangelists.[40]

In the case of some detractors, even the most energetic efforts to solicit their opinions and accommodate their objections will not lessen their opposition. In this situation, transparency is key and includes broad representation among the stakeholders and an open development process. You should be ready to freely discuss the CDS program benefits and costs (for example, as outlined in Figure 1-3), a strategy that can help neutralize potential objections. Some objections might be that the CDS program represents the wishes of a few individuals or that decision support knowledge established as effective elsewhere lacks sufficient customization to be effective locally.

Solid clinical leadership can help minimize the negative effects from issues that cannot immediately be resolved. This leadership involves clearly setting goals and expectations, communicating often and effectively, and modeling and reinforcing desired behaviors regarding the CDS program. When your program produces specific target-focused CDS interventions, there may be additional resistors and detractors that arise, so the points previously outlined are relevant to Part II as well.

Building Capabilities for CDS Measurement and Tracking

A successful CDS program, by definition, has a mechanism for measuring success. There is actually quite a bit to track and measure about the CDS program, including what interventions are launched and why, how they are performing over time, whether their content remains current and appropriate, and many other dimensions.

Chapter 3 provides more detail on measurement capabilities needed for CDS programs (that is, building measurement into the planning, implementation and refinement of every intervention), and Chapter 4 discusses tracking and maintaining CDS content and interventions over time. We mention these core capabilities now because they should be filtered in to the earliest stages of CDS program development; as you assemble the CDS Team, consider goals and engage stakeholders. For example, measurement and knowledge management can be foundational elements in your CDS Charter (see sidebars following, focused mainly on larger organizations but also adaptable for smaller settings), and you'll also need to have resources dedicated to these functions.

Foreshadowing deeper discussion in the next chapter, here are some initial considerations about metrics for CDS programs:

- The measurement approach, tools and specific metrics should be based on broader organizational improvement efforts and strategic priorities. This helps ensure that the CDS program activities align with and support the broader initiatives.
- Measurement details should be determined prior to designing specific CDS interventions so that baselines can be established against which CDS intervention effects can be assessed.
- Improvement goals should be objective and quantifiable, for example, "Our goal is to improve that rate at which appropriate VTE (venous thromboembolism) prophylaxis is ordered in patients undergoing hip and knee surgery from 48% to 85% within 12 months after the VTE prophylaxis CDS intervention package is launched" vs. "Our goal is to improve VTE prophylaxis."
- Build the capability to ensure that all your key measurements are relevant, accurate, believable, and visible at all levels of the organization (especially with leadership). This will help garner resources and build support for further interventions.

Change Management

As pointed out in this book's Foreword, successful CDS programs require a balance of work with *people, processes* and *technologies*, and collaborating successfully with *people* to drive changes in the other two areas is the most difficult. Technology certainly presents many important opportunities and challenges to improve outcomes with CDS, and the CDS Team must manage these well. CDS effort success or failure also depends heavily on your CDS Team's ability to drive and manage change more broadly, for example, gaining consensus on improvement targets, and full engagement on applying new care processes and tools to achieve shared objective, as discussed earlier.

A recent study[41] examining factors related to disease-specific hospital death rates provides an important lesson on this theme for CDS Teams. Site visits and in-depth interviews with top- and bottom-performing hospitals found that use of care guidelines and protocols didn't differentiate these groups. However, high-performing hospitals were characterized by an organizational culture that supported broad improvements in the disease measures. The implication for your CDS efforts is that, in order for interventions that increase adherence to guidelines and protocols to improve outcomes, they should be delivered into an environment where improvement is a cultural priority. In many cases, this will require as much attention from CDS (and related performance improvement) initiatives to the cultural environment as to supporting workflow and technology enhancements (which can be challenging in themselves).

Heifetz has written extensively on managing change in individuals and organizations. He notes that it is important to gauge "adaptive reserve"—the capacity to take on new changes in workflow and process. This reserve is dependent on baseline stress levels and how well individuals are managing the existing "core structure"—the current day-to-day processes and operations.[42] The CDS program should consider your organization's capacity to absorb change in considering the overall pace of CDS activities, as well as the rate at which specific CDS interventions will be released. In the latter, for example, you might consider factors such as:

- Current end-user clinical volume (perhaps related to seasonal workload variability);
- Other organizational initiatives that may distract or consume time from end users or others affected by the CDS intervention (for example, by requiring new staffing patterns and models or new care procedures).

Another helpful framework for managing change can be found in John Kotter's Eight Step Model:[43]

- Establish a sense of urgency: Create a compelling reason as to why the change is needed and compelling stories as to what could happen if the change is not instituted.
- Create a guiding coalition: Establish the team that has the right amount of knowledge, power and authority to accomplish the change.
- Develop a vision and strategy: Organize the change so everyone clearly understands the overall vision and the strategy and how it relates to the overall organizational goals/vision.
- Communicate the change vision: Determine how to effectively communicate the change within the organization.
- Overcome barriers and empower broad-based action: Identify all the barriers to change and work through them, including resistance and workflow barriers.
- Generate short-term wins: Accomplish quick wins that can then be publicized to generate excitement for the change and acceptance of future change.
- Consolidate gains and produce more change: Use the short-term quick wins to learn what went well and what didn't, and build off of them to create further change.
- Anchor new approaches in the culture: Reinforce the change(s) and the success throughout the organization and ensure ongoing leadership support.

These steps resonate with the approach outlined in this Guide for effective CDS programs and also for the CDS interventions the program uses to improve outcomes (discussed in Part II).

CONSIDERATIONS FOR HOSPITALS/HEALTH SYSTEMS

While the General Approach previously outlined can be applied to any size organization, there are significant additional complexities involved in applying them in a hospital or health system. These complexities result from the greater number of stakeholders and political considerations in a larger organization. To more fully address these issues, the Hospital and Health System Considerations in this chapter are presented in a discussion format (rather than the bulleted format used in other chapters).

Leadership and Support

Successful CDS efforts require support from all levels of the organization, particularly senior officials and groups that set policies and allocate resources. In larger organizations, this includes the medical and administrative leadership. On the medical side, the Medical Executive Committee—which represents and sets policy for the medical staff—plays an important role in physician engagement with and input to the CDS program and activities. Because this group can help manage and address expectations that physicians have of the CDS program, and vice versa, you should cultivate a strong relationship with leaders and members of this committee.

You should likewise work closely with senior administrative leadership on the CDS program goals and activities. This includes educating them about CDS benefits and strategies (such as the CDS Five Rights approach), getting their input on CDS goals and targets, and enlisting their support in CDS execution. Specific senior roles to work with include: the chief executive officer (CEO), chief financial officer (CFO, to ensure financial support), chief operating officer (COO, to ensure support for process changes), chief nursing officer (CNO), chief medical officer (CMO, to provide oversight and support with medical staff), and the quality officer. Interactions should be both informal (such as ad hoc discussions), as well as more formal dialog with and presentation to the operating groups these leaders manage.

The board of trustees, whose members often have personal relationships and communicate with members of the medical staff, is another important leadership stakeholder group with which you should cultivate fruitful collaboration. The time and attention that the board gives to quality issues are associated with hospital performance,[44] and helping this group understand and support the CDS program's role in enhancing quality can bode well for the attention and resources the program receives. An indication that you've successfully engaged the board is if members can correctly articulate the CDS program goals (and how they support broader organizational goals) and provide a very high level overview of CDS activities to support those goals.

The Clinical Decision Support Committee

In the General Approach section of this chapter, we discussed the CDS Team as the core group directly responsible for the CDS activities. In larger organizations, CDS management may be divided into different functions for addressing program oversight and execution management, with groups responsible for either or both functions referred to as "the CDS Committee." When the group handles the oversight function in a hospital/system, it is often a formal subcommittee of the medical staff or the hospital/system management team. More execution-oriented CDS Committees might fit within the CMIO's office. There isn't a single 'right' configuration for organizing CDS management functions; structures will vary depending on the organization's approach to related governance functions (such as for clinical activities, HIT implementations and the like). Next, we outline some sample approaches, including considerations useful in a broad range of configurations.

A sample governance structure that illustrates where a higher-level CDS Committee might fit in the overall organizational structure is shown in Figure 2-4.

The CMIO typically chairs oversight-oriented CDS Committees. More execution-oriented CDS committees may be led by the CMIO, a physician champion or a clinician suited to managing CDS development and deployment activities.

Well-rounded CDS oversight committees should have representatives from a variety of key departments. These can include physicians from various specialty groups, pharmacists, nursing, risk management, infection control, quality, case management, administration, information systems, and other stakeholders as appropriate. Organizational leadership should endow this group with enough authority and mandate to give it access to the necessary people, infrastructure and other resources to ensure that CDS interventions are developed and deployed in a manner that delivers the expected, measurable value in targeted areas.

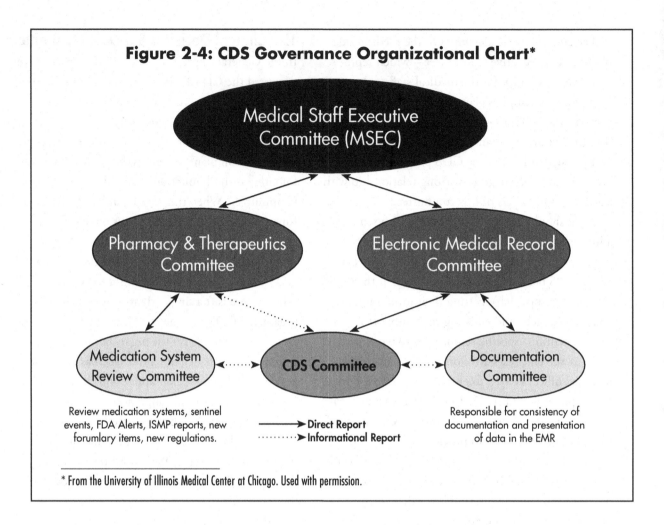

Figure 2-4: CDS Governance Organizational Chart*

Medical Staff Executive Committee (MSEC)

Pharmacy & Therapeutics Committee

Electronic Medical Record Committee

Medication System Review Committee

CDS Committee

Documentation Committee

Review medication systems, sentinel events, FDA Alerts, ISMP reports, new forumlary items, new regulations.

→ Direct Report
·····► Informational Report

Responsible for consistency of documentation and presentation of data in the EMR

* From the University of Illinois Medical Center at Chicago. Used with permission.

A typical CDS Committee might include the following roles and stakeholders:

- CMIO or the physician champion;
- Representation from primary and specialty care;
- Representation that includes all major stakeholder groups;
- Residents, if a teaching hospital;
- Mid-level providers (typically heavy users of the system);
- Nursing and nursing informatics;
- Ancillary departments (pharmacy, respiratory therapy, lab, etc.);
- Medication safety officer;
- Quality officer;
- Consider unofficial "opinion leaders" on the medical staff or in the practice;
- Consider including those who are vocal resistors to technology and standardization of care ("Keep

your friends close, and your enemies closer," Sun Tzu, *The Art of War*, 6th century B.C.).

Specialty-oriented interventions (for example, related to radiology test ordering) will require leadership from clinicians who are directly involved, so be sure that these stakeholders are directly represented on the CDS Committee or that the Committee has ready access to them.

As noted earlier in the chapter, this Committee should meet regularly to develop strategy, guide execution, monitor progress and results, and address challenges that arise in the CDS program. These responsibilities extend continuously throughout planning, implementation, evaluation and continuous improvement phases. As opposed to only including clinicians who primarily function in administrative roles, it is important to include representation from actively practicing physicians, nurses, pharmacists, and other clinicians (and ideally champions from these groups) on the CDS oversight committee. By involving actual users of the interventions that will be deployed, you will help ensure that this critical constituency's needs and constraints are addressed in CDS program planning and management.

Similar considerations to those just outlined apply for more execution-oriented CDS Committees and subcommittees. In these cases, you will have more analysts who create rules and other CDS interventions, as well as other technical and deployment roles. For example, a typical core team (often a sub-team of the CDS Committee) executing CDS interventions for medication management might consist of a physician, pharmacist, nurse, IT specialist and a team leader (who may also fill one of the other roles). It is very helpful to have one or more team members with formal clinical informatics skills and experiences: that is, expertise in how clinical and technology capabilities can be applied together in addressing care delivery needs.

Figure 2-5 lists CDS program and intervention stakeholders that you should consider for membership in, or close collaboration with, your CDS Committee.

Figure 2-6 illustrates roles and responsibilities typically required for success of a CDS program in a large organization. You can consider these in constituting (and refining) your CDS committee membership and in documenting the group's governance approach.

Decision-making and Governance

You should understand how "decisions are made" and "how work gets done" within your hospital or health system, including how resources are allocated (for both systems and personnel) and which individuals and committees are the true decision makers. This understanding can help you prioritize targets for CDS interventions to ensure you have appropriate representation on the CDS Committee. Approaching the decision makers through official channels (such as formal committees) and through unofficial communication with influential stakeholders can greatly enhance CDS program alignment with broader organizational direction.

Here's an example of these dynamics at work. A large organization had implemented CPOE and full medication bar code administration. The pathology/laboratory medicine department strongly advocated to the CDS Committee for a solution to eliminate mislabeled lab specimens. The CDS Committee was intrigued by the challenge and believed that a solution was possible, albeit expensive. However, discussions at the senior management level clearly did not place a high priority on mislabeled lab specimens, which had a very low incidence at the institution. Without this "political insight" and communication, the CDS Committee might have begun a major initiative without the support and resources needed for success. More fundamentally, this anecdote highlights the need for formal mechanisms—sanctioned by organizational leadership—to vet and prioritize requests to the CDS Committee for specific target-focused interventions. We'll say more about this strategic prioritization shortly.

Cross-fertilization with Other Committees/Departments

Interplay with other committees and departments will help you build awareness and understanding of the CDS efforts and the potential impact on the organization. You can achieve this by involving the CMIO or CDS physician champion on departmental Quality Assurance/Quality Improvement/Performance Improvement Committees. Involvement of the physician champions from other IT initiatives (CPOE, EHR, etc.) and other quality/patient safety initiatives should also be considered.

Cross-fertilization will allow you to identify potential opportunities for CDS efforts and also reduce the risk that CDS is used inappropriately (see earlier discussion of where CDS should not show up).

An example illustrates this point. A Quality Improvement Committee was evaluating the appropriate use of order sets. It was suggested that

Figure 2-5: Stakeholders for Overall
CDS Program and Individual CDS Interventions

Committees

- Board of directors
- Pharmacy and therapeutics (P&T)
- Quality improvement (organization-wide)
- Quality (departmental)
- Patient safety
- Utilization review (organization-wide or departmental, such as blood product use)
- Medical staff/executive
- Residency/training
- Clinical information systems (for example, implementation, oversight, benefits realization)
- Guideline/practice standards, clinical strategy, disease/care management
- Medical records
- Infection control
- Service line–focused

Positions

- Medical director of CDS
- CMO/medical director
- CMIO/medical director of information systems
- Chief information officer (CIO)
- Pharmacy director/chair of P&T committee
- CNO/director of nursing informatics
- Quality officer
- Patient/medication safety officer
- Risk management officer
- Department chairs
- Residency/training directors
- Independent Practice Association (IPA)/physician group chairs
- Legal counsel

Other CDS Stakeholders

- Clinicians vocal on clinical computing/CDS issues (positively or negatively)
- Clinical thought leaders
- Patients/patient representatives
- Other clinician, trainee, and non-clinician end users of CDS interventions
- Non-end users who will be affected by a CDS intervention (such as radiology staff that will have to accommodate interventions that will increase the frequency of particular imaging studies)

Figure 2-6: Generic Outline of CDS Program Stakeholder Groups and Responsibilities

Board and Executive Leadership: Set Strategy and Priorities, Clinical Standards, Allocate Resources

- Overall board and members with quality/safety interests: help set overall organizational agenda (including quality/safety focus), improvement priorities, resource allocation
- Executive leadership: sets a more specific improvement agenda, priorities, resource allocations

Management/Oversight: Manage Processes Related to CDS Program

- Healthcare organization departments/functions: responsible for processes/outcomes that will be affected by CDS program (see Figure 2-2)
  - Clinical departments (for example, laboratory, pharmacy, nursing, medicine, surgery and infection control) and service lines
  - Organized medical staff
  - Cross-cutting functions (for example, quality, safety, disease management, case managers and risk management)
  - Clinical director of information systems/medical informatics
  - Other organizational committees and departments
- CDS oversight/benefits realization committee: supports execution and evaluation of CDS initiatives; educates senior executives and board of directors on importance and impact of CDS efforts
- CIO/IT steering committee and IT department: responsible for IT infrastructure that underpins CDS interventions

Implementation/Project Management: Develops, Deploys, Monitors CDS Interventions

- CDS-specific: overall responsibility to deploy/maintain CDS knowledge assets, collect and analyze evaluation data
- General IT: overall responsibility to support/maintain CISs

End Users and Related Positions: Perform Patient Care Activities Affected by CDS

- End users: recipients of CDS interventions (for example, patients, nurses, pharmacists, physicians, others on the care team and case managers)
- Related staff: generate data for, or are affected by, interventions
- Subject matter experts: clinical authorities for content in CDS interventions
- Clinical thought leaders and champions (such as clinicians respected and listened to by colleagues): help ensure interventions meet needs and are successfully adopted

---

to improve compliance, the choice of order sets be driven by the admitting diagnosis. Most of the administrative personnel at the meeting approved the idea. The CDS representative at the meeting appropriately pointed out that admission diagnoses were not captured in the current CIS during the admission process, and therefore this was not a viable option. This interplay therefore prevented significant wasted effort pursuing a non-viable solution.

The challenge of keeping all stakeholders involved and informed is greatly increased in a large hospital or health system. Building the shared appreciation for the value of CDS and preparing the targeted end users should occur throughout the planning and implementation phases. It is important to ensure that all stakeholders understand the challenges involved in large-scale change and the expected outcomes and impact on patient safety and quality.

Specific tactics to build shared support include:
- Developing and distributing a bibliography of key articles that support the value of CDS. This is useful when resistance is raised using the "show me the data" approach. The Chapter 1 section "Evidence Base for CDS Value" contains rich pointers to this literature.
- Compelling CDS success stories (including small wins), such as avoiding important omission or commission errors though well-executed CDS interventions, will often evoke strong responses, since clinicians typically relate well to the clinical anecdotes being told by colleagues.
- Open discussions about value added through CDS (reduction in call backs from the pharmacy, faster dose calculation times, etc.) will provide balance to the concerns regarding potentially increased "clicks" (which will hopefully be minimized through careful CDS design) and time required to learn new workflows.

CDS Committee Charter

The shared vision and coordinated effort required to successfully apply CDS in addressing priority needs does not happen by accident. As opposed to a document with no real buy-in or execution, a living CDS charter or mission statement can help, especially when you manage this charter within a governance model that fully leverages and optimizes pertinent organizational resources in carrying out the charter.

Successful CDS efforts often use such a CDS mission statement, or charter, to formalize the program's goals and overall approach. When appropriately developed with stakeholder input and incorporated into an organization's broader culture and activities, such a statement can add focus, credibility, and urgency to CDS initiatives and provide a natural framework for CDS activities. Following are sample generic CDS charters that might be of use in developing or enhancing one in your organization.

You can use these as a template, as well as Worksheet 2-2, to help you create or enhance your CDS Committee Charter.

Strategic Context for CDS
External Drivers

Many of the healthcare improvement drivers mentioned in Figures 1-4 and 2-3 have direct financial implications for hospitals by linking reimbursement to performance. As a result, hospital leaders are devoting increasing attention to optimizing particular outcomes that carry major financial implications. This attention can be a favorable backdrop for discussions between these leaders and the CDS Committee about how the CDS program and specific interventions can contribute to performance improvement.

Value-based purchasing and related clinical quality initiatives rely on quality measures to assess and report performance—and help drive improvements. These measures address the extent to which healthcare services shown to improve outcomes are actually being delivered to patients for whom they are indicated. For example, both The Joint Commission and the Centers for Medicare & Medicaid Services (CMS) require hospitals to report quality measures, such as the percentage of eligible patients with acute myocardial infarction that are prescribed aspirin and beta blockers at hospital admission and discharge, and the percentage of patients admitted to the hospital with congestive heart failure who have a documented assessment of their left ventricular ejection fraction.[45] The Agency for Healthcare Research and Quality (AHRQ) maintains a clearinghouse of evidence-based quality measures,[46] and the National Quality Forum (NQF) endorses quality measures.[47]

Improving performance on these measures presents excellent targets for CDS programs and interventions, especially in circumstances when such improvement has a directly measurable return on investment (e.g., through a value-based purchasing initiative or HIT Meaningful Use program). An important step in identifying objectives for your CDS program is, therefore, to carefully assess external and internal quality, safety, regulatory and reimbursement initiatives that are affect-

Sample Generic CDS Charter*

Overview
Well-executed Clinical Decision Support (CDS) is essential for Health System to realize full value from its substantial investments in health information technology (HIT) and to address Health System's overall mission and vision.

Mission Statement
The mission of Health System's CDS program is to continuously improve the safety, quality, and efficiency of patient care at Health System by ensuring that the care delivery team has the information needed to drive good decisions and actions that lead to optimal outcomes.

Principles
- Aim to measurably improve key organizational performance metrics.
- Leverage the full spectrum of CDS interventions and the full capabilities of the deployed health information technology to maximize CDS usefulness and benefits.
- Develop and deploy CDS in a user-focused manner to optimize user acceptance and clinical workflow; use best evidence and documented best practices when available.
- Proactively manage CDS knowledge assets to ensure their currency, relevance, and consistency, and continuously monitor and enhance their effectiveness.

Methods
Governance
- Core CDS efforts are focused on addressing goals established and prioritized by the Health System clinical and executive leadership.
- The Decision Support Strategic Planning Committee (DSSPC), a subcommittee of the system-wide HIT Physician Advisory Council (PAC), is responsible for the oversight and direction of the Health System CDS Program.
- The Decision Support Working Group (DSWG) is responsible for managing the CDS program execution and operates under the direction of the DSSPC.
- Specific DSWG responsibilities include prioritizing and addressing requests for CDS support received from various departments, developing and maintaining CDS interventions, monitoring CDS system implementation and results, and ensuring currency, consistency, and appropriateness of Health System CDS assets.

CDS Intervention Strategy
- *Begin with the end in mind:* the starting point for considering CDS interventions is a clear, shared understanding by pertinent stakeholders of the target that the planned CDS approach is intended to address.

---

* Adapted from: The University of Pittsburgh Medical Center CDS Mission Statement. Used with permission.

continued on next page

Sample Generic CDS Charter *continued*

- *Key parties at the table:* the intended users and other affected parties play a key role in each step of the development, launch, evaluation, and improvement loop. There is meticulous attention to affected workflows and processes during each of these steps in the CDS intervention lifecycle. Good use is made of champions.
- *Right tool for the job:* a range of possible CDS intervention types (for example, alerts, order sets, referential information, focused data gathering, review tools, etc.) are considered in developing an optimal strategy for ensuring that targeted goals are achieved most efficiently and effectively.
- *Deliver high-value information:* patient- and context-specific information available in deployed HIT systems is fully leveraged to optimize the applicability and usefulness of CDS information and guidance delivered to the recipient.
- *Measure and improve:* intervention monitoring is considered at each step of the intervention lifecycle. Effects of deployed interventions (both desirable and otherwise) are monitored; progress toward each intended objective is tracked, and the portfolio of interventions focused on the objective is refined, as needed.

Knowledge Asset Portfolio Management and Value
- The DSWG maintains an inventory of deployed CDS interventions and regularly monitors their currency, appropriateness, and consistency. For example, there is at least a yearly review of each CDS rule.
- To complement the review of interventions focused on specific objectives, the DSWG monitors overall performance of the Health System CDS program on an ongoing basis to ensure continued function as intended.
- DSWG will collaborate with pertinent experts within the Health System, affiliated academic programs, and outside agencies, as appropriate, in evaluating the CDS program.

ing your organization, or might be soon. Figures 1-4 and 2-3 and Worksheet 2-1 can help you gather and document this information. Keep in mind though that performance-related measurement and reimbursement is rapidly evolving, so you will need to carefully track programs from primary sources such as healthcare payers, accreditors and regulators.

Strategic Prioritization

One advantage of implementing CDS in a large organization is that you can use departmental or subject-matter committees and experts to help prioritize targets and develop and maintain CDS interventions to address them. This will provide broad-based input, facilitate communication and awareness of the CDS efforts, and identify potential barriers long before implementation. Although this additional outreach may increase challenges related to communications and consensus-building, it will benefit your CDS efforts in the long run by fully tapping available expertise and support.

Because addressing priority goals can require significant investment (especially in a large orga-

A More Concise
CDS Charter Sample*

- Focus on clinical interventions for which strong evidence and/or best practices have been demonstrated.
- Develop solutions that are useful and usable, focusing on those things that truly make a difference. Align priorities with overall organizational goals for safe, timely, effective, efficient, and equitable patient-centered care.
- Recognize the applications and limitations of decision support, while respecting the clinical expertise of nurses, physicians, and other staff.
- Pursue systemness when it enhances value, allowing latitude for legitimate local variation.
- Create an organizational model that is sustainable over the long-term and offers rapid support and problem-resolution for Texas Health Resources' (THR) clinicians.

---

*Source: Texas Health Resources, Arlington TX. Used with permission.

nization), you should build formal mechanisms for considering the ROI—both financial and non-financial—from addressing each target with CDS. Chapter 5 discusses selecting and prioritizing CDS interventions in more detail (see, for example, Figures 5-1 and 5-2). The pertinent issue for this Part I discussion is building the organizational capability to select and prioritize targets and interventions.

The CDS program benefit and cost dimensions outlined in Figure 1-3 can be applied to specific CDS interventions as well, and your intervention selection and prioritization approach may utilize them. Published CDS ROI data to inform your processes (for example, in populating the intervention desirability formula in Figure 5-2) are relatively scant, but some are available. As an example, Brigham and Women's Hospital, Boston, MA, has reported some details on CDS ROI (total benefit per year listed in parentheses after each item):[48]

- Renal dosing ($2.24 million);
- ADE [adverse drug event] prevention ($1.05 million);
- Guidance related to special or expensive drugs, such as Human Growth Hormone and vancomycin ($880,000);
- ADE monitoring ($760,000);
- Converting medication route from intravenous to oral ($740,000);
- Automated medication summary at hospital discharge ($100,000);
- Guidance for dosing in the elderly ($50,000);
- Guidance on need-to-order drug levels ($20,000).

An extension of these findings is provided in the report "Saving Lives, Saving Money" from the Massachusetts Technology Collaborative.[49]

Communication Strategies and Building Support for the CDS Program

The larger the organization, the more important it is for the CDS Committee—and its many connection points to all the other stakeholders in the organization—to act as evangelists and feedback channels for the CDS program goals and activities. There are many more people who can become resistors or detractors for this work, or prevent its full value from being delivered by not understanding needed care processes changes. Heightened attention to the engagement and communication strategies outlined in this chapter's General Approach section can minimize these risks; for example, acting promptly and transparently to address major concerns raised by stakeholders.

A 'communication amplification' approach can also be helpful. This may include one or more physician champions working closely with the CDS Committee, who then engage in formal and informal dialog about the CDS program with their peers, who in turn engage their peers. This can increase the flow of critical information and support both to and from the CDS Committee. Remember also to phase interactions over time and develop other outreach strategies to engage personnel who are not in the hospital on a daily basis, such as physicians who round intermittently.

CONSIDERATIONS FOR SMALL PRACTICES
People (Stakeholder Involvement)

- A small practice is also a business. You should incorporate CDS use into the practice business plan as a tool to assist in achieving financial, clinical and operational goals. The entire practice should contribute to the business plan to ensure buy-in and collaboration. They must understand this means a new approach to information and how information is used to make decisions in care. The plan's language should reflect and encourage a "culture of change." Transparent and communicative leadership are critical aspects of this culture.

- Seek out CIS/CDS software providers with appropriate expertise and resources to offer them support for shaping and guiding essential provider staff roles needed for CDS success (e.g., CDS intervention design, development, implementation and evaluation).

- The plan should ensure that all participants are aware of their roles and responsibilities regarding CDS and underlying data entry. If there are multiple people within each role (physicians, nurses, office staff), there should be a leader to keep others who share that role on track.

- Throughout this Guide, we emphasize the role of diverse stakeholders in supporting CDS-related activities. An example pertinent to office practice is the successful role that nurses can play in facilitating CDS-mediated quality improvement in practices with EHRs. Similarly, front desk

personnel desk can play a key role in supporting CDS. They will update basic non-clinical structured data, including the preferred pharmacy. This last action is particularly important to facilitate efficient e-prescribing. You should think creatively about these models and other approaches to fully engaging all those in the practice in optimizing your efforts.

- Approach CDS as a team sport—even in solo physician offices. CDS success will be related to the extent to which this team is working together toward mutually desirable goals, such as care safety, quality and efficiency. The appearance or reality that one group is '*doing* the CDS interventions' to another (especially for strictly selfish purposes) undermines the team approach and reduces efficiency and effectiveness. Clinical decision support is not an appropriate or effective tool for reinforcing 'command and control' management in healthcare in either large or small care settings.

- In smaller organizations, especially private practices, it is important to *not* limit champions to the clinician-owners of the practice. The multiple roles of the clinician-owner may lead to the staff accepting a system that fits the practice poorly because "that's what the boss wanted." Successful practices often enlist champions from among the ancillary clinical staff and other office staff members. Some practices even instruct staff members to voice their thoughts without regard to what the clinician-owners might prefer. As with any safety- and quality-focused enterprise, this openness is an important ingredient for the full participant engagement and support needed for high CDS performance.

- In a small practice, many of the key CDS program and intervention functions will require external support, such as from the Regional Extension Center (REC),[50] consultant, and/or EHR vendor. Nonetheless, you should identify at least one individual within the practice to take 'ownership' of the CDS-related activities. This person should oversee and coordinate the external support that's needed and ensure that all the activities support the practice's performance improvement goals (as discussed next).

Planning

- The CDS program, and CDS interventions used within the program, should be approached in the context of the practice's broader performance improvement efforts; for example, addressing quality-related payment drivers and efforts to improve efficiency. CDS is a very valuable tool set for these efforts, and these drivers provide justification and resources for CDS efforts.
- Make sure the CDS plan includes oversight mechanisms for the various strategic and tactical decisions, such as initiating and approving target-focused interventions, and outlines the role that each practice member plays in selecting, configuring, launching, using, monitoring, maintaining and improving CDS interventions.
- Your documented CDS plan should be a meaningful, living document for all those who work in the practice. They should see it as accurately reflecting how their efforts contribute to achieving important practice goals and how, in turn, this participation benefits them personally.
- Small practices have limited time and finances for CDS-related work, and the CDS program activities should be approached with this in mind. If possible, have a practice member keep tabs on ROI considerations (including both clinical and/or financial benefits) for the program overall and the CDS interventions it provides. Figure 1-3 contains some ROI dimensions to consider that can be applied to both. Your small practice typically won't have resources to calculate these in detail, but you should nonetheless consider "guestimates" to help inform where to focus your CDS energies. In any case, prepare to pay careful attention to measurement and evaluation to track and accelerate progress toward goals.
- Seek to ground the CDS program and interventions in the pertinent evidence base (see Chapter 1, section entitled CDS Promise and Pitfalls: A Peek at the Literature); that is, focusing on CDS

deployment strategies shown to be useful, and on specific CDS interventions that reinforce evidence-based clinical practice. CDS interventions that lack evidence for the recommended clinical approach may be rejected more easily and considered less useful. There should be strong consensus among all those affected in the practice that the right targets have been chosen and (as discussed in more detail in Part II), that the CDS approach to these targets are the right ones.

- Recognize how outside sources can help the practice to achieve its goals. Vendors, vendor user-groups, CDS collaboratives (see the Epilogue), RECs, other successful practices similar to your own that have successfully used CDS, and other resources can be of great help. Don't reinvent the wheel.

Capabilities (Systems)

- Valuable results from technology implementation, such as achieving Meaningful Use and otherwise improving care processes and outcomes, depends critically on successful CDS. Therefore, make sure that your practice's efforts to implement an EHR and related systems go hand in hand with the CDS program and intervention development activities outlined in this book.

Communication

- Your practice may already have set up regularly scheduled meetings to address EHR issues. CDS should be on that agenda, and the meeting should provide an open platform for all staff members to express their concerns and share what is working. If you don't have such a regular meeting, consider starting one.
- Even in small practices where everyone is in close proximity, communications about important issues—including those related to the CDS program—might not be as rich as you would expect, or might even be inadequate for optimal performance. If your practice is like this, you should take special care to ensure that *everyone* is aware of important CDS-related decisions and actions and has an opportunity to provide feed-

back. Don't assume that silence indicates consent. Communication channels can include internal newsletters (printed or online), standing agenda item during practice meetings, email or bulletin boards, scheduled group lunches, messages within the practice EHR, and many others. Leverage everyone in the practice's creativity and energy to identify the best approaches for the group.

CONSIDERATIONS FOR HIT SOFTWARE PROVIDERS
People (Stakeholder Involvement)

- If you don't have one already, consider fostering a user group among your client base that focuses specifically on using and enhancing your CDS-related tools. This can include enabling them to share CDS best practices, leveraging frameworks (such as Worksheets 6-2 and 6-3) outlined in this Guide.
- Continually enhance your client collaborations to understand their CDS-related needs, both short term (such as related to Meaningful Use) and longer term (such as optimizing specific value-based purchasing performance measures related to patient safety, care quality and patient engagement).

Planning

- If there are appropriate expertise and resources in your organization, consider offering support for implementers in shaping and guiding essential provider staff roles needed for CDS success, such as CDS intervention design, development, implementation and evaluation. For providers (such as small practices) that won't have such staff, consider ways to support these functions on their behalf.
- If appropriate to your organization's culture and client relationships, explore with your clients ways you might engage more deeply and helpfully in their CDS strategic planning and execution efforts.

WORKSHEETS

Worksheet 2-1

Stakeholders, Goals, and Objectives

Worksheet 2-1 is used to document your discussions with stakeholders about their priority clinical goals and objectives, as outlined in this chapter. Careful attention to all key stakeholders cannot be overemphasized. List each stakeholder in the first column.

In the next column, indicate the role that this person or group will play in the CDS program (e.g., from Figures 2-5 and 2-6). You should also note whether they are a potential champion or resistor/detractor for addressing a particular goal or objective (that you will list in the next columns) with CDS interventions, and whether they might play a key role in obtaining resources or funding. If they are a resistor or detractor, add principal concern or objection.

In the third column, list the high-level clinical goals that emerged from your discussions as important to this person or committee. These goals define broad care processes or outcomes that you will address with CDS interventions. Besides listening for spontaneously offered stakeholder priorities, use the sources in Figure 5-1 to probe for organizational focus on the goals in Figures 2-2 and 2-3.

In the fourth column, break down the goals you have elicited into their component clinical objectives. The more specific and quantifiable you make these objectives, the more likely you will be to devise interventions that produce measurable results. For example, an objective such as "Improve prescribing practices for heparin" will likely be less useful than a more specific one, such as "Decrease incidence of heparin overdose."

Stakeholder(s)	Role in CDS Program	High-level Goals	Clinical Objectives
James C. (Chief Quality Officer)	Proponent, general quality leader	Disease-specific prevention (outpatient)	• Improve checking of urinary protein and eye exams in diabetics • Improve prescription patterns for asthmatics on inhaled steroids
		Antibiotic utilization (inpatient)	Improve compliance with antibiotic prescriptions based on culture data
Claire D. (Chief Nursing Officer)	Detractor Concern = potential increased workload for nurses	Nursing documentation accuracy	Improve likelihood that advance directives are reviewed with patients
			Improve accuracy of allergy documentation
Ken V. (Director of ICU)	Proponent, clinical thought leader	Ventilator management	Reduce number of patients receiving paralytics
			Reduce ventilator-associated lung injuries
		Managing pressor use for blood pressure support	Reduce use of high-dose norepinephrine, as opposed to multiple pressors

continued on next page

Worksheet 2-1 *continued*

Stakeholder(s)	Role in CDS Program	High-level Goals	Clinical Objectives
Eric E. (Director of Oncology Service)	Proponent, clinical thought leader	Managing patients in bone marrow unit	Decrease likelihood that high-dose chemotherapy is started too late after admission
			Reduce vancomycin over-utilization in patients with neutropenic fever

Synthesize and validate a working list of CDS goals, and clinical goals and objectives for your CDS program. Define baseline and target performance for the clinical objectives.

The analysis in Worksheet 2-1 of current and potential clinical goals within your organization provides the foundation for synthesizing and prioritizing the CDS program goals. Prioritizing can be important if limited resources or other factors tightly constrain the number of issues that the CDS program can contemplate at one time. It might be useful to first begin developing detailed clinical goals and objectives for the CDS goals and focus areas that are expected, based on Worksheet 2-1 data, to be of greatest importance to your organization.

In Worksheet 2-1 you began breaking down clinical goals into measurable objectives based on stakeholder discussions. It is important to think more comprehensively about the range of objectives that might be helpful in achieving the goal. To help prepare for measuring progress toward CDS targets, Worksheet 5-1 (which builds on Worksheet 2-1 to support next steps in CDS intervention development) includes a column for documenting measurable baseline performance levels and desired outcomes.

Worksheet 2-2

Checklist for Clinical Decision Support Goal Charter*

Once you have identified goals and objectives on which to focus CDS attention, you might consider making a formal charter for the targets, individually or collectively. There are different ways to approach templates for project charters, and the following checklist is one example. For this worksheet sample, we have provided notes about the type of information that could be used for some of the elements in a charter focusing on the objective of reducing preventable allergic reactions. See also the sample charters presented earlier in this chapter, which can be used as templates for broader CDS program activities.

Check		Section	Details
❏	1.	Overview	
❏	1.1	Purpose Statement	What are the reasons for addressing this goal? For example, antibiotics given to patients who are allergic to them result in significant morbidity and mortality.
❏	1.2	Goals and Objectives/ Expected Outcome	What are expected returns from addressing this goal/objective? They need to be important and worthwhile! For example, prevent patients from getting antibiotics to which they are allergic, and reap corresponding returns.
❏	1.3	Scope	What are the boundaries for this project? For example, 1. Actions from this initiative will affect major nodes in the medication management process—prescription, dispensing, administration. 2. Will only focus on antibiotic medications. 3. Non-antibiotic medications will not be considered, although we may favor actions that are scalable to other medication groups.
❏	1.4	Critical Success Factors	What are factors needed for success? For example, 1. Education to all, especially to frontline stakeholders 2. Easy CDS system use with minimal disruption of current workflow 3. Quantifiable reduction in preventable adverse events
❏	1.5	Assumptions	What are assumptions related to the technology, resource, scope, expectation, or timeline assumptions for addressing this goal/objective? For example: 1. Adverse events from antibiotics are detectable and preventable. 2. We have statistical methods that can determine whether our actions are effective, even if the event rate is very low.
❏	1.6	Constraints	What are the constraints related to budget, resources, timeline, and technology? For example, 1. This project needs to be completed within 12 months. 2. Action plan must be efficient for frontline stakeholders. 3. Leadership support is critical.

* Adapted from: State of Texas Department of Information Resources. *Project Charter*. Available online at: http://www.dir.state.tx.us/pubs/framework/gate1/projectcharter/index.htm.

continued on next page

Worksheet 2-1 *continued*

Check		Section	Details
❏	2.	Authority and Milestones	
❏	2.1	Funding Authority	Who or what is funding efforts toward this goal? For example, this project is funded by hospital capital budget.
❏	2.2	Oversight Authority	What committee is responsible for this goal/objective? For example, the Quality Improvement, Patient Safety and/or P&T Committee could be the oversight authority for an objective that focuses on decreasing preventable allergic reactions.
			It is important that the CDS Committee not take full authority for all interventions. Involving more stakeholders at the front lines will increase acceptance.
❏	2.3	Major Milestones	What are the major points of success and deliverables that will define progress toward this objective? For example:
			1. Get buy-in from oversight authority and executive committee.
			2. Define feasible data management strategy.
			3. Formulate action strategy and timeline.
			4. Execute action strategy.
			5. Analyze and interpret results.
❏	3.	Organization	
❏	3.1	Committee Structure	Graphically represent committees pertinent to this goal/objective and their interaction.
❏	3.2	Roles and Responsibilities	Three-column table stating the member, their role, and responsibilities
❏	3.3	Facilities and Resources	What are the facilities and resources needed; for example, office space, computers, personnel?
❏	4.	Points of Contact	Who is the primary and back-up contact for the project?
❏	5.	Glossary	Define all terms and acronyms used in the project charter.
❏	6.	Revision History	Track all changes to the charter document.
❏	7.	Appendices	Include any additional relevant information, for example, charts, tables, lists.

REFERENCES

1   Kaplan R, Norton D. Using the balanced scorecard as a strategic management system. *Harv Bus Rev*.1996; 74(1):75-85.

2   Wright A, Sittig DF, Ash JS. Governance for clinical decision support: case studies and recommended practices from leading institutions. *J Am Med Inform Assoc*. 2011 Mar 1; 18(2):187-94.

3   Krall MA. Clinician champions and leaders for electronic medical record innovations. *The Permanente Journal*. 2001; 5(1):40-45. Available online at: http://xnet.kp.org/permanentejournal/winter01/HSchamp.html. Accessed June 16, 2011.

4   Lorenzi NM, Kouroubali A, Detmer DE, et al. How to successfully select and implement electronic health records (EHR) in small ambulatory practice settings. *BMC Med Inform Decis Mak*. 2009 Feb; 23;9:15.

5   Eichner J, Das M. Challenges and Barriers to Clinical Decision Support (CDS) Design and Implementation Experienced in the Agency for Healthcare Research and Quality CDS Demonstrations. AHRQ Publication No. 10-0064-EF; 2010 March.

6   For a list of topics identified nationally as high priority for this type of program see the following: Institute of Medicine (IOM). *Priority Areas for National Action: Transforming Health Care Quality*. 2003. (a summary is available online at: http://www.ahrq.gov/qual/iompriorities. htm; the full report is available at http://www.nap.edu/books/0309085438/html); see the AHRQ priority topics for research at http://www.ahrq.gov/about/mmarsrch.htm. Accessed June 16, 2011.

7   For example, note the Institute of Medicine report: Institute of Medicine (IOM). *Knowing What Works in Healthcare: A Roadmap for the Nation*. 2008. This report emphasizes the importance of synthesizing and applying to practice the evidence about healthcare interventions known to do more good than harm. Available online at http://books.nap. edu/catalog.php?record_id=12038. Accessed July 26, 2011.

8   Such as JCAHO/NCQA accreditation and quality measures (e.g., NCQA/HEDIS) and those in the National Healthcare Quality Report available online at: http://www.ahcpr.gov/qual/nhqr02/premeasures.htm), and the National Quality Forum hospital performance measures, also available online: http://www.qualityforum.org/Measures_List.aspx.

9   See, for example, United Kingdom's Quality and Outcomes Framework, available online at: http://www.ic.nhs.uk/statistics-and-data-collections/audits-and-performance/the-quality-and-outcomes-framework, Accessed June 16, 2011.

10   Theory and Reality of Value-Based Purchasing: Lessons from the Pioneers. Agency for Healthcare Research and Quality website: http://www.ahrq.gov/qual/meyerrpt.htm http://www.ahrq.gov/qual/meyerrpt.htm. Accessed May 27, 2011.

11   Hospital Quality Initiatives Overview. Centers for Medicare and Medicaid Services (CMS) website: http://www.cms.gov/HospitalQualityInits/; see also Roadmap for Implementing Value Driven Healthcare in the Traditional Medicare Fee-for-Service Pogram: https://www.cms.gov/QualityInitiativesGenInfo/downloads/VBPRoadmap_OEA_1-16_508.pdf. Both accessed July 27, 2011.

12   See state-based reports aggregated by the National Association of Health Data Organizations, available online at,: http://www.nahdo.org/map , and AHRQ: http://statesnapshots.ahrq.gov/snaps09/map. jsp?menuId=2&state=. Both accessed October 23, 2011.

13   Physician Quality Reporting System Overview. Centers for Medicare and Medicaid Services website: https://www.cms.gov/PQRS/. Accessed May, 27, 2011.

14   See Hospital Quality Initiatives Overview. Centers for Medicare and Medicaid Services website: http://www.cms.gov/HospitalQualityInits/. (Scroll down the page to see the variety of quality measurement and improvement initiatives.)

15   Rewarding results: aligning incentives with high-quality healthcare. Available online at: http://www.leapfroggroup.org/about_us/other_initiatives/incentives_and_rewards/rewarding_results Accessed June 17, 2011

16   National Committee for Quality Assurance website: http://www.ncqa.org/. Accessed May 27, 2011.

17   CMS EHR Meaningful Use Overview. Centers for Medicare and Medicaid Services website: https://www.cms.gov/EHRIncentivePrograms/30_Meaningful_Use.asp. Accessed May 27, 2011.

18   Certification Commission for Health Information Technology website: http://www.cchit.org/media/news/2010/09/commission-launches-onc-atcb-certification-program. Accessed May 27, 2011.

19   2010 Electronic Prescribing Incentive Program – Adoption/Use of Medication Electronic Prescribing Measure. Centers for Medicare and Medicaid Services website: http://www.cms.gov/ERxIncentive/Downloads/2010GPROeRx%20_Specifications_Document_111009.pdf. Accessed June 16, 2011.

The Medicare ePrescribing Incentive Program. American Medical Association website: http://www.ama-assn.org/ama/pub/eprescribing/medicare-eprescribing-incentive.shtml. Accessed June 16, 2011.

20 Shared Savings Program Overview. Centers for Medicare and Medicaid Services website: http://www.cms.gov/sharedsavingsprogram/. Accessed May 27, 2011.

21 Draper A. Managing bundled payments. *Healthcare Financial Management.* 2011 April; 110-118.

22 Demonstration Projects & Evaluation Reports: Medical Home Demonstration. Centers for Medicare and Medicaid Services website: http://www.cms.gov/demoprojectsevalrpts/md/itemdetail.asp?filterType=none&filterByDID=0&sortByDID=2&sortOrder=ascending&itemID=CMS1199247. Accessed May 27, 2011.

23 See also "Evidence base for CDS Value" in Chapter 1.

24 Agency for Healthcare Research and Quality. Evidence-based practice recommendations, available online at: http://www.ahrq.gov/clinic/epcix.htm. Accessed July 29, 2011.

25 Garg AX, Adhikari NKJ, McDonald H, et al. Effects of computerized clinical decision support systems on performance and patient outcomes: a systematic review. *JAMA.* 2005; 293:1223-1238.

26 Kaushal R, Shojania K, Bates D. Effects of computerized physician order entry and clinical decision support systems on medication safety: a systematic review. *Arch Intern Med.* 2003; 163:1409-1416.

27 Weingarten SR et al. Interventions used in disease management programmes for patients with chronic illness: which ones work? Meta-analysis of published reports. *BMJ.* 2002; 323:925.

28 Rundall TG, Shortell SM, Wang MC, et al. As good as it gets? Chronic care management in nine leading US physician organizations. *BMJ.* 2002; 325:958-961.

29 U.S. Pharmacopeia, National Database for Medication Errors. Both available online at: https://www.medmarx.com. See also America's riskiest drugs. *Forbes.* February 24, 2003. http://www.forbes.com/2003/02/24/cx_mh_0224risk.html. Accessed June 16, 2011.

30 Agency for Healthcare Research Quality. Patient safety reporting systems. Available online at: http://www.psnet.ahrq.gov/primer.aspx?primerID=13. Accessed October 23, 2011.

31 McGlynn EA, Mularski RA, Shrank WH , et al. The quality of healthcare delivered to adults in the United States. *New Engl J Med.* 2003; 348:2635-2645.

32 National Committee for Quality Assurance. *The State of health Care Quality.* 2010. Available online at: http://www.ncqa.org/tabid/836/Default.aspx. Accessed July 26, 2011.

33 Gurwitz JH, Field TS, Harrold LR, et al. Incidence and preventability of adverse drug events among older persons in the ambulatory setting. *JAMA.* 2003; 289:1107-1116.

34 Dovey SM, Phillips RL, Green LA, et al. Types of medical errors commonly reported by family physicians. *Am Fam Physician.* 2003; 67:697.

35 Strom BL, Schinnar R, Aberra F, et al. Unintended effects of a computerized physician order entry nearly hard-stop alert to prevent a drug interaction: a randomized controlled trial. *Arch Intern Med.* 2010 Sep 27; 170(17):1578-1583.

36 Sittig DF, Teich JM, Osheroff JA, et al. Improving clinical quality indicators through electronic health records: it takes more than just a reminder. *Pediatrics.* 2009 Jul; 124(1):375-377.

37 Lobach D, Kawamotok K, Houlihan CA, et. al. Enabling Health Care Decision making through Clinical Decision Support and Knowledge Management. AHRQ Effective Healthcare Program. Evidence Report/ Technology Assessment. 2011. Available online at: http://www.effectivehealthcare.ahrq.gov/ehc/products/278/607/Decision%20Support_Draft%20Report%2012-06-2010.pdf. Accessed June 16, 2011.

38 Levick D, Lukens HF, Stillman PL. You've led the horse to water; Now how do you get him to drink: Increasing utilization of computerized order entry. *J Healthcare Information Manage.* 2005; 19(1):70.

39 Bhattacherjee, A, Hikmet, N. Physicians' resistance toward healthcare information technology: a theoretical model and empirical test. *European Journal of Information Systems* 2007; 16;725–737.

40 Ash JS, Stavri PZ, Dykstra R, et al. Implementing computerized physician order entry: the importance of special people. *Int J Med Inform.* 2003 Mar; 69(2-3): 235-250.

41 Curry LA, Spatz E, Cherlin E, et. al. What distinguishes top-performing hospitals in acute myocardial infarction mortality rates? A qualitative study. *Ann Intern Med.* 2011; 154(6):384-390. See also coverage of the article in the May 2011 issue of Today's Hospitalist, available online at: http://todayshospitalist.com/index.php?b=articles_read&cnt=1226. Accessed July 28, 2011.

42 Heifetz R, Linsky M. *The Practice of Adaptive Leadership.* Alexander Grashow, ed. HBR Press, 2009

43 See the website for Kotter International, available online at: http://www.kotterinternational.com/KotterPrinciples/ChangeSteps.aspx. Accessed August 29, 2011.

44 Jha AK, Epstein AM. Hospital boards and their relationship to quality of care. *Health Aff.* 2010; 29(1):182-187.

45 Both JCAHO and CMS require reporting of "core measures." They are working toward convergence of these requirements; details can be found online at: https://www.cms.gov/HospitalQualityInits/. Accessed October 23, 2011.

46 AHRQ National Quality Measures Clearinghouse: http://www.qualitymeasures.ahrq.gov. Accessed July 29, 2011.

47 National Quality Forum website: http://www.qualityforum.org. Accessed July 29, 2011.

48 Kaushal R, Ashish K, Jha A, et al. Technology evaluation: Return on investment for a computerized physician order entry system. *JAMIA*. 2006; 13:261266 doi:10.1197/jamia.M1984

49 Massachusetts Hospital CPOE Initiative. Saving Lives, Saving Money: The Imperative for Computerize Physician Order Entry in Massachusetts Hospitals; The Clinical Baseline and Financial Impact Study. February 2008. Available online at: http://www.masstech.org/ehealth/cpoe/cpoe08release.html. Accessed July 29, 2011.

50 Regional Extension Centers are federally funded programs in the U.S. that provide assistance to small and mid-sized practices in the selection, configuration (including workflow and process re-design), and implementation of ambulatory EHRs. Each state has at least one REC providing services for a minimal fee or at no cost to the practice. See the ONC webpage for locating Regional Extension Centers: http://healthit.hhs.gov/portal/server.pt/community/healthit_hhs_gov__rec_program/1495. Accessed July 29, 2011.

Chapter 3

Other Key CDS Program Building Blocks: Systems, Workflow and Measurement

Tasks

Systems

- Prepare an inventory of the information technology assets in your organization relevant to delivering CDS interventions. (Worksheet 3-1)
- Assess your HIT systems' CDS capabilities and compatibility with standard vocabularies.
- Develop a roadmap for acquiring and enhancing information technology systems to meet your organization's CDS goals.

Workflow

- Make sure you have the capability to carefully map clinical workflows to be enhanced by CDS—both current and desired future state. (Worksheet 3-2)
- Think broadly about who the stakeholders are in key workflow processes. Ensure your CDS team has the skills needed to meticulously document what actually happens in these processes through direct observations, instead of relying on interviews and written policies and procedures alone.

Measurement

- Make sure you have the capabilities and resources for assessing intervention effects as core components of your CDS program. (Worksheets 9-1 and 9-3)
- Align your approach to measuring intervention performance against organizational goals and objectives with broader initiatives to track and improve clinical, operational and financial performance.
- Leverage CDS governance processes to establish reasonable measurement goals and expectations for improvement.

KEY LESSONS

Systems

- Reliable, fast and usable information technology infrastructure is essential for robust CDS interventions.
- CDS depends on access to structured (coded) data, use of standard vocabularies and ability to aggregate information from multiple sources.

Workflow

- What CDS intervention developers and others *think* is happening as care processes unfold is often quite different from what is *actually* happening. Effective CDS interventions require knowledge of the latter, which depends on direct observation supplemented by interviews and other data-gathering tools.

Measurement

- Many organizations do not allocate enough time or resources to build adequate capability to address CDS intervention effects, but increasing global drivers for measurable healthcare performance improvement makes this essential.
- Appropriately evaluating positive and negative CDS effects requires both quantitative and qualitative approaches.

GENERAL APPROACH

In Chapter 1 we introduced the CDS Five Rights' framework, which asserts that to measurably improve care processes and outcomes with CDS interventions you must get:

- *The right information*
- *To the right person*
- *In the right CDS intervention format*
- *Through the right channel*
- *At the right point in workflow.*

To build a CDS program that reliably achieves these objectives, you must have a strong handle on the systems and applications that comprise your technology infrastructure, since they provide the intervention formats and channels through which interventions are delivered. Similarly, you need strong capabilities to understand and enhance workflow. You also must be able to measure processes and outcomes so you can know where to focus your CDS

efforts and whether or not these efforts are making a difference.

This chapter offers information and guidance on strengthening these three major building blocks for successful CDS programs: systems, workflow and measurement. They are covered next in this General Approach section.

Systems

When you select interventions to meet specific clinical objectives (as discussed in Chapter 6), you will see that CDS-related capabilities in your core CIS applications influence key intervention features. Likewise, your hardware and network environment determine how these interventions can be delivered. Using the CDS Five Rights framework, this means that your technology infrastructure heavily influences how you can configure and use the intervention *format* and *channel* dimensions.

For example, some intervention types that use patient-specific data, such as certain alerts and reminders, depend heavily on having these data available—often in a structured and coded format—in your EHR and related systems. Thus, considering CDS targets as part of CIS procurement and updating requirements can help ensure that, over time, the tools needed for optimal CDS effectiveness will be available. Strategic planning that involves IT and business and clinical leadership, and anticipates this interdependent relationship between CIS and CDS, can help your organization navigate the expensive and potentially risky challenges associated with CIS procurement, deployment and updating.

As discussed in Chapters 1 and 2, the CDS program will be most effective in addressing priority goals if you staff and manage it as a key strategic initiative, rather than as a subcomponent of information system deployment. Helpful guides on clinical information systems implementation are available[1] and can be used in conjunction with this Guide to ensure that the CIS and CDS efforts are optimally effective and synergistic. Fortunately, certification requirements and processes (discussed below) are emerging that will ensure that systems have a common suite of essential functionality, including elements related to CDS. There are mechanisms for public stakeholders to influence how these requirements evolve, and we encourage implementers to use them.

We next consider features of your IT infrastructure—and related standards and drivers. Your CDS team needs to understand these well—and ideally catalog the technology components—since they underpin your CDS efforts. CDS capabilities depend on both CIS application features and available hardware and software infrastructure. You should consider them independently and how they inter-relate. The remaining material in this "Systems" chapter subsection provides information needed to assess, catalog and leverage the information system infrastructure pertinent to your CDS efforts.

Hardware and Networks

The computer network performance, workstation and mobile device availability, wireless coverage, system reliability, and similar features are important enablers (or impediments) for deploying an effective CDS intervention portfolio. It is important, therefore, to assess the basic features and stability of your computing environment. Key elements to consider are outlined in Figure 3-1.

Significant problems or limitations with these features in your environment might warrant attention early in CDS program planning to minimize problems later during intervention implementation. For example, it would be unwise to begin developing CDS interventions that deliver information over the network to clinicians via workstations or portable devices if users don't have convenient access to these systems. Similarly, those CDS access points, and the network that delivers the interventions, should be free from maintenance problems and unacceptable downtime.

CIS Applications

CDS interventions are most effective when tightly integrated into workflow. Generally, this involves incorporating them into the CISs that underpin patient care processes. Figure 3-2 lists a broad range of CISs that can serve as channels for delivering CDS interventions. Clinicians and patients interact directly with some of these systems, making them important conduits through which CDS content can be delivered. Other systems that might not be within typical clinician or patient workflow, such as scheduling or billing systems, can provide patient-related demographic information that will be used in CDS interventions. Most organizations have some applications that provide medical knowledge to clinicians and patients (e.g., via an intranet or the Internet). These should be considered as well.

Regulatory Backdrop: HITECH and Meaningful Use

The passage in the U.S. of the HITECH Act in 2009 provides powerful incentives for the adop-

Figure 3-1: Information System Infrastructure Characteristics

Hardware/software	• *Number* of workstations/terminals, handheld/portable devices, printers—per bed/exam room, per clinician • *Quality*: age, software/operating system version • *Reliability*: e.g., percent uptime, maintenance issues • *Performance*: speed of the core applications, as perceived by users
Network connectivity	• *Number* and proportion of computers connected to Internet and high-speed internal communications
Wireless/remote systems	• *Number* and use of wireless devices: alphanumeric pager, smart phones, tablet computers, laptops • *Telemedicine* infrastructure (e.g., remote monitoring or data-gathering from patients at home via machines that measure blood pressure or blood sugar) • *Remote access* to information systems by clinicians
Medical devices that generate patient data	• *Number* and *type* of medical instruments that gather and deliver data about patients (e.g., electrocardiogram machines, automated blood pressure monitors, smart infusion pumps)
Integration among clinical systems	• *Number* of different terminals/workstations/windows required to access the full portfolio of available applications.

tion and Meaningful Use of certified EHRs in both inpatient and outpatient settings.[2] The HITECH Act includes in its definition of a certified EHR[3] "the capacity to provide clinical decision support" and federal regulations established to implement the Act include increasingly stringent CDS-related requirements. Most of the CISs described in the previous section, whether as part of a single software product or an aggregation of separate applications, collectively make up an EHR system. They are, therefore, foundational for interrelated activities around CDS and Meaningful Use.

The online site HealthIT.gov referenced earlier contains important details about the incentive program and certification process that provide important context for how CISs in the U.S. should be leveraged within CDS programs. Your CDS team should therefore work closely with others in your organization who are responding to Meaningful Use incentive programs.

An important Meaningful Use theme pertinent to the discussion in this chapter (and book as a whole) is that it is necessary, but not sufficient, to *deploy* information systems that have certain features; it is necessary to also ensure that these features are *used*. In addition, implementers must ensure that this use is *meaningful*, that is, that it drives measurably better outcomes. You should keep this imperative in mind during the information system inventory described next. In other countries, there are analogous national performance improvement forces at work, so CIS/CDS implementers outside the U.S. should likewise understand this pertinent national context as they catalog and leverage the information systems that underpin their CDS efforts.

Cataloging CDS-related IT Infrastructure

To document and leverage your CDS team's familiarity with the hardware, network and application environment for your CDS interventions, you should consider formally cataloging this infrastructure. The hospital information services department, or the pertinent vendor(s) for small practices, may already have material useful for this purpose.

Figure 3-2: CIS Applications Pertinent to CDS Interventions

Departmental data management	• Pharmacy information system • Laboratory information system/results-reporting system • Radiology information/results-reporting system
Clinical records and patient management	• Electronic health records: ambulatory, inpatient, for patients (i.e., personal health record/PHR) • Department-oriented records (e.g., anesthesia, cardiology) • Care-tracking systems: emergency department, operating room • Medication administration and documentation
Ordering	• Computerized practitioner order entry • Other order entry systems
Data aggregation	• Data warehouse • Clinical data repository • Dashboards for performance management • External and internal registries (e.g., disease-specific registries and government immunization registry)
Clinical content	• Order sets • Alerts, such as for drug interactions, disease management • Reference/knowledge sources for clinicians • Health information for patients • Health risk assessment tools
Financial/administrative	• Charge capture system • Billing system • Scheduling/registration system • Directories: physician on-call and coverage schedules and contact numbers, clinician and patient email addresses

The goal is to understand the information ecosystem available to support CDS functionality. This encompasses identifying the infrastructure that can be leveraged to obtain data needed to drive CDS interventions, providing the user interface to deliver this information, conveying the content that will be delivered to end users, and supporting analytics needed to assess intervention use and effects. In building the catalog, you should classify the information types entered, managed and displayed in the CIS (such as lab information, patient demographics, etc.), as well as the underlying terminologies, coding systems and other standards (discussed below). You

should list the CIS users and the utilization (adoption) rate. This list will include physicians, nurses, pharmacists, patients and their families, and others.

Core clinical systems are a good starting point for your catalog; these may include applications that handle documentation, order entry, medication management and results review. Consider especially clinical content resources such as drug-reference information, drug interaction databases, order-set content, and alerts and alert configuring tools. These will be important starting points for your efforts to enhance CDS value and use. Also examine clinical and administrative business-intelligence software and associated data warehouses, reporting tools and dashboards. These will play an important role in assessing CDS intervention results. You can use Worksheet 3-1 to help your CDS team analyze and document pertinent applications, and also use it as a model for a similar hardware and network catalog.

Using the Infrastructure Catalog

Later in this chapter, we say more about workflow into which system use fits, and in Part II we describe in detail using available systems to provide valuable CDS interventions. For now, we provide some issues about technology infrastructure that are important to consider in developing and refining CDS programs.

To maximize CDS effectiveness, it is key to ensure that system users have adequate access to devices required to interact with the CISs and their CDS functionality. For example, physicians unable to access a device for CPOE may be forced to give a verbal order or write the order on paper, potentially bypassing prescriber-focused CDS capabilities. Monitoring clinical workflow and speaking to stakeholders will typically indicate whether access to devices is adequate.

Along similar lines, good wireless connectivity is critical in settings in which wireless systems are used for CDS-related applications. Unreliable wireless access can discourage CIS use at the point of care, and the resulting physical separation between information delivery and targeted care activities can render CDS features less effective. The interplay between CDS interventions and system performance raises similar issues. For example, as you add CDS interventions, you need to ensure that they will not degrade CIS response times for end users. This could engender user frustration and resistance to CDS efforts, which can significantly impair your CDS team's ability to achieve goals. We will offer guidance on assessing impact from specific CDS interventions on CIS performance through pre- and post-implementation measurement in Chapter 9.

It is helpful in the IT inventory process to consider how introducing or expanding CDS in the various information systems will affect workflow. To optimize care efficiency and user acceptance, the sequence and details for enabling CDS features in each system should be based on a careful workflow assessment for that system and the care processes it mediates (as discussed later in this chapter). For example, an interruptive alert displayed at an inopportune step in EMR workflow can distract the clinician from the current task, increase the likelihood that the notification will be dismissed without action, and potentially result in an error by disrupting thought flow. The salient point for this discussion is that CIS tools and workflows provide a foundation for CDS-mediated enhancements, so building capacity to understand and leverage CIS details is an important task for CDS programs that can reliably produce helpful CDS interventions within available information systems.

You should also consider overall system usability, that is, users' baseline interactions with the underlying hardware and software that will convey the CDS interventions. Users should be trained on effectively using these devices and programs, and any usability problems should be fixed before adding CDS interventions, since these problems will likely hinder successful CDS. Beyond just being able to successfully interact with the information systems, users should be comfortable with them to the greatest extent possible. Remember that individuals have a limited capacity for absorbing new skills and changes to routine. Adding new CDS-related tasks on top of shaky interactions with the underlying systems can undermine the success of both. Again, the capacity to assess and address these issues needs to be built into your CDS program.

Addressing CDS-related Standards

We recommend in the previous discussion and in Worksheet 3-1 that you pay careful attention to standards and codes handled by your information systems. They figure into certification and Meaningful Use requirements, and affect data and functions available to your CDS interventions—and how users interact with them. As such, these standards should be considered when selecting, acquiring and installing pertinent CIS components, as well as when designing and deploying CDS interventions that use these systems. In the following discussion, we describe several types of standards pertinent to infrastructure for your CDS program overall, and to specific interventions.

Standard Vocabularies

A robust CDS program will likely involve a variety of specific interventions delivered via several different information systems or system components. Even a single intervention, such as a clinical alert, might require information from several systems (such as laboratory, pharmacy or CPOE) and perhaps also from external electronic knowledge sources. Integrating the various CDS intervention components, such as pertinent patient data and clinical knowledge, often requires a common underlying vocabulary and coding scheme, as well as a variety of other standards for data elements and inter-system communication.

Far from being an arcane technological detail, standard vocabularies are key to achieving "semantic interoperability" across systems that must communicate to produce a CDS intervention's intended result. That is, the standards ensure that data—such as a lab test result or medication—have the same meaning in whatever system they are recorded, displayed, or used. For example, semantic interoperability means that when a clinician records in an EHR a piece of data (such as an abnormal physical finding identified during a clinical examination), this information can be copied into other systems (such as a clinical data repository, discussed shortly) and interpreted by other applications (such as a CDS rule) with the meaning intended by the clinician preserved. A standard vocabulary used across these systems facilitates interoperability by providing an unambiguous code for tagging what the data element is and what are its dimensions (such as units of measure). Interoperability made possible by coded data is crucial to most CDS interventions, since they typically require specific and unambiguous clinical data on which to operate. Likewise, precise terminol-

ogy can be helpful for CDS interventions that query knowledge sources.

A robust vocabulary typically is more than just a controlled list of codes matched to their names. Instead, a structured vocabulary provides relationships among the concepts and details about those concepts. This, in turn, permits CDS interventions to automatically aggregate and intelligently interpret related data. For example, a drug vocabulary may contain a class or grouping that identifies all penicillin-like antibiotics for use in drug-allergy checking. It may also contain the manufactured dose forms to facilitate drug ordering in a CPOE system.

Universally accepted vocabularies related to CDS do not exist yet, but some consensus is beginning to emerge. For example, there are codes for medical and nursing diagnoses and procedures, laboratory and radiology tests, and medications. Many of these coding systems have been endorsed by various U.S. government agencies, including by units of the U.S. Department of Health and Human Services (HHS) acting under its authority provided by two key statutes: the HITECH Act of 2009 (discussed earlier) and the Health Insurance Portability and Accountability Act (HIPAA). Additional consensus has been provided in the U.S. through the work of the Health Information Technology Standards Panel (HITSP) and HHS, and by additional agencies cooperating under the Consolidated Health Informatics effort.[4] Figure 3-3 highlights several vocabulary standards relevant to CDS. Unfortunately, there is currently no single, comprehensive reference for learning more about all these various standards. Individual countries may have bodies that address authoritative HIT standards for national purposes; in the U.S., the HIT Standards Committee[5] plays this role.

While consensus on specific vocabularies for particular classes of data may be emerging, overlap remains where multiple terminologies address the same data class. For example, both the International Classification of Diseases, Ninth Revision, Clinical Modification (ICD-9-CM) and the Systemitized Nomenclature of Medicine—Clinical Terms

(SNOMED CT) contain codes for diagnoses and problems. The former has achieved ubiquity in the U.S. because of its widespread use for billing purposes, although it was designed for epidemiological documentation and not for clinical use. By contrast, SNOMED CT was designed in part to facilitate clinical documentation, but it has not yet come into widespread use. This is an example where an organization may need to leverage whatever coding is available in their systems in order to provide CDS—and then migrate toward better terminologies as they become available.

While Health Level Seven (HL7)[6] is known primarily for its messaging standard, the organization maintains a suite of standards that address knowledge representation, structured documentation and other domains. In addition, as part of its messaging standard that defines a syntax for communicating clinical data, HL7 provides a relatively small set of standard codes that can be used to tag data in messages, such as codes related to marital status, family relationships and the like. Figure 3-3 contains common vocabulary standards pertinent to CDS and the information types they cover.

HL7's Common Terminology Services (CTS) standard defines a minimum set of services that a terminology server should provide in order to help realize the goal of interoperability in an overall information system architecture. Information systems can use a terminology server that is compliant with the CTS standard, in combination with appropriate vocabularies, to translate from one code set to another and to look up a code given its name (and vice versa). Such translations can be important during CDS intervention execution—such as when a system is querying a repository for patient data.

Using consensus or standard vocabularies facilitates data reporting to regulatory and accreditation agencies. It also allows data exchange among organizations without the need to translate from one non-standard coding scheme to another. For example, a government agency may require your organization to report laboratory test results regarding human immunodeficiency virus (HIV) infection using

Figure 3-3: Some Standard Vocabularies Pertinent to CDS

Vocabulary	Coverage
Systemitized Nomenclature of Medicine — Clinical Terms (SNOMED CT)	Multiple areas (including allergies and diagnoses)
International Classification of Diseases Clinical Modification (ICD-9-CM, ICD-10-CM)	Diagnoses
Current Procedural Terminology (CPT-4)	Procedures
Logical Observation Identifiers Names and Codes (LOINC)	Laboratory tests
Healthcare Common Procedure Coding System (HCPCS)	Supplies, non-physician services
Code on Dental Procedures and Nomenclature (CDT)	Procedures
National Drug Codes (NDC)	Drugs: Names
RxNorm	Drugs: Names + dose forms
National Drug File-Reference Terminology (NDF-RT)	Drugs: Mechanism of action, physiologic effects
HIPAA code sets	Billing, administrative functions
Unified Code for Units of Measure (UCUM)	Units of measure, such as laboratory test results
Health Level Seven (HL7)	Demographics and others
Healthcare Provider Taxonomy Codes (HPTC)	Provider types (used in billing in the U.S.)

LOINC codes. This allows the agency to aggregate data from many places and still understand what each data element means. If your laboratory does not use these codes, your staff may have to translate your local codes into the LOINC standard before the agency will accept them as fulfilling regulations.

Coded data in your CIS can facilitate use of CDS interventions that use those same coding schemes to refer to data used by the knowledge intervention. Even if standard codes are used, each healthcare organization may need to represent certain local concepts with codes not found in a standard vocabulary. These codes might include concepts unique to a local organization (such as physical locations referenced by the logic of an alert) or vendor-supplied codes in ancillary systems.

Keep these issues in mind as you consider what coding schemes are used in your CIS and how these might interplay with CDS interventions you may wish to deploy. If your systems do not use standard vocabularies and they are needed for a CDS intervention, one option is to work with the CIS vendor to convert or map them to standard schemes. Some healthcare organizations create a local vocabulary that maps local or CIS vendor codes to standard

schemes. Whatever approach you take, it is important to maintain up-to-date information about the coding schemes used by all the pertinent CDS interventions and CISs. During and after intervention deployment, it is also important to keep in mind that coding schemes sources may abruptly reuse codes and thereby change their meaning and corresponding intervention behavior.

OTHER STANDARDS

In addition to standard vocabularies, other standards are important for collecting, transmitting and integrating data identified by these vocabularies. While incorporating these standards into information systems in your organization is not absolutely required, their use increases the possibility that you will be able to exchange data and knowledge—such as CDS rules—with other organizations, or transmit data to regulatory or professional organizations without having to translate those data to another format. Several of these standards are listed in Figure 3-4.

Standards for CDS Knowledge and Interventions

There have been efforts over many years to realize a universally accepted standard for representing com-

Figure 3-4: Standards Other Than Vocabularies Pertinent to CDS, or the Systems from Which the CDS Intervention Gathers Data

Standard	Coverage
National Council of Prescription Drug Plans SCRIPT	Retail pharmacy transactions
IEEE 1073	Bedside device messaging
Digital Imaging and Communications in Medicine (DICOM)	Imaging data
ANSI X12	Claims/encounter data
Health Level Seven (HL7) messaging standard	Clinical data
Clinical Document Architecture (HL7 CDA)	Clinical reports
Clinical Context Object Workgroup (HL7 CCOW)	Desktop inter-application communication
Infobutton Standard	Communication between an EHR and a knowledge source to display contextual CDS information
Decision Support Services Standard (HL7 DSS)	Communication between an EHR and a CDS system
Continuity of Care Document (a constraint on HL7 CDA)	Patient summary document

putable knowledge that can be used to provide CDS. A number of formalisms have been created and some standards endorsed, but unfortunately there is no single CDS knowledge representation standard. As these efforts have evolved, two important approaches to this domain have been developed: structuring the knowledge itself for sharing, and encapsulating the knowledge and providing access to it via a service-oriented architecture (SOA).

In the first approach, a knowledge representation formalism is used to encode the CDS knowledge in a way that can be shared among different organizations. This means that the executable logic and the unambiguous references to data processed by that logic, encoded using standard vocabularies, could be composed in one place and used in many other organizations. Examples of standard formalisms that have been used in practice include the HL7 Arden Syntax and GELLO standards, as well as the ASTM Guideline Elements Model (GEM) standard.

However, for a variety of reasons—including lack of universal agreement on vocabularies, varying structure for clinical data repositories, the need for locally customizing the knowledge, and the use of different computer platforms for executing the knowledge—such knowledge-sharing is not widespread, even when a standard formalism is used.

To avoid these challenges in CDS intervention knowledge-sharing, a second approach to knowledge representation has been developed that standardizes the services that a CDS system provides and elaborates a standard interface for communicating with such services. CDS services would include requesting that a specific knowledge module (e.g., based on evidence and guidelines about immunizations or cancer screening) be invoked using a specific patient's data, with recommendations sent back to the calling system. In this way, you need not move the actual computable knowledge among different organizations and computing platforms but instead centralize it, with different EHRs and CDS interventions requesting those services via standard mechanisms. There is increasing interest in the use of SOA

for CDS.[7,8] One such effort is the HL7 Decision Support Services (HL7 DSS) standard.[9]

Neither of these knowledge and CDS representation and sharing approaches has achieved the full healthcare penetration envisioned by their proponents. With national healthcare initiatives increasingly addressing CDS (such as Meaningful Use in the U.S.), existing and/or new CDS knowledge and format standards may become much more widely used. Keeping an eye on the national HIT standards and certification activities mentioned earlier will ensure that you are aware of CDS intervention standards that might be useful in your efforts.

NQF Quality Data Model and eMeasures

An emerging framework worth noting in the context of CDS-related standards is the National Quality Forum's (NQF) Quality Data Model (QDM). Developed through guidance from the NQF Health Information Technology Expert Panel, the QDM is a framework for the developing, using and reporting quality measures from EHRs.[10] The framework specifies how data elements derived from an EHR such as diagnosis, medication, laboratory value, etc. can be incorporated into the definition of a quality measure that can be processed by electronic systems (eMeasure). These data elements can be reused in different contexts to specify different eMeasures, which is the format required for quality measure reporting under Meaningful Use.

An eMeasure itself is represented using the HL7 Health Quality Measures Format (HQMF), which allows quality indicator data and logic to be expressed unambiguously. This enables quality measurement results to be compared across different organizations. Since an important target for CDS is improving performance on specific measures (such as those reported for Meaningful Use), the QDM and related eMeasure specifications can be leveraged to inform CDS intervention design. Preliminary research has demonstrated value from this approach.[11]

Integrating Data from Multiple Systems

Decision support guidance about a particular patient should ideally be based on *all* the pertinent information about that patient. Often this information is housed in a variety of different information systems, leading many healthcare organizations to aggregate data from various ancillary systems or applications into a common database or repository. The way in which this is done can have implications for what types of CDS interventions may be delivered and how they are created.

When data are not aggregated, but instead distributed among various software applications, mechanisms for retrieving and combining the data will have to be explicitly developed for CDS interventions that require this disparate data. In this situation, you must determine whether the applications have modules that enable messaging or some sort of communication capability that provides access to needed data. The ease with which data can be exchanged will be determined, in part, by whether the access methods are compliant with any standard, as discussed earlier. In some cases, specific applications may have these modules, but they may not have been installed or activated at a particular location. Doing so may require additional cost or further negotiation with a vendor.

Even in those settings in which data may be aggregated continuously into a central clinical data repository (CDR), the properties of this repository will have an impact on the design of the CDS intervention. Key issues to consider include:

- What types of data are available?
- How quickly is the repository updated after data appears in the individual source systems?
- Does the repository make use of standard vocabularies (such as SNOMED-CT or LOINC), or are the data stored with their original vendor terminology?
- Are the CDR data organized so that needed data of a given type from all sources can be retrieved together?

Keep in mind that any changes in the vocabulary (for example, through the installation of a new laboratory information system) or the database organization may affect any CDS interventions that rely upon it. For example, the laboratory information system may store test results of kidney function (e.g., serum creatinine) using a particular code. To retrieve those results from the database to generate an alert for worsening kidney function, the CDS rule would be written to query all those results with that particular code. If the laboratory subsequently changed the code for the test, the CDS system would be able to retrieve only old results and not more recent ones, thus rendering any processing of those data inaccurate. Therefore coordinating any such information system changes with CDS implementers is important.

Some organizations maintain a distinct data warehouse into which data are stored periodically, but not necessarily in real time. Data warehouses often are used by administrators for quality assurance and by researchers to perform scientific studies. While the data warehouse may not be as up-to-date as the clinical data repository at any given moment, the warehouse may be used for CDS when the interventions are not necessarily urgent or time-sensitive (e.g., to prepare a list of outpatients overdue for an indicated screening test). Using a data warehouse for this type of intervention can help reduce the processing load from CDS interventions on real-time information systems used for direct patient care.

Many larger organizations create registries of information about patients with chronic diseases to help manage these patients. Disease registries can be powerful assets for a CDS program because they contain key information about the process and outcomes of care for clinical conditions that are the focus of performance improvement efforts. Like data warehouses, you can use these registries in CDS interventions alone or in combination with EMRs or other CISs (e.g., to provide data for alerts to clinicians about patient events requiring attention).

Drivers to improve care processes and outcomes in a patient-centered manner across delivery settings are increasing the attention that is paid to health information exchange (HIE) among those who care for individual patients. Such clinical data exchange is an explicit requirement for Meaningful Use. Similar considerations regarding CDS and data aggregation apply as outlined earlier, though the situation is more complex because different business entities are involved.[12] Some pioneering organizations are reporting success using CDS in an HIE context,[13] and these approaches will likely undergo much more development and spread in the next few years.

Coordinating Your CIS and CDS Roadmaps

The work on CDS goal selection outlined in Chapter 2, together with results from your information system infrastructure analysis outlined earlier in this chapter, should give you a gross sense of where you want your CDS program to take your organization and the tools you have to get there. Both the goals and tools will be dynamic, as internal and external improvement drivers and deployed systems evolve. It is important, therefore, to develop mechanisms to ensure that your roadmaps for information technology deployment and CDS-related activities are aligned and remain in sync over time. The governance processes described in Chapter 2 provide the mechanisms for this—for example, through formal interplay between groups managing the CDS program and CIS deployments.

This interplay is particularly important given the inter-relationship between CDS and CIS deployment featured in CIS incentive and measurement programs. One prominent example is the CMS EHR incentive program, in which CDS elements are central to the evolving Meaningful Use definition.[14] Another high-level framework that can inform a joint CIS-CDS roadmap is the HIMSS Analytics EMR adoption model (EMRAM™), which defines three CDS levels corresponding to stages in an organization's overall EMR system maturity[15]:

- Stage 3 - "Level 1" CDS: drug-drug, drug-lab, etc., interaction checking;
- Stage 4 - "Level 2" CDS: evidence-based protocols;
- Stage 6 - "Level 3" CDS: guidance for all clinician activities related to protocols and outcomes in the form of variance and compliance alerts.

Another goal for the combined CIS-CDS roadmap might be to demonstrate, using the Leapfrog CPOE evaluation tool (discussed in Chapter 9), effective CDS capabilities in the CPOE system to intercept common and serious prescribing errors.

Consider CIS-CDS Interplay During CIS Configuration

Interconnecting CIS and CDS management is important not only for future planning but also as your organization deploys and maintains CIS applications. This tactical work should unfold with careful attention to how the CDS components help ensure that goals for the CIS implementation are realized, and vice versa.

For example, certain CDS interventions are available as "standard" certified EHR features but often require local configuration. Examples include drug-drug interaction checking, infobuttons, and embedded references. Note that CDS content and interventions available commercially are typically not "plug-and-play" but still require significant time and effort to validate, localize, coordinate and maintain. Deploying these CDS components within CIS without careful attention to how the knowledge interventions will support specific improvement goals will often prevent these goals from being achieved. An article entitled "High rates of adverse drug events [ADEs] in a highly computerized hospital"[16] illustrates a case in point. Despite deploying CPOE with CDS—along with other sophisticated electronic medication management systems—this hospital failed to achieve desired results. This was due, in part, to not having the CDS optimally focused on the ADEs' underlying causes. Again, tightly integrating CIS and CDS strategy and execution can help avoid misses like this.

WORKFLOW

The organizational capacity to document, understand and improve how care delivery activities (that is, clinical workflows) are carried out is essential for a successful CDS program. This is because these activities are the context into which CDS interventions are delivered and the avenue through which their benefits are realized. Clinical workflows include care steps performed at different points in time by different people (including patients and their caregivers), where these steps may be sequential or simultaneous. Workflows occur at different levels within an organization; there are workflows for an individual provider (or patient), for the care team, and for the care delivery organization as a whole.

Because CDS interventions are tightly coupled with workflow, a central goal of intervention development is to ensure their successful integration into pertinent clinical activities. Effective CDS programs should routinely add value to these workflows through enhanced automation of knowledge- and data-intensive processes. In some cases, this involves selecting or adapting an intervention(s) to fit an already successful workflow; in other cases, a workflow must be improved to optimally leverage the additional intervention support. It is a mistake to choose interventions that map into current workflows without first considering whether these workflows are well-suited to the task at hand.

In assessing your CDS program's capabilities around workflow analysis and improvement broadly—and in relation to configuring and deploying specific interventions—consider the following:

- Whether you have—and how you create and use—maps that document current and desired future workflows;
- How you do—or will—decide which workflow should be mapped;
- Who on your team has expertise to document, interpret and enhance key workflows (in addition to staff, consider vendors, consultants, RECs and others outside the organization who might be able to provide support);
- What tools and conventions (such as format and level of detail) you will use for workflow mapping;
- When in the CDS goal and intervention development process you will conduct workflow mapping.

The following discussion provides further information and guidance on building strong workflow-related capabilities into your CDS program. These issues also come into play in the context of specific CDS interventions, as we discuss in Part II.

Benefits from Workflow Mapping

Workflow analysis provides several important benefits to CDS program and intervention activities, and you should cultivate these as you build your workflow mapping capabilities:

- Engages intervention end users and other stakeholders in the performance improvement process, and helps ensure that solutions will meet their needs;
- In organizations where care is delivered across several sites, makes explicit how processes across the sites are similar and different;
- Highlights improvement opportunities related to CIS/CDS and overall operations;
- Provides input for those configuring CDS interventions and related information systems, as well as those making policies related to these tools;
- Provides realistic scenarios for creating scripts to test, and user training materials for, the CDS interventions;
- Clarifies effects—both positive and negative—that CDS interventions are having on the care activities they are intended to support.

Workflow considerations should be omnipresent throughout processes related to assessing improvement opportunities addressable with CDS, and then designing and implementing and evaluating the resulting CDS intervention. This focus will help ensure that the benefits noted earlier are fully realized.

Doing Workflow/Process Mapping

People, engaging in specific processes pertinent to their role on the care team, play an important role in determining the extent to which care delivery is safe, effective and efficient. CDS programs and interventions seek to systematically improve these processes, which depends heavily on a detailed and accurate picture—shared among the CDS team and other stakeholders—about what is happening during care activities. Workflow mapping is an invaluable tool to make these care processes explicit, so they can be examined and improved.

In Chapter 2, we outlined stakeholders in developing and managing the *CDS program*. For workflow mapping, it is important to carefully consider all those involved in the *clinical processes* that you plan to augment with CDS. In small practices, these individuals will be obvious. In larger organizations, clinical managers, staffing lists, directly observing care delivery and other approaches can be used to clarify exactly who will be affected by specific intervention. As your CDS program matures, the speed and accuracy with which you identify these stakeholders should increase.

Once you identify the stakeholders in the pertinent care delivery process—including patients, nurses, pharmacists, physicians and other members of the care delivery team—workflow mapping helps identify the roles they play in addressing performance improvement targets. Mapping helps you identify not only the detailed workflows for each stakeholder but also their needs and perspectives pertinent to supporting clinical care with CDS.

Workflow/process mapping is a method by which activities pertinent to a specific objective are identified and represented in a visual manner. The maps depict how information and tasks flow from one stakeholder to another. They help to identify how data originate and are reused and highlight potential areas of vulnerability and improvement related to outcomes such as care quality, safety and efficiency. When there are multiple actions taken by multiple users within each process, it is most useful to create a cross-functional process map, as will be illustrated shortly.

When considering and mapping workflows, keep in mind that there may be important differences between how processes are designed to work (such as reflected in clinical policies), how participants describe what they do, and what they actually do. Ideally these should be the same, and workflow mapping can help ensure this is the case. Gathering objective data (for example, based on directly observing care activities) is an important foundation for understanding steps participants *actually take* in clinical practice. These observations can serve as a foundation for reconciling with participants any differences with their mental models about their workflow and/or with formal organizational procedures for accomplishing the care-related activity.

A variety of software tools that generate flowcharts are available for workflow mapping.[17] Worksheet 3-1 in this chapter contains a sample blank flowsheet and symbol key that might be useful for your mapping efforts.

Techniques for gathering the data that underpin creation of workflow maps include *structured interviews* and *observations*.

Structured Interviews

This approach involves conducting team sessions or one-on-one interviews to identify individual tasks performed by each stakeholder. Asking about other participants in tasks related to key clinical work processes that are CDS targets can help ensure that all pertinent stakeholders are considered.

As an example, pharmacists play a central role in processing medication orders and are a logical starting point for analyzing this task. The following is an example of the different steps that a pharmacist performs in a particular hospital when processing orders using a pharmacy IS. In this case, some prescribers enter orders via CPOE and others handwrite orders or deliver them verbally (that is, as spoken orders). Task lists of this sort as shown next might be gathered by interviewing one or more pharmacists:

- Pull up CPOE orders or scanned copy of written orders.
- Pull up correct patient medication profile in pharmacy system.
- Identify drug from the scanned order.
- Pull up the right drug order.
- Enter and verify in the pharmacy system the correct route, dosage, and frequency.

Based on this interview, other non-pharmacy stakeholders and their tasks will be identified. Continuing this example:

- The physician (or other ordering clinician) gives a written, verbal or electronic order for medication. (Note that verbal orders can introduce opportunities for error and decrease use of prescriber-focused CDS, so care should be taken to avoid the spoken ordering mode when possible. Interviews and observation can help characterize such improvement opportunities and determine approaches that minimize risks.)
- Nursing accepts the written order, or in the case of the verbal medication order, reads it back to the ordering clinician, and writes it down. The nurse may scan the written order into the pharmacy application, or ask the unit clerk to do this. (Handwritten orders should be avoided when possible, since they can be more prone to misinterpretation.)
- If not already done by the nurse, the unit clerk takes the written medication order and scans the order into the pharmacy application.

Observations

This method involves directly observing all the participants involved in a particular clinical task and documenting workflow and information flow related to the improvement target at hand. The method can also include discussion with those being observed to address observer questions that arise about workflow activities and issues. If you have conducted interviews prior to direct observation, remain alert for any differences between results gleaned from the two methods. One approach used by some organizations is to conduct time-motion studies to directly observe the impact of CDS interventions on clinician efficiency. Keep in mind the potential for a Hawthorne Effect, in which a process temporarily improves or changes due to outside observation.

Interviews and observations should complement each other in creating an accurate "before picture" into which CDS-enabled improvements will be introduced. Smoothing out any identified inconsis-

tencies or rough spots prior to CDS launch can help increase intervention success.

When multiple stakeholders perform one or several steps within a process, it is helpful to illustrate this interrelationship in a cross-functional workflow map in which each functional band represents a different stakeholder. Figure 3-5 illustrates what a cross-functional process map would look like for the medication order management workflow outlined earlier.

Explicit, high-level workflow maps, such as this one, provide a foundation for deeper, step-by-step analyses and maps pertinent to specific improvement goals (such as decreasing preventable ADEs) and objectives (such as reducing drug dosing errors and drug-drug and drug-allergy interactions). Such explorations may require additional high-level workflow maps—in this case, for example, related to drug-dispensing, administration, patient education and other medication management activities.

Workflow Analysis as a Collaboration-building Tool

The resulting maps—together with annotations about the nuances concerning how various key steps actually happen—can then be used to underpin discussions with pertinent stakeholders about where and how CDS interventions can be introduced into workflow to improve processes and outcomes. Highly visible stakeholders in care processes (besides the patient) include physicians and nurses, but many others should be considered as well. In ambulatory settings, this may include receptionists and other office staff, and those in the patient's support network who help care for them. In inpatient settings, this might include pharmacists, respiratory therapists and many others on the care delivery team.

Keep in mind that workflow analysis comes into play at many stages during the CDS program and intervention lifecycles. Early in each cycle, it clarifies how work gets done currently and how CDS can help improve these processes generally. As specific improvement targets are chosen, the mapping helps ensure that your CDS interventions will be a useful

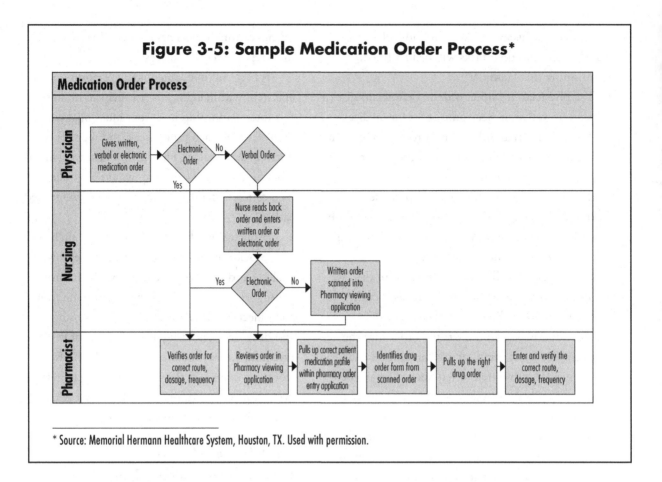

Figure 3-5: Sample Medication Order Process*

* Source: Memorial Hermann Healthcare System, Houston, TX. Used with permission.

enhancement to workflow. Remember that, given the functional limitations of CISs, it is not always possible to maintain the same workflow process—some changes may be unavoidable. However, the new CDS-supported workflows should provide important benefits to each stakeholder. After launch, the workflow mapping demonstrates what effects (both good and bad) the interventions *actually have* on care processes.

Our admonition about doing CDS *with* stakeholders and not *to* them applies to workflow analysis at each of these stages. You and your CDS team will learn a lot about care processes and intervention needs and effects by *observing* people doing their work. However, you should also leverage the analysis activities to *create dialog* that deepens the shared understanding and collaborative approach between the CDS team and other stakeholders about the CDS program's goals, methods and results. For example, using the workflow investigations as a

chance to work together to identify shared improvement goals and determine how CDS interventions (individually and collectively) can best be developed and incorporated into workflow to achieve these goals. This dialog sets up subsequent rich collaboration with pertinent stakeholders to solidify intervention details and workflow changes required for intervention success. These points about collaboration tie back to the discussion in Chapter 2 on Engaging Stakeholders, and points forward to the guidance in Chapter 8 on Change Management around the launch of specific interventions.

Use Case Scenarios

Workflow processes mapping, and related analyses and conversations, will generate rich hypotheses about CDS interventions that may improve care processes and outcomes. As you translate these hypotheses into intervention designs, use-case scenarios can support the design process by helping make explicit exactly how these improvements will occur. *Use-case scenarios*[18] are step-by-step written descriptions of how users interact with an intervention, and the interactions results. For example, consider the case in which an alert is chosen to reduce a specific commission error, such as ordering a medication to which the patient is allergic. Use-case scenarios can help make explicit how the alert is expected to occur in workflow, what the range of responses is likely to be, and whether these notifications and responses will help achieve the desired objective.

Use-case scenarios for an intervention should cover several different examples of likely user-system interactions and can be divided into a low, medium, and high complexity progression. This hierarchy can help you isolate areas in which the intervention might perform well or poorly based on a specific design approach, which can then be modified if needed.

You should review use cases with all pertinent stakeholder groups to ensure a shared understanding about the intervention purpose and mechanics. This review can help uncover incorrect assumptions about how the interventions will work or what they will accomplish. Obtaining this input early in the development process can make it far easier to address any problematic issues that arise. Keep in mind that as intervention development unfolds, you might need to add stakeholders to ensure that all parties affected by the intervention are included in reviewing the use cases.

Use cases developed for design will underpin testing and validation for the corresponding interventions, as will be discussed in Chapter 7. Often changes to the use cases will occur as review and input broadens during intervention development and vetting. This evolution should be handled through formal processes for managing the changes.

Workarounds

When end users consider CDS interventions to be unhelpful speed bumps in their workflow, they will predictably find "workarounds." Halbesleben defines workarounds as "work patterns an individual or a group of individuals create to accomplish a crucial work goal within a system of dysfunctional work processes that prohibits the accomplishment of that goal or makes it difficult."[19] For instance, if a clinician cannot easily find a condition or medication in a drop-down list within a specific CDS intervention (such as an order set or documentation tool), then he or she may put the information in a textbox instead. Because such free text information (as opposed to the structured/coded information from the dropdown list) is frequently not processed by CDS interventions, this workaround will bypass decision support that may be associated with the medication or condition.

A workaround may be the response to ineffective work processes, poorly designed interventions, and sometimes to an emergency situation (such as the need to administer medication before entering it into the EHR). Because workarounds for CDS interventions can subvert all the benefits that the interventions are intended to deliver, it is important to detect when they are occurring. Or better yet, to avoid them through the careful workflow analysis and related dialog, as was previously outlined. Keep in mind that it may be difficult for you to discover where workarounds occur simply by looking at reports: as we've emphasized throughout this section, your CDS team should be directly observing end users at the front line. A good collaborative atmosphere with end users and other stakeholders are other components of an effective early warning system that interventions are adversely affecting workflow. Part II explores channels and approaches for gathering this feedback.

MEASUREMENT

You must carefully analyze the effects of CDS interventions to ensure that the considerable resources required for their implementation yield the intended results. This analysis will demonstrate whether interventions are being used as expected and are valuable. In addition, it can help you quantify ROI, both financially and clinically. The analysis may require comparing post-intervention data with pre-intervention baselines concerning clinical processes/ workflow, patient and clinician satisfaction, specific healthcare outcomes, or other measures

Evaluation permeates the entire CDS lifecycle, from selecting targets through assessing results. Because the clinical environment and clinical knowledge base are so dynamic, this analysis must be ongoing. Figure 3-6 demonstrates this cyclical process graphically. With each iteration through the cycle, your CDS program should enhance its capabilities and tools for cultivating measurably better outcomes.

A common pitfall in CDS efforts is not giving adequate attention to CDS-related measurement and evaluation at either the programmatic level, or in specific CDS interventions. This situation arises when all the focus goes to building and releasing interventions without careful forethought into baseline performance levels on the intervention's targets, and/or how the team will know whether and how the interventions are affecting that performance and the care processes that feed into it. When queried about such seemingly inadequate attention to measurement, these imple-

menters provide explanations such as 'We don't have the resources/expertise/time to do this evaluation." This begs the question, if the improvement target warrants CDS intervention, isn't it necessary to determine whether or not the intervention is effective?

This section discusses CDS measurement principles and approaches pertinent to your CDS program; Chapter 9 builds on this foundation to cover measurement pertinent to specific CDS interventions. In particular, this chapter addresses why you should measure, what you should measure, and some considerations about personnel and capabilities needed for useful measurement.

Why Measure?

The following are major reasons to measure:

- Ensuring that the CDS tools provided to clinicians and patients are helping to improve care;
- Determining whether the interventions are working as expected and not disrupting workflow or negatively affecting care;
- Learning continually from end-user experience and feedback, and using these insights to refine

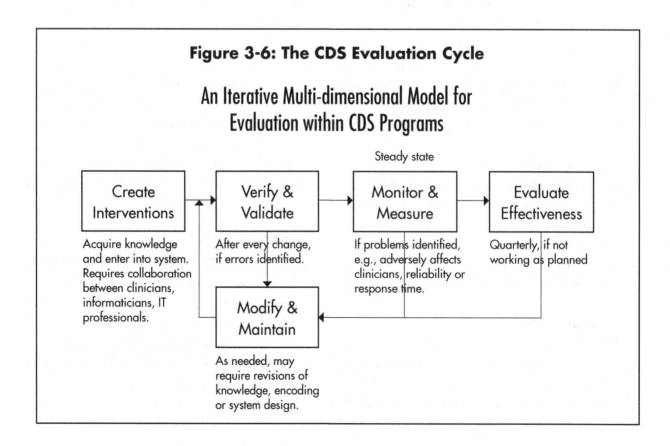

Figure 3-6: The CDS Evaluation Cycle

An Iterative Multi-dimensional Model for Evaluation within CDS Programs

Steady state

Create Interventions	Verify & Validate	Monitor & Measure	Evaluate Effectiveness
Acquire knowledge and enter into system. Requires collaboration between clinicians, informaticians, IT professionals.	After every change, if errors identified.	If problems identified, e.g., adversely affects clinicians, reliability or response time.	Quarterly, if not working as planned

Modify & Maintain

As needed, may require revisions of knowledge, encoding or system design.

the interventions and their value in addressing priority targets;

• Determining whether the interventions are cost-effective, and communicating that information to organizational leaders—for example, justifying the CDS investments to chief executives in the hospital, practice or health system;

• Creating new knowledge about best implementation practices so you can improve more quickly (and, if you share your results, so others can learn from your efforts).

You should build a plan to measure effects and respond accordingly into the core of every process design and redesign effort—and this is no less true for CDS programs and interventions. It is important to begin considering evaluation issues at the earliest CDS planning stages. For example, how will you know what effects the overall program and specific interventions have had, especially regarding targeted goals and objectives? As new interventions are developed, associated data collection procedures and measures should be prepared in conjunction with them. Because improvement can and should be an ongoing process, evaluation efforts are never finished; project planning and resource allocation need to account for this critical component.

The following are some background points about evaluation to keep in mind:

• Measuring and reporting errors in diagnosis and treatment is not new, and this history provides a conceptual foundation for the topic at hand. For example, in 1911, Boston surgeon Ernest Codman developed the "End Result Hospital." Within this hospital "All errors in diagnosis and treatment were recorded for every patient."[20] In addition, all patients were followed for many years after discharge to evaluate the final results of their care.[21]

• Donabedian's work on measurement and quality improvement has been influential in more recent efforts, including his improvement definition: The systematic measurement and evaluation of predetermined outcomes of a process and the subsequent use of that information to improve the process based on customer expectations.[22]

• As noted in Chapters 1 and 2, there is intense international focus on *measurably* improving care processes and outcomes. This emphasis is increasingly reflected in compensation arrangements such as value-based purchasing and Meaningful Use, which require accurate and useful performance measurement and reporting. These requirements relate to your CDS program to the extent that you provide interventions that affect care processes, and are focused on outcomes that overlap with reporting requirements.

• The National Quality Forum (NQF) is a leading public-private partnership "created to develop and implement a national strategy for healthcare quality measurement and reporting."[23] To complement its role as the national standard-setting organization for performance measures, NQF formed the National Priorities Partnership "to establish national priorities and goals for performance measurement and public reporting."[24] The National Priorities Partnership is providing input into the U.S. National Quality Strategy,[25] further reinforcing the importance of NQF's work to measurement activities in provider organizations; for example, by influencing the performance dimensions that providers need to assess and improve.

• NQF has also contributed to the knowledge base for assessing Health IT—and CDS—effects through a 2010 consensus report "Driving Quality—A Health IT Assessment Framework for Measurement."[26] This report discusses a method for expressing data that can be captured by health IT systems to understand and measure their effectiveness. The goal of this work is to increase the level of standardization to allow for development of more "clearly defined measures with reliable, consistent, and achievable results while reducing the effort required to assess clinical system effectiveness by system vendors, implementers, or users of such systems."

- Note that in some cases, there may be a close relationship between quality measurement and improvement activities carried out strictly to improve care, and for the purposes of research and reporting in the literature. For the latter, there are strict requirements surrounding the need for a local Institutional Review Board (IRB) to approve the research protocol. Failure to obtain proper approval prior to commencing research activities can trigger intervention by federal authorities.[27] Organizations should consult their legal counsel and IRB if questions arise about whether local measurement and improvement efforts would require such approval.

What to Measure
PERFORMANCE GAPS AND BASELINES

As discussed in Chapters 2 and 5, selecting intervention targets (in collaboration with other organizational stakeholders) is a core CDS program function. A key selection factor is large, addressable gaps between current and desired performance in specific areas, and decision makers need detailed, accurate data about these gaps that they can accept and act on. Although these assessments and measurement capabilities may come from outside your CDS team, the team must still understand and have confidence in them, since they heavily influence CDS activities and how results are evaluated. If your CDS goals are aligned with top organizational priorities, then there should be significant leadership incentive to ensure that the measurement resources and attention needed for CDS-mediated outcome improvements are available.

Once CDS targets are selected, you need reliable baseline data about care processes and outcomes related to those targets so you can establish the starting point against which to measure intervention results. Data capture from paper-based systems can be difficult, so you should fully leverage available processes and systems to obtain the most accurate baseline data and follow-up measurements possible. Be careful how you interpret baseline data. Often, implementing CDS interventions in newly launched HIT systems will result in negative comparisons to previous results, due to the fact that significantly more complete data will be captured using the new HIT systems. Since clinical performance improvements depend critically on detailed measurements, don't become discouraged if improved measurements in this case make it appear initially that performance is worsening.

When considering CDS measurement targets and capabilities, keep in mind emerging care delivery models that may have special requirements. For example, the patient centered medical home (PCMH) and accountable care organization (ACO) may need to emphasize quality measures that emphasize improved care coordination (e.g., reduction of avoidable admissions and readmissions) and corresponding clinical decision support capabilities that may extend across multiple care settings.

FOUR SPECIFIC METRIC TYPES

Discussions about healthcare quality measurement typically refer to structure, process and outcome metrics and are rooted in Donabedian's work.[28] Next we consider issues pertinent to establishing CDS intervention assessment capabilities in each of these categories—though we may have used these categories somewhat differently than readers deeply steeped in them might expect. We also discuss system response time as a separate measure. The brief overviews presented here are revisited in much more detail in Chapter 9, which offers guidance on evaluating these metric types for specific CDS interventions.

System Response Time Measurement

A basic system-oriented CDS intervention feature is how quickly the CIS/CDS system processes any triggering data from end users (or various other ISs) and displays the intervention—that is, the system response time. You should consider this metric when evaluating the system capacity necessary to deploy CDS interventions effectively. Not surprisingly, a slow system response can have deleterious effects on the end-user opinion of the CDS interventions. Your

CDS team should have arrangements with your IS staff, and/or HIT vendors, to enable you to track this important information. You can also supplement automated response time measurement and tracking with directly observing uses interacting with the system to ensure that any delays aren't unacceptable. In a small office practice, such direct observation may be all that is needed.

Structure Measurements

Your 'CDS structure' includes the CDS tools and interventions available in your systems. Your CDS team needs to understand this foundation for developing new interventions and for measuring and interpreting effects from those you've already deployed. For example, as a starting point for configuring new interventions, you should be able to lay out which system might display the intervention (EHR, CPOE, smart pumps), its format (alert vs. data display vs. other) who will receive it (physician, nurse, pharmacist), and what actions will be possible after the intervention is presented (overriding, ordering, no action).

Worksheets 6-2 and 6-3 can help with this documentation and planning for specific interventions, but the point here is that your CDS team needs a menu of available options, such as delivery channels and formats, to complete this work. Likewise, when you seek to understand what effects your alerts, order sets and other interventions are having, you must start with a detailed picture of what exactly you have deployed. Your HIT inventory (discussed above under Systems and in Worksheet 3-1) provides many important details about your CDS structure. Likewise, the knowledge management approaches discussed in Chapter 4 will help you understand and evaluate the knowledge and intervention components of that structure.

Process Measures

CDS interventions help achieve improvement targets when they positively influence care processes, so measuring these process changes is central to evaluating and improving CDS effects. Process measures

can be more complex than system performance and structural metrics and therefore require special attention to measure and monitor appropriately. In particular, there are two key processes to measure: intervention use and effects, and end-user's time and satisfaction. These two processes are often interrelated, as intervention non-use or misuse often correlate with end-user's time (and satisfaction).

When considering how end users view CDS interventions, you might consider conducting a culture survey.[29] This can help determine users' beliefs, attitudes and skills regarding the use of CISs and related hardware at different implementation phases—such as before and after training, and after implementation. This information is useful, since these systems typically provide the channel through which the CDS is delivered, so user interactions with them may influence their responses to the CDS interventions. The survey could also assess user perceptions about how easy and valuable it is to access and use the CDS tools themselves.[30] For example, user perceptions about tolerable system and user response times can help shed light on strategies for managing these times to optimize CDS acceptance and use. On the other hand, it's important to set an expectation that feedback obtained from these surveys won't necessarily translate into immediate actions taken to address improvements. Nonetheless, the CDS team should strive to be seen by stakeholders as responsive as possible to their needs and concerns.

The key issues here for CDS program development is ensuring you have adequate capacity to assess CDS effects on care processes. The tools and approaches outlined earlier under Systems and Workflow will play major roles.

Outcome Measures

This is a particularly important metric category since a primary CDS goal is to improve healthcare delivery results. You should consider CDS intervention effects on care efficiency, safety, quality and cost—as well as patient and clinician satisfaction. Because the link between technology and healthcare delivery and outcomes is complex, it can be difficult to conclusively determine whether and exactly how CDS interventions may have affected any of these results. For example, CDS interventions are often just one facet of an organization's clinical improvement effort, so attributing improvements specifically to CDS activities can be tricky.

Chapter 9 provides guidance on dealing with these issues. For now, the point is that your CDS team must ensure that your organization has capabilities to measure and track outcomes that are important to the CDS program's improvement efforts.

Additional Metric Considerations

For each metric type previously outlined, you should define specific, objective measurements that will be useful in bringing your organization closer to desired goals. An acronym that can serve as a helpful guidepost for your evaluation effort is "METRIC"; Measure Everything That Really Impacts Customers.[31] For our purposes, "customers" includes all CDS intervention stakeholders—for example, the organization's leadership, front-line clinicians, other key ancillary and clinical support roles, and patients. Although this ideal may not always be attainable, the acronym helps focus attention on measurement priorities.

Even if not tied to a financial ROI, CDS measures should be quantitative—for example, reduction in medication errors, reduction in VTE incidence, improved patient throughput. Keep in mind that subjective dimensions such as clinician or patient satisfaction can be assessed quantitatively through techniques such as surveys in which these dimensions can be rated numerically.

Here are some additional considerations to keep in mind about optimizing measurement capabilities within your CDS program:

- Make the measurements visible and transparent.
- Seek usefulness, not perfection, in measurement.
- Use a balanced set of measures (that is, a combination of clinical, financial and satisfaction indicators, as well as both qualitative and quantitative data).

- Keep measurement simple so that it can be performed in the context of daily work with a minimal requirement for additional dedicated resources.
- Measure small but representative samples when broader measurements are prohibitively expensive or difficult so that CDS intervention impact can be assessed quickly to enable rapid cycle improvements.

Who Will Measure?

As we have emphasized, you should develop your CDS program's evaluation plan early on, after determining which organizational roles will be responsible for creating and executing the plan. In assigning these tasks, you should consider whether the individuals have the appropriate skills and training to succeed in these efforts and from what source(s) you will obtain the resources to fund the evaluation.[32]

Responsibility for CDS measurement activities will depend on how your organization manages the various CDS program components. For example, some use one team that manages all CDS aspects, including implementation, development, training, communication, process redesign, and system evaluation. Others separate the work and have very specific measurement duties performed by a select few who do not have other responsibilities in the process.

LEVERAGING AVAILABLE RESOURCES

A key step in building CDS-related measurement capabilities is to assess evaluation processes and responsibilities in place within your organization. The following are questions to consider:

- Who currently performs measurements related to the broader CDS program and to structure, process and outcome measures related to specific aspects of care delivery? Are nurse managers measuring near-misses or actual adverse events? How are they capturing this information? More than likely, your organization is already performing pertinent measurements. It is critical that you thoroughly document and evaluate these efforts.

Also, ensure that those currently conducting the measurements are able to continue to do so once new CDS-related technology and processes are implemented. Ideally, CDS should enhance their ability to measure.

• What tools, such as analytical applications and databases with pertinent information needed for the metrics, are currently in place to support needed measurements? Who has access to them, and what processes are they currently using to collect and analyze information? Are there synergies that can be cultivated between these current efforts and new CDS interventions and related measurement activities? Reducing the total time and staff it takes to gather and analyze data needed for CDS and other priorities—for example, through better leveraging an EHR, data warehouse, or similar data gathering and analysis application—can have a significant ROI.

Next, identify additional resources that could potentially assist with evaluation efforts. These might include:

• Motivated and engaged end users, such as, nurses, pharmacists, and physicians. For example, hospitalists are increasingly playing important roles in such performance improvement (PI) activities;

• Managers, including unit/department and specialty managers;

• Existing committees and departments, especially pharmacy department and pharmacy and therapeutics committee, quality assurance, and of course the CDS Team.

Figure 3-7 presents a skeletal outline of some key roles that might assist with evaluation activities,

---

Figure 3-7: Skeletal Outline of Different Stakeholders and Their Potential Evaluation Role

Who	What	Why
End users		
Physicians	Order sets for specific diseases	Determine usefulness of the order sets and the use patterns for each
Nurses	User feedback — what's working and what's not	Understanding from a user standpoint how the CDS affects workflow is key
Pharmacists	Medication errors Medication turnaround time	Pharmacists are central figures in the medication management process
Managers		
Unit/department	Departmental usage statistics	Has the system been adequately customized for this department?
Specialty	Usage statistics Override rates	Has the system been adequately customized for this specialty; has the right content been developed?
Quality Team		
Core team members	Core quality measures Patient safety measures	Is the CDS system helping the organization achieve desired quality and safety goals?
CDS Team		
Core team members	Entire evaluation program	Well-positioned between clinical and IS to gather performance, structure and process metrics, and coordinate efforts on outcome metrics

the types of issues for which these roles might be helpful, and why this support might be useful. This material is intended to serve as a trigger for broader and deeper thinking about pertinent roles and activities in your organization.

Other important considerations include:

- Determining who wants to—versus who should—measure; some managers will want to measure for their own purposes, such as to evaluate personnel or departments.
- Coordinating all evaluation efforts to limit inefficiency or duplication, ensuring that all goals are being met (organizational, departmental, individual), and leveraging available resources appropriately to address evaluation needs. A well-documented and vetted evaluation plan can help.

Whether you select centralized versus local data collection depends on whether your organization is a small practice, a single hospital, or a multi-facility IDN. The goal in all cases is to maximize resources and allow for appropriate autonomy. Some local departments or facilities may want to do their own collection and measurement rather than rely on a central team from larger multi-facility organization. Either way, it is extremely beneficial when you can agree on measure details and definitions (see "What to Measure" earlier in this chapter and in Chapter 9). Once consensus has been achieved, measures can be compared across locations and/or interpreted correctly within an individual facility. Without this explicit consensus, there may be subsequent disagreement about what the measurements mean and what should be done about them.

Whatever team is responsible for setting and reporting on the CDS performance measures must be clearly and tightly connected to appropriate governance mechanisms within your organization (see Chapter 2). For example, the evaluation effort should be linked to new or existing structures responsible for CDS and related PI and HIT infrastructure activities. This connection is necessary to coordinate pertinent internal communication, external reporting, and refinements aimed at the CDS interventions and/or broader quality improvement activities.

ENSURING ACCESS TO NEEDED EVALUATION SKILLS

You might not find all of the skills required to evaluate CDS performance metrics in your organization's current staff, and at least some skills typically must be brought in from outside. Pertinent skill sets to inventory and seek for the evaluation team/function include:

- **Technical:** At a minimum, the person(s) who performs application-derived measurements will have the technical skills to run reports from several different systems, such as the EMR, CPOE, pharmacy system, data warehouse, business intelligence systems, and other such tools your organization has developed or acquired from vendors. Ideally, they'll also know how to build and configure those reports and be able to identify potential problems and create solutions for improved reporting capabilities. These technical staff may or may not be the same as those who configure and maximize the CDS interventions within the CIS infrastructure.
- **Clinical:** At a minimum, the evaluation team must understand all pertinent clinical workflows and potential CDS effects on each. This familiarity is necessary to address the clinical complexity and nuances that will inevitably arise from developing and evaluating the performance metrics. Ideally, the team should therefore include clinicians (pharmacists, physicians and/or nurses and others) who together are sensitive to these issues and can work well with each type of clinical end user throughout the evaluation process.
- **Data analysis and presentation:** Besides pertinent clinical expertise, rich analytical skills are required to deal appropriately with the metric complexities, statistical considerations and the like. Individuals with expertise in multiple quantitative and qualitative data collection techniques, data and statistical analysis, and interpretation skills should be included on the team, or at least be readily available to it. Similarly, conveying CDS interventions effects in a clear and credible way to all pertinent stakeholders (leadership,

end users, clinical and technical implementation staff, etc.) is essential to help the organization understand and enhance results from the program. Individuals with the communication skills and credibility to accomplish this should also be included on the team.

- **Cross-functional:** The tasks previously outlined do not occur in isolation; they are highly interdependent. As a result, team members must not only have adequate competency in the respective functions but also have appreciation for the needs and challenges associated with other evaluation program components. Good collaboration skills, and ability to work with others who have complementary expertise and responsibilities, is key. Increasingly, team members with formal clinical informatics training will be a part of this mix.[33]

SECURING FUNDING FOR EVALUATION

Before leaving this "who" section on measurement, we consider briefly who will financially support evaluation activities. Many organizations do not allocate adequate funding at the CDS program outset for ongoing maintenance and (especially) for evaluating CDS interventions after their initial deployment. This is often true more broadly for IT-enabled process changes. Strategies to avoid this problem include the following:

- Create and present both the quality/safety and financial business case to pertinent executives within the organization (CMO, CFO, CEO, and board, if necessary) at the beginning of the process, and formalize the CDS efforts in a charter (see Chapter 2).
- Document baseline measurements to provide comparison points for each alert and other interventions and to reinforce that the goal is measurable improvement in these priority targets.
- Ensure that each evaluation team member has sufficient dedicated time to perform his or her pertinent duties. These activities should be core position responsibilities and not merely "add-on tasks as time allows," since the targets being evaluated should include organizational priorities.

- Outline expected resource needs from the very beginning, knowing that CDS interventions will likely require as many resources, if not more, to maintain and evaluate as they did to implement. Resources may include headcount and their time, funds to acquire additional needed expertise as outlined earlier, and analytic software tools and databases, among many others.
- Communicate to all appropriate executives that driving improved outcomes with CDS is not a "once and done" effort but is a process that continues throughout the organization's lifetime.

CONSIDERATIONS FOR HOSPITALS AND HEALTH SYSTEMS
Capabilities (Systems)

- Because technology infrastructure is a foundation for delivering CDS interventions, the IT department has historically been the initial home for many CDS programs. This makes sense to the extent that the systems, staff and budget pertinent to the program are managed there. However, the CDS program should be more than an IT project subsumed under CIS purchasing and implementation. This is especially true in the current environment where CDS is increasingly recognized as a key strategic initiative for addressing mounting pressures for measurable performance improvement. Nonetheless, addressing the systems, workflow and measurement tasks outlined in this chapter requires close collaboration between the CDS team and the IT department.
- To optimize your CDS program and intervention value, make sure to consider how other clinical systems in addition to your core applications such as CPOE and EHR can help achieve CDS program and organizational goals. For example, as you conduct your CDS application inventory, consider ancillary systems supporting specific departments and clinical areas, such as pharmacy, laboratory, radiology, therapy services, food and nutrition, cardiology (including diagnostic and interventional), blood bank, and operating room

(anesthesia, intra-operative documentation, for example), and others. Hospitals and health systems typically use a complex and multifaceted web of systems—often not integrated—to support clinical workflows, and your CDS program should leverage these to the greatest extent possible.

- Develop a roadmap for acquiring and enhancing information technology systems to meet CDS goals.

- Having established a sound CDS organizational infrastructure as described in Chapter 2, hospitals, large physician practices, and integrated healthcare delivery systems will be well-positioned to operationalize the principles described in this chapter. Because of their size, these organizations need to formally take into account the resource implications of undertaking the tasks of selecting, acquiring, assessing, and configuring the systems that support the CDS program, conducting and documenting the workflow analysis, and establishing a robust measurement program. All of this requires time, budget and skilled personnel.

Workflow

- Think broadly about who the stakeholders are in key workflow processes, and ensure skills in meticulously documenting what actually happens in these processes through observations, instead of relying on interviews and written policies and procedures alone.

- Once you have determined who all these players are, it may be helpful in the case of a larger organization to appoint a clinical liaison or champion from each stakeholder group. These individuals ensure those constituents' needs and constraints regarding CDS will be fully addressed as CDS interventions suggested by workflow analyses are developed.

- In large practices and health systems that consist of entities that are geographically dispersed, variations in technology infrastructure and clinical processes are not uncommon and must be addressed. Many such organizations resulted from

consolidating or acquiring several independent practices and hospitals at different technology adoption stages. You will need to make important decisions regarding the extent to which these organizations will seek to minimize complexity by reducing the number of disparate clinical systems. Even when providers are all on the same technology platform, there are often differences in clinical workflows that can have an impact on CDS effectiveness. This underscores the importance of conducting a detailed workflow analysis across all representative clinical settings, rather than relying on a sample, for interventions that will be mandated across the system.

People (Measurement)

- There are several approaches to assigning responsibility for measurement. These are not mutually exclusive and include:
  - **Option 1:** CDS implementation team performs measurement.
  - **Option 2:** A separate "CIS Benefits Realization Team" is established to perform measurement. This group may be part of the formal EHR/CIS project structure but separate and independent from the CDS Implementation Team.
  - **Option 3:** The organization's performance improvement and or patient safety departments, which have organization-wide responsibility for quality/safety outcomes measurement and analysis, perform the measurement.

CONSIDERATIONS FOR SMALL PRACTICES

Limited resources in small practices require a scaled-down approach and increased reliance on external support (such as EHR vendors and RECs) to address the CDS program infrastructure activities outlined in this chapter. However, your needs in these areas are also typically less complex than in larger organizations. In any case, the principles outlined under the General Approach section in this chapter remain relevant to all size organizations, and you can adapt the details to your small practice's needs and constraints.

Systems

- Catalog and make sure you understand the CDS-related capabilities in your EHR and other pertinent systems. For example, what features are easy and hard to implement and configure? Examining and documenting these details serves as an important starting point for leveraging these tools in your efforts to improve outcomes with CDS. The number of these tools in your small practice should be more manageable than in a large organization, and your system vendor(s) should be able to help provide the pertinent documentation. RECs can also serve as a valuable resource.

- In most cases in the U.S., your small practice would do well to select EHR systems that have been certified for satisfying Meaningful Use criteria, including those related to CDS and quality measure reporting. Implementing an ONC-ATCB certified system[34] means that functionality related to achieving Meaningful Use and other CDS-related quality improvement activities will be present. In addition to these CDS benefits, using certified systems is also important for receiving incentive payments and avoiding penalties related to the Meaningful Use regulations.

- Small practices typically lack the clout that larger institutional EHR customers have with their vendors in requesting system modifications to better address workflow and other practice needs and constraints pertinent to CDS. Working with the REC and/or vendor user group, however, can enable many practices to come together and present a stronger voice to the EHR vendor and thereby increase the chances that the system will evolve toward increasing value to your practice.

Workflow

- Even in small or solo practices, clinical workflow can be complex and nuanced. Documenting workflows before and after CDS interventions can help you ensure that all affected staff are fully on board with the new routines and tools and adapt successfully. You need to build your capacity to anticipate and address "upstream" and "downstream" activities that need to happen before and after physician-focused CDS for interventions to have their intended effect. For example, you must ensure ample supplies of flu shots and nurse time are available to handle a desired uptick in flu vaccination rates in response to CDS focused on this target.

- Physicians in office practice may function quite autonomously (as compared to hospital staff physicians), so you should consider this variability and filter results into your workflow evaluation and enhancement activities. These activities should likewise account for potentially limited IT support for system changes. RECs, EHR vendors and colleagues can be helpful resources for optimizing your approach to documenting and enhancing workflows.

- Those in specialty practices may wish to engage the services of a consultant. Increasingly, assistance in these areas is being provided through participation in an independent practice association (IPA) or physician hospital organization (PHO).

- Local hospitals can be a source for EHRs and CDS applications, but it's important to consider carefully practice workflow, culture and clinical needs, and how these externally supplied tools fit into this mix. There are useful synergies between hospitals and practices that shared CDS and related tools can support, but keep in mind that there may also be important differences in objectives, needs, and approach. Exploring these openly with the hospital—bringing in as appropriate support from the EHR/CDS supplier, REC, and local colleagues—can help ensure that potential CDS-related collaborations with the hospital are smooth and valuable for the practice.

- A new toolkit, funded by AHRQ and prepared by the University of Wisconsin-Madison's Center for Quality and Productivity Improvement, can assist small- and medium-sized practices in workflow analysis and redesign before, during and after health IT implementation. Workflow Assessment for Health IT includes tools to analyze workflow, provides examples of workflow analysis and redesign, and describes the experiences of other organizations.[35]

Measurement

- Although performance improvement drivers are leading to better measurement functionality, capturing and using data for CDS-related metrics from office-based systems can be difficult and time-consuming. You should consider these data and reporting needs carefully as you implement and maintain EHRs. RECs and EHR vendors may be able to help with strategies and tools.

- In the absence of automated systems to run reports on intervention effects, your practice should create a system (e.g., calendar reminders, spreadsheet documents and the like) to make sure reports are run at appropriate intervals and to manage and share the results.

CONSIDERATIONS FOR HIT SOFTWARE PROVIDERS

As emphasized throughout this chapter, healthcare providers increasingly need technology partners—rather than just suppliers—to help them optimally leverage systems, manage workflows and address measurement needs. We believe that successful HIT vendors will increasingly be those that are sensitive to their clients' clinical workflows—and help ensure that they can deploy CDS interventions that measurably enhance those processes and the resulting outcomes.

While respecting and protecting proprietary intellectual capital, we encourage HIT vendors to amplify current efforts to collaborate—with each other, with informatics organizations, with government agencies and non-government organizations, and with their customers—to advance the usefulness and value that your technologies bring to CDS implementation. Such collaboration has been fruitful in promoting progress in HIE and is needed to fully realize CDS' outcome-improving potential. This collaboration can create new market opportunities, as well as improve the efficiency and effectiveness of your product development efforts.

Capabilities (Systems)

- CDS implementers base their efforts on the technology infrastructure available in their settings—that is, on currently deployed clinical information systems and CDS capabilities—and we have recommended that they develop and maintain an explicit inventory of these resources. As CIS and CDS suppliers, you ideally should (individually and collectively) help them assemble these action-oriented information systems catalogs, as well as documenting the systems' CDS tools and functionality. For example, these catalogs should cover deployed system capabilities related to alerts, order sets, documentation tools, relevant data display, context-sensitive reference information display, and other CDS intervention types. Implementers would likewise appreciate guidance you can provide on resources (both internal and external to your organization) that can assist them with CDS intervention development and deployment activities related to your system.

- Just as implementers have standard building blocks they need to have in place, HIT suppliers (in collaboration with implementers and national bodies) should have certain CDS building blocks in place. For example:

  - Ensure that CDS features in your systems are compatible with data element standards, as well as other emerging CDS standards (see Figures 3-3 and 3-4). Follow (and perhaps contribute to) national efforts (such as from NQF, ONC and AHRQ) on standardizing CDS-related components, nomenclature, terminology and intervention structure. Consider especially data element requirements needed to address reportable quality measures, and ensure those elements can be readily captured within workflow.

  - Support interplay with local health information exchanges and the requirement for identity matching, e.g., capability to match patients based on multiple demographic criteria; import data from external systems—and related capabilities important to cross-facility CDS.

– Develop a repository of client-developed interventions that are sharable with the entire client base. Place particular emphasis on sharing these interventions in expedited fashion when clients have developed workarounds for known CDS-related shortcomings in your software that have significant patient safety implications.

Workflow

- Consider opportunities to leverage insights and tools from across your client base to help individual clients with approaches to analyzing and enhancing the clinical workflow related to CDS interventions.
- To the extent possible, ensure that your systems don't rigidly dictate CDS-related workflow, but rather are accommodating and enhance (in a user-defined manner) existing workflow.

Measurement (Processes and Outcomes)

- Implementers need tools and support for measuring intervention availability, use, response and effects; these measurement and reporting capabilities should be built into or accompany CIS/CDS applications and be user-friendly and needs-focused (see also Chapter 9 regarding intervention-specific capabilities).
- Built-in capability to measure CDS use and response (and ultimately impact)—minimizing the need for manual measurement work—is becoming essential for providers, and should be a high HIT supplier priority. For example, as of this 2011 writing, it is anticipated that upcoming Meaningful Use requirements will require that CDS interventions be evaluated, both with respect to their actual operation (for example, user responses to the intervention) and their impact on care practices and outcomes. These measurements should not be made in a vacuum, but should reflect the pertinent clinical context—adding further requirements to measurement details and capabilities.

- Measurement capabilities should closely track and support quality measure reporting requirements, such as those for Meaningful Use, value-based purchasing and similar high-impact programs.
- Measuring CDS availability, use and outcomes is not only essential for regulatory purposes but is critical internally for providers to document CDS intervention impact and ROI. As providers continue to embrace formal process improvement methodologies (such as Lean, Six Sigma and others), the ability to measure CDS intervention effects will be important for driving ongoing improvements and directing resources to CDS efforts. You should ensure that your systems capture and transmit data that is appropriately structured and granular to enable providers to both accurately track CDS results and facilitate care delivery. Similarly, the systems should address competing demands related to displaying key patient data for clinician overviews (where summarization may be helpful) vs. automated surveillance for attention-requiring clinical situations (where access to the full data detail may be important).
- Consider the NQF report "Driving Quality—a Health IT Assessment Framework for Measurement" (cited earlier) in approaching measurement capabilities. This model is based on an *Action – Actor – Content* data triplet to record exactly what the HIT application did, who did it, and what happened as a result of this action.
- Consider collaborating with your provider clients to aggregate data about CDS intervention use and results, and apply that learning to accelerate CDS-enabled performance improvement efforts.

WORKSHEETS
Clinical Information System Inventory

Conduct and document an inventory of your organization's CIS that could play a role in delivering CDS interventions. For each system, note pertinent CDS capabilities, coding systems, and current usage.

This worksheet helps you survey the CIS applications in your organization to determine what information technology infrastructure is available to help you achieve the goals outlined in Chapter 2. Think broadly about what applications might be pertinent, using Figure 3-2 as a guide. In larger organizations, key executives or staff in your IT department can be a good starting point for gathering information about the breadth and details of pertinent systems. In small practices, your EHR vendor may be able to help.

Include in your survey all the different clinical content and knowledge resources that are available in your organization to support clinical care and decision making. This might include content that has been developed locally, such as clinical protocols and guidelines or content that is licensed from content vendors, such as clinical reference databases or knowledge components integrated into the CIS. While in most cases the information will be in electronic format and delivered via electronic clinical information systems, remember that paper-based CDS interventions (e.g., relevant data summaries, order sets) can be effective and may have a role in your program.

Your organization's clinical knowledge resources provide an initial content base for achieving the clinical goals within the CDS program. Some of these assets might be stand-alone reference databases, while others might be tightly integrated into specific clinical systems (for example, drug interaction detection within CPOE). Additional content (developed locally, shared with other institutions, or acquired from CIS or content vendors) may be required to optimally address the CDS program goals.

Worksheet 3-1

CIS Inventory

In the first column of this worksheet, list the name and system type for all the CIS components that you have identified in your survey of IS pertinent to your CDS efforts (see discussion in chapter). Consider subdividing the list by IS type. If there are many available systems, you might initially focus on those that appear most relevant and powerful for achieving your priority CDS objectives. Keep in mind that the more comprehensively you outline your infrastructure, the easier it will be to identify potential CDS intervention options that are available in your environment.

In the second column, begin noting which of the CDS intervention types that each system can deliver or facilitate. CDS intervention types are described in detail in Chapter 5 and Figure 5-5. You can review those briefly now if you haven't already been over that material.

This book emphasizes that coded data are important in certain CDS interventions. In the third column, document the information types the system handles and any coding schemes used. Pay particular attention to key items, such as laboratory test names, drug names and patients' clinical problems.

The fourth column is for documenting the system user types and how well the system is penetrated into that user population. The Notes column can be used to document other key system features, such as any knowledge bases it contains and its interoperability with other key systems.

continued on next page

Worksheet 3-1 *continued*

System Name/Type	CDS-related Functionality	Information Types (Coding System)	System Users and Usage	Notes
Ordering				
See clinical records, next				
Clinical records and patient management				
Better Care Inc./Inpatient EMR and CPOE	• Order sets • Documentation templates • Relevant data display • Alerts	• Diagnosis information (ICD-10) • Order information (CPT) • Lab results (LOINC) • Imaging results (homegrown scheme)	Nurses, doctors, and pharmacists; 50% of physicians are currently using	Uses drug knowledge base from XYZ Corp. for drug interaction and allergy alerting
Outpatient Computer Corp.	• Order sets • Documentation templates • Relevant data display • Alerts	• Visit diagnosis (ICD-10) • Problem lists (ICD-10) • Medication lists (National Drug Code [NDC]) • Visit notes (Text)	25% of outpatient clinics, mostly primary care	Not yet exchanging data well with inpatient system
Given Meds Corp.	• Alerts • Documentation templates • Relevant data display	• Date/time for medication administration • Medications (NDC) • Dose administered	100% of nurses at two hospitals	Linked to handheld devices
Departmental data management				
Get Your Labs, Inc.	• Relevant data display • Alerts	• Lab results (LOINC) • Anatomic pathology results (Text)	Doctors, nurses, pharmacists all use it frequently	
Clinical content				
Know-it-all Reference	• Disease and drug reference — info-buttons capability	• Disease management info (ICD-9) • Drug reference info (NDC)	Doctors, nurses, pharmacists all use it frequently	Linked to handheld devices

Workflow Process Mapping

The following is a flowcharting template example you can use for mapping workflows pertinent to the priority clinical decision support targets you will be address-ing with your interventions. The chapter text outlines considerations for creating such maps. See also the refer-ences on the following pages on flowcharts[17] and the AHRQ "Workflow Assessment for Health IT Toolkit."[35]

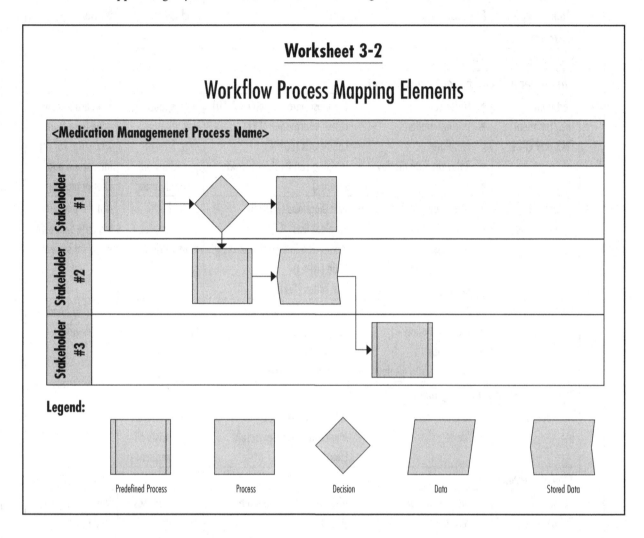

Worksheet 3-2

Workflow Process Mapping Elements

<Medication Managemenet Process Name>

Stakeholder #1

Stakeholder #2

Stakeholder #3

Legend:

Predefined Process   Process   Decision   Data   Stored Data

REFERENCES

1 See, for example: College of Healthcare Information Management Executives. *The CIO's Guide to Implementing EHRs in the HITECH Era.* CHIME. 2010. Available online at: http://www.cio-chime.org/advocacy/CIOsGuideBook/CIO_Guide_Final.pdf. Accessed August 1, 2011.

2 See the HealthIT.Gov website for information for a Meaningful Use definition, and information about certification and incentive programs authorized by HITECH: http://healthit.gov/providers-professionals/ehr-incentives-certification. Accessed August 1, 2011.

3 See HITECH Legislation, Section 3000: Definitions. Subsection 13. Qualified Electronic Health Record. Available online at: http://waysandmeans.house.gov/media/pdf/111/hitech.pdf. Accesssed August 1, 2011.

4 See discussion of the Consolidated Health Informatics initiative on the DHHS website: http://www.hhs.gov/healthit/chiinitiative.html. Accessed August 1, 2011

5 See the HealthIT Standards Committee page on the ONC website: http://healthit.hhs.gov/portal/server.pt/community/healthit_hhs_gov__health_it_standards_committee/1271. Accessed August 1, 2011

6 See the HL7 website: http://www.hl7.org, and the All HL7 Standards page: http://www.hl7.org/implement/standards. Both accessed August 1, 2011.

7 Kawamoto K, Lobach DF. Proposal for fulfilling strategic objectives of the U.S. roadmap for national action on decision support through a service-oriented architecture leveraging HL7 services. *J Am Med Inform Assoc.* 2007 Mar-Apr; 14(2):146–155.

8 Wright A, Sittig DF. SANDS: a service-oriented architecture for clinical decision support in a National Health Information Network. *J Biomed Inform.* 2008 Dec; 41(6):962-981.

9 See HL7 website page on Service Oriented Architecture: http://www.hl7.org/Special/committees/soa/index.cfm. Accessed August 2, 2011.

10 National Quality Forum Consensus Report: Health Information Technology Automation of Quality Measurement. Available online at: http://www.qualityforum.org/Publications/2009/11/Health_Information_Technology_Automation_of_Quality_Measurement__Quality_Data_Set_and_Data_Flow.aspx. Accessed June 26, 2011

11 See the eRecommendation project description page on the AHRQ website: http://healthit.ahrq.gov/structuring_care_recommendations_for_CDS. Accessed August 10, 2011.

12 Sittig DF, Joe JC. Toward a statewide health information technology center (abbreviated version). *South Med J.* 2010 Nov; 103(11):1111-1114. Unabridged version available online at: http://www.uth.tmc.edu/schools/med/imed/patient_safety/members/documents/2010SittigTowardaStatewideHITCenter.pdf. Accessed August 2, 2011.

13 See, for example, the Indiana Health Information Exchange Quality Health First Program webpage: http://www.ihie.com/Solutions/quality-health-first-program.php. Accessed August 2, 2011.

14 Medicare and Medicaid Programs: Electronic Health Record Incentive Program. Available online at:http://edocket.access.gpo.gov/2010/pdf/2010-17207.pdf Accessed June 26, 2011

15 HIMSS Analytics EMR Adoption Model. Available online at: http://www.himssanalytics.org/hc_providers/emr_adoption.asp. Accessed June 26, 2011

16 Nebeker JR, Hoffman JM, Weir CR, et. al. High rates of adverse drug events in a highly computerized hospital. *Arch Intern Med.* 2005; 165:1111-1116.

17 For example, see Wikipedia. *Flowcharts.* Available online at: http://en.wikipedia.org/wiki/Flowchart. Accessed June 17, 2011.

18 See, for example, Wikipedia discussion of use cases. Available online at: http://en.wikipedia.org/wiki/Use_case. Accessed August 5, 2011.

19 Halbesleben JR, Wakefield DS, Wakefield BJ. Work-arounds in health care settings: Literature review and research agenda. *Health Care Manage Rev.* 2008 Jan-Mar; 33(1):2-12. Review. PubMed PMID: 18091439.

20 Neuhauser D. Codman EA. *Qual Saf Health Care.* 2002; 11(1):104-105.

21 Codman EA. *A Study in Hospital Efficiency: As Demonstrated by the Case Report of the First Five Years of a Private Hospital.* 1st ed. Oakbrook, IL: Joint Commission on Accreditation of Healthcare Organizations Press; 1995.

22 Donabedian A. Quality of care: problems of measurement. II. Some issues in evaluating the quality of nursing care. *Am J Public Health Nations Health.* 1969; 59(10):1833-1836.

23 National Quality Forum. *About Us.* Available online at: http://www.qualityforum.org/about/, Accessed June 17, 2011.

24 National Quality Forum. *NQF National Priorities Partnership.* Available online at: http://www.qualityforum.org/Home/New/National_Priorities_Partnership.aspx Accessed June 17, 2011.

25 See NQF's page on the National Priorities Partnership, which discusses its role in proving input into the U.S. National Quality Strategy. Available online at: http://www.qualityforum.org/Setting_Priorities/NPP/National_Priorities_Partnership.aspx. Accessed August 5, 2011.

26 National Quality Forum (NQF), *Driving Quality—A Health IT Assessment Framework for Measurement: A Consensus Report*, Washington, DC: NQF; 2010. Available online at: http://www.qualityforum.org/WorkArea/linkit.aspx?LinkIdentifier=id&ItemID=52609. Accessed August 5, 2011.

27 See the Health and Human Services Office for Human Research Protections (OHRP) Frequently Asked Questions page regarding quality improvement research. Available online at: http://www.hhs.gov/ohrp/policy/qualityfaqsmar2011.pdf. Accessed June 26, 2011.

28 See, for example, the "What types of measures can we use" section of the *Understanding Quality Measurement* document on the AHRQ website: http://www.ahrq.gov/CHToolBx/understn.htm#typesa. Accessed June 17, 2011

29 Callen J, Braithwaite J, Westbrook JI. The importance of medical and nursing sub-cultures in the implementation of clinical information systems. *Methods Inf Med*. 2009; 48(2):196-202. Epub 2009 Feb 18.

30 Sittig DF, Kuperman GJ, Fiskio J. Evaluating physician satisfaction regarding user interactions with an electronic medical record system. *Proc AMIA Symp*. 1999; 400-404.

31 We learned of this acronym from Mark Granville, Senior Vice President, Client Experience, Thomson Reuters Healthcare.

32 Thompson DI, Henry S, Lockwood L, et al. Benefits planning for advanced clinical information systems implementation at Allina hospitals and clinics. *J Healthcare Inf Manag*. 2005; 19(1):54-62.

33 Educational programs such as those from AMIA seek to ensure an adequate workforce of appropriately trained individuals for these roles. See, for example AMIA 10 x 10™. Available online at: http://www.amia.org/education/10x10-courses. Accessed August 5, 2011. Note also that in the U.S., the federal government is investing heavily in HIT workforce development; see the ONC's HIT Workforce development webpage: http://healthit.hhs.gov/portal/server.pt/community/health_it_workforce_development_program:_facts_at_a_glance/1432/home/17051. Accessed August 5, 2011.

34 See ONC's Certified Health IT Product List, available online at: http://onc-chpl.force.com/ehrcert. Accessed August 5, 2011.

35 For more information and a copy of the toolkit go to the AHRQ National Resource Center for Health IT webpage: "Workflow Assessment for Health IT Toolkit." http://healthit.ahrq.gov/workflow. Accessed August 5, 2011.

Chapter 4

Knowledge Management for Clinical Decision Support Programs

Tasks

- Put CDS knowledge management governance structures and processes in place—for example, to make decisions about how you will acquire, monitor and maintain CDS interventions.
- Use this governance system to create and execute an explicit approach for managing your CDS content portfolio's lifecycle. This includes ensuring that CDS interventions have an appropriate scope to achieve improvement goals, are current with evidence-based best practices, and are internally consistent.
- Catalog your CDS interventions and their key attributes, and use this documentation to monitor and maintain your CDS content portfolio. (Worksheet 4-1)
- Document important decisions and actions related to managing your CDS intervention assets so that you can build on this learning and justify knowledge management activities if needed.

KEY LESSONS

- A systematic, cyclic process for managing your CDS knowledge assets is essential and includes people, procedures and information systems.
- Knowledge management activities are an important subcomponent of your CDS program activities, and leverage decision making and management approaches and tools from those broader activities.
- A knowledge management infrastructure should be established before beginning any CDS implementation.
- External support for knowledge management activities may be available from vendor personnel or consultants and should be used to supplement internal staff efforts as needed.

GENERAL APPROACH

One constant about knowledge to guide care delivery is that it changes. New treatments are discovered. Old treatments are superseded by new ones or are proven ineffective or unsafe. New diagnostic tests are invented. Clinical practice continually changes in response to many forces, including new evidence-based clinical practice guidelines, changes in healthcare regulations, evolving healthcare delivery best practices, and changes in the law. In addition, information system deployments evolve, and this affects how the clinical knowledge and guidance gets incorporated into technologies and workflows. Because successful CDS requires that you deliver to clinical decision makers the *right* information in the *right* fashion, all of this change means that you must actively manage your CDS interventions to ensure that they remain in harmony with all these dynamic forces.

Knowledge Management Drivers and Definition

It is helpful to consider your organization's CDS content assets as a single portfolio of knowledge resources. These assets might exist in several different forms, such as order sets, alerts, rules/reminders, reference information and documentation templates (see Figure 5-5, Taxonomy of CDS Intervention Types). They may be stand-alone or integrated into CISs, such as CPOE and EMRs. In addition, virtually all organizations have both paper-based and electronic medical reference information available for clinicians and patients that also should be considered as portfolio components.

This universe of deployed content assets may come from various sources, including published clinical guidelines and research, internal content experts, CIS vendors (provided directly with the system or shared among their institutional users), governmental agencies and clearinghouses, other healthcare institutions, publicly accessible websites, and commercial CDS content vendors (that can include print reference publishers). This information may be accessed and used in different ways by clinicians and patients in your organization. This diversity in sources, distribution and formats makes managing CDS knowledge currency, appropriateness and internal consistency a challenge.

How this knowledge is incorporated into your information systems, and integrated with patient-specific clinical data, also requires careful attention. For example, changes in technology details—such as data format, coding, terminology, messaging, clinical data repositories and information systems that record clinical observations used in CDS—all can affect computer-based knowledge execution (see Chapter 3, section entitled General Approach/Systems). Similarly, your different ISs may have different tools and approaches for imbedding knowledge into CDS interventions (such as order sets and clinical rules)—and these may evolve over time.

Given all this flux, you need a systematic process to ensure that your CDS interventions—and the knowledge and data on which they are based—remain appropriate for meeting your organizational goals and in sync with your technology infrastructure. This approach should address how you acquire and maintain CDS interventions and related underlying clinical knowledge. It should be based on formal mechanisms for deciding about, and making and documenting changes to, this CDS asset portfolio. These activities comprise your CDS program's *approach* to *knowledge management;* here is how we defined this term in Chapter 1:

Knowledge Management: A comprehensive process for acquiring, adapting and monitoring information for use in clinical decision support that keeps it up-to-date with current clinical evidence, expert consensus and local conditions including pertinent health information system implementation(s).

Keeping CDS interventions appropriate for "local conditions" includes making sure they continually add value to achieving targeted improvement goals and objectives. This means linking your knowledge management activities to feedback you are getting about intervention effects. We discuss foundational measurement capabilities for CDS programs in the Chapter 3 Measurement section and for individual CDS interventions in Chapter 9.

The sections that follow provide guidance on applying a systematic approach to CDS knowledge management.

Establishing Knowledge Management Governance Structures and Processes

Knowledge management activities within your CDS program involve significant collaborating among participants, appreciating medical knowledge and information systems nuances, and using tools (such as from your EHR vendor, or more general data management applications such as spreadsheets, databases, and word processors) to manage your CDS interventions. These activities draw on the stakeholder engagement and governance approaches outlined in Chapter 2, and the systems-related capabilities outlined in Chapter 3. Following are some key elements:

- *A governance structure* that allocates decision-making authority and defines processes for selecting and maintaining CDS interventions and related clinical knowledge.
- *People*—technical, clinical and management—to oversee and execute knowledge management processes.
- *An administrative workflow* that seamlessly executes the lifecycle for clinical knowledge and related CDS interventions—from acquisition, to vetting, implementation and monitoring, and ultimately to modification, retirement or replacement.
- *Software tools* to track deployed knowledge resources, knowledge and intervention versioning, and knowledge management decisions and actions.

Effective CDS programs invest significantly in people and time to manage CDS-related knowledge,[1] which includes addressing these elements. At the core, someone or some group in your organization must take responsibility for ensuring that your CDS content portfolio is monitored for ongoing accuracy and internal consistency, and compli-

ance with clinical practice guidelines and regulations. They must also ensure smooth interplay with organizational information systems (such as EHR upgrades) and processes (such as broader performance improvement activities). In addition, this person or group must determine and manage the mechanisms for accomplishing these goals.

Knowledge management governance and accountability details vary depending on your healthcare organization's size and complexity. In small practices with only one or a few physicians, a single individual may assume overall responsibility, sharing specific tracking and updating work with other physicians or office staff. In this case, support from vendors or consultants (such as your Regional Extension Center) may be particularly helpful. In larger, more complex environments, various committees may participate in knowledge management activities, possibly supervised by a single, executive-level committee with final responsibility for reviewing and approving changes to CDS interventions and content (see Figure 2-4 and related governance discussion in Chapter 2).

In any case, the governance approach should clearly assign accountability for the CDS intervention portfolio overall, as well as for individual interventions. This can help when there is uncertainty about the decision-making process for configuring and implementing an intervention or when questions arise about its clinical meaning. Larger organizations may accomplish this by identifying a clinical lead for interventions grouped by coverage, for example, oncology vs. cardiology. An overall lead for the intervention portfolio may be assigned to coordinate the interplay between different CDS content areas, such as the shared interest among surgeons, internists, infectious disease specialists and others in CDS for catheter-associated infections.

In addition to specifying and documenting CDS knowledge management structures, people and processes, your CDS program should include mechanisms for documenting work related to managing the CDS intervention lifecycle. This includes tracking dates, actors and discussions for key decisions and actions about acquiring and maintaining interventions. This helps you base subsequent decisions on earlier work and justify content-related actions if needed (see Appendix, Medico-legal Considerations).

For example, a CDS intervention package focused on diabetes management should be accompanied by documentation about how the content for alerts, order sets, documentation tools, and the like were configured and/or vetted; what key decisions were made, including why and by whom; when and how these interventions were monitored, and by whom; and the justification for decisions made along the way. This effort will help you efficiently optimize the intervention package appropriateness and value over time. It will also enable you to reconstruct the process in case you run into future problems such as interventions failing to work as expected, legal or regulatory issues, and questions regarding clinical correctness or legitimacy. Many of the worksheets in Part II can help with this intervention-related documentation, but the organizational commitment to complete and use this documentation is a CDS program function. Later in this chapter, we say more about tools for tracking information about your CDS interventions.

As illustrated in the Sample CDS Charter sidebar in Chapter 2, some organizations explicitly mention their commitment to CDS knowledge management in their CDS program charter. This should be based on discussions up front with leadership about the significant time and resources required to keep CDS interventions useful and valuable. Their support helps ensure that adequate resources are available for essential knowledge management activities.

We next describe in more detail program tasks related to obtaining and maintaining your CDS content portfolio.

Obtaining Needed CDS Content and Interventions

Our definition for clinical decision support includes using organized clinical knowledge to enhance decisions and actions (see Chapter 1). From a knowl-edge management perspective then, obtaining the knowledge and interventions that will be used in this process is a key CDS program function.

Knowledge to guide clinical and health behavior may reside in a variety of formats and tools. These may include electronic rule collections within clinical software such as EHRs and clinical surveillance applications; textbooks, including electronic versions thereof; domain-specific treatises such as drug prescribing aids or references; order sets; scientific papers; and clinical practice guidelines. In a few cases, these may be developed entirely locally, but in most situations, this knowledge and intervention portfolio underpinning your CDS program will largely come from various sources outside your organization. These knowledge and intervention units may reside on external websites, in government and professional clearinghouses, on paper in library collections, with EHR or CDS vendors, in partner care delivery organizations, and elsewhere.

How, and from which of these sources, should you acquire knowledge and interventions needed for your CDS program? The answer, which is not mutually exclusive even for any given CDS intervention, comes down to building them within your organization, buying them from a company, or acquiring them through sharing.

Build vs. Buy vs. Share: Relative Advantages and Disadvantages

Several different factors inform your decision about how best to acquire CDS-related content. These may include price, comprehensiveness, access to local clinical experts or others to work on content; customizability for local priorities and circumstances; suitability for particular information system platforms; and others. The answer for your organization may be a balance among all these factors that results in a mix of knowledge sources. While each approach is considered here separately for clarity, most organizations will end up with a hybrid that includes CDS tools commonly purchased from vendors (such as a drug-drug interaction knowledge base or an electronic textbook) and artifacts created, or at least customized, by the organization itself (such as order sets).

Whatever CDS content sources you use for your performance improvement efforts, you will typically incur substantial time and monetary costs to obtain and maintain them. Tracking and optimizing these costs is important in maximizing your CDS program's ROI, as discussed in the measurement section in Chapter 3 and in Chapter 9.

BUILDING YOUR OWN

Building your own CDS knowledge resources and interventions, such as clinical guidelines and order sets, offers several advantages,[2] many involving the ability to customize the material from the outset exactly for local conditions. More specific benefits include:

- Aligning intervention (such as alert and order set) wording to reflect local clinical test names, as well as clinician and referral center names;
- Harmonizing patient-specific intervention triggering and data display features with data elements and codes available locally in electronic format;
- Selecting intervention parameters (such as alerting messages) and formatting most desirable for your end users;
- Adapting to local needs factors such as the frequency and urgency with which specific CDS interventions are displayed;
- Ensuring that intervention details are fully consistent with local practice patterns, especially when these may vary (for justifiable reasons) from a specific clinical practice guideline.

To this last point, there may be a number of acceptable approaches for diagnosing and treating a particular clinical condition when there is no definitive evidence from clinical trials on preferred approaches. Building a knowledge base on this condition's treatment locally would allow your organization to specify exactly which options will be incorporated into your CDS interventions based on your organizational goals and clinical expertise and consensus.

For example, in delivering an order set based on a pneumonia diagnosis, your organization may prefer a particular first-line antibiotic among several equally acceptable choices from a national evidence-based guideline. This choice may be based on cost savings that result from a bulk-purchase agreement with the manufacturer. An order set provided by a national organization or vendor using that guideline may not reflect this local preference, but when your healthcare organization builds a knowledge base itself, it can incorporate these local factors directly into the intervention from the start.

Despite these advantages, building CDS interventions and knowledge bases yourself also carries significant disadvantages. Perhaps most importantly, a build-it-yourself approach can be very expensive in terms of time and labor. For example, researching different clinical options, implementing resulting recommendations as CDS interventions in your information systems, and keeping this information up-to-date can be very costly.[3]

In addition, your local clinicians may not have the experience or expertise in a particular clinical domain to appropriately inform CDS tools. Similarly, deviating from specific evidence-based recommendations in national clinical practice guidelines to align well with local practice may reduce the beneficial impact from adapting these guidelines into CDS interventions. Also, because some knowledge vendors program their knowledge to interact with specific information system platform components such as data structures, coded data, and display approaches, building it yourself may disrupt the interoperability that knowledge bases constructed on a more national level may provide.

As we'll discuss next, though, buying or obtaining interventions from sharing sources still requires some local vetting, so the associated review and maintenance costs can't be completely avoided by not creating your own CDS content.

BUYING COMMERCIALLY

Purchasing CDS tools such as order sets, reference sources, drug safety-checking software, and others from a commercial source that specializes in these areas offers several advantages. A key feature is that vendors can access clinical expertise that may not be readily available to your organization. This expertise can improve the evidence and best practice foundation on which your CDS interventions rest and thereby enhance intervention quality and value. Also, commercial vendors can bring to bear the resources needed to tailor knowledge to specific, high-profile use cases, such as preventing certain 'Never Events,' the adverse clinical events that should never occur.[4]

By bringing about economies of scale, vendors can spread the substantial content development and maintenance costs over many clients, which can greatly decrease costs compared to doing this work yourself. That is, your organization's total investments in people, time and dollars to create, integrate and keep CDS content up-to-date can be significantly less if you license this material from your EHR supplier and/or CDS vendors. Ideally, these vendors should update their CDS content and interventions periodically (in near-real-time for high-impact changes) and disseminate these updates for you to review and deploy into your ISs (with at least some automation support). Also, note that some EHR and CDS vendors partner with their clients to develop CDS-related content. By purchasing content from these vendors, you can benefit from this broader input into intervention development and may be in a position to contribute your content and expertise into the offering for some rewarding return.

Purchasing CDS interventions and related content from your information system suppliers (or CDS suppliers whose offerings are well-integrated into those systems) can make it much easier to incorporate this material into your applications. Because there are few, if any, widely adopted standards for incorporating CDS interventions into HIT applications (see Chapter 3, Systems), this integration may be very difficult without such a greased path. For example, it may require access to those systems' source code or computer programming details, including their data message and database storage structures. The HIT/CDS industry's relatively early

evolutionary state is such that incorporating CDS interventions into ISs can even be cumbersome in some circumstances when the content comes from your HIT supplier or one of their partners.

Just as with creating CDS content yourself, buying it commercially also has important disadvantages. Many are the inverse of the advantages to building the knowledge yourself. For example, because CDS content vendors often attend to a large national or even an international audience, it may be harder to customize their CDS content to meet your specific needs or for you to have updates at the frequency you would prefer.[5]

Also, the advantages provided by a vendor do not come free; initial CDS content purchase price and an ongoing subscription may be considerable and that may be a challenge for your budget—even if the approach reduces overall costs. In addition, relying on a particular vendor may be problematic in a dynamic economy, especially if that vendor is the sole source for many of your core CDS content needs. If that vendor goes out of business (or is acquired by another company in a manner that negatively affects their product[s] that you use), transitioning to a new vendor, or picking up knowledge maintenance tasks in the meantime, can be difficult, time consuming and expensive.

As just noted, buying commercially does not necessarily eliminate the effort required to make sure the content is appropriate for your specific organization or to integrate it into your information system(s). If your CDS supplier does not have a seamless integration interface, you will still need to do some work locally to upload the intervention(s) (such as rules, alerts, order sets) into your system. You will need to consider any data coding schemes used by the vendor and whether these match those used in your systems that will be handling this content.

Similarly, if the interventions include computable knowledge, you must ensure that it is in a version and format that your systems can use. For example, a vendor may supply a set of alerts and reminders as a knowledge base of HL7 Arden Syntax medical logic modules. While this represents a highly structured clinical knowledge representation, your organization may lack the software needed to execute these modules.

Because your CDS program requires many different intervention types—such as alerts, order sets, patient education materials and other reference information, documentation tools, and others—this may require business arrangements and content integration work with at least several CDS content suppliers. This can further add to content acquisition and use costs.

You should also consider legal issues related to responsibility for maintaining the underlying knowledge and liability for adverse clinical outcomes that may arise from using the knowledge. While this is frequently addressed through warranties and hold-harmless clauses in contracts, you must make this clear when acquiring and using vendor-supplied knowledge. These CDS contracts typically place the medico-legal burden on the clinically licensed content user, and this may seem daunting to the uninitiated. However, there is evidence that EHR (including CDS) users realize a medical malpractice liability benefit because this technology can enable clinicians to deliver higher quality care than those who do not use it. Further comments and references on CDS-related liability issues are presented in the Appendix: Medico-legal Considerations.

USING SHARING SERVICES AND SOURCES

Many care delivery organizations voluntarily share their CDS material for other implementers to use. In some cases, this occurs informally among organizations, particularly those that use the same information system vendor. This common infrastructure reduces the implementation burden by increasing the likelihood that the coded data, database pointers and other technical details are the same in the receiving organization as in the originating one.[6] Your EHR and CDS content vendor may support forums wherein their clients share CDS interventions that they have locally developed or customized. You should seek these out and determine whether those

that are available would support your efforts, if you haven't done so already.

This information-sharing has several typical features, which reflect advantages and disadvantages associated with this route to acquiring CDS content:

- It is free or has a nominal cost for the receiving organization to obtain the material;
- The organization providing the content doesn't promise to maintain or update it, or help adapt it to the receiving organization's needs;
- The content is offered "as-is" without warranty.

Large scale CDS content sharing to extend this informal foundation has been discussed in the informatics community for many years. More recently, CDS use has become widely recognized as a key enabler for many national healthcare performance improvement initiatives, and this has accelerated interest in—and funding for—work toward broad CDS-sharing resources. For example, in the U.S., ONC[7] and AHRQ[8] are supporting various projects to advance CDS sharing, as are other U.S. and international efforts, such as the Morningside Initiative[9] and OpenClinical.[10] These efforts include work toward platforms and clearinghouses that would allow organizations both to share knowledge they have created and to acquire knowledge created by others. Despite some progress, there are currently no robust sharing solutions that incorporate different knowledge types from multiple sources for use in different systems. Given the stakes and interest, we encourage readers to keep an eye on progress on national CDS sharing initiatives.

Another sharing type that complements CDS content exchanges among care delivery organizations is when non-profit entities—such as government agencies, specialty societies and clinical condition-oriented organizations—provide knowledge and other content useful for CDS interventions. For example, AHRQ's National Guideline Clearinghouse[11] provides free access to many structured clinical practice guideline summaries, but these are generally not in an executable format and would require considerable work to make them so. On the other hand, MedlinePlus Connect from the

U.S. National Library of Medicine is a free service that uses the HL7 Infobutton standard to deliver information about drugs, laboratory tests, disease and health topics and others into EHRs.[12]

In addition, some AHRQ and ONC projects noted earlier that are related to CDS-sharing infrastructure also provide content for CDS interventions focused on targets such as Meaningful Use requirements. Examples here include a list of clinically important drug-drug interactions developed by ONC's Advancing CDS project[13] and the structured, coded logic statements developed by AHRQ's eRecommendations project[14]—among others described in the AHRQ and ONC project pages referenced earlier.

A final topic worth noting in this CDS-sharing discussion is internal sharing—that is, re-using CDS content or interventions for a different purpose than originally intended. For example, if your organization is implementing alerts about improper medication dosing, the rule underlying the alert will need to determine if a particular patient suffers from chronic kidney disease (CKD). You can create a module that brings together different data in order to ascertain whether a patient has CKD, and its severity.

However, that module also may be useful for CDS interventions to minimize harm from imaging contrast agents, certain antibiotics, and other medications that can harm kidneys—especially already-damaged ones. Here, a CDS tool implemented for one purpose can be used for another, and this CDS content reuse can increase efficiencies in your CDS program. This applies in outpatient settings too, for example, with CDS modules related to blood pressure management that might be useful for CDS intervention packages focused on cardiovascular risk reduction, diabetes management and other topics. Because different organizational units (especially within small hospitals and practices) may share common policies and information systems, complexities associated with cross-institution sharing aren't often a problem.

Factors to Consider When Integrating Content from Multiple Sources

In many clinical settings, particularly in a large hospital or health system, your CDS content will come from at least several sources and will involve building (or at least adapting) it yourself, buying commercially and using sharing sources.

While this mixing is typical and avoids a single potential failure point for your entire CDS knowledge pipeline, you should consider certain factors to maximize success in integrating diverse knowledge sources to achieve positive clinical outcomes and accomplish other related organizational goals. First, content elements from different sources may have been developed for different computer platforms, so you need to make sure that new content acquisitions closely match your technical infrastructure. This assessment is not just theoretical; it should be based on experiences of other consumers like your organization—keeping in mind even then that nuanced system differences between reference sites and your environment could lead to different experiences using the 'same' content in the 'same' application.

You may need to adjust technical factors—such as code sets and terminology, as well as knowledge format—for externally-acquired content to function smoothly in your setting. For example, intelligent data capture forms in your hospital's nursing care documentation system database may use one code set to label and store clinical observations, while a rules knowledge base that analyzes such observations may use another, and this disparity may adversely affect how your CDS interventions serve their intended function. Indeed, disparities even between different versions of the same software, or that arise when CDS content has been customized for other organizations, can make it difficult for you to incorporate this material into your systems.

In addition, even when CDS content has been vetted elsewhere, your organization is still responsible for ensuring that it is appropriate for your needs and circumstances. This requires at least some local expertise and time to review and vet the content at a level adequate to assess adherence to your local policies, practice patterns and norms set by other CDS content already deployed. An important consideration when obtaining CDS content from outside sources is, therefore, ensuring that it is accessible in a user-friendly form that allows review by clinical experts without special computer skills. If not, this will confound your internal vetting process and may complicate how you integrate the content with other parts of your CDS infrastructure. Also, if the content needs tailoring before you can apply it, such a "black-box" property may make this integration even more difficult for you.

Addressing CDS Content Already in Place

Even if your organization attends to the knowledge management principles just outlined, you will likely have some CDS content that was deployed before you began carefully tracking these knowledge assets, and the decisions and action taken about them. For example, your organization may have acquired and customized order sets without clearly documenting how they were customized, what scientific evidence and other reference material was used, and who made and approved these changes. In addition, this previously-acquired knowledge may represent significant investment in terms of money and time, and the details—including the return on this investment—may be unclear. Accordingly, even as new knowledge is acquired, vetted, tailored, used and maintained, your organization must deal with this legacy knowledge, in part to ensure that it is clinically consistent internally and with newer content.

Many of the same considerations that go into selecting sources for new knowledge and maintaining that material apply to gathering, analyzing and maintaining legacy CDS content. This work begins with establishing provenance, which means determining where the content originated; what expertise those who created it had; the scientific evidence and guidelines that were used; what was done to evaluate and vet that information; and how the content (and pertinent clinical knowledge base) have changed

since the material was first acquired. Knowing this information will help you identify what additional changes, if any, are required and how that material will fit into your knowledge maintenance schedule and routines.

In addition, as your knowledge management program evolves, you may develop new intervention mechanisms or change current ones, and this raises similar legacy content issues. For example, acquiring a new CPOE system should provide additional powerful ways to deliver tailored knowledge to providers. However, it also means that, in order to avoid losing prior content investments altogether, you have to integrate the old interventions and content with the new delivery mechanism. This may include updating hyperlinks in a new system to point to previously acquired internal knowledge sources (or vetted external sources on the Web), or adjusting the codes or other order set content to make it usable by your new CPOE system.

Keeping What You Acquired Up-to-Date

Once you have acquired and/or identified the CDS interventions and related content in your program's portfolio, protecting that investment (which may be an expensive one) is a key task for your knowledge management efforts. A comprehensive program to keep CDS content up-to-date will help you ensure that it remains helpful to clinicians and other healthcare personnel and that it serves broader goals—such as supporting better care delivery decisions, actions and outcomes.

Although initially you may be able to track interventions informally, this will eventually become impossible to do effectively as your deployed CDS asset portfolio becomes larger and more complex. Loosely tracking and coordinating CDS content that is manually "hard-coded" into systems (for example, specific links to Web-based resources or rules that are maintained locally) can be particularly challenging. Even with CIS and CDS vendor-supplied systems, the search and cataloging capabilities may not easily support collecting these data about what CDS is actually deployed.

It may not be possible to easily obtain and track all the information you would like about your CDS content, but you should strive in your CDS program to use a systematic, coordinated and thorough process to manage this information about the interventions, as well as the interventions themselves. After all, your organization has made substantial investments in this CDS content and much is at stake. At some point, successfully managing information about CDS interventions used in your environment will require special tools.

Tracking Your CDS Assets

Earlier, this chapter covered knowledge management governance and processes; for these to be optimally effective, your CDS program should provide tools for tracking all the CDS interventions and content—as well as decisions and actions concerning this material.[1]

One sophisticated tool for this tracking and management is a CDS knowledge repository. Although very few organizations currently have such software, how such pioneers use these repositories points toward where the industry is going and where you should steer your knowledge management efforts.

CDS knowledge repositories catalog in a single resource all the CDS interventions and related content within a healthcare organization. This repository contains information about what interventions are deployed in each information system. CDS knowledge repositories, or other tools for cataloging CDS interventions, should use some taxonomy to classify different CDS knowledge types.[16] This helps you retrieve different CDS content elements and document their properties.

In addition, the repository is used to record and track CDS knowledge and intervention features needed to manage these assets. Figure 4-1 lists CDS intervention dimensions you should consider tracking, and Worksheet 4-1 is a tool for documenting these intervention portfolio features.

CDS knowledge repositories may also contain intervention content itself—such as order sets,

production rules that drive alerts and reminders, nursing care plans, electronic textbooks and drug knowledge bases. Centrally managing CDS content in this way can yield many important benefits, such as supporting internal content reuse as described earlier under sharing sources. This can have important patient safety implications, for example, by ensuring that critical information (such as drug dosages) are presented in similar ways across different systems to help avoid user errors from misinterpreting this guidance.

An additional desirable knowledge repository feature (either for local or national repositories) is feeding individual CDS interventions directly into target CISs. Some AHRQ and ONC CDS-sharing research and demonstration projects mentioned earlier take steps in this direction. Also, some CDS vendor products that deal narrowly with specific intervention types (such as alerts and order sets) perform this integration function.

There are few, if any, vendor-supplied knowledge management tools that perform all the knowledge repository functions previously outlined.[17] In addition, most organizations find their CDS content buried in, or tightly integrated with, specific software modules, and not in a separate structure from the applications in which they are embedded. This can make it difficult to catalog and manage CDS content assets as a whole.

As a result, you will likely need to parcel out CDS content tracking and maintenance tasks among different software applications. In this situation, the repository becomes a virtual one, based on pointers in some tracking tool to where the knowledge resides. By pointing to specific applications or knowledge bases where all the various CDS content assets are deployed, this tracking tool enables you to more easily find, view, vet and update the assets. For example, a rules-based decision support system may include a module for classifying, listing and tracking the rules in the knowledge base. You might also adapt software change-tracking or versioning tools for this purpose. Lacking any suitable vendor-supplied intervention tracking tools, your organization may have

Figure 4-1: Key Attributes to Track for Deployed CDS Interventions

Acquisition and Maintenance

- Source, versions;
- Acquisition and maintenance costs;
- Technical dependencies related to the content, such as controlled terminology codes and database references;
- Process for initial vetting, localizing and approval/adoption (who, when, how);
- When the content was acquired, reviewed, modified (including change details) and approved for use in your systems; this includes leadership signoff details and stakeholder discussions leading to these decisions and actions, as well as associated technology modifications (such as changes to data coding schemes to ensure compliance with underlying information systems);
- Monitoring and maintenance plan (who, when, how) includes content "expiration/review date" and process for making changes (either locally or requesting from vendor);
- Citations to clinical evidence and authoritative sources underpinning the content, and changes to it.

Scope

- Specific populations covered (for example, for specialty- or pediatric-specific interventions);
- Specific practice locations affected (for example, alerts may be generally deployed but switched off in emergency department (ED) or intensive care unit (ICU) locations due to impact on time-critical workflows);
- Primary end-user targets for intervention/knowledge (such as patient, pharmacist, nurse or physician).

Delivery

- Content deployment status (e.g., development vs. testing vs. production system vs. retired);
- Intervention type (for example, order sets, alerts and infobutton links to reference materials);
- Presentation format (for example, alerts that either do or do not interrupt workflow);
- Systems through which knowledge/intervention is delivered (such as Web, EMR, CPOE and departmental system);
- End-user intervention champion;
- Knowledge formalism used, such as the HL7 Arden Syntax for alerts and reminders or HL7 Infobutton standard;
- Format used to import knowledge into or export it from various ISs;
- Coding or terminology standard for patient data used by the CDS intervention;
- Intervention effects on key processes and outcomes.

to craft its own by using general purpose spreadsheet, database or word processing software.

You should ideally link your knowledge repository (or related tracking tool) to other change management systems and activities in your organization. This may include mechanisms for HIT software versioning, clinical policy and procedure management, and pertinent staff committee minutes. By linking knowledge management tools and approaches with other organizational change management systems (possibly through a shared repository or decision-making process), you can further ensure that your CDS program's content assets are well maintained and aligned with broader organizational goals and processes.

Maintaining Your CDS Assets

Your CDS knowledge repository—or related tracking tools—provide the foundation for monitoring and maintaining your CDS asset portfolio. The knowledge management governance mechanisms discussed earlier in this chapter should establish a regular schedule to ensure that each CDS asset is reviewed at an appropriate interval and that the overall portfolio remains valid and internally consistent. This might include requiring expiration or mandatory review dates for each intervention. Local experts can help determine the appropriate "shelf life," which may range from a few months to a few years depending on how fast the pertinent knowledge base changes. The software tools just discussed can then be used to generate reminders to examine the intervention to ensure ongoing content appropriateness. Chapter 9 discusses monitoring interventions for other key features such as deployment efficiency and value, and these evaluations should be coordinated with the content review.

Unless your organization's clinical activities are focused on a very narrow clinical specialty, the expertise required to review and revise individual content units across your entire CDS portfolio will likely be quite broad. Your governance mechanisms should find ways to engage individuals whose expertise and interests align most closely with each intervention's topic to assume responsibility for this content. To optimally leverage limited resources, you should prioritize an intervention's review frequency and intensity based on its impact—for example, focusing more intensely on high-stakes interventions that frequently affect workflow. Content that crosses domains may involve review by multiple individuals or departments. Examples include collaboration between a hospital's medical department and the pharmacy department or pharmacy and therapeutic committee for a CDS intervention related to a high-risk medication, or between a multi-specialty clinic's gastroenterologist and internist for CDS interventions related to diagnosing and managing peptic ulcer disease.

An overall CDS committee that has representation from all departments and stakeholders may conduct a secondary review or approval for individual interventions, as well as maintain ultimate responsibility for the overall portfolio. In a small practice,

this may include consulting with clinical experts elsewhere or a group discussion by the members of a practice at a periodic meeting. No matter how many content review layers you have, you should faithfully conduct the review and maintenance activities called for in your knowledge management plan, following the established protocol for upkeep accountability and decision making and using the decision-making authority as determined for each content asset. Because this is time consuming, those doing the maintenance should provide ongoing feedback to the team about how the review and maintenance work can be better prioritized and made more efficient and effective.

In addition to time-based content CDS portfolio monitoring and updating activities, you should establish a notification scheme so that changes in information system properties will trigger a review as necessary. In a hospital or health system, this may involve shared committee membership (such as between CDS, IT and medical staff committees) or at the least, regular messages among different groups to ensure that changes to IT systems are reviewed with an eye toward assessing the impact on deployed CDS interventions. In a small practice, this may involve discussing with your software vendor how system updates may affect other installed CDS interventions. Make sure to look for changes that affect knowledge and data interoperability; for example, changes related to data codes, message formats, database structure, user interfaces, telecommunication protocols (such as new smart phones) and the like. Testing for effects related to launching new CDS interventions is a related consideration and is discussed in Chapter 8.

More broadly, your knowledge management approach should include evaluation approaches to ensure continued proper CDS portfolio functioning.[18] One useful way to do this is to monitor CDS intervention use or output across the portfolio. For example, if alerts regarding a particular medication fall suddenly from some prior steady-state level, that may suggest that data coding has changed, a message format has been altered, or other system parameters have been modified in a way that adversely affects rule triggering or execution. Monitoring intervention activity in this way can provide useful feedback about intervention status across many intervention types, for example, accesses to a website for a commonly used reference source (to ensure proper hyperlink functioning), and to individual order sets or documentation templates (to ensure their unhindered availability). Other forces besides technical factors can acutely affect intervention use (see Chapter 9), so you should keep this in mind when interpreting these statistics. But these too (for example, changes in clinical circumstances) have implications for your intervention maintenance efforts as well.

Your CDS portfolio monitoring and updating mechanisms must also have an outward-looking component to supplement internal facing surveillance. For example, you should establish protocols to regularly review external CDS-related knowledge—such as that in clinical practice guidelines or in the regulatory pronouncements of government agencies or professional societies—to determine whether changes in these practice standards require changes in your CDS interventions. Larger hospitals and health systems may have formal departmental mechanisms for keeping healthcare delivery in sync with evolving clinical evidence and best practices, and these should be tapped for CDS maintenance as well. Similarly, in smaller hospitals and practices, clinicians' continuing education activities—including reading journals, attending courses and researching specific patient care-related questions—can provide signals that specific CDS interventions may require review and updating.

Periodically you will need to withdraw a particular information unit or CDS intervention from your portfolio, and you should have procedures in place for doing this. In some cases, you will retire CDS content after your regular, proactive surveillance determines that it is no longer useful or appropriate. For example, this would be the case when a new guideline provides strong evidence that a different patient management protocol than the one supported by your current intervention is needed.

In other cases, this need to withdraw an information unit will be proactive. For example, when a drug is withdrawn from the market, you must remove it from each CDS intervention where it appears. EHR tools may help with this to some degree, but this situation emphasizes how important it is to have a CDS knowledge repository—or at least a robust intervention tracking tool. Another example where you need to manipulate your knowledge base before a regular review cycle is when a medication is temporarily in short supply. Here you might need to replace in pertinent CDS interventions the unavailable medication with an appropriate substitute, and change things back when the original drug is again available.

As we emphasize throughout this chapter, it is important not only to manage your CDS assets well, but also to track the decisions and actions taken during that work. For this knowledge maintenance discussion, this involves documenting who reviewed what; what decisions were made and why; the chain of command followed in approving or revising knowledge; and the justification for decisions made along the way. This effort will help you address subsequent revisions and to reconstruct the process in case you run into future problems such as system failure, improper output, legal or regulatory issues, and questions regarding clinical correctness or legitimacy.

Using a systematic content maintenance approach allows you to track and manage all the inevitable challenges to intervention portfolio use and value. These challenges—and the necessity to respond quickly and effectively—become increasingly important as your CDS intervention portfolio grows. Increasing interplay between more—and more complex—CDS interventions can increase your maintenance effort exponentially, making a thoughtful, proactive approach critical. Again, prioritizing for action those knowledge maintenance activities that will have the greatest impact on top goals—such as good patient outcomes and care delivery efficiency—is an important knowledge management strategy.

Knowledge Maintenance in Specific Situations

To further illustrate the knowledge maintenance approaches previously outlined, we next briefly consider a few specific areas where you will typically apply these principles.

MEDICATION-RELATED CDS

Supporting appropriate medication use is among the most common CDS focus areas because drugs are a central tool in healthcare delivery, and they carry tremendous potential benefits and harms. In addition, the systems for acquiring patient data (such as pharmacy systems), and knowledge bases for generating recommendations based on those data (such as drug prescribing knowledge bases), are widely available and used. Because medication-related CDS is so common and important, your knowledge management activities should pay particular attention to these interventions—and the knowledge base on which they depend.

Major changes to medication availability, use or formulary status are good focal points. This includes carefully tracking new drug approvals and accepted indications, both by regulatory authorities and by local pharmacy and therapeutics committees. You should also track drug withdrawals from the market for safety and other reasons—the former may provide opportunities for CDS-enhanced patient outreach. Likewise, your CDS maintenance effort should track when drugs are removed or reclassified in local formularies for cost or other reasons so you can modify pertinent CDS interventions accordingly. Similarly, newly published "black-box" warnings that incorporate crucial safety information should prompt your CDS Team to consider rules and other interventions to address patients who may be newly classified as being at increased risk for adverse drug events. These changes may affect many order sets, alerts and reminders, intelligent data collection forms, and other CDS intervention types and instances.

TESTING-RELATED CDS

While new studies—laboratory analyses, imaging studies and the like—are currently developed less frequently than new drugs, these changes to clinical practice also can affect your organization's CDS portfolio. For example, changes to a laboratory analytic method may produce a different reference range for a particular laboratory test, and this in turn may have an impact on alerts and reminders driven by those data, and conditional orders in order sets (for example, when an order appears only if a specific condition—such as an abnormal test result—is present). As a result, you must carefully consider when new tests (which may alter preferred diagnostic or monitoring protocols) or reference ranges are introduced whether these changes require modifications to deployed CDS interventions.

Similar considerations apply to other diagnostic tools, such as imaging studies, where how the test is used and associated risks may have important implications for current CDS interventions—or suggest the need for new ones. As mentioned earlier in this and the preceding chapter, you should also carefully examine the effect that a new laboratory information system may have on your CDS portfolio. For example, you need to ensure that any new coding terminologies or messaging formats don't adversely affect deployed CDS interventions.

CARE PLAN RELATED CDS

Care plans are helpful tools for ensuring that patients with certain specific conditions receive appropriate care. These plans are typically based on clinical practice guidelines, augmented with local policies and procedures. The plans themselves may be considered knowledge assets within the CDS program, and there may be specific CDS interventions—such as documentation templates, order sets, and surveillance rules and reminders—to help implement the care plan.

Changes in underlying policies or guidelines may therefore affect the related CDS interventions. Similarly, changes in resources used to execute the care plan—such as specific tests, medications, clinical consultants or therapy providers—may affect how pertinent CDS interventions are configured or deployed. Close communication and collaboration between those responsible for the care plan and the CDS Team can help ensure that care plan-related CDS interventions optimally support care plan goals.

Putting It All Together: Suggestions for Successful Knowledge Management

Although successfully managing a rich CDS content portfolio will become increasingly essential for performance improvement efforts in care delivery organizations, there are relatively few models for doing this well. In addition, CDS knowledge management tools and approaches will (hopefully) undergo significant evolution in the coming years as corresponding CDS tools and best practices mature. Your CDS assets constitute in some sense your CDS program's "family jewels," so despite this uncertainty and flux, you should attend carefully to managing them well today—and to doing better going forward.

Earlier discussion in this chapter outlines approaches to setting up CDS knowledge management governance structures and processes and using these to acquire and maintain your CDS assets. The following bullets highlight some of the key recommendations:

- Develop and empower a dedicated team to create and maintain CDS interventions. Ensure there is a published and transparent governance structure for this team.
- Engage clinical content experts to support the CDS Team's work. It is not reasonable to expect the CDS Team to have comprehensive clinical knowledge about all CDS interventions that will be deployed.
- Aim for a single reference knowledge version for CDS interventions, and insert this into various interventions from that source. As a rule of thumb, acquire knowledge once, and use it consistently many times. Specific knowledge elements should be changed once (for example, in updating) and then that version should cascade through pertinent interventions and systems.
- Work toward automatically migrating content from your knowledge management repository

into your CIS applications. Begin by understanding your CIS supplier's import specifications and having your knowledge management tools export in these formats.
- Develop a formal process for exporting deployed interventions from the CIS applications into the knowledge management environment for updating (if your CDS-related information systems do not provide adequate tools for this task).
- Use knowledge management tools suited to your needs, according to formal policies and procedures, to help manage CDS assets and processes.
- Utilize a collaboration environment that allows asynchronous discussion, capturing consensus, version-tracking and maintenance activities for knowledge management. The maintenance activities should be automated to facilitate content currency, for example, through notifications about content expiration dates. Explore ways to provide automated notification when underlying CDS content needs to change based on regulations, drug withdrawals, new strong clinical evidence and the like.
- Try to use standard medical vocabularies for tagging your CDS assets and available interoperability standards for moving them across systems (see Figures 3-3 and 3-4).
- Use tools that facilitate feedback on CDS interventions. Ideally, these can be accessed within the intervention so that end users do not need to use a separate application to provide feedback.
- Consider analytics-enabled approaches to generate new insights about clinical care and CDS effects from the clinical database, and use these to improve the delivery of care and CDS.
- Explore methods to share clinical content and strategies with other institutions to accelerate individual and collective progress toward priority objectives.

To help you determine how well your CDS knowledge management activities are performing, Figure 4-2 contains questions about your CDS content assets, as well as the processes for managing those assets, that your CDS program should

---

Figure 4-2: Questions That CDS Knowledge Management Programs Should Answer

CDS Content Assets

- What intervention types are deployed throughout your organization? (See Figure 5-5)
- How many of each type is deployed, and what domains/topics are covered?
- What are the attributes for each intervention (for example, as outlined in Figure 4-1)?
- Are the clinical information and recommendations consistent across interventions?
- Is there an appropriate balance of content that is developed locally, shared, obtained from free sources, and purchased from commercial vendors?
- Is available CDS content optimally leveraged to meet CDS goals given available CIS infrastructure?

Processes

- How do subject matter experts, CDS implementation staff, and others collaborate on determining and implementing CDS interventions and workflow modifications, and communicate about these with leadership and other stakeholders?
- How are individuals (such as subject matter experts) compensated for their role in developing and maintaining the knowledge assets (since this may affect quality/quantity of available expert input and will affect total CDS program costs)?
- Is there an audit trail for decisions about the content assets, and why and how they are made? Who maintains this trail, and how is that done?
- What tools are being used to manage the content asset repository (for example, applications for content authoring, storing, updating, editing and change tracking)? Who is responsible for these tools, and how are content versions managed?
- How is feedback from end users managed?

---

be should be able to answer. Not explicit in this figure—but covered in detail in the Chapter 3 Measurement section and in Chapter 9—is the 'punch line' question, "To what extent is your CDS content portfolio bringing your organization closer to its improvement goals?"

In addition to addressing these questions about the *portfolio overall*, your tracking tools and maintenance processes should document and address issues pertinent to *individual interventions*. Figure 4-1, presented earlier, highlights several key issues, and Worksheet 4-1 is a model for how you might begin to document this information.

CONSIDERATIONS FOR HOSPITALS/HEALTH SYSTEMS
Planning (Tasks)

- Approaches to CDS knowledge management have historically been best developed in large care organizations with the budgets, expertise, and

personnel to focus on these issues. Comprehensive knowledge management in this setting involves leveraging different parts of your organization—including the information systems department, medical staff committees, administrative personnel and structures—to work with the CDS Team to acquire, vet, implement, test, evaluate, and revise knowledge. Taking into account your organization's overall goals and objectives, you should establish administrative structures and a chain of command to evaluate and update knowledge periodically. You must task specific people or groups to carry out these evaluations and identify system and knowledge changes needed to keep up with system evolution and changes in clinical knowledge.

People (Stakeholder Involvement and Governance)

- Your organization may vest this responsibility in a single individual or committee, but more commonly, the responsibility is divided among several groups: an executive-level committee may hold final responsibility for reviewing changes to knowledge and approving them, while clinical staff committees in each department or service line may supervise knowledge in their own area and pass the results to the supervising executive, safety or clinical practice committee. In addition, you may charge the information systems department, or possibly its liaison with the clinical enterprise (such as a chief medical information officer) with establishing a schedule that monitors proposed changes to ISs. These include changes to terminologies, messaging formats, database schemas and user interfaces, and it must be determined if they will affect the ability of CDS-related systems (such as EHRs and CPOE modules), to execute deployed CDS interventions as expected.

- Your CDS knowledge management activities must account for the fact that in a large, diverse setting with a variety of clinical practice patterns and opinions regarding clinical knowledge and recommendations, consensus may be challenging. For example, it may take time and excellent facilitation skills to obtain agreement about content for a particular CDS intervention—especially when there is limited compelling clinical evidence to guide the approach. Even when there is strong evidence, representatives from different specialties may differ on how that evidence should be interpreted and applied in your setting.

- Finding ways to broadly connect all affected staff to your CDS content maintenance efforts can help ensure that the interventions will remain high quality, personally relevant and useful, and heeded. For example, good use of champions (as discussed in Chapter 2) and communication channels such as email updates, periodic newsletters and department meetings (as discussed in Chapters 2 and 8) can surface input about updating and other maintenance needs from stakeholders, as well as provide outgoing information to them about content updates and other changes to the CDS portfolio.

- There are many ways in which your hospital or health system can leverage internal and external sources in managing your CDS content portfolio. For instance, your hospital may contract with a CDS vendor for a subscription to inpatient order sets. At the same time, because it is a center of nursing excellence, hospital administration may leverage local expertise and innovation to build and maintain its own nursing protocols and care plans. Finally, as part of a consortium with other hospitals, your hospital may borrow executable alerts and reminders from other hospitals in the consortium and share its own content in return to spread out the cost of developing such interventions. In all cases though, the content will need some vetting to ensure content quality and local applicability before being put into production systems.

CONSIDERATIONS FOR SMALL PRACTICES

Your practice will likely be limited in human and financial resources for acquiring and maintaining CDS content and other knowledge management tasks. Nonetheless, a proactive and systematic CDS approach is essential for your CDS activities to achieve their performance improvement goals.

Planning (Processes)

- Your CDS Team should work with the practice to develop, document and apply a plan to ensure that your CDS intervention portfolio and related content remain current, accurate and appropriate. For example, you should ensure that alerts, order sets, documentation tools and the like remain consistent with the evolving medical knowledge base, as well as clinical and CDS best practices. They should of course also be aligned with office policies and clinician preferences to the extent possible and appropriate. EHR and CDS suppliers can help with this work through their policies, procedures, expertise and tools.

- Determine if your information system and CDS suppliers have an environment for sharing, and communicating with other practices about, CDS content and interventions. This can be helpful in local knowledge management efforts, but you should take care to ensure that material and experiences are applicable in your setting. Explore whether your REC has tools or approaches that can likewise support your knowledge management needs.

People (Stakeholder Involvement)

- Even though EHR and CDS suppliers will handle many content updating tasks, clinicians in your practice should play some role in monitoring deployed CDS interventions for appropriateness and currency. This helps reinforce that the CDS interventions and program are for achieving *shared* goals and increases clinician ownership in the CDS content, processes and results.
- Clinicians in your practice will typically track updated guidelines and new literature as part of ongoing professional competency and continuing education requirements.[19] You can leverage this work to support your CDS content maintenance activities. For example, practice clinicians—supported by your CDS Team—can establish formal processes to leverage their clinical knowledge surveillance activities to help monitor deployed intervention content and update these assets as needed.

Maintenance

- Make the CDS portfolio simple and easy to manage—for example, by focusing on interventions to address high-priority improvement needs (see goal and objective selection discussions in Chapters 2 and 5, respectively) and trying to get the most value from a limited number of content suppliers.
- In addition to (or as part of) CME-related content surveillance activities mentioned earlier,

monitor key sources for updates to guidelines and other information and interventions pertinent to your practice. This might include the CMS EHR Meaningful Use Overview website,[20] which contains pointers to CDS-related Meaningful Use requirements and specific condition-oriented organization's websites.[21] As you gain comfort and skill in this monitoring, you can track additional resources.

CONSIDERATIONS FOR HIT SOFTWARE PROVIDERS
Capabilities

- Provide user-friendly tools for providers to develop new CDS interventions and manage existing CDS content deployed in your systems. This is essential.
- Provide user-friendly tools for providers to track deployed CDS content in your systems. Consider pertinent intervention attributes that providers need to track (see Figure 4-1), especially who is responsible for maintaining the intervention and how long it has been since it has been updated or reviewed.
- Provide capability to export the clinical knowledge used in CDS interventions in a human-readable form so that any interested person can easily review the clinical logic used in any CDS intervention.[22]
- Provide standard Application Programming Interfaces (APIs) (such as for infobuttons) to support providers in using third-party content sources within your information systems.
- Follow—and engage as appropriate in—emerging national projects related to standardizing EHR interfaces to CDS content and national repositories and sharing services for CDS rules and other interventions (for example, ONC and AHRQ demonstration project referenced earlier).

WORKSHEET

Worksheet 4-1

CDS Knowledge Asset Inventory

In this chapter, we have recommended managing your deployed CDS interventions as a portfolio. In Figure 4-1, and other worksheets throughout this guidebook, we describe key data about one or more interventions that you might want to record and track.

There is no "right way" to monitor your CDS portfolio; this worksheet is intended to provide another sampling of variables you might consider using to create a working overview of your deployed CDS assets. Consider also other key dimensions outlined in this and previous chapters and needs you have uncovered in your own organization. Data to complete this worksheet will flow from your knowledge management activities and are also reflected in various other worksheets.

Asset Name	Source/ Entity Responsible for Review (Version)	Delivery System	Go-live Date (Action)	Date of Last Review	Date of Next Review/ Review Frequency	Target Population, Role, Location	Purpose of Intervention	Intervention Effects (Process/ Outcomes)	Actions/ Comments
Drug allergy alert trigger rules	CPOE alerts committee (v1)	CPOE	4/25	(none since launch)	5/25; annual	Prescriber entering orders for pediatric population in the wards	Eliminate preventable allergic reactions to drugs	Early feedback that triggering frequency is acceptable to end users; override rate 30%; outcome data pending	Continue close monitoring
Drug-drug interaction database	[commercial vendor]	CPOE, Pharmacy system	2/20	(none since launch)	2/20	Prescriber, pharmacist	Eliminate serious DDIs	Early feedback that triggering frequency is somewhat excessive; override rate 70%; outcome data pending	Task force to monitor and consider options for further refinement

REFERENCES

1 Wright A, Sittig DF, Ash JS, et al. Governance for clinical decision support: Case studies and recommended practices from leading institutions. *J Am Med Inform Assoc.* 2011 Mar 1; 18(2):187-194.

2 Payne TH, Hoey PJ, Nichol P, et al. Preparation and use of preconstructed orders, order sets, and order menus in a computerized provider order entry system. *J Am Med Inform Assoc.* 2003 Jul-Aug; 10(4):322-329. Epub 2003 Mar 28.

3 Wright A, Sittig DF, Carpenter JD, et al. Order sets in computerized physician order entry systems: An analysis of seven sites. AMIA Annu Symp Proc. 2010 Nov 13; 2010:892-896.

4 Never Events. AHRQ Patient Safety Network. Available online at: http://www.psnet.ahrq.gov/primer. aspx?primerID=3. Accessed June 24, 2011.

5 Kuperman GJ, Reichley RM, Bailey TC. Using commercial knowledge bases for clinical decision support: Opportunities, hurdles, and recommendations. *J Am Med Inform Assoc.* 2006 Jul-Aug; 13(4):369-371.

6 Wright A, Bates DW, Middleton B, et al. Creating and sharing clinical decision support content with Web 2.0: Issues and examples. *J Biomed Inform.* 2009 Apr; 42(2):334-346.

7 See ONC's CDS webpage: http://healthit.hhs.gov/portal/ server.pt/community/healthit_hhs_gov__cds/1218, especially the Advancing CDS project description. See also the SHARP C 2B project on the SHARP C webpage: http://www.uthouston.edu/nccd/projects.htm. Both accessed August 9, 2011.

8 See the AHRQ CDS Initiative website, especially the eRecommendation and CDS Demonstration initiatives: http://healthit.ahrq.gov/portal/server.pt/community/ ahrq-funded_projects/654/clinical_decision_support_ initiative/13665. Accessed August 9, 2011.

9 Greenes R, Bloomrosen M, Brown-Connolly NE, et al.The morningside initiative: Collaborative development of a knowledge repository to accelerate adoption of clinical decision support. *Open Med Inform J.* 2010; 4:278-290. Epub 2010 Dec 14.

10 Open Clinical: Knowledge Management for Medical Care. Available online at: http://www.openclinical.org/. Accessed June 24, 2011.

11 National Guideline Clearinghouse website: http://www. guideline.gov/. Accessed August 9, 2011.

12 MedlinePlus Connect webpage describing this service: http://www.nlm.nih.gov/medlineplus/connect/overview. html. Accessed August 9, 2011.

13 RAND Advancing CDS webpage: http://www.rand.org/ health/projects/clinical-decision-support.html (see 'Task 3'). Accessed June 26, 2011.

14 See AHRQ webpage describing the eRecommendations project: http://healthit.ahrq.gov/structuring_care_ recommendations_for_CDS. Accessed August 9, 2011.

15 Sittig DF, Wright A, Simonaitis L, et al. The state of the art in clinical knowledge management: An inventory of tools and techniques. *Int J Med Inform.* 2010 Jan; 79(1):44-57.

16 Wright A, Sittig DF, Ash JS, et al. Development and evaluation of a comprehensive clinical decision support taxonomy: Comparison of front-end tools in commercial and internally developed electronic health record systems. *J Am Med Inform Assoc.* 2011 May 1;b18(3):232-242.

17 Sittig DF, Wright A, Meltzer S, et al. Comparison of clinical knowledge management capabilities of commercially-available and leading internally-developed electronic health records. *BMC Med Inform Decis Mak.* 2011 Feb 17; 11:13.

18 Sittig DF, Campbell E, Guappone K, et al. Recommendations for onitoring and evaluation of in-patient Computer-based Provider Order Entry systems: Results of a Delphi survey. AMIA Annu Symp Proc. 2007 Oct 11: 671-675.

19 See, for example, the American Medical Association's webpage for the Physician's Recognition Award (PRA), which outlines widely accepted continuing medical education activities: http://www.ama-assn.org/ama/pub/ about-ama/awards/ama-physicians-recognition-award.page. Accessed August 10, 2011.

20 CMS EHR Meaningful Use Overview website: http:// www.cms.gov/EHRIncentivePrograms/30_Meaningful_ Use.asp#TopOfPage. See especially Meaningful Use Specificiation Sheets. Accessed August 10, 2011.

21 See, for example, practice guidelines and other CDS-related information on the American Diabetes Association webpage: http://www.diabetes.org/. Note especially the 'For Professionals' page and links to 'Clinical Practice Recommendations' and 'Professional Resources' pages from this page. Accessed August 10, 2011.

22 Sittig DF, Wright A, Ash JS, et al. A set of preliminary standards recommended for achieving a national repository of clinical decision support interventions. AMIA Annu Symp Proc. 2009 Nov 14; 614-618.

Part II

Selecting, Configuring and Implementing CDS Interventions

Hope is not a strategy.
—Original author unknown

Chapter 1 presented several examples where CDS efforts failed to show benefit, and even caused harm. Such undesirable results are not uncommon, and they are much more likely to occur when implementers do not appropriately follow all the steps that are necessary to select, configure, test and deploy CDS interventions in a goal-oriented fashion.

Chapters 5 through 9 in Part II provide detailed guidance on the steps necessary to ensure that your organization's target-focused CDS efforts achieve specific, desired objectives. As outlined in Figure PII-1, these chapters cover building a shared understanding with stakeholders about specific CDS-enabled improvement strategies and optimal targets; selecting, configuring, testing and deploying CDS interventions for maximum usability, acceptance, and impact; and finally, measuring and improving the results.

Part I and Part II go hand-in-hand. It is important to select and design individual CDS objectives and interventions properly, and this requires an appropriate organizational context—a CDS program—that supplies necessary governance structures, stakeholder engagement, technology infrastructure and other core capabilities as outlined in Part I.

We continue in this Part II Introduction with the community hospital and small practice case studies presented in the Part I Introduction. Here we illustrate how these organizations build on the CDS program foundation they established (as described in Part I) to select, deploy and evaluate CDS interventions to address specific improvement goals.

Again, these scenarios bring to life the guidance presented in the chapters, and you can refer to them before, while, or after you work through the corresponding chapter materials. Each scenario section is introduced by a "Task" that relates to the material presented in the chapters. These headings help make explicit the key points that are being illustrated.

CASE STUDY FOR HOSPITALS: REDUCING POTENTIALLY PREVENTABLE INPATIENT VTE INCIDENCE

Select the targets for which your intervention package will be focused; understand the fundamental CDS intervention elements, including the CDS Five Rights and the ten basic intervention types.

Having determined the care process for VTE-at-risk patients and published a general guideline for VTE prophylaxis at Grandview Hospital, the QI Team began working directly with the CDS Committee to tackle the job of incorporating this knowledge into a process that made it 'easy to do the right thing.' Although they had worked hard to achieve consensus for the guideline from surgical and medical services, the team realized it was unlikely that overburdened doctors would remember the consensus decisions or reference the guideline—even when it was posted in a highly visible area. Somehow these recommendations had to be incorporated into the workflow so that the necessary information for any given step would be presented just at the time it was needed.

By reviewing the process maps developed by the quality department, together with subsequent joint brainstorming, representatives from the CDS Committee and QI Team were able to identify the most effective points in the process—and personnel involved—where CDS interventions would be valuable (see Figure 6-1). The group understood that improvements would be more likely if participants in the care processes process 'owned' the workflow changes and were held accountable for better results.

In meetings that followed the workflow mapping, the CDS Committee identified other issues where CDS could bring value in supporting VTE treatment, such as interventions to assist with the transition from intravenous heparin to oral warfarin, or monitoring unfractionated heparin effects. However, they agreed that focusing initially on the imperative to improve VTE prophylaxis rates—and deferring other CDS opportunities at this time—

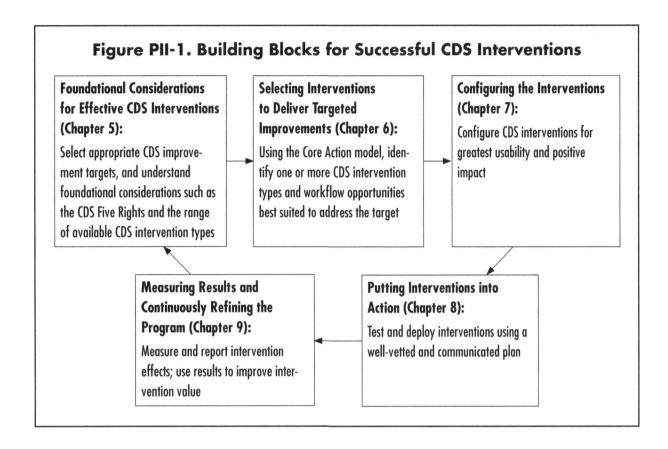

Figure PII-1. Building Blocks for Successful CDS Interventions

Foundational Considerations for Effective CDS Interventions (Chapter 5):
Select appropriate CDS improvement targets, and understand foundational considerations such as the CDS Five Rights and the range of available CDS intervention types

Selecting Interventions to Deliver Targeted Improvements (Chapter 6):
Using the Core Action model, identify one or more CDS intervention types and workflow opportunities best suited to address the target

Configuring the Interventions (Chapter 7):
Configure CDS interventions for greatest usability and positive impact

Measuring Results and Continuously Refining the Program (Chapter 9):
Measure and report intervention effects; use results to improve intervention value

Putting Interventions into Action (Chapter 8):
Test and deploy interventions using a well-vetted and communicated plan

would increase the likelihood that the initial CDS interventions would be well received and would effectively address top priority concerns. This success could then provide a solid foundation for important add-on efforts to better support VTE-related care. The group selected as their CDS focus initial VTE risk assessment and prophylaxis ordering on admission and during care transitions, based on this generic workflow:

- Identify patients at risk;
- Select prophylactic regimen;
- Order and administer selected prophylaxis.

After much discussion, the QI Team concluded that physicians should perform the initial risk assessment upon admission or following surgery, evaluate the patient for contraindications, and order the appropriate prophylaxis. However, to achieve high reliability in the process, they focused on redundant processes, including having nurses conduct a daily risk-assessment to identify any changes in each patient's VTE risk. Lastly, using reports generated by the pharmacy system, the pharmacy department would review patients who were not on any VTE prophylaxis. These redundant safety layers—built into physician, nurse and pharmacy workflows—would ensure that they achieved their initial goal to have greater than 90 percent of patients receive appropriate VTE prophylaxis. Having determined the desired processes and pertinent players, the CDS Committee now needed to develop the CDS tools to facilitate these processes.

Determine which intervention types to use based on the core action type, information handling, and clinical workflow that you need to affect. Consider the different intervention types and their properties, with special attention to ease of deployment, acceptability to the clinical users, and impact on achieving the objective.

Hospitalist Goldsmith, the physician lead, and the CDS Committee began considering CDS interventions to support the key VTE prophylaxis steps on which they were focusing. This involved selecting approaches that were most likely to be effective and easiest to implement, given available infrastructure.

After some initial exploratory work on their own, the CDS Committee then engaged front-line staff to help develop the intervention—seeking out not only those they knew would be excited about the performance improvement initiative, but also those they suspected might be resistant to process changes.

In their meetings, hospitalist/physician lead Goldsmith and the CDS Committee outlined the key steps they would follow in selecting and developing their VTE prophylaxis CDS intervention package, many of which had already been started:

1. Identify VTE prophylaxis rates as an improvement priority—create the proverbial "burning platform" to garner institutional support.

2. Identify champions and form a team specific to the VTE intervention.

3. Get baseline data, care process map and identify areas for improvement.

4. Set aggressive but realistic goals.

5. Review evidence, guidelines, and best practices for VTE prophylaxis, and analyze gaps between Grandview's actual and desired performance.

6. Define, with meaningful frontline staff involvement, an intervention package to close gaps between current and desired VTE prophylaxis practices.

7. Present this CDS plan to committees (such as medical staff, hospital performance improvement and others); get their formal approval.

8. Start and quickly iterate PDSA (Plan-Do-Study-Act) cycles* to develop the interventions, and release them when there is broad agreement that they will be used and useful.

9. Monitor intervention effects with both process and outcome measures; recognize work-arounds, and identify appropriate protocol deviations—revising the protocol when necessary.

10. Define mechanisms whereby the CDS Committee and others can ensure that results from ongoing monitoring can be translated into needed enhancements. Recognize that intervention launch is more a beginning than an end (as the IT department might understandably want it to be); more effort will likely be required for maintenance than was required to prepare the intervention package for launch.

11. Keep a sharp focus on the CDS end goal—substantially better VTE prophylaxis rates (and correspondingly lower preventable VTE incidence)—in efforts to increase CDS intervention use and effectiveness.

Since their process improvement approach involved different workflow points for different care team members (as is typically required for complex targets such as this one), the CDS Committee recognized that it would take multiple CDS interventions to achieve their goals. Grandview's CDS Committee took a systematic approach to selecting these interventions, relying on an approach outlined in a guidebook for CDS implementers (see Chapter 6, especially Figures 6-2, 6-3 and discussion that follows under "Deciding among Several Available Intervention Types," as well as Worksheets 6-1 through 6-3).

This process led to two interventions that the CDS Committee agreed to develop initially: a VTE prophylaxis order set and a real-time unit-based 'dashboard' of VTE prophylaxis.

Figures PII-2 and PII-3 illustrate intervention package configuration worksheets that the CDS Committee developed for its VTE prophylaxis CDS efforts (including subsequent steps beyond the initial interventions they considered as described earlier). The diagram in PII-2 helped the CDS Committee visualize where in workflow their VTE prophylaxis CDS interventions would intervene and what intervention type might be most useful at each step. The table in Figure PII-3 helped them to discuss and specify the interventions in greater detail so that the essential questions (who, what, when, where, how and why?) were apparent throughout the intervention package development, deployment and enhancement.

Design interventions, by taking into account the many design strategy nuances that are

---

* See "How to Improve" webpage on the Institute for Healthcare Improvement website: http://www.ihi.org/knowledge/Pages/HowtoImprove/default.aspx. Accessed August 16, 2011.

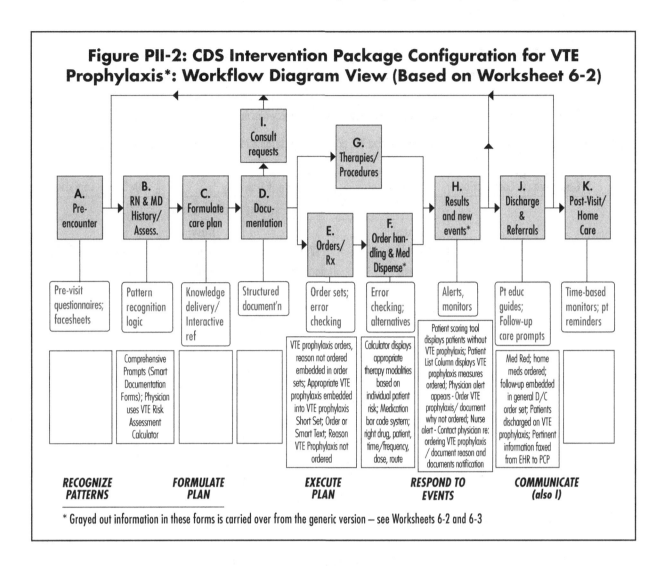

Figure PII-2: CDS Intervention Package Configuration for VTE Prophylaxis*: Workflow Diagram View (Based on Worksheet 6-2)

* Grayed out information in these forms is carried over from the generic version — see Worksheets 6-2 and 6-3

important for usability and functionality, begin to validate and vet the intervention with key stakeholders.

This CDS Committee began developing the CPOE order set using the published guideline as reference. An initial version was created in a checklist format with embedded recommendations, depending on which items were checked. This would allow decision branches to present appropriate orders based on the specific patient's risk level. For example, if a patient was identified as 'low risk,' a secondary query was launched showing the user a VTE-risk factors list to ensure that the patient was actually low risk. The order set incorporated the risk assessment scheme the VTE PI Team developed (low risk, moderate/high risk, and very high risk) and then presented appropriate treatment choices with

an option to order the treatment directly from the list. The order set also had the ability to document contraindications to VTE prophylaxis and addressed specific patient populations—such as those with renal disease—that require different pharmacologic options. Realizing that they could not include every circumstance in which the typical VTE prophylaxis approach should be modified, they focused on making the order set appropriate for 80% of patients. The order set provided opportunities to deviate from the recommended protocol when necessary and allowed the reasons to be documented.

After obtaining appropriate buy-in and approvals, the CDS Team submitted the written order set to the IT department to develop into the first electronic version. IT delivered this electronic order set back to the committee for review on schedule,

Figure PII-3: VTE Prophylaxis: CDS Intervention Package Configuration, Table View (Based on Worksheet 6-3)

Current Performance: 45% of inpatients receive *any* VTE prophylaxis when indicated; 25% receive *appropriate* prophylaxis

Target Performance: >90% of inpatients receive VTE prophylaxis according to hospital consensus protocol

Objective	Core Action	Workflow	Content Delivery		Delivery Logistics	
			CDS Five Rights dimensions			
		When[1] (Workflow Step)	What (Information)	How[2] (Intervention Type)	Who[3] (Person)	Where[4] (Channel)
	Recognize patterns	Pre-encounter **A**	Demographics, conditions, care gaps, self-progress	Per Worksheet 6-1	Patient, admin, case manager	PHR/ Registry/ EHR
	Recognize patterns/ formulate plan of care	RN & MD history/assess **B**	History/Physical data, medications, prior data review, inferred conditions		Nurse/ physician	EHR, flowsheets, data facesheets
VTE risk assessment			Answers to comprehensive prompts enable some fields within VTE risk calculator to autopopulate	Comprehensive prompts (smart documentation forms)	Nurse	EHR
Appropriate VTE prophylaxis			Calculator displays appropriate therapy modalities based on individual patient risk	VTE risk assessment clinical calculator (relevant data summaries)	Physician	EHR
	Formulate Plan of Care	Formulate Care Plan **C**	Guidance on best-practice approach to workup and management		Nurse/ physician/ patient	EHR, smart reference, shared decision making
	Execute Plan	Documentation **D**	Appropriate and complete documentation of observations, assessment, plan		Physician/ nurse	EHR (Clinical docu. tools)
	Execute Plan	Orders/Rx **E**	Appropriate, correct and complete orders for evaluation and therapy		Physician/ prescriber	CPOE, eprescribing

Figure PII-3 *continued*

Objective	Core Action	Workflow	Content Delivery			Delivery Logistics	
			CDS Five Rights dimensions				
		When[1] (Workflow Step)	**What** (Information)	**How[2]** (Intervention Type)	**Who[3]** (Person)	**Where[4]** (Channel)	
Adherence to standards of care by making the right thing the easiest to do			VTE prophylaxis orders, reason not ordered embedded into admission order sets	Order sets	Physician	CPOE	
			Appropriate VTE prophy-laxis measures embedded into VTE prophylaxis short set	Order sets	Physician	CPOE	
			Order or smart text: reason VTE prophylaxis not ordered	Order sets; smart documen-tation form	Physician	CPOE/EHR	
	Execute plan	Order handling and med dispensing F	Safety and appro-priateness checks on medications and other diagnostic and therapeutic interventions		Physician/ nurse/ pharma-cist/ other clinicians/ patient	EHR/ CPOE/ pharmacy system/ medication dispensing and admin systems	
Pharmacy and/or nursing inter-vention(s)			Patient scoring tool displays patients without VTE prophylaxis	Relevant data summary	Nurse/ pharmacist	CPOE/EHR	
			Patient list column displays VTE prophylaxis measures ordered	Relevant data summary	Nurse/ pharmacist	CPOE/EHR	
			Calculator displays appro-priate therapy modalities based on individual patient risk	Relevant data summary	Nurse/ pharmacist	CPOE/EHR	
Prevent errors of commission			Medication bar code system: right drug, patient, time/frequency, dose, route	Alerts	Nurse	BCMA	

Figure PII-3 *continued*

Objective	Core Action	Workflow	Content Delivery		Delivery Logistics	
			CDS Five Rights dimensions			
		When[1] (Workflow Step)	**What** (Information)	**How[2]** (Intervention Type)	**Who[3]** (Person)	**Where[4]** (Channel)
	Execute plan	Therapies/ procedures **G**	Reference information and relevant data pertinent to safe and effective procedures and techniques		Physician/ nurse/ other clinicians	Reference tools, EHR modules
	Respond to events	Results and new events **H**	Inferred hazards and improvement opportunities from lab and imaging results		Physician/ nurse/ patient	EHR/PHR, HIE, alerting devices
Prevent errors of omission			If VTE prophylaxis not ordered or reason not documented within eighteen hours post admission: Physician alert Order VTE prophylaxis/ document why not ordered; Nurse alert appears Contact attending physician regarding VTE prophylaxis/documenting why not ordered Nurse documents notification in "Physician Notification Flowsheet" row	Relevant data summary (flowsheet, highlight problems) filtered reference information and knowledge tools (for results interpretation)	Physician/ nurse	EHR
	Communicate	Consult requests **I**	Guidance on appropriate use of consultation and best exchange of information to/from consultant		Physician	EHR, HIE, reference tools (referral guidance)

Figure PII-3 *continued*

Objective	Core Action	Workflow	Content Delivery		Delivery Logistics	
			CDS Five Rights dimensions			
		When[1] (Workflow Step)	**What** (Information)	**How[2]** (Intervention Type)	**Who[3]** (Person)	**Where[4]** (Channel)
	Communicate	Discharge & referrals **J**	Discharge instructions, medication instructions, home care and continuing care information		Physician/ nurse/ patient	Discharge modules, medication reconcilia- tion apps
Prevent errors of omission			EHR medication reconcili- ation; home medications ordered to include VTE chemoprophylaxis if appropriate	Order sets	Nurse	EHR
			Patient discharge instruc- tions to include handouts generated from EHR	Reference infor- mation, relevant data summary	Nurse	EHR
			Follow-up embedded into discharge order set	Order set	Nurse	EHR
			Patients discharged on VTE chemoprophylaxis; pertinent information faxed from EHR to PCP	Relevant data summary	Nurse	EHR
	Respond to events	Post-visit/ home care **K**	Patient guidance on self-care, data gathering for condition monitor- ing; abnormal conditions requiring attention		Patient/ caregiver, case manager, visiting nurse	PHR, online portal, smart pillbox, home data monitors

since they had been engaged early in the planning and were able to allocate necessary development staff when needed. The formatting and flow were signifi- cantly changed in going from the paper version to the CPOE version, and it required several iterations between the CDS Team and the IT staff to render

the order set in the CPOE system in a manner con- sistent with the clinical intent.

After multiple revisions over several weeks, the order set was then presented to clinical providers outside the development team for feedback. This review uncovered new areas that were considered confusing to front-line clinicians and new patient populations that were not addressed with the original order set. After these issues were addressed, the order set was ready to be piloted in real patient care on a small scale, with the goal to broaden its use over time and after addressing any additional user feedback. Physician lead, Dr. Goldsmith, took on additional responsibility as the 'intervention owner' for the order set, and her contact information was placed on the CPOE order set form to reinforce project team accountability and encourage user feedback.

After the order set was developed, the CDS Committee began work on how it would be appropriately triggered and used for patient care. They embedded the order set into all admission, post-operative and transfer order sets—and removed all other references to VTE in other order sets—to help ensure that a carefully developed and vetted management approach was consistently applied.

In preparing to go live with the order set, the CDS Committee considered ways to monitor its utilization and effectiveness. They decided that "Effectiveness" would be based on whether order set use led to the appropriate risk assessment and VTE prophylaxis choice. "Utilization" would be measured by the percentage of admitted patients who had the order set activated for use by the ordering clinician. The team anticipated different potential monitoring results, for example, that the order set could be highly utilized but not effective. Alternatively, it might be highly effective but underutilized. Each potential scenario would require a different CDS Committee response. The team met with the IT department to determine how best to gather and process these data, which led to interactions with other departments where these data are manually abstracted and generated. The goal moving forward would be to automate process and outcome data collection for this order set intervention, as well as other interventions the CDS Committee launches.

The next intervention in the CDS Committee's initial VTE CDS package was the real-time dashboard for reviewing patients not on pharmacologic prophylaxis. The goal here was to create ongoing situational awareness about which patients in each Grandview unit were—or were not—on appropriate prophylaxis. Meetings were held with the IT and pharmacy departments to build a report viewable by any EHR user and categorized by floor and medical service—building on the lessons learned from the related work on measuring order set use and effects. For example, the dashboard intervention included modules to assess each patient's VTE risk and to query the EHR to identify patients already receiving anticoagulants or mechanical treatments to prevent VTE.

End users and others engaged in developing the VTE dashboard emphasized that it had to be very simple to understand and use. The consensus was that the best approach would be to categorize patients on the display into three groups identified by colored boxes next to their names and room numbers: red boxes next to patients with no pharmacologic prophylaxis and no known contraindication; yellow boxes for patients with no pharmacologic prophylaxis with contraindications or those considered 'low risk'; and finally, green boxes for those on appropriate pharmacologic prophylaxis. This report would be automated and run in real time, with the results displayed along with other quality indicators on a large screen easily visible to nursing and physicians on the floor (but not visible to others, in accordance with patient privacy regulations).

In addition to putting much thought and user input into *designing* the intervention itself, the CDS Committee likewise invested heavily in crafting the role-specific workflows associated with *using* the dashboard. For example, they developed mechanisms to ensure that the right person responded in the proper fashion to gaps highlighted in the dashboard so that these gaps were closed before adversely affecting patient care. For example, the CDS Committee and clinical stakeholders decided together that each floor's charge nurse and pharmacist would take primary responsibility for monitoring this list and contacting providers for any patients who fell in the 'red zone.'

Develop and execute intervention deployment plan.

After six months of preparation and development work, the committee was finally ready to implement its two new clinical decision support interventions: (1) a VTE-prophylaxis order set containing a risk-assessment tool; and (2) a real-time unit-based VTE-prophylaxis dashboard. Early on, the committee communicated key information about the projects—covering key questions about the interventions including "why, what, when, who, how, where." They used multiple channels to generate interest and engagement including newsletters, hospital committee meetings, and rich communications facilitated by 'clinician champions' who had been engaged early in the project as additional liaisons between the project team and frontline staff. They also shared with each floor the patient audit results, including prophylaxis rates compared to other floors and national benchmarks. They widely publicized their stretch goal of greater than 90 percent appropriate prophylaxis while ensuring it was aligned with unit-based goals and incentive plans.

The committee decided to pilot the two interventions on one floor each for two weeks to get feedback in a real work environment before hospital-wide rollout. The medicine unit began using the admission order set, and the orthopedics floor launched the real-time dashboard. Clinical leader Goldsmith set up feedback sessions with the hospitalist group after one week of using the order set and worked with IT to incorporate their revisions into the order set. The team also solicited feedback from nursing on the assessment processes and on usability issues. Order set ease of use and presentation clarity became major focus areas after several pilot users reported that they found the order set overwhelming and confusing to navigate. Group discussion among the project team and frontline users surfaced ideas for better formatting, for example, using larger headers to introduce each order set section, and organizing the order set into clearly identified 'steps.' For example: "Step 1: Determine your patient's risk level;" "Step 2: Review contraindication list." These steps were followed by relevant information or orders.

The dashboard pilot went pretty smoothly. Nursing and physician staff liked having the information display visible at the nursing station in the location and orientation that had been carefully planned during the prelaunch work. Everyone was pleased that stories recounting immediate action taken on patients who were in the 'red' had already begun to surface and spread among staff on and beyond the pilot floor.

Some glitches surfaced too during the dashboard pilot, but fortunately they were quickly identified and straightforward to fix—thanks to careful monitoring (including directly observing the dashboard's use in action) by the CDS Team and close collaboration with other intervention stakeholders. For example, some patients did not have contraindications to pharmacologic prophylaxis adequately documented, so the display showed them as 'red'—even though withholding these drugs was clinically appropriate. The team worked with orthopedic physicians to develop and implement documentation forms that captured contraindications better, and with IT to use these forms in the dashboard display algorithm to ensure that patients for whom anticoagulants were contraindicated were not displayed red. These patients were, however, displayed as yellow so they could be closely monitored for status changes.

The CDS Committee set a date to deploy both the order set and dashboard house-wide, and developed plans to expand intervention effect-monitoring and stakeholder communications accordingly. They also provided in-service programs to educate nurses, physicians and pharmacy staff about the new tools. This included sharing anecdotes (outlined earlier) about successes and lessons learned during the pilot launches, reinforcing that this performance improvement project was a collaborative effort. On launch day, the EHR displayed a message on the system login screen to alert users that the new tools were available.

In the first month, the CDS Committee made sure that there were extra staff available to monitor and support post-launch use. Frequent 'rounds' on the floors by CDS Team members created a good communication channel whereby team members could receive feedback about the interventions. This included asking frontline staff if the tools met their needs and if there were any new issues the team needed to address to ensure optimal intervention use and usefulness. The CDS Team made an extra effort to appear (and actually be) receptive to feedback provided spontaneously by staff, as well as to seek out issues not verbalized but uncovered just by monitoring workflow. Through this enhanced presence, the team responded to many user questions, provided pointers on optimizing intervention use and value, and made additional minor changes to the order set and dashboard display to smooth out additional rough edges that surfaced. They continued intensive communication, education and awareness programs through the first month post-launch, while the quality department began executing plans to formally track outcomes and process measures.

Use a formal plan for identifying, tracking, measuring and addressing intended and unintended intervention behavior and effects.

The VTE QI Team was now ready to put into action the plan they had developed (in collaboration with the CDS Team, IT and other departments) for a quality dashboard to display the VTE prophylaxis performance metrics they had agreed upon earlier. The quality dashboard presented monthly "run charts" to monitor process and outcomes measures, such as order set utilization rates, appropriate VTE prophylaxis rate and the frequency of preventable VTE. The team also implemented plans to measure order set effectiveness through chart reviews by pharmacists to see if clinicians selected the appropriate risk level and corresponding orders. These measures were helpful for a pay-for-performance agreement that Grandview and insurers had arranged.

One month after launch, the committee found encouraging signs that the order set was delivering desired results: when used, 95 percent of patients received appropriate prophylaxis. However, clinicians were using the order set, on average, for only 50 percent of patients, and in some services, this use was less than 10 percent. Physician lead Goldsmith met

with services that had low utilization to investigate the causes. During her meeting with neurosurgery staff, she learned that they were concerned that the order set didn't adequately address patients with epidural catheters. These surgeons felt that the order set would expose these patients to specific blood thinners that, although they can prevent VTE, would carry unacceptable neurological risks. Working with the neurosurgery department, the CDS Team and IT staff were able to modify the order set to account appropriately for this patient population. Everyone was pleased to see prophylaxis rates rise toward targets on this service as a result.

These conversations with 'low order set utilizers'—and subsequent order set revisions informed by available clinical evidence and Grandview clinician consensus—continued until the order set was used for more than 90 percent of patients. The time and re-work required for these 'post-launch' revisions reinforced for the CDS Team that more broadly engaging affected stakeholders *during the planning process* was much more efficient. Although they had done significant outreach during intervention development, they agreed to substantially intensify these efforts early in their next major CDS initiative.

Quality dashboards for specific floors showed a significant increase in appropriate prophylaxis rates in the two months after launch, but then there was a gradual decline. Observations and stakeholder conversations uncovered that some floors had stopped following established response procedures for patients flagged as yellow and red on the VTE prophylaxis dashboard. Staffing shortages made it easier to overlook this important work. Following through on its commitment to transparency in achieving shared VTE prevention goals, the hospital staff and physicians agreed that each floor's VTE prophylaxis rates would be published in a monthly report. This triggered competition among floors and increasing VTE prophylaxis rates.

The VTE QI Team assumed ongoing responsibility for monitoring and improving VTE prophylaxis rates. The CDS Committee planned to formally re-evaluate the VTE CDS tools on a yearly basis, while continuing more rapid improvement cycles until they worked out all the initial kinks. This annual evaluation would ensure (in collaboration with the VTE QI Team) that the interventions remained consistent with the evidence base and best practices for VTE prevention. It would also check for needed revisions based on other factors such as new information system functionality, clinical workflows or other changes suggesting a need to modify the interventions. The VTE QI Team and CDS Committee also established protocols for reacting quickly to any major interim changes to clinical knowledge, workflows or systems that would require revisiting the VTE CDS interventions.

At the end of the first year post-launch for the two CDS interventions, the VTE QI and CDS Teams met to comprehensively evaluate and address the VTE-related performance data. The teams were very pleased to recap that VTE prophylaxis was being used appropriately in 85 percent of patients in Grandview—a dramatic increase from the 25 percent benchmark where they started! The order set was being used in more than 90 percent of admissions and preventable VTE rates had dropped by 20 percent. In addition, all floors reported increased staff efficiencies resulting from the VTE prophylaxis dashboard bringing together and processing important information needed for clinical decision making. These compelling results had required significant time, energy and financial resources but played an important role in addressing Grandview's mission (which includes striving for the safest possible care delivered efficiently), and financial strength (through CDS-enhanced compensation from the pay-for-performance program).

But the work wasn't finished (and never is for deployed interventions). The knowledge management protocol established for the VTE CDS interventions triggered the CDS and VTE QI Teams to review the evidence underlying the order set. A Grandview medical librarian worked with the groups on a literature search to identify any new practice-changing clinical guidelines or evidence.

They also performed a financial analysis to ensure that any medication choices were the most cost-effective ones available. The review determined that very few changes were necessary. After these changes were made and approved, the order set's formal review/approval date was updated. Physician lead Goldsmith agreed to continue for another year as the order set's owner, and she entered a reminder in her calendar to initiate next year's formal VTE intervention review. The VTE prophylaxis dashboard intervention was likewise reviewed for content, workflow and technical issues; no concerns or new improvement opportunities were identified. It too was scheduled for another formal review the following year.

This effort to apply CDS in addressing an organizational improvement imperative—decreasing hospital-acquired VTEs by dramatically increasing appropriate VTE prophylaxis rates—touched many people, processes and technologies in the Grandview organization. The CDS Committee and the quality improvement staff developed important new performance improvement skills, processes and collaborations. For example, they became much more facile leveraging functionality within their information systems to enhance care processes. More importantly, they learned to combine these capabilities with change management approaches aligned with the Grandview culture in ways that made a measurable difference for its patients and staff. Executing this project successfully built the CDS Committee's confidence—and credibility within the hospital leadership and frontline staff—and laid a strong foundation for future CDS-enhanced performance improvement initiatives. In fact, the VTE prophylaxis CDS results and experiences were discussed in many pertinent hospital committees, and there was widespread agreement to apply this learning to other organizational priorities. Facing this increasing visibility and demand, the CDS Committee began developing with the hospital executive and medical staff committees an approach to prioritize where else it would focus its efforts going forward.

CASE STUDY FOR SMALL PRACTICES: IMPROVING DIABETES CONTROL IN THE OUTPATIENT SETTING

Select the targets for which your intervention package will be focused; understand the fundamental intervention elements, including the CDS Five Rights and the ten basic intervention types.

The Elm Heights Vision for CDS-enhanced performance improvement had taken hold nicely with the practice. Work by the CDS Team (PI leader Dr. Franks, nurse Beck, and practice manager Matthews) to understand and enhance capabilities and infrastructure to address improvement opportunities made everyone eager to dig in on a specific CDS project. Franks and Beck led a brainstorming session on this topic at a practice meeting. They began by reviewing the Elm Heights Vision document and considering how its elements could be used to advance specific clinical, operational and financial aspirations outlined in the practice's business plan.

They discussed disease-management targets used by the local Physician Hospital Organization, a quality improvement process used by one of the local payers and the local hospital's process-improvement activities. The group understood that to improve outcomes for chronic conditions, multiple therapies and preventative screenings are often necessary—but that implementing multiple new CDS interventions for each one may be too taxing considering the limited resources.

The Elm Heights clinicians discussed three chronic conditions prevalent within their practice, each a high priority for CDS support: asthma, diabetes and chronic heart failure. They chose diabetes care as their initial CDS focus. This decision was driven by an anecdotal sense that there was a substantial care process and outcome improvement opportunity here and that given emerging initiatives from their payers, there could be significant financial upside from doing better with these patients (see Figures 5-1 and 5-2).

PI leader Franks pointed out that better data on their actual performance would be very helpful for subsequent CDS target prioritization and selection rounds and would be critical for their diabetes CDS work. She noted that the CDS Team had anticipated these issues, and work was underway with their EHR vendor to ensure that Elm Heights would have ready access to the process and outcome data they needed for their improvement efforts.

After discussing diabetes care dimensions on which they could focus—patient lifestyle modifications, blood pressure and lipid control, among many others—they decided to concentrate CDS efforts initially on optimizing glycemic control. They believed that the needed lab test information would be readily available and that making headway against this target would be valuable to the patients and practice.

Diving down further into specific objectives they could address with CDS interventions, they noted that effective glycemic control requires several steps, such as ensuring that HbA1c is measured in each diabetic patient at an appropriate interval, that abnormal results are recognized and attended to, and that effective therapies to reduce elevated levels are appropriately instituted and monitored. Recounting advice from a colleague in a small practice with a highly effective CDS-enhanced diabetes care program, PI leader Franks suggested that the practice first seek a "small win" to build skills and momentum before attacking more—and more complex—objectives.

The practice's emphasis on population management led naturally to a decision to begin by harnessing CDS interventions to ensure that each patient had HbA1c levels checked and documented at intervals recommended by authoritative clinical guidelines. This would provide a strong foundation for subsequent efforts to reduce abnormal levels across *all* patients. In addition, the needed laboratory test data were relatively easy to obtain (now that the lab interface was in place, thanks to the CDS Team's earlier analysis and work). CDS approaches seemed at first glance to be straightforward, and the measurements and improvements would position the practice well for increased reimbursement from payers' reporting and improvement programs. Though it would add complexity and therefore make success more difficult, they also agreed that this initial CDS effort must include interventions to ensure that abnormal HbA1c results didn't 'fall through the cracks.'

There were differing opinions initially about the HbA1c threshold that should trigger notification. Some wanted any abnormal value to trigger alerting in order to help drive levels across the entire population into the normal range. PI leader Dr. Franks suggested that this would likely lead to 'over-alerting' since many abnormal results were likely already known to the clinician—and building the ability to detect this into the rule would be difficult. Further, the practice's limited resources required that they carefully prioritize where they would focus their attention. The group agreed to make the HbA1c notification threshold 9.0 mg%, which corresponds to the value used in a measure they will use for performance reporting.

Another physician in the group noted that more patients could be helped by using CDS to ensure that critical elements of effective diabetes care (e.g., having a care plan for each patient) were in place for every patient with diabetes. It was agreed that this warranted further consideration but that finding and addressing significantly abnormal HbA1c levels was an appropriate focus for this first major CDS effort. Everyone left the meeting excited that they had agreed upon very specific and important targets for their CDS efforts and that, if successful, they could realize significant clinical, operational and financial rewards.

In a follow-up meeting, the CDS Team began considering in broad terms how they might approach using CDS to address their HbA1c measurement and notification objectives. They noted that there are multiple actors in the underlying care processes (including the patient, physician, nurse and others). Further, different information systems presenting information through various CDS intervention types at appropriate workflow points could help make sure

these objectives were accomplished (see the CDS Five Rights sidebar, Chapter 5). To lay a foundation for intervention development to follow, the CDS Team members began informal conversations with other practice members about how these CDS Five Rights dimensions were currently being utilized in caring for diabetic patients (for example, by using paper-based patient handouts about diabetes management issues, such as the need for regular HbA1c testing) and what improvement opportunities might exist.

From their earlier work to assess and enhance their CDS capabilities, the CDS Team knew that they had a rich—though far from perfect—toolkit for configuring CDS interventions to leverage these dimensions. They brushed up on available CDS intervention types (see Figure 5-5 and text that follows that figure) in preparation for making sure that they fully leveraged these capabilities in their information systems when they began planning their enhanced CDS approach to glycemic monitoring and control.

The CDS Team also revisited the assessment capabilities and specific metrics they would need to drive and track their progress. For example, they would need to identify individual patients at risk of becoming overdue (or actually overdue) for HbA1c testing to drive corresponding CDS interventions, and report—for the practice overall and for each physician—the percent of patients whose testing is in compliance with recommendations. Likewise, they would need metrics to identify and report patients with HbA1c levels above the threshold and, ideally, information about whether and how these abnormal levels were addressed. Eventually, metrics such as average HbA1c across all diabetic patients in the practice—and how this and other outcome measures track over time—would be important. They researched how other practices were handling these issues and found some compelling models for measurements and interventions.* Since a health information exchange (HIE) was forming in their

---

* See, for example, the Southeast Texas Medical Associates (SETMA) webpage, "Public Reporting of Provider Performance on Quality Measures" (http://www.setma.com/PublicReporting.cfm - accessed August 18, 2011), as well as links from the "Public Reporting" tab on this webpage to further details on SETMA physician performance on diabetes and other measures, and CDS interventions used in the SETMA practice to enhance performance on these measures.

community, they agreed to keep an eye on how that infrastructure might help them track important data related to their diabetes and other CDS efforts.

Determine which intervention types to use based on the core action type, information handling and clinical workflow that you need to affect. Consider the different intervention types and their properties, with special attention to ease of deployment, acceptability to the clinical users and impact on achieving the objective.

Conversations with other practices farther along in applying CDS to diabetes care, in light of the CDS Five Rights framework, had prepared the CDS Team for the possibility that they might ultimately need several CDS interventions working together as a "package" to fully address individual improvement objectives. Armed with a good background on frameworks and strategies for selecting specific interventions to enhance decisions, actions and workflow (see Chapters 5 and 6), the CDS Team decided the next step was to gather objective information about workflows pertinent to their CDS objectives.

They agreed nurse Beck and practice manager Matthews would spend an hour or two over a few days observing practice workflows and speaking with staff about their activities related to HbA1c ordering and monitoring. These meetings would include, for example, examining with different staff when, where and how the test is ordered; the chain of events surrounding HbA1c results posting in the EHR, how these results are reviewed and communicated, and how these reviews are documented; and specific steps different practice members take to respond to abnormal HbA1cs—and document these actions. They correctly anticipated that observing and recording what is *actually happening* would inform planning and conversations within the practice about how CDS can be applied most fruitfully to support these processes and close gaps. The CDS Team's earlier work with their EHR vendor to better understand system capabilities was expected to help trigger ideas during the observation period about how specific CDS tools could be brought to bear.

The CDS Team was rewarded well for the workflow analysis and prior research. They saw people approaching the same basic task in different ways, and many inefficient and problematic processes. This surfaced many opportunities to apply CDS interventions that would make information flow more efficient and make it harder to inadvertently fail to order an HbA1c test—or respond to a significantly abnormal result. Several different EHR subsystems and capabilities would serve these needs well. They began documenting these intervention ideas on a workflow-anchored worksheet (see Figure PII-4).

Design interventions by taking into account the many design strategy nuances that are important for usability and functionality; begin to validate and vet the intervention with key stakeholders.

The workflow analysis reinforced to the CDS Team that they would need to design—with input and buy-in from the entire practice—new CDS-enhanced workflows. In a series of CDS Team and full-practice meetings, they developed explicit care protocols for processes related to their objective—for example, how often the HbA1c test should be performed in different clinical situations (informed by evidence-based guidelines); who should order the test; how and where it will be documented in the EHR; who will be responsible for monitoring results (and how this review will be documented); and how follow-up actions in response to HbA1cs above the threshold will be documented.

The CDS Team recognized that these new workflows would provide the foundation onto which new CDS interventions would be layered and that the new interventions would, in turn, influence workflow details. With this in mind, they used a worksheet (see Worksheet 6-3) to begin sketching out the interplay between clinical workflow and the intervention configuration dimensions they would layer on those workflow steps. For example, they considered different intervention types, including order sets, single and multiple patient data displays, and different alert types (see Figure 5-5, and discussion that follows this figure)—as well as issues in

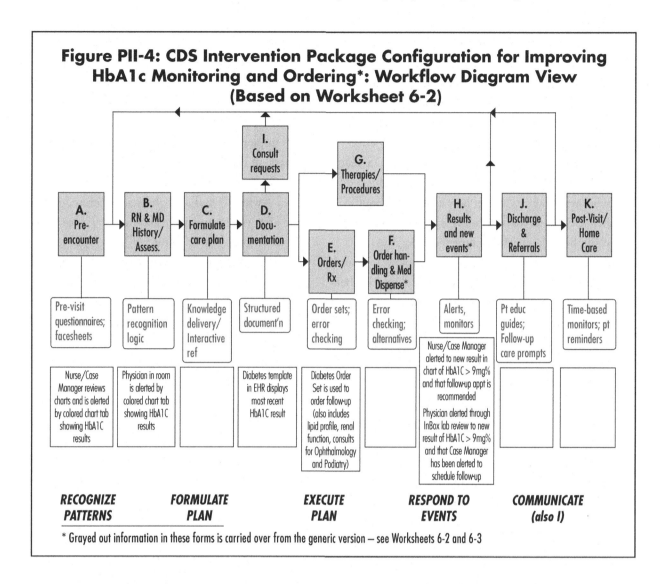

Figure PII-4: CDS Intervention Package Configuration for Improving HbA1c Monitoring and Ordering*: Workflow Diagram View (Based on Worksheet 6-2)

* Grayed out information in these forms is carried over from the generic version — see Worksheets 6-2 and 6-3

using these different intervention types (see Chapter 6 discussion "Deciding Among Several Available Intervention Types"). They were particularly sensitive to whether these interventions would be considered helpful or unwelcome workflow changes by end users.

The practice's EHR has alerting functionality that seemed promising for both the HbA1c ordering and monitoring objectives. For example, a reminder can be displayed via a highlighted tab within the patient's chart. The tab is green if an HbA1c test should be ordered, yellow if the test is not ordered within 5 five days of the due date, and red if the test is overdue. This approach to alerting is less invasive than alerts that pop up on the EHR screen and must be dismissed by the user. The practice believed that

this gentler approach to alerting would be better for their current objectives, especially since they would be using other intervention types to help ensure proper HbA1c ordering and monitoring. For example, they would use diabetic flowsheets that conveniently displayed data needed to manage diabetic patients (including HbA1c test dates and results) and diabetic patient return visit order sets that made it easy to order the test and contain information about recommended testing frequencies.

They even planned to involve patients by providing them with enhanced educational materials so they would better understand—and help ensure—appropriate HbA1c monitoring and follow-up. Similarly, they considered how to enhance their process for communicating to patients that testing was due or results were abnormal. Typical channels included office visits, phone calls and postal mail, but to improve the speed and efficiency of information flow and action, they explored options to automate the process through EHR-generated letter creation and secure e-mail.

Figure PII-5 contains notes that the CDS Team took as they worked through the essential questions (who, what, when, where, how and why) about their CDS intervention configuration—and how it would help them achieve targeted objectives. This form supported the team's internal explorations and discussions and then served as a helpful tool in their discussions with the rest of the practice to refine and approve the configuration they would ultimately launch. They used other worksheets to capture in more detail stakeholder responsibilities regarding the interventions (see Worksheet 5-3), and other key intervention details (see Worksheet 7-2).

Develop and execute intervention deployment plan.

Because they had worked closely with the full practice to select and configure the new diabetes CDS interventions—and with the vendor pre-launch—they were optimistic that there wouldn't be any major surprises. They had even involved several diabetic patients to ensure that the enhanced educational tools would, in fact, be useful for helping them make sure that they receive appropriate testing and follow-up.

Nurse Beck took personal responsibility to ensure that everyone in the practice was ready for the new interventions and protocols and how these affected each person's workflow. He used vendor-supplied EHR training modules that were pertinent to the interventions and lined up vendor staff to jump in if major system problems arose after launch.

The CDS Team would have preferred to evaluate their new interventions in a test environment before general release, but they didn't have the systems or personnel to do this. Because they would have to 'go-live' directly, they developed plans to carefully monitor the intervention and system behavior—as well as workflow effects—after launch. This included

a plan to "back-out" one or both interventions if necessary if, for example, there was significant negative impact on system response time, the interventions did not function as planned, or there were unanticipated problems with workflow.

Implementation efforts by nurse Beck and others on the CDS Team were informed by the mantra "Communicate, communicate, communicate"—with all staff and physicians before, during, and after the interventions launched. For example, they reinforced the "Culture of Value" as a key driver for the interventions and workflow changes and worked with the practice to ensure that this value equation was, in fact, optimized. They identified and communicated specific actions that could be taken if the user had questions or encountered a problem with the process. They even drafted (with full practice input) sample scripts for how clinicians could describe to patients new interventions, such as the enhanced diabetes patient education materials. Looking ahead, they knew that their communication approach would again be very important when the time came to gather, analyze and respond to data about intervention effects.

All this preparation (see Chapter 8) paid off well, and the new interventions were launched without any major problems. There were some minor glitches—such as the yellow chart tab not displaying properly in certain circumstances. However, because the CDS Team had anticipated that such technical problems might arise and planned accordingly, the vendor was able to rectify the problem quickly when nurse Beck contacted them.

Everyone was pleased that the intervention go-live went so well. During the first several weeks, other workflow and technical issues related to the new interventions arose, but the CDS Team handled them smoothly.

Use a formal plan for identifying, tracking, measuring, and addressing intended and unintended intervention behavior and effects.

The CDS Team and others in the practice believed that the new diabetes management tools were adding value, but they knew the proof would

Figure PII-5: Improving Diabetes Control: CDS Intervention Package Configuration, Table View (Based on Worksheet 6-3)

Current Performance: Robust data are not available, but random chart reviews suggest that as many as 50% of diabetic patients might not have an HbA1c recorded within the recommended interval, and 50% of those with HbA1c >9 do not appear to have any specific corrective action taken within 3 months of that abnormal result.

Target Performance: 80% of patients with diabetes have HbA1C measured at recommended intervals and recorded in the EHR, and some corrective action (such as follow-up visit scheduled, patient counseled, medication changed) is taken and documented within 1 month in 80% of cases where HbA1c result >9 is recorded.

Objective	Core Action	Workflow	Content Delivery		Delivery Logistics	
			CDS Five Rights Dimensions			
		When[1] (Workflow Step)	**What** (Information)	**How**[2] (Intervention Type)	**Who**[3] (Person)	**Where**[4] (Channel)
	Recognize patterns	Pre-encounter **A**	Demographics, conditions, care gaps, self-progress	Per Worksheet 6-1	Patient, admin, case manager	PHR/ registry/ EHR
Appropriate identification of pts with DM requiring A1c testing			Date of most recent A1c or if one is overdue to be done	List of all patients with overdue A1c (multi-patient monitor)	Nurse or case manager	EMR
	Recognize patterns / formulate plan of care	RN & MD history/assess **B**	History/physical data, medications, prior data review, inferred conditions		Nurse/ physician	EHR, flowsheets, data facesheets
Appropriate identification of pts with DM requiring A1c testing			Date of most recent A1c or if one is overdue to be done	Colored chart tab in EMR (relevant data summary)	Physician	EMR
	Formulate plan of care	Formulate care plan **C**	Guidance on best-practice approach to workup and management		Nurse/ physician/ patient	EHR, smart reference, shared decision making

Figure PII-5 *continued*

Objective	Core Action	Workflow	Content Delivery		Delivery Logistics	
			CDS Five Rights Dimensions			
		When[1] (Workflow Step)	**What** (Information)	**How[2]** (Intervention Type)	**Who[3]** (Person)	**Where[4]** (Channel)
	Execute plan	Documentation **D**	Appropriate and complete documentation of observations, assessment, plan		Physician/ nurse	EHR (Clinical docu. tools)
Appropriate documenttation of most recent A1c and resulting plan			Result of most recent A1c and date of test	Displayed in diabetes documentation template	Physician or nurse/case manager	EMR
	Execute plan	Orders/Rx **E**	Appropriate, correct and complete orders for evaluation and therapy		Physician/ prescriber	CPOE eprescribing
Appropriate screening orders for pts with DM			DM Screening recommendations (includes A1c, lipid profile, renal function, ophthalmology and podiatry consults	DM Screening Order Set	Physician or nurse/case manager	EMR
	Execute plan	Order handling and med dispensing **F**	Safety and appropriateness checks on medications and other diagnostic and therapeutic interventions		Physician/ nurse/ pharmacist/ other clinicians/ patient	EHR/ CPOE/ pharmacy system/ medication dispensing and admin systems
	Execute plan	Therapies/ procedures **G**	Reference information and relevant data pertinent to safe and effective procedures and techniques		Physician/ nurse/ other clinicians	Reference tools, EHR modules

Figure PII-5 *continued*

Objective	Core Action	Workflow	Content Delivery		Delivery Logistics	
			CDS Five Rights Dimensions			
		When[1] (Workflow Step)	**What** (Information)	**How[2]** (Intervention Type)	**Who[3]** (Person)	**Where[4]** (Channel)
	Respond to events	Results and new events **H**	Inferred hazards and improvement opportunities from lab and imaging results		Physician/ nurse/ patient	EHR/PHR, HIE, alerting devices
Appropriate F/U for at-risk patients			Lab results	Alert of incoming results with HbA1c > 9.0 mg%	Physician or nurse/case manager	EMR
	Communicate	Consult requests **I**	Guidance on appropriate use of consultation and best exchange of information to/from consultant		Physician	EHR, HIE, reference tools (referral guidance)
	Communicate	Discharge & referrals **J**	Discharge instructions, medication instructions, home care and continuing care information		Physician/ nurse/ patient	Discharge modules, medication reconciliation apps
	Respond to events	Post-visit/ home care **K**	Patient guidance on self-care, data gathering for condition monitoring; abnormal conditions requiring attention		Patient/ caregiver, case manager, visiting nurse	PHR, online portal, smart pillbox, home data monitors

be in the performance metrics they agreed to track. When things settled down after the new diabetes intervention package and workflow changes were launched, the CDS Team returned to the monitoring plan they developed as they were configuring the interventions. They had worked closely with the full practice and the vendor on the 'why, how,

who, when' measurement issues (see Chapter 9), and the task now was to put that plan into action. They adapted worksheets (see Worksheets 9-1 through 9-5) to help document and track their results and built into their regular practice meeting a schedule for reviewing and discussing their diabetes management CDS efforts.

Everyone in the practice recognized that frequent changes in the diabetes clinical knowledge base required that they closely monitor their new interventions' currency and appropriateness, in addition to their effects on performance metrics. Inevitable flux in their clinical information systems and the broader healthcare regulatory and reimbursement environment amplified this need for ongoing intervention surveillance and maintenance. The CDS knowledge management plan that the CDS Team had established as they were building their CDS program capabilities (see Part I Introduction, Case Study for Small Practices) would now come into play.

They plugged into that framework specific resources and routines pertinent to their new diabetes interventions. For example, they used diabetes-focused searches in PubMed and the National Guideline Clearinghouse to identify new systematic reviews and guidelines on diabetes management, as well as updates from the American Diabetes Association, the National Institute of Diabetes and Kidney Diseases and the practice's electronic reference sources for other pertinent clinical updates. They also established mechanisms to track relevant new material from the practice clinicians' continuing education activities, from their EHR vendor's user group, and from their regional extension center. Knowing that changes in their EHR and data feeds can affect their CDS intervention accuracy, they worked with their EHR vendor and reference labs on plans to smoothly detect and respond to HbA1c reference value changes or other such modifications that might interfere with the interventions.

Internist Shelby Burnham had a particular interest in diabetes management literature, and she volunteered to take primary responsibility for monitoring the intervention content currency and evidence-base. She agreed to serve as the focal point for receiving information from the sources just noted, and presented new information and recommendations to the group to determine what, if any, changes they would need to make to the diabetes CDS interventions and/or related workflows. Dr. Franks, practice

manager Matthews, and Dr. Burnham worked together to create calendar reminders to signal the need for periodic intervention review tasks and coordinated this with the broader staff meetings schedule for reviewing progress toward intervention objectives. Delegating this knowledge management role to someone outside the CDS Team helped to further broaden 'ownership' for the CDS interventions and prepare the practice to scale its CDS efforts to other priority improvement areas.

Everyone was excited when PI lead Dr. Franks formally presented the diabetes CDS status update at the 9-month post-launch practice meeting. Appropriate screening rates improved from roughly 50 to 75 percent of patients, and there was clear documentation that HbA1c results >9 mg % were attended to within one month in 60 percent of patients. Progress had been made, but there was more work to be done. The group discussed what was working well about the interventions, as well as opportunities for improvement. The latter included better documenting responses to abnormal HbA1c levels so they would 'get credit' for follow-up actions that weren't being captured by their reporting tools (as revealed by some manual chart reviews). In addition, further workflow analyses by nurse Beck revealed opportunities to further tweak the interventions and workflows to yield better results. The CDS Team agreed to follow-up in the next meeting with specific improvement proposals. Near the end of the meeting, Dr. Burnham suggested that the CDS program should next tackle actually lowering the percentage of patients with grossly abnormal HbA1c levels, and the group agreed to explore this in detail at the next practice meeting.

A short while later, a new physician joined the Elm Heights internal medicine practice from a different medical group that was not as sophisticated as Elm Heights in applying CDS to performance improvement. After being introduced to the Elm Heights diabetes-related CDS interventions and related workflows, he commented to the practice staff and physicians that he thought they were very helpful. He was particularly impressed by measurable results they delivered—and all the programmatic elements that supported those results. When he reflected back to the practice members some key performance-related policy, attitude and behavior differences between his prior group and Elm Heights, they realized that improving outcomes with CDS was becoming core to their culture.

Chapter 5

Foundational Considerations for Effective CDS Interventions

Tasks

- Solidify your organization's foundational understanding of CDS concepts, including the 'CDS Five Rights' framework, to prepare for choosing and configuring CDS interventions.
- Narrow the high-level improvement goals identified in Chapter 2 (Worksheet 2-1), selecting those that have the most organizational support and are most likely to succeed. Start small and build to more complex goals with experience. (Worksheet 5-1)
- Identify specific CDS objectives to achieve each high-level goal. From these objectives, choose those that have the highest potential for impact and for which CDS interventions will be most practical and effective. Gather baseline data about performance on selected objectives, and work closely with stakeholders on all these activities. (Worksheets 5-1 through 5-4)
- Familiarize yourself with the wide range of CDS intervention types. Keep these in mind as you select your objectives, recognizing that any objective may be addressed through a single CDS intervention or through a package of interventions.

KEY LESSONS

- The CDS Five Rights approach provides a framework for considering the what, who, how, where and when dimensions in configuring effective CDS interventions. This framework should underpin the CDS Team's efforts, including collaboration with stakeholders.
- For many important objectives, using more than one CDS intervention (a CDS package), triggered at different points in the clinical workflow for different end-user types, will produce a greater impact.
- CDS interventions can be grouped into ten different types. Understanding these intervention types, their advantages and disadvantages, and how they can work together to optimize care processes is critical in selecting and designing optimal CDS approaches to accomplish specific objectives.
- There are several steps in the CDS intervention lifecycle after determining which goals and objectives to address; these include selecting, configuring, vetting, testing, implementing and measuring effects. We delve into these in greater detail in subsequent chapters.

GENERAL APPROACH

Part I of this Guide provides strategies for developing an effective clinical decision support program. Part II now focuses on how to develop and apply CDS interventions to address clinical, operational and financial improvements that your CDS program has determined to be priority goals. This chapter will help you select high-level CDS goals, more specific objectives, and to understand CDS intervention strategies and tools. The following chapters in Part II cover selecting appropriate intervention types for particular objectives, configuring and implementing the interventions, and then monitoring, maintaining and refining them. It is important to note that while some discussions may focus on interventions as individual entities, in practice many major targets you are trying to improve will be best addressed with a package of CDS interventions, as we discuss later in this chapter.

Clinical decision support can be used to enhance many care processes and outcomes, so your CDS Team should begin target selection by fully appreciating this breadth. Many clinicians and implementers think narrowly about CDS in terms of medication safety alerts or order sets, but the CDS toolkit and application range are much broader. While therapeutic CDS is most prevalent (for example, medication alerts or clinical care recommendations), CDS interventions may be applied to the entire care spectrum from health maintenance to diagnosis to therapeutics to end-of-life care. It is also useful for overall process optimization, which may cut across these care phases. CDS interventions focused on these phases can work together; for example, you can integrate diagnostic CDS tools into your therapeutic CDS interventions by confirming that the condition's diagnostic criteria are met before delivering the therapeutic recommendations. Considering this full spectrum of CDS use will help ensure that you don't overlook important opportunities as you select CDS targets and that you fully leverage frameworks (such as the CDS Five Rights and CDS intervention type taxonomy) that we present in this chapter.

As stressed in Part I, keep in mind that successfully using CDS requires not only CDS-specific expertise but also broader tools for organizational leadership and governance, change management, and quality and process/workflow improvement. This is true at the broad CDS program level and also in using specific interventions to drive targeted improvements. We revisit these management themes from Part I here in Part II; the point for now is that you should approach specific CDS interventions with appropriate attention to *people, process*, and *technology*. Many organizations have tried to jump straight to the technological 'fix' without taking the necessary steps to fully engage appropriate stakeholders and understand the relevant current state and organizational processes. As we will emphasize throughout Part II, you must collaborate with stakeholders to build a strong, shared understanding about current and desired processes. This shared vision and purpose then drives joint efforts to select improvement opportunities and successfully capitalize on them with CDS interventions.

We next discuss selecting CDS goals and objectives and then provide two frameworks useful for CDS interventions to address these targets. These frameworks are the CDS Five Rights, which reinforce fundamental components of an effective CDS intervention, and a broad CDS intervention taxonomy to help that you fully leverage available information delivery formats.

Selecting Clinical Goals and Objectives for CDS Intervention

A critical initial step in targeted CDS efforts is ensuring that you select appropriate goals and objectives. For example, if you choose targets that are not aligned with organizational and stakeholder priorities, then it will be difficult to muster financial support and engagement needed to configure, deploy, monitor and maintain the interventions. Similarly, if you choose objectives that are too difficult or expensive for your organization to handle—or just not well suited to CDS interventions—it will be hard to succeed.

Figure 5-1: Some Internal Sources for Identifying CDS Targets

- Organizational analyses of quality, safety, patient satisfaction, cost and regulatory problems (for example, from standing committees such as pharmacy and therapeutics, quality assurance, patient safety or utilization review—or reporting under the Physician Quality Reporting System [PQRS] in ambulatory settings);

- Planning activities for responding to specific environmental drivers, such as accreditation requirements, pay-for-performance and quality/improvement initiatives;

- Analyses of available data on care and outcomes at the organization;

- Interviews with clinicians, medical directors and other stakeholders regarding key issues and approaches (other than via CDS) currently in use, such as manual pharmacist interventions to avoid medication errors;

- Directly observing unfilled information needs and related workflow problems that are creating challenges in care delivery, supplemented with stakeholder surveys and dialog about these CDS needs and opportunities;

- Community-based priorities and programs, such as local smoking cessation campaigns, and related cardiovascular risk-reduction initiatives.

Chapter 2 discusses identifying high-level clinical goals and objectives for CDS intervention development that align with your organizational goals. Refer back to Figures 2-2 and 2-3—as well as Worksheet 2-1—to help gather improvement priorities for your organization overall, as well as for key individuals and roles. Figure 5-1 provides additional suggestions about internal sources for identifying CDS targets.

You may find that there are many competing priorities; this stresses the importance of governance processes for target prioritization and related strategic decision making. Organizational drivers will likely surface target themes, such as a special emphasis on decreasing or eliminating patient harm, increasing patient flow (such as through improved provider efficiency), or improving performance measures with significant financial implications for the organization or providers. We next discuss several considerations for selecting specific goals and objectives on which to focus CDS intervention efforts.

Select Goals and Objectives That Optimize Impact

Your organization should choose high-level CDS clinical goals in a manner that evaluates and opti-

mizes clinical, operational and financial benefits. For instance, what is the potential impact on morbidity, mortality or other *clinical* outcome measures from providing CDS interventions for each goal? If the interventions are successful, how will this *financially* impact your organization, considering the cost to build the intervention and the potential return on investment? This return might not only be expressed in dollars but also in length of stay, decreased utilization of overburdened resources, or increased patient satisfaction (which may improve market share). Also, what is the *opportunity cost* from choosing one target over another that may be easier to implement? Lastly, but equally important, what is the *operational* benefit or cost? Will the targeted intervention(s) result in improved workflow, improved staff satisfaction or efficiency? Weigh the positive and negative attributes for each of these clinical, operational and financial components to determine which targets could yield the greatest benefits.

Similar considerations apply to selecting specific CDS objectives to address a higher-level goal. For example, you might choose to focus on improving adherence with specific testing, therapeutic or patient education recommendations for a particular

---

Figure 5-2: Factors Affecting the Desirability of a CDS Objective

Clinical Objective Value Score* = (P+O+C+N+G)-(D+C)

P= Patient impact (individual/population) (positive, for example, higher quality, safe, cost-effective care; improved morbidity and mortality; improved patient satisfaction)

O= Organizational impact (positive, for example, regulatory or audit compliance [such as alignment with Meaningful Use requirements], appropriate resource use, support for internal improvement priorities, reduced liability, financial return)

C= Clinician impact (for example, enhanced workflow/compensation, support for consensus practice patterns and operations, improving care capabilities, projects of particular interest to clinicians)

N= Number of patients positively affected

G= Gap between ideal and actual behavior and outcomes pertinent to the objective

D= Difficulty associated with addressing the objective (for example, related to intervention configuration, adoption and use)

C= Cost of addressing the objective (such as from procuring and maintaining intervention content and technology)

---

* Consider the strength of systematic evidence about the magnitude of the variable when practical.

---

condition to address the broader goal of improving disease management for that condition—as called for in a value-based purchasing initiative. Similarly, if your clinical goal is reducing readmissions, your objectives might include identifying patients at risk for readmission before they are discharged, improving discharge paperwork and processes, or improving patient education and follow-up. These specific objectives are the targets on which your CDS interventions focus to achieve broader goals, and you should choose objectives that maximize impact. The next chapter discusses selecting objective-focused interventions in detail.

Figure 5-2 lists factors related to how desirable it will be to use CDS interventions to address a particular objective. Difficulties and costs associated with addressing an objective will depend on the specific intervention approach you select, which we haven't covered at this point. You can make rough guesses about these 'negative' factors or defer considering them until you are farther along in evaluating specific intervention options (such as outlined in Chapter 6 and Figure 6-4).

Your CDS governance should provide an explicit mechanism for stakeholders to consider objective desirability factors such as these and formally prioritize CDS objectives. Different organizations use different prioritization schemes and weighting factors, but they typically involve factors such as those in Figure 5-2. These processes should evolve over time as needed.

You can use Worksheets 5-1 and 5-2 in developing your own tools to select and prioritize CDS goals and objectives and to clarify the specific actions you need to influence. This exercise sets up the discussion in Chapter 6 about selecting interventions to address the objectives and desired actions. The worksheets include space to document baseline performance against goals and objectives, which we discuss next. Worksheet 5-3 can help your CDS Team begin thinking about stakeholders in achieving each objective and the role they could play in your CDS intervention efforts. As we repeatedly emphasize, it is essential to engage all pertinent stakeholders at each stage in the CDS intervention lifecycle (see Figure PII-1)—beginning with selecting appropriate targets.

Consider Which Objectives Lend Themselves to CDS Approaches

Before moving on to determine CDS intervention specifics in subsequent chapters, keep in mind that some objectives lend themselves very well to CDS techniques, while others do not. As you prioritize the CDS intervention development and implementation, make sure you are prioritizing targets based on their suitability for CDS intervention, as well as on the pure target priority.

In general, CDS is well-suited when the objective or process can be improved through information delivery approaches such as:

- *Reinforcing* important specific patient facts and clinical knowledge that are relevant to properly managing a given situation;
- *Supporting* diagnostic and therapeutic decision making that consistently applies a previously determined best clinical approach to a problem;
- *Ensuring* proper details and parameters for clinical orders, such as medication dosage or imaging test specifics;
- *Making* short "course corrections"—based on new data or circumstances—to a process that is already underway;
- *Helping* to organize and prioritize among multiple tasks based on incoming data;
- *Monitoring* one or many patients for possible omissions and gaps in the care process;
- *Spotting* trends or variances in a care process that has already been applied to multiple patients, to help drive any necessary process changes.

On the other hand, CDS is not always suited to every improvement need, and you should consider for each potential objective and desired clinical action whether CDS is an appropriate tool. Situations in which CDS interventions might not be the best approach include those where information-based support *is not* the primary need, and those that involve more than a *supportive* role, such as:

- *Substituting* for the physician or nurse in assessing the patient;

- *Overriding* a physician's or nurse's overall plan of care after it has already been established;
- *Making* decisions based on data that are subjective or not easily available to the electronic health record;
- *Requiring* that users enter extensive information—or face other workflow burdens—before any decision support is provided.

In addition, it is important to have adequate communication with and agreement by the users on any new policies and process changes before implementing a CDS approach. "The computer does not make policy"; if the first time a clinician sees a new policy is when the intervention restricts him or her from taking a planned action, dissatisfaction and resistance will likely occur. You should focus first on direct conversation, education and consensus with all relevant clinical staff. Once policies and best practices related to an objective have been agreed upon, CDS interventions can ensure that those policies are reinforced at relevant moments in the care process.

Assess Baseline Performance against Objectives

Because your organization should focus CDS efforts on objectives for which there is an important improvement opportunity, you'll need to have some idea about current practice and performance pertinent to potential objectives. This will help in assessing gaps between current and desired states and prioritizing which gaps to address. For example, there is no reason to take on projects for which you already have good performance and there is only minimal room for improvement, compared to those with a high-impact potential. Your baseline performance data then become the starting point for measuring effects caused by CDS interventions implemented to address targeted objectives.

Chapter 9 provides a detailed discussion on measurement. For now, keep in mind that careful attention to measuring key CDS-related parameters is essential throughout the CDS intervention lifecycle, starting with these early objective selection steps.

Start Simple and Build from There

As with any complex skill, it is important to learn by mastering the basics and building on this solid foundation. Do not take on very complex CDS objectives until you have achieved success with more basic CDS-mediated improvement projects, for example, ones that address what your organization considers 'simple' improvement objectives that already have good stakeholder support and awareness. Although we have recommended that you select objectives to optimize impact, carefully consider how hard intervening will be (as per Figure 5-2). As you are building basic CDS intervention skills, try to avoid especially difficult objectives—even if they provide substantial value—unless you have strong and broad internal support (for example, addressing what your organization considers imperatives, such as Meaningful Use-related CDS requirements).

Seek targets that have well established and accepted guidelines that are proven to lead to the desired clinical or process outcome. Avoid starting with a target that is based on controversial expert opinion, whether at a local or national level. It is important for your team to have an early victory that is easy to see; this will help build a culture that expects successful CDS efforts. Choosing a process that is seen as simple, necessary and easily measurable—such as improving pneumococcal vaccine administration to inpatients with chronic obstructive pulmonary disease (COPD), or other core measures—will also show your team how many stakeholders and complexities there are even in 'simple' healthcare processes. Aim for an intervention that will benefit patients and not just improve administrative measures.

It is more important to make a small difference in something that matters to the organization than to aim for a large impact on something that is not a priority. Frontline users must see CDS interventions as valuable to patient care quality improvement and not just something that makes 'the numbers' look better. Similarly, the CDS interventions must produce personal benefits that end users personally consider valuable, such as saving them time or making their workflow more efficient or effective.

You can use a 2x2 table to help complement the equation in Figure 5-2 for considering factors to guide objective selection. For example, Figure 5-3 plots Feasibility vs. Potential Impact (or the axes can be Ease of Implementation vs. Effectiveness) for different potential objectives. If you map CDS objectives your organization is considering into this diagram, it helps call attention to objectives that are highly feasible and have a high potential impact. This is your 'low hanging fruit.' Over time, you can work your way up to those objectives that are also high impact but more difficult or those that are feasible but maybe less valuable. Naturally, you should avoid objectives that are difficult to implement and have a low potential impact.

The objective selection process is an important early milestone in establishing/deepening collaborations between your CDS Team and other CDS inter-

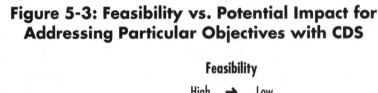

Figure 5-3: Feasibility vs. Potential Impact for Addressing Particular Objectives with CDS

		Feasibility	
		High →	Low
Impact	High	Do Now	Plan to Do
	Low	Do Next	Avoid

vention stakeholders. Everyone should recognize that there will be challenges and setbacks, and the goal is to learn from them. Each successful intervention for an important target will enhance this collaboration, the shared expertise and skill on which it draws, and everyone's enthusiasm for further CDS efforts.

Begin Anticipating CDS Intervention Packages for Selected Objectives

You should recognize that effective decision support for a specific improvement target is not always accomplished through a single CDS intervention. Many clinical goals and outcomes require a set of CDS interventions, which we refer to as a CDS intervention package. Although subsequent chapters at times discuss designing and implementing individual CDS interventions, keep in mind that often a package of two or more interventions, applied at different points in the workflow and perhaps directed to different persons, will be more effective for addressing an objective. In the next section we provide a framework for CDS intervention packages for specific performance targets. To exemplify a multifaceted approach to important CDS objectives, Figure 5-4 shows one organization's CDS package for addressing core measures. Part II emphasizes thinking about measuring effects in concert with developing interventions, and the figure includes notes about potential measurement data sources.

Begin Considering Current Workflow Challenges and Opportunities Related to Objectives

Once your organization selects a high-level clinical goal and its associated objectives, your CDS Team can begin considering factors contributing to current performance and opportunities to improve workflow and other outcome determinants. In subsequent chapters, we discuss collaborating with stakeholders to examine outcomes data, directly observe target-related processes, and map pertinent workflows to fully understand factors that drive the results you are trying to improve. For now, you can review the workflow discussion in Chapter 3 and peek ahead at

the CDS in Clinical Workflow section in Chapter 6. This will help prepare you for thinking in more detail about appropriate CDS interventions useful for selected objectives (which is covered in detail in Chapter 6).

For example, your CDS governance may select better pain control for hospitalized patients as a high-level goal; in addition to its importance for good patient care, pain control is a publically reported patient satisfaction measure and incorporated into value-based purchasing programs. Your organization may determine that enhancing physician ordering and nursing administration of PRN (as needed) pain medications are the two most promising improvement objectives to reach this goal. Carefully mapping care processes associated with these two objectives will help identify potential intervention opportunities. Results from such analyses provide clues to configuring effective intervention packages; we next discuss a framework for this task.

A Framework for Effective CDS Interventions: The CDS Five Rights

A useful framework for configuring and deploying valuable CDS interventions is the CDS Five Rights approach. Do not confuse it with the Five Rights of medication use, which speak to ensuring that the right patient gets the right drug, at the right dose, via the right route, and the right time.[1] The CDS Five Rights model states that we can achieve CDS-supported improvements in targeted healthcare outcomes if we communicate:

1. The *right information:* evidence-based, suitable to guide action, pertinent to the circumstance;

2. To the *right person:* considering all care team members, including clinicians, patients and their caretakers;

3. In the *right CDS intervention format:* based on the intervention types described in the next section, such as an alert, order set, documentation tool, data display or reference information;

4. Through the *right channel:* for example, through an electronic health record (EHR), personal

Figure 5-4: Sample CDS Package with Measurement Data Sources for CHF Core Measures*

Core Measures Description	Measurement Data Sources	Clinical Interventions for Decision Support — Examples
Discharge instructions for congestive heart failure (CHF) patients	1. Discharge orders for review of medication list, recommended activity level, recommended diet, recommended weight monitoring, follow-up and management of worsening symptoms 2. Documented tasks that the above items were reviewed 3. Audit trail that education materials, discharge instructions, medication list, etc. were printed is connected to above tasks as relevant	1. CHF discharge order set with orders for performing discharge tasks including medication list review, activity level review, follow-up appointment review, diet review, weight monitoring review, and management of worsening symptoms instructions 2. Discharge tasks that are populated by nursing care plan or orders to capture completion of the discharge tasks 3. Printable materials for education, medication list, etc. as HTML links associated with above tasks that log when materials were printed for a given patient
Evaluation of left ventricular systolic dysfunction (LVSD)	1. Admission, pathway or discharge orders for echocardiogram 2. Intra-admission echocardiogram result posted to clinical data repository	1. Admission, pathway or discharge orders for echocardiogram as component of CHF management order sets and pathways 2. Discharge clinical documentation check list or task list that ensures cardiac echo is scheduled at discharge if not completed during admission 3. Decision support rules that check for the presence of completed echocardiogram during admission and post task to nursing discharge task list if not performed
Angiotensin-converting enzyme inhibitor (ACEI) or Angiotensin II Receptor Blocker (ARB) for left ventricular systolic dysfunction	1. For ACEI, electronic medication administration record 2. For patient contraindications, clinical documentation, allergies, laboratory data, problem list 3. For LVSD, echo report has discrete field that indicates LVEF< 40%	1. Discharge order set with ACEI on discharge order if LVSD present 2. Rules that cause ACEI order to be defaulted if echo report or problem list include LVSD 3. Documentation template in echo report with coded field for EF < 40% 4. Documentation template for ACEI contraindication capture
Smoking cessation advice/counseling for CHF patients	1. Nursing and/or physician documentation template	1. Congestive heart failure admission order set containing smoking cessation counseling order 2. Documentation template for smoking cessation counseling

* Source: Partners HealthCare, Boston, MA. Used with permission.

health record (PHR), or a more general channel such as a website or a mobile application;

5. At the *right time in workflow:* when it is most needed to make a decision or take action.

These five intervention dimensions cover the what, who, how, where and when for CDS interventions focused on given objective. For each care delivery activity, you can consider how to apply these CDS Five Rights to ensure that the activity is accomplished with optimal effectiveness, safety, clinician/patient satisfaction and resource use. Chapters 6 and 7 will explore in detail how to address these parameters to achieve specific objectives.

We next explore these five (the CDS Five Rights) dimensions in further detail to lay the foundation for choosing and implementing successful CDS interventions.

The Right Information (What)

A core consideration for any CDS intervention is what information will be communicated to the user to support decision making and related workflow activity. Especially in early CDS program stages, it is vital to focus on well recognized and established guidelines and performance measures supported by appropriate clinical evidence. Expert opinion alone should be avoided as this can damage a young CDS program's credibility. That said, strict evidence-based guidelines are available for only a fraction of common clinical decisions. As your program matures, it will be easier to gain consensus on using CDS interventions to help consistently apply agreed-upon expert recommendations.

Your intervention ideally should be based on evidence (obtained by your CDS Team and/or your content supplier) that establishes the relationship between the desired action or outcome and the information the intervention will communicate. When you supply this information within the CDS intervention itself, be sure to relay enough—but only enough—material to support the user's clinical decision or task. For example, including a full drug product label does not help the user decide if the drug is appropriate for his or her patient, and this

information overload is as detrimental as providing inadequate support. If the information presented is not concise and useful, many users will ignore the information entirely. You can strike an appropriate balance by providing brief summary information or recommendations in the intervention, supplemented with references and links to primary sources and other details that the user can access if desired. If possible, provide an option to review the material outside of busy patient care activities.

It is important to adapt guidelines and primary literature to your local environment and make the information specific to your patient population (see Chapter 4). Do not blindly apply tools and information from other organizations without considering whether they are appropriate, or need modification, for your local setting. For many CDS interventions, you must first develop an agreed-upon guideline or protocol within your organization for optimal care in a particular clinical situation. You can then reference this guideline and use it as a basis for the pertinent information to be delivered with your CDS intervention.

In summary, be sure to consider that the information being communicated is:

- Based on appropriate evidence;
- Useful for guiding decisions/actions;
- Concise and pertinent; and
- Consistent with recipients' core beliefs or values and local policies.

The Right Person (Who)

Even in small practice settings, there are at least several different care team members—each with different roles in the care process. CDS interventions must communicate information to these individuals—physicians, nurses, pharmacists, patients and their caregivers, and others—that supports decisions and actions pertinent to their role. Information given to a care team member who is not in a position to act on it will not result in the desired outcome and can be bothersome and even counterproductive. For example, presenting a nurse with an alert advising renal dose adjustment for a medication when it is being administered is ineffective. The nurse will have no way to know if the ordering physician or pharmacist had already adjusted the dose.

Keep in mind that your organization may opt—with appropriate stakeholder support—to use CDS interventions that alter traditional care team member roles and authority. For example, some CDS programs empower nurses or pharmacists who gather data necessary to trigger a CDS intervention with authority to action indicated by that data. A case in point: the nurse evaluates patients for flu-shot eligibility with support from a CDS rule, then administers the shot—as per prior approved protocol—to patients for whom it is indicated. When nurse-empowering protocols have not been established, the intervention may guide the nurse to contact a prescribing clinician, though these extra steps will likely decrease overall effectiveness. For example, in one program, a standing order coupled with decision support given to the nurse was more effective than a physician reminder in promoting vaccination.[2] A compelling video[3] from another organization likewise illustrates how creatively considering potential CDS intervention recipients—in this case, notifying an allergy clinic receptionist about a patient's overdue mammogram—can have profoundly positive patient effects.

The Right CDS Intervention Format (How)

Later in this chapter this Right is covered in detail; it explores the range of CDS intervention types and the circumstances in which they are appropriate. These intervention types provide a 'toolbox' you can draw from to affect care; it is very important to choose the right tool for the job and to consider the full range of intervention types in making your selection. Avoid the management proverb 'If you have a hammer, every problem looks like a nail'—which results in relying excessively on any specific intervention format. Different types of interventions are best for different problems and needs, and the correct tool selection is vital to its success.

Make sure your CDS Team and organization understand each intervention type thoroughly—

including whether and how each is currently available in your systems (see Chapter 3, especially Worksheet 3-1)—and incorporate them in your improvement efforts when appropriate. Chapter 6 offers detailed guidance on selecting intervention types for a given objective. In particular, be aware of the potential to over-use alerts, and recognize when alerts are more or less effective versus other tools. For example, other intervention types can be utilized earlier in the workflow to help ensure that the right care is delivered in the first place. Alerts can be an effective safety net when earlier decision support fails but shouldn't be relied upon as a primary approach to ensuring proper action.

The Right Channel (Where)

The right channel refers to how the information will be delivered to the user. As the EHR becomes more encompassing and integrated, the user will likely see this as the primary channel, but also consider other methods including PHRs that patients use, and stand-alone medical information and data tools including mobile and cloud-based applications. It is often the case that a specific module (such as clinical documentation, CPOE, patient status summary page) in an EHR is a powerful channel through which an intervention can be applied. But remember that this may not always be the case; Chapters 6 and 7 explore this assessment in detail.

As noted in Chapter 3 (especially Worksheet 3-1), a detailed inventory covering your available information systems will help ensure that you consider all available options in selecting the "Right Channel" for an intervention. In resource-limited environments, paper-based tools such as documentation forms, printed flowsheets, reminder labels on charts, and the like can be effective delivery channels.

The best channel for delivering a CDS intervention may depend on the circumstances and data that trigger the intervention and what tools the user is working with during a particular workflow step. If the trigger occurs during patient intake, the right channel might be the administrative intake application. It may also be a PHR that interacts with your organization's EHR, if the trigger occurs in an electronic registration form that the patient is filling out.

Information processing complexity also helps determine the right delivery channel. A simple intervention may only need a simple channel, while more complex decision making may require information access and logic processing available only online or through an EHR. For instance, when it is necessary to pull from multiple data sources to trigger a CDS rule, the EHR might be the only source that has all this information. Likewise, it may be the most appropriate workflow-integrated user interface to communicate this information to the user.

The EHR offers extensive functionality that you should understand and apply in configuring channels for your CDS interventions—again, refer back to Chapter 3 for further details. In some cases, you may want to build or enhance a specific intervention delivery channel, or work with the vendor to design the capability you need to reach the right user with the right information. Do not allow the current system limitations to inhibit you from exploring what would be an ideal intervention for a given need, and communicating the idea to your vendor or IT department. In some cases, you have to be very inventive regarding how you use the features currently available in information systems to achieve your goals.

The Right Time in the Workflow (When)

'Timing is everything.' A well-intentioned intervention delivered too early or too late in the workflow will be ineffective. For example, it will be less effective to alert a physician that a patient is allergic to a medication after all details of that medication order have been filled out and the order finalized; a more effective point would be as soon as the medication class or name is selected in the order entry system. Similarly, it is much better to detect and address a discharge plan that cannot be accomplished as soon as possible after admission, rather than on the discharge day. Conversely, alerting a physician as soon as he or she opens the chart that the patient is overdue for a preventive service might not be the

best time to convey this information because it is outside the typical ordering workflow. To properly design and implement an intervention, you must understand the workflow and process for appropriate care and clinical decision making.

Besides considering when it will be most effective to deliver an intervention into broad workflow activities, also consider finer decision-making steps as intervention opportunities. For example, in many cases your CDS interventions will seek to mimic and support decision-making steps that experienced clinicians follow in addressing a particular care task, such selecting an initial workup and management plan for a severe new symptom with an unclear cause. CDS focused on supporting this challenge should consider the steps an expert would take, the information the expert would need to make an optimal decision, and when that information should be made available.

Workflow analysis and mapping, as described in Chapter 3 (Worksheet 3-2) helps your CDS Team understand broad and more focused care process. Chapter 6 discusses using these analyses to develop specific interventions and intervention packages that achieve objectives by supporting workflows and decision making. The analysis outlined there can help you decide both which interventions should be deployed and when they can be optimally provided within care processes.

Using the CDS Five Rights

Your CDS program should ensure that your CDS Team and organization share an understanding about the CDS Five Rights framework for using CDS interventions to achieve improvement goals and objectives. This shared framework will help the various stakeholders consider which objectives are appropriate to address with CDS interventions, as well support them in providing useful input and informed validation for your CDS intervention plans. Finally, when the interventions are launched, it provides a framework for stakeholders to assess how the interventions are affecting care processes and for providing input to make them better.

The next two chapters present details about selecting and configuring CDS interventions; before diving into those specifics, you might revisit the Part I Introduction to reinforce what it looks like when the CDS Five Rights approach is applied to specific clinical objectives. Specifically, the summary tables with CDS configurations for VTE prophylaxis (Figures PII-2 and PII-3) and diabetes management (Figures PII-4 and PII-5)—together with the related text—illustrate important end products from your CDS intervention planning efforts. Generic versions of the diagrams and tables in these figures are provided as Worksheets 6-2 and 6-3; you might peek ahead to that material to stimulate your CDS Team's thinking about how you might approach your chosen CDS objectives through available CDS intervention configuration dimensions.

You can also begin thinking about who will be affected by the new CDS objectives and corresponding interventions. We discuss this further in Chapters 6 and 7, but as a backdrop for that work, you might start meeting with these people and documenting (in forms such as Worksheet 5-3) results from your explorations. Similarly, you can begin considering the systems you have available to deliver interventions that address targeted objectives and using forms such as Worksheet 5-4 to document that information.

As you select objectives and prepare to develop interventions, you should confirm that key participants understand and are applying the CDS Five Rights framework. For example, it is a useful exercise to ask at the beginning, middle, and end of intervention configuration: "To accomplish our goal of '_____,' is this the right CDS intervention (package) communicating the right information to the right person(s) through the right channel(s) at the right time(s)?"

Fully leveraging the CDS Five Rights framework requires a detailed understanding of the palettes underlying each configuration dimension. Chapter 2 provides details about CDS program stakeholders (who), and Chapter 3 discusses pertinent systems (where). The specific information delivered (what) will depend on the improvement target. Workflow opportunities for CDS intervention (when) were introduced in Chapter 3 and are covered further in the following chapter. We next explore in detail the decision support formats (how) that are available to provide CDS interventions. Chapter 6 covers how to apply these formats to address specific objectives.

Clinical Decision Support Intervention Types

As stated before, it is essential to fully understand the intervention-types toolbox to ensure that you are applying the right intervention type—or package of intervention types—to meet specific improvement needs. There are different ways to classify the CDS intervention types in the toolbox, and there is currently no universally accepted categorization scheme. Previous editions of this Guide introduced a taxonomy based on broad use cases; since that time, feedback and new contributions from clinical users, academic informatics laboratories,[4] and multi-stakeholder panels[5] have helped to expand and reshape the list. For example, additional categories such as diagnostic decision aids and analytic tools have been more prominently included. The updated classification presented in Figure 5-5 and described next maintains the strategy used in earlier guidebook editions; that is, dividing interventions into easily recognized types based on their typical presentation and user interaction. In this updated version, the intervention types are further grouped by typical workflows in which they appear.

For each intervention type within these four major groupings, we next outline their benefits and give several examples of specific interventions within that type.

CDS During Data-entry Tasks
Smart Documentation Forms
Benefits: Provide complete documentation for care quality/continuity, reimbursement, legal requirements; reduce omission errors by making sure the clinician thinks about the items displayed on the form; reduce commission errors by ensuring criti-

---

Figure 5-5: Taxonomy of CDS Intervention Types

A. CDS during data-entry tasks
   1. Smart documentation forms
   2. Order sets, care plans and protocols
   3. Parameter guidance
   4. Critiques and warnings—"immediate alerts"

B. CDS during data-review tasks
   5. Relevant data summaries (single-patient)
   6. Multi-patient monitors
   7. Predictive and retrospective analytics

C. CDS during assessment and understanding tasks
   8. Filtered reference information and knowledge resources
   9. Expert workup and management advisors

D. CDS not triggered by a user task
   10. Event-driven alerts (data-triggered) and reminders (time-triggered)

---

cal data—such as allergies—are captured; provide coded data for other data-driven CDS interventions; in some cases, provide calculated risk scores based on entries made in the form. Provide prompts to acquire specific information in the format desired (for example, displaying "kg" for weight to ensure capture in the metric system as needed for subsequent dose calculation).

Examples:
- Checklists for a given procedure or workflow;
- Structured documentation forms for a given problem or presentation that help guide proper care and facilitate documentation for quality reporting;
- Clinical documentation forms that adjust their items based on the patient's condition;
- Patient self-assessment forms;
- Pre-visit questionnaire that captures health problems and current medications;
- Nursing documentation forms that also inform the care plan by the items that are checked;
- Online health risk appraisals;
- Medication administration record forms that automatically help track whether medications have been missed;
- Intelligent referral forms that ensure that proper information is passed along;
- Data flowsheets for viewing and entering a patient's preventive care or immunization information (usually a mixture of data entry forms and relevant data summaries).

ORDER SETS, CARE PLANS AND MULTI-STEP PROTOCOLS

Benefits: Promote adherence to care standards by making the right thing the easiest thing to do. They facilitate compliance with previously agreed-upon care policies, best practices and locally designed clinical pathways. Because they usually are quicker to use than "a la carte" ordering, they often rate high in physician acceptance, increasing the likelihood that they are used and their benefits realized. Multi-step protocols can include collected order sets or care plans that are designed to be used in sequence.

Examples:

- Order sets and care plans for standard and ICU inpatient admissions, ambulatory problem management and pre- and post-operative care;
- Conditional order sets that adjust for patient conditions, allergies, comorbidities or other variations;
- Recommender programs that suggest likely order sets and care plans based on admission diagnosis or other patient factors;
- Protocol helpers that lead a clinician to the various 'order sets' that are part of a multi-step pathway;
- Support for managing clinical problems over long periods and many encounters, such as a computer-assisted management algorithm for treating hyperlipidemia over many outpatient visits.

PARAMETER GUIDANCE

Benefits: When writing orders or prescriptions (whether using an order set or not), these *proactive* interventions help ensure that drug doses and frequencies, as well as other diagnostic and therapeutic ordering parameters, are complete and correct. Parameter guidance may be provided as simple lists (such as for recommended drug dosages) or via more complex algorithms.

Examples:

- Suggested drug and/or dose choice lists integrated into ordering function—possibly modified by patient's kidney or liver function and age;
- Guided dose algorithms based on weight, body surface area (BSA) and other key parameters;
- Forms that facilitate entering complex orders such as insulin sliding scales and prednisone tapers (this can also be done as an order set but often is implemented within a single order in CPOE applications);
- Displays that help guide an order, for example, displaying hematocrit and crossmatch status when ordering blood products, or displaying kidney function when ordering medications where dosages must be adjusted if this function is abnormal;

- Template to ensure complete documentation of reasons and alternative options when ordering physical or chemical restraints;
- Total parenteral nutrition (TPN) ordering forms with built-in calculators to transform total sodium, potassium, calorie and CO_2 requirements into the appropriate solutions;
- Displaying additional important parameters, such as patient allergies, relevant lab test results, drug formulary status and/or drug costs when ordering a medication.

CRITIQUES AND WARNINGS (IMMEDIATE ALERTS)

Benefits: These *reactive* interventions prompt the user to immediately address possible errors, hazards or quality improvement opportunities related to new data or orders just entered into an information system; they help enforce care standards and prevent adverse events. They also may provide critiques to help ensure that additional documentation or orders necessary to make an order safe and complete are entered.

Note: Because this intervention type is so easily recognized and relatively simple in structure, it is easy to overuse. See the discussion on "alert fatigue" in Chapter 7. Effectiveness requires careful attention to workflow and ensuring that critiques are only presented when the likelihood is high that the user will use it to change management.

Examples:

- Drug allergy warnings;
- Drug interaction warnings, for example, in response to a newly prescribed drug's interaction with other drugs, pregnancy, laboratory results or food;
- Inappropriate therapeutic duplication warning;
- Underdose/overdose alert after an order has been entered (often for checking total dosage of some component, which may derive from multiple orders);
- Critique asking for additional data entry to ensure that a radiology study is ordered for the right reasons;

A Note about the Term 'Alert'

The "alert" intervention type is commonly understood to mean any highly focused and important message that pops up more or less unexpectedly. Two important alert subtypes include:

- *Immediate critiques and warnings* that are urgent requests for clarification, correction or different action—often related to an order or prescription—based on an action the user just took or data they entered;[6]
- *Event-driven reminders and notifications* that are driven by asynchronous events, that is, care-related occurrences that occur outside care team members' workflows. These events include when highly abnormal test results are posted in the laboratory system, or when too much time passes after a particular test or clinical event without appropriate follow-up. Reminders and notifications are used to make the clinicians and patients aware that such events have occurred.

Because these alert subtypes relate to workflow in different ways, we have tried to address them separately. We would prefer to give them different terms altogether, but the generic term 'alert' is too well entrenched to easily replace or modify. In addition, it is important to link these alert types to the work directed toward preventing 'alert fatigue' (which largely speaks to excessive immediate critiques, such as drug-drug interaction warnings). Thus, we are keeping the word 'alert' in both names, while also offering terms that distinguish these two intervention types and their very different applications. Immediate critiques and warnings are described next, and event-driven reminders and notifications are the last intervention type discussed.

- Warning that a consequent order is probably needed: for example, for drug levels when ordering certain antibiotics or for premedication when ordering certain drugs or procedures;
- Suggesting more cost-effective drug, regimen or formulary-compliant option than the medication being ordered.

CDS During Data Review Tasks
RELEVANT DATA SUMMARIES (SINGLE-PATIENT)

Benefits: These concise presentations of important data optimize decision making for a specific patient's circumstances by ensuring all pertinent data are noted and considered. They organize complex data sets to help care team members better understand the overall clinical picture and to highlight needed actions.

Examples:

- Health maintenance flowsheet presented when the patient returns for an ambulatory visit, showing fulfilled and needed screening tests;
- Chart that displays a patient's immunization status and highlights vaccinations that are due or overdue;
- Quality-metric status sheet (for example, related to patient-specific Meaningful Use and value-based purchasing quality measures) that shows which care requirements are completed and needed for a particular patient overall or for a certain aspect of their care (such as for diabetes management);
- Patient rounding or action lists organized to highlight patient-specific items needing attention, such as abnormal or new values;

- ICU electronic "status board" that provides a filtered view of a patient's critical physiologic parameters, ventilator settings, intravenous medication delivery rates and other information to facilitate 'at-a-glance' decision making;
- Key parameters such as a patient's heart rate and pain level presented to the nurse prior to medication administration;
- Displaying the current level of care/evaluation and management (E&M) score given current level of documentation for the patient encounter.

Multi-patient Monitors

Benefits: Like single-patient relevant data summaries, these provide a filtered, organized, "at-a-glance" look at key parameters and facilitate using the right information for decision making from a large data set covering several patients. In these multi-patient situations, for which resources must be prioritized and clinician attention constantly re-directed, this proactive intervention prevents many omission errors and permits much faster response to important events. Like the relevant data summary, this type does not necessarily require an immediate clinician response.

   Examples:
- Emergency department tracking system highlighting new patients, critical lab results, admission and disposition process, and other patient care and patient flow parameters;
- Operating room status monitor showing the procedure progress in each room, to facilitate rapid transitions and efficient resource utilization;
- Whole-service display of International Normalized Ratio (INR) values and warfarin dosing for an orthopedic post-op service;
- Patient-controlled analgesia service display, showing the current dosing and status for all patients on service, permitting changes to be made on all patients from one screen;
- Inpatient unit status monitor that lets the nurse see which patients have pending orders, due medications, or transfer/discharge events.

Predictive and Retrospective Analytics

Benefits: Whereas monitors display organized, real-time data elements in one place, analytics display data over time, compare them to benchmarks, enable users to drill down into data details to understand root causes, and in many other ways facilitate broad quality improvement projects. They can be used to help find the causes for results that CDS interventions are producing (for example, which clinicians are and are not adhering to care guidance supported by specific CDS interventions) and to monitor improvement trends. Predictive analytics use related techniques but can be applied to individual patients to risk-stratify them and to raise awareness about clinical hazards and opportunities. Analytics interventions may use much more sophisticated calculations and algorithms than is typical for most other CDS intervention types.

   Examples:
- Retrospective displays of performance, control charts, benchmarks for strategic guidance and problem-spotting;
- Syndromic surveillance and biosurveillance tools to identify disease patterns, outcomes changes and epidemics;
- Predictive tool to stratify pressure-ulcer risk in individual patients, thus directing resources to those at highest risk;
- Tools for comparing performance of different practices or subgroups in a particular quality or safety objective, or assessing (via control charts) whether a clinical pathway or other intervention or intervention package has successfully improved care process and outcome metrics;
- Displays comparing which initiative—among three or four possible broad alternatives—has the greatest potential for driving improvement.

CDS During Assessment and Understanding Tasks
Filtered Reference Information and Knowledge Resources

Benefits: Clinicians experience frequent information needs in caring for patients, and many of these are difficult to answer.[7] The information needs are diverse and span trying to integrate patient data into an accurate diagnostic picture and formulate an overall plan, to more focused needs such as understanding a medication's effects or proper dose, determining the best testing procedure, formulating a differential diagnosis, or deciding between several therapeutic options. Patients also experience many clinical information needs, and likewise experience important difficulties addressing them.[8] Many of these clinician and patient information needs can be addressed by material available in reference sources such as textbooks or guidebooks, journal articles, guidelines and other resources.

CDS reference interventions deliver information from these sources into clinician and patient workflow. Ideally, they filter the information based on patient and situational factors (such as care setting and intervention recipient), and deliver the most useful information in the most practical manner. This filtering is often accomplished through infobuttons or evidence links; the HL7 infobutton standard[9] is a mechanism to broker this information exchange between a reference source and a clinical application (such as an EHR or PHR) that delivers the information to the end user. Other information tools deliver images, charts, visually oriented reference, or specifically deliver relevant updates from recent research. The information itself may come from commercial references, such as drug information resources; from public resources, such as national guideline websites; or from local sources within a care delivery organization.

Examples:
- Infobutton linking from each entry in an active medication list in an EHR to a display for clinicians containing side effects and/or dosing for that medication; related links to drug information for the patient that can be printed and/or securely emailed to the patient;
- Infobutton linking from problem-list entry or review in an EHR to recent evidence-based treatment overviews for that problem;
- Link from patient's problems and medications in a PHR to self-management guidance and drug information sheets;
- Link from an immunization flowsheet to table listing standard immunization intervals;
- Links to calculators and nomograms, such as for drug dosing, within a CPOE system;
- Service that notifies clinicians and/or patients about recent research updates relevant to a patient's problems or medications;
- Order set links to explanatory information and evidence supporting the orders presented in the set;
- Health risk assessment results that generate a set of information resources and educational programs to be used by the patient.

Expert Workup and Management Advisors

Benefits: These applications typically use patient data from an EHR or (more commonly as of this writing) from direct user entry, to suggest diagnoses that may not have been considered; they also can suggest tests and workup steps that can further clarify the diagnosis. Although they are most commonly used for diagnostic purposes, the same model can be used to advise on recommended therapies specific to the patient's situation.

Examples:
- Diagnostic decision support program that accepts symptoms, signs and general test findings and suggests a ranked list of possible diagnoses;
- Workup advisor that suggests best next tests for patients, given their clinical findings;
- Visual dermatology guide that helps clinicians identify rashes based on characteristics such as color, size and texture;
- Antibiotic advisor that assesses, for a particular infection, the likely pathogens, local antibiotic sensitivities, and drug contraindications in order to provide recommended treatments.

CDS Not Triggered by a User Task
Event-driven Alerts and Reminders

Benefits: As noted in the sidebar presented earlier, these alert subtypes raise awareness about events that are occurring outside routine, patient-specific workflows. These events can include newly posted abnormal lab results that suggest significant patient danger,[10] a new admission or discharge for a primary care physician's patient, and many others. These interventions can also detect important *non-events*, that is, when important events have *not* occurred in a prescribed time period or as indicated. For example, detecting and notifying that a patient has not had a particular cancer screening or disease-monitoring test, or health-maintenance exam, within the recommended time period. Similarly, they can detect and notify when a particular medication is indicated for a specific condition, and the patient has not received it. Alerts and reminders prevent omission errors and promote faster response to critical situations.[11]

Typically, important event-driven alerts must reach the target user through a notification mechanism (see Chapter 7), such as text message, secure email or appearance on a notification screen (see relevant data summaries and multi-patient monitors previously presented). Lower-urgency reminders that can wait for the patient's next in-person clinician encounter can be displayed on the patient's EHR facesheet and/or via their PHR.

Examples:
- EHR, text message or pager alert about an abnormal and critical lab result;[12]
- Notification about an abnormal mammogram or Pap smear finding;
- Reminder that a patient is due for a flu shot or other immunization;
- Alert that a critical follow-up lab test has not been performed within the recommended time period;
- Notification that restraint orders or indwelling catheters must be renewed after a specific time period has elapsed;
- Program that generates standard letters to patients about their lab results, with varied text, depending on whether the result is normal or abnormal;
- Adverse event detector that monitors proxies for adverse events, such as when antidotes for overdoses and allergic reactions (such as naloxone, diphenhydramine) are used;

- User-requested notification when an important lab result is available or other key event has occurred;
- Disease management alert; for example, notification that there are needed therapeutic or monitoring interventions based on guidelines/evidence and patient-specific factors.

Chapter 6 explores in more detail how to select from among these intervention types to efficiently and effectively meet your improvement objectives. For now, you can begin considering which intervention types are available in your information systems and which would be most implementable, usable, valuable and cost-effective for the different improvement targets you have selected.

Other Interventions/Considerations
Manage the CDS/CPOE Interplay
In some organizations that are early in their CDS program efforts, clinicians might consider CDS and CPOE to be the nearly the same. This occurs especially when there is major organizational attention to a new CPOE rollout, and there is intense focus on developing and rolling out imbedded order sets and alerts. While there is certainly positive interplay between CDS interventions and CPOE applications, it is important for clinicians and other stakeholders to understand that they are different. The CDS Five Rights framework can be helpful in clarifying important distinctions: CPOE is a *delivery channel* for *CDS interventions* which may include alerts, order sets and other *intervention types*, that convey *information* about drug prescribing safety concerns and support evidence-based orders for a particular situation.

Ideally, you should gain organizational comfort with—and begin implementing—CDS interventions before the CPOE launch date. CPOE is a difficult enough change process to manage without the additional stressors associated with a newly deployed CDS program. If possible, have your organization adopt protocol-driven care and CDS interventions delivered via other channels before adapting these approaches for the CPOE channel. Otherwise, a failure in one will be seen as a failure in both. For example, if a CDS tool is developed without a firm basis in good clinical evidence or workflow realities, clinicians will see this as a CPOE failure. Conversely, if the CPOE system is hampered by poor usability and poor acceptance, clinicians may associate imbedded CDS interventions (even if they are carefully developed) with this failure.

While CDS and CPOE are interdependent in important ways, your organization should ensure that they are on strong independent footing, and your CDS Team should try to lay a solid CDS foundation before utilizing the CPOE channel. If you have already launched CPOE and are still in the early CDS program development stages, you should carefully address the issues outlined in Part I to ensure that your CDS efforts optimally support your CPOE-related efforts, and vice versa.

Understand and Manage Organizational Politics

CDS programs—and interventions launched by those programs—typically create the perception in organizations that power and control are shifting, and you should anticipate and address this as early as possible. Changes in clinical policy that precede and follow CDS interventions must be made in collaboration with frontline clinicians at each development and deployment step.

Consider who will be affected, both positively and negatively, by the objectives you have selected—and resulting CDS interventions—and establish and maintain communication, shared understanding, and stakeholder buy-in throughout the improvement process. Failure to do this will inevitably lead to problems when those who perceive that new interventions have negatively affected them in some way (such as through decreased autonomy or increased workflow burden) respond accordingly.

Identify your champions/enablers/detractors in advance and engage them closely (see also the discussion about these important stakeholders in Chapter 8), and take pains to ensure that top leadership is highly supportive and willing to help you through the

inevitable rough spots at the beginning. Liberally use process mapping and workflow analysis (as discussed in Chapters 3 and 6) to ensure that your CDS Team remains close to the both clinical and political realities that will determine whether or not your interventions will be successful.

Ensure That Your CDS Team Is Prepared to Manage the Full Intervention Lifecycle

Just as many people carefully consider beforehand all the responsibility and necessary investments associated with having children, your CDS Team should likewise carefully consider in advance all that will be required to successfully apply CDS to your chosen objective(s). Figure PII-1 in the Part II Introduction summarizes major elements in the CDS intervention lifecycle. These building blocks outline major tasks and investments that will be required; not just to select, configure and launch the interventions but also to monitor and maintain them over time. Contrary to what beginning implementers typically think, it is often true that the latter efforts (which are cyclical by nature) are more impactful and resource intensive than the former.

Before embarking on the activities outlined in subsequent chapters, your CDS Team should step back and consider among its members—in consultation with organizational leadership and other stakeholders—whether there is adequate commitment to proceed with the work and investments that will be needed for success. If this exploration raises questions or concerns, you should pause to address them and re-evaluate as needed whether or not to proceed with the effort to apply CDS to your chosen objective. It is much wiser to pull back and redirect CDS energies than to proceed with an effort that lacks resources and commitment required for success.

CONSIDERATIONS FOR HOSPITALS/HEALTH SYSTEMS
People (Governance)

- With multiple committees affecting CDS program decisions (see, for example, Figures 2-4 through 2-6), each committee's politics and different priorities may cause difficulty in gaining agreement on fundamental CDS concepts such as how the CDS Five Rights apply to targeted objectives in an integrated way across domains. As Chapter 2 suggests, having CDS Committee members represented on other committees (P&T, EHR, Medication System Review, etc.)—and vice versa—can help you unify how the CDS framework is understood and applies across the entire organization. Individual outreach from CDS Team members, champions and others can likewise help build an effective shared framework.

- Across different departments or different hospitals (if the CDS Committee is centralized within a health system) the high-level CDS goals may be different. To begin building overall understanding and buy-in, you should try to address a goal that is common to many departments, if possible. Feedback from multiple departments for the same high-level goal will provide the CDS Team with important insights into how to approach the intervention (package) in as unified a manner as possible, as well as how to best adapt it for each particular department or hospital.

People (Stakeholder Involvement)

- Ensure that appropriate end-users (generalist and specialist physicians, nurses, pharmacists, and other individuals including patients, if appropriate) provide input to determine which objectives are most important to the high-level goal. Their support will be critical to achieving improvement targets, and this will be garnered to the extent that they see personal value from achieving the objective(s).
- As suggested in Chapter 2, it is very helpful to have one or more team members working on the intervention who possess formal clinical informatics skills and experiences; that is, expertise in how clinical and people/process/technology capabilities can be applied together in addressing care delivery needs. Understanding both the clinical needs and the informatics capabilities will be key to match-

ing objectives with interventions. Chapter 6 provides more detail on accomplishing this match.

CONSIDERATIONS FOR SMALL PRACTICES
Focusing/Refining (Goal and Intervention Selection)

- Apply your practice's systematic approach to prioritizing improvement targets to select focal points for your CDS intervention efforts. Specific macro drivers—such as CDS and performance improvement–related requirements for achieving Meaningful Use, and value-based purchasing initiatives—will largely inform priority targets for CDS intervention.
- Recognize that achieving better outcomes for specific conditions means treating and monitoring a cluster of clinical parameters more effectively, and CDS interventions may be focused on several different parameters. For example, a pertinent diabetes cluster and CDS approach might include interventions to ensure that foot and eye exams are done at appropriate intervals, that hemoglobin A1c and LDL levels are appropriately monitored and managed, and that patients receive appropriate guidance on self-management. Intervention packages (perhaps including alerts, order sets, relevant data summary, reference information, documentation tools and other intervention types) can be used to address these targets individually and collectively.

Capabilities

- Understand the CDS Five Rights dimensions and how each is applicable to developing effective CDS interventions in your practice; for example, the specific information delivery channels and CDS intervention types available in your EHR and other information systems.
- Work with your EHR and CDS suppliers (either directly or via intermediaries such as RECs) to ensure that their content and delivery channels work smoothly together as a foundation for your new CDS interventions. In the coming years,

there will be increasing pressure for these suppliers to better integrate their interdependent offerings, since the combined functionality is often critical, yet problematic for small practices.

Planning (Tasks)

- Many key steps in the CDS intervention lifecycle—that is, selecting, configuring, monitoring and maintaining target-focused interventions, will be highly dependent on the tools and services provided by your EHR supplier. Nonetheless, you should keep all pertinent individuals in the practice engaged as appropriate throughout the cycle to ensure that the CDS is done *with* them and not *to* them and that the tools available are appropriate for your objectives and practice circumstances.

CONSIDERATIONS FOR HIT SOFTWARE PROVIDERS
Capabilities

- Consider that your provider clients—whether small practices or large health systems—will need support from their information systems, and system suppliers, to accomplish many or most of the major tasks associated with the CDS intervention lifecycle.
- Strive to be optimally receptive to clients' needs for improved functionality that is essential to better address improvement imperatives. Deepening your knowledge about these drivers and your collaborations with clients around them can help address this business imperative (see Epilogue). In circumstances where needed enhancements can't readily be provided, advise clients on alternatives that best leverage available capabilities.
- Your CDS-related tools should track with national improvement priorities (see Chapters 1 and 2) to help providers rise to the substantial challenges they create. This should be obvious, but consider ways to improve your collaborations with your CDS/CIS supplier counterparts and provider clients to better to ensure that CDS content resources and delivery channels work

smoothly together to meet implementers' deployment and improvement needs. Better integration between interdependent offerings from CDS content and CIS system providers should be a high priority, since the joint functionality for implementers is often critical yet problematic.

- In addition to the broader CDS-related standards mentioned in the Considerations for HIT Software Providers section in Chapter 3, consider opportunities to foster collaborations among CIS and CDS system suppliers and implementers on intervention-specific standards and tools; for example, covering infobuttons, rules, order sets and other intervention types.
- Consider developing/increasing support for CDS modules that use Service Oriented Architecture (see Chapter 4).

Planning (Processes)

- Explore ways to collaborate with clients to provide them with mentorship, tools and tactics to manage the complex process of successfully implementing CDS capabilities in your systems.
- Consider opportunities to shorten software development and release cycles to enable more rapid evolution in how well the systems support performance improvement needs.
  - Most large and successful CIS/CDS applications have evolved over many years. This has produced very complex legacy systems that make it difficult to conduct rapid improvement cycles—both clinical and technological. This and other legacy systems limitations have led to calls for radically different approaches to developing and deploying clinical information systems—more akin to the modular, plug-and-play application platform model used in smartphones.[13]
  - It is difficult for large system suppliers to quickly change technology models—especially if they are successful and have a large installed customer base. Nonetheless, given accelerating demands on provider for measurable performance improvement (see Chapter 1), both

suppliers and implementers need to find ways to enhance CIS/CDS effectiveness faster.

• Develop or enhance capabilities and/or services that enable clients to share CDS content and/or strategies and configurations between sites.

Too often implementers start at ground level when they should be building off of each other's successes and failures. Explore business models that provide incentives for your organization to encourage and facilitate such collaboration.

WORKSHEETS

Worksheet 5-1

Selecting and Prioritizing CDS Goals

Worksheet 5-1 helps integrate, prioritize, and refine your stakeholder survey about clinical goals into a foundation for action. You can extract from the stakeholder-centric Worksheet 2-1 the strong themes regarding CDS-facilitated improvement opportunities that emerge from your interviews and analysis. To this candidate list, add other potential targets identified from the internal and external survey of improvement opportunities as discussed in the chapter, as well as in Chapters 1 and 2. List the most promising targets in the first column of this worksheet. In the second column, list the rationale for why you've included each target. This might include the stakeholder(s) who emphasized the target, the mandatory external (such as regulatory) or internal (such as practice leadership or hospital board-level) driver behind it, or the pertinent organizational momentum (for example, from a major CIS deployment such as CPOE motivated by addressing the target).

In the third column record information about the organizational priority for addressing the target through the CDS program. The prioritization approaches outlined in the chapter should be helpful here. In the fourth column, indicate any baseline performance data available for the target. Be as quantitative as possible, considering data-gathering approaches as outlined in this chapter and Chapter 9. In the fifth column, record a desired performance level to be achieved through CDS implementation. Determining this target will require consulting with key stakeholders and governance entities, and the specific goal may be further refined during the subsequent implementation steps outlined in the next chapters. When possible and appropriate, try to specify a timeframe during which the goal will be achieved.

In the Notes column include items that might be useful in justifying or executing the CDS effort directed toward the target, such as synergies with other organizational initiatives, available information about the benefit/cost ratio of addressing the target, and the like.

Target	Rationale	Priority	Baseline Performance	Desired Outcome	Notes
Increase appropriate use of VTE prophylaxis	Part of P4P contract; VTE is a hospital-acquired condition for which CMS is not providing additional reimbursement	1	76% appropriate prophylaxis use	>90% appropriate use within 12 months	Coordinate CDS efforts with major organizational PI effort on this topic
Prevent patients from getting medications to which they are allergic	Recent high-profile sentinel event; significant documented costs associated with this preventable ADE	2	3% of prescriptions are to allergic patients	0% of prescriptions are to allergic patients within 12 months	Coordinate CDS approach with recent launch of CPOE and eMAR system

An explicit and detailed picture of CDS-sensitive care improvement opportunities emerges from the completed Worksheet 5-1. These opportunities should trigger a thoughtful gap analysis, i.e., an effort to understand the care structure and processes that result in the difference between the current and desired performance (see Chapters 3 and 6).

This analysis is an essential prerequisite to developing successful improvement strategies that will help uncover promising modifications to information management and workflow. These strategies may include CDS interventions, but do not assume that this will always be the case. Despite the focus of this Guide on these knowledge-based interventions, it is important to recognize that these might not always be the best or first approach to addressing every performance gap; the analysis will help identify their proper role.

Once your CDS Team has identified priority high-level goals on which to focus CDS efforts—and developed a shared appreciation with stakeholders about why these performance gaps exist—the next step is to determine more specific objectives for targeted CDS intervention. Following is a sample worksheet that illustrates the process of articulating clinical objectives and desired actions necessary to accomplish selected high-level clinical goals. Processes for selecting higher levels goals and more specific objectives are similar, so the worksheets are likewise similar. You can complete such worksheets for your CDS program over time—building, refining, prioritizing and validating their contents during multiple meetings with internal stakeholders and based on other research as discussed in this and other chapters.

Worksheet 5-2

Objectives to Achieve Goals

You can generate a separate Worksheet 5-2 for each priority high-level clinical goal you documented in Worksheet 5-1, and list this goal at the top. The data needed to complete this worksheet come from your gap and processes analyses with stakeholders and committees.

In the first column, list clinical objectives required to achieve the goal. In the second column, identify care processes and actions needed to accomplish each objective. For each action, use the third column to document (as quantitatively as is practical) the baseline performance on that action. The fourth column is used to record the desired outcomes (again, ideally in a quantifiable way) that would indicate success in achieving the objective.

Several key issues mentioned previously should be recorded in the Notes column. These include rationale for pursuing the objective, key stakeholder(s), and major initiatives currently in place to address this objective. In addition, matters pertinent to CDS cost justification (such as inefficiencies and opportunities in current approaches) should be documented as well.

Clinical goal: Use anticoagulation drugs more safely and effectively

Clinical Objective	Desired Action	Baseline Performance	Desired Outcomes	Notes
Improve adherence post-op heparin prophylaxis recommendations	Entry of physician order for subcutaneous heparin	Reviewing inpatient order entry data reveals approximately 62% compliance on the three surgical wards	100% compliance for appropriate patients, defined as no history of neurosurgery or other major bleeding risk and no history of heparin-related allergy or problem in the past	Objective is big push for quality officer; lots of time and attention being devoted to the gap; interest in exploring CDS to help make current improvement approach more efficient and effective
Improve PTT monitoring for anticoagulant effect on a timely and regular basis	Order for PTT entered by physician	88% of reviewed patients have PTT ordered within the first six hours	100% compliance	
	Collection of PTT by nursing	66% of reviewed patients had PTT collected within the first six hours	100% compliance	Some wards are not staffed with nursing assistants, leading to delays in drawing the PTT

continued on next page

Worksheet 5-2 *continued*

Clinical Objective	Desired Action	Baseline Performance	Desired Outcomes	Notes
	Abnormal PTT posted by lab acknowledged and addressed by clinical staff	39% of inappropriate PTT values [define thresholds] addressed within six hours	75% compliance, allow for some delay based on time of day and lab reporting schedule, but only one hour leeway	Shift changes seem to have a big effect on the delay in addressing inappropriate PTT values
Improve compliance with care guideline for enoxaparin.	Order for enoxaparin in patients admitted with DVT without embolism	75% of hospitalized patients with DVT still receive IV heparin	100% compliance with enoxaparin and DVT policy	

Worksheet 5-3

Roles and Responsibilities of Clinical and Non-clinical Stakeholders

As we have emphasized, those who are affected by the CDS goal—such as patients, nurses, pharmacists, and physicians—should be engaged all through the intervention lifecycle. Their successful participation in selecting, configuring, validating, launching, using and monitoring the interventions can dramatically increase the likelihood that outcomes will improve. Mapping the roles that these stakeholders should play in this change management process—in collaboration with the CDS Team—can help ensure that these stakeholders are effectively engaged and their efforts are coordinated. You can use this worksheet to help get that process started; additional change management considerations and tasks associated with intervention launch are addressed in Chapter 8.

List the improvement goal at the top of the worksheet to provide context. Copy into the first column each objective from Worksheet 5-2 for which you will develop CDS interventions. If you are addressing more than one objective, you can use additional worksheets for each, or combine them into a single worksheet.

In the second column, outline the tasks that the CDS Team needs to address for intervention success. Use the remaining columns to assign corresponding roles in developing the intervention to other stakeholders. Continue adding columns as needed for additional stakeholders, such as quality officers or committees. Figures 2-1 and 2-6 provide information about stakeholder roles and responsibilities, and you can refer to them in filling out this worksheet.

continued on next page

Worksheet 5-3 *continued*

Goal: Reduce preventable ADEs						
CDS Objective	**CDS Team**	**Patient**	**Nurse**	**Physician**	**Pharmacist**	**Clinical IT Advisory Committee**
Prevent patients from getting drugs to which they are allergic	• Document and validate changes to workflow • Determine/validate data flows needed to manage allergy information • Provide and validate database to be used for checking • Develop/implement intervention and evaluation plan • Prepare preliminary training/communications for broader stakeholder community	• Know and communicate their allergies (develop tools and strategies to support this—such as gathering information from previous admissions and office visits for prompting)	• Help develop, finalize and accept intervention plan • Help test and validate workflow that involves accurately recording medication list and allergies on outpatient visit or admission to floor • Define nursing constraints • Convey the process to other frontline nurses • Help create implementation plans	• Help develop, finalize and accept intervention plan • Define prescriber workflow constraints (time, efficiency) • Convey process to colleagues • Help create implementation plans • Advise on intervention management such as override handling for alerts	• Validate workflow components and identify gaps • Help develop, finalize, and accept intervention plan • Help with intervention testing and validation • Educate colleagues • Verify drug information and intervention strategy • Help create implementation plans	• Coordinate intervention management and updates • Oversee development, rollout and monitoring, help with problem solving

Worksheet 5-4

Linking Systems and Objectives

Thinking about your available information systems (see Worksheet 3-1)— together with your selected CDS objectives and performance gap analysis results (Worksheets 5-1 and 5-2)—will help trigger initial thoughts about how your available CIS and CDS assets can be applied to improve performance. You can use Worksheet 5-4 to help document those notes.

In the first column, list your priority clinical decision support objective(s) from Worksheet 5-2. In the second column, list some potential ideas for CDS interventions that could help address that objective (Chapter 6 covers this in detail). In the next three columns, bring forward information from Worksheet 3-1. In the last two columns, record information about whether and how the currently available systems can enable the desired CDS functionality and clinical outcomes. You can revisit this worksheet after reviewing recommendations and worksheets in the next two chapters.

Clinical Decision Support Objective	CDS Intervention	System Name/Type/ Vendor	Information Type	System User and Usage	Adequacy to Complete Intervention (Good, Need Upgrade, Need Replacement)	Notes
Prevent prescription of medication to allergic patients	Prescription allergy alert window	Better Care CPOE	Medication list (NDC), allergy list, XYZ Corp Drug Database	Physicians	Need upgrade— Alert functionality needs to be modified to trigger at moment of order submission, medication list user interface needs to be friendlier	Accurate medication list is critical, need to discuss alert trigger rules—consult clinical IT advisory committee
Prevent prescription of medication to allergic patients	Pharmacy med check	Safe Drugs Pharmacy System	XYZ Corp Drug Database, drug formulary, allergy list	Pharmacist	Need upgrade— EHR and drug database interfaces need to be built, pharmacist alert feature needs to be built	Allergy content— consult clinical IT advisory committee for vetting

REFERENCES

1   Institute for Healthcare Improvement. The Five Rights of Medication Administration. http://www.ihi.org/knowledge/Pages/ImprovementStories/FiveRightsofMedicationAdministration.aspx. Accessed September 14, 2011.

2   Dexter, et al. Inpatient Computer-Based Standing Orders vs Physician Reminders to Increase Influenza and Pneumococcal Vaccination Rates. *JAMA*. 2004; 292(19):2366-2371.

3   See "Mary Gonzales' Kaiser Permanente Story" on YouTube: http://www.youtube.com/watch?v=qKiD-4deFPQ. Accessed June 14, 2011.

4   Wright A, Sittig DF, Ash JS, et al. Development and evaluation of a comprehensive clinical decision support taxonomy: Comparison of front-end tools in commercial and internally-developed electronic health record systems. *J Am Med Inform Assoc*. 2011, Mar 17; PMID: 21415065.

5   See, for example: "Driving Quality and Performance Measurement—A Foundation for Clinical Decision Support." National Quality Forum CDS Expert Panel Report. http://www.qualityforum.org/Publications/2010/12/CDS_Report_full.aspx. Accessed June 1, 2011. And: "Clinical Decision Support Workshop Meeting Summary, August 2009", ONC report http://healthit.hhs.gov/cds . Accessed June 1, 2011.

6   See, for example, a systematic review of drug alerts: Schedlbauer A, Prasad V, Mulvaney C, et. al. What Evidence Supports the Use of Computerized Alerts and Prompts to Improve Clinicians' Prescribing Behavior? *J Am Med Inform Assoc*. 2009 Jul-Aug; 16(4): 531–538.

7   See, for example: Ely JW, Osheroff JA, Ebell MH, et al. Analysis of questions asked by family doctors regarding patient care. BMJ. 1999 Aug 7;319(7206):358-361.; and Smith R. What clinical information do doctors need? *BMJ*. 1996; 26;313(7064):1062-1068.

8   Halvorsen PA. What information do patients need to make a medical decision? *Med Decis Making*. 2010 Sep-Oct; 30(5 Suppl):11S-13S.

9   See the HL7 wiki page on Product Infobutton: Product Brief - Context-Aware Knowledge Retrieval (Infobutton). http://wiki.hl7.org/index.php?title=Product_Infobutton. Accessed September 13, 2011.

10   Singh H, Wilson L, Reis B, et al. Ten strategies to improve management of abnormal test result alerts in the electronic health record. *Journal of Patient Safety*. 2010.6(2):121-123.

11   Kuperman GJ, Teich JM, Bates DW, Hiltz FL, Hurley JM, Lee RY, Paterno MD. Detecting alerts, notifying the physician, and offering action items: a comprehensive alerting system. *J Am Med Informatics Assoc*. 1996; 3(suppl):704-708.

12   Hysong SJ, Sawhney MK, Wilson L, et al. Understanding the management of electronic test result notifications in the outpatient setting. *BMC Medical Informatics and Decision Making*. 2011; 11:22. http://www.biomedcentral.com/1472-6947/11/22/abstract. Accessed September 15, 2011.

13   Mandl KD, Kohane IS. No small change for the health information economy. *N Engl J Med*. 2009; 360:1278-1281.

Chapter 6

Selecting Interventions to Deliver Targeted Improvements

Tasks

- Use results from your objective-related care process mapping to build a shared understanding with stakeholders about the workflows—and related decision support needs and opportunities—pertinent to your selected improvement objective(s).
- Understand the five CDS Core Actions that help link your objective to specific intervention types and specific steps in the workflow that are likely to be effective in addressing it.
- Consider which Core Actions apply to your objective, and for each that does, examine intervention types and workflows to see which are relevant to objective-related care processes. Use Figures 6-1 through 6-3 for details and examples. (Worksheet 6-1)
- Choose specific interventions to address your objective based on implementation factors: ease of implementation, acceptability and impact—balancing these factors based on your organization's CDS experience and resources. (Worksheets 6-2 and 6-3)

KEY LESSONS

- Five CDS Core Actions—recognizing patterns, formulating a plan, executing the plan, monitoring and responding to events, and communicating—broadly cover care delivery activities and the ways in which information systems can augment this work. One or more Core Actions can be identified for a given clinical objective, and each Core Action is associated with CDS intervention types that can facilitate that action.
- Additionally, the Core Actions typically take place at different workflow points. If you understand which Core Actions drive performance on your objective, then you can identify not only some likely CDS intervention types to apply, but you can also identify when they should be applied.
- The better you understand how current care processes affect performance on your target objectives, the better able you will be to provide CDS interventions that improve outcomes. Often, the causes of high or low performance are multifactorial, and in those cases, a package of two or more interventions applied at different times can improve effectiveness more than just a single intervention.

KEY LESSONS *continued*

- Each intervention type has its characteristic properties, such as how easy it is to implement, how acceptable users find it to be, and how effective it is at improving outcomes. When choosing among several intervention types that can address a given objective class, different organizations will have different optimal choices based on these properties.
- At this intervention selection stage, as at the subsequent stages outlined in the next chapters, it is vital to communicate your actions to key stakeholders and get their input into the planning and decisions.

GENERAL APPROACH

Chapter 5 discussed selecting specific objectives to achieve the goals established by your CDS program. The objective may be narrowly focused, such as improving the number of patients who are appropriately given smoking cessation advice during an office visit, or perhaps broader and multi-factorial, such as preventing venous thromboembolism in postoperative patients. CDS can help across this spectrum. The question for implementers in any case is, which CDS interventions, applied in what way, are going to be most acceptable, easiest to implement, and most effective? In this chapter and the next, we present steps to help you choose effective interventions and configure them for greatest impact.

In this chapter, we discuss a structured method for understanding the Core Actions that clinicians and patients take at different care process steps, and how these actions play a part in achieving your objectives. Since these Core Actions are also closely associated with the specific CDS intervention types (discussed in Chapter 5), this approach helps you to find the CDS intervention types that are most useful to address your objective.

The Core CDS Actions

If you are trying to improve VTE prophylaxis rates in surgical patients (see Case Study for Hospitals in Part II Introduction, including Figures PII-2 and PII-3), you should start by considering how clinicians handle VTE prophylaxis without CDS:

- Identify patients who are likely to be at high risk, so you can ensure that those patients who can benefit most receive prophylaxis. During initial assessment and data gathering, *recognize the patterns* that suggest high VTE risk, based on type of surgery to be performed, the patient's age, and whether the patient is obese or has circulatory problems. In addition, recognize whether the patient has had bleeding problems that would argue against aggressive clot prevention therapies.
- Having recognized that a particular patient in a particular situation needs additional management, clinicians then *formulate a plan*. They need to choose the best therapy, perhaps deciding among warfarin, unfractionated heparin and low-molecular-weight heparin. If necessary, they may also choose the best additional tests and studies to assess the risk level.
- Having decided on a therapy plan—perhaps to start oral warfarin, as well as apply a passive range-of-motion device after orthopedic surgery—clinicians *execute the plan*: they order the warfarin, order any tests deemed necessary, perform the surgical procedure itself, and apply the range-of-motion device. In doing this, they are constantly checking to see that these actions have been taken correctly and have not introduced adverse events.

- Postoperatively, clinicians constantly monitor, detect and *respond to events*—making sure that the patient has appropriate drug levels drawn, and responding to abnormal results by changing doses or applying other therapies, if monitoring identifies such needs.

- In all cases, clinicians are *communicating* and coordinating activities with the primary care team, and any other services involved with the patient. If the patient is getting ready for discharge and rehabilitation services, clinicians make sure that this process is started in a timely fashion, at least a day or two before the actual discharge.

Whenever you see the following wording, "recognize a pattern," "making sure," "actions taken correctly," "monitor," or "detect/respond to events," you are likely to find benefit with CDS interventions that are tuned to those specific actions. These activities map closely to a few CDS intervention types and to one or two typical places in the workflow, as we illustrate in the next section. The Core CDS Actions reflect ways that information systems can augment human information processing capabilities. Next, we outline in more detail these actions and their CDS implications.

1. **Recognize patterns.** When assessing or re-assessing a patient, clinicians process available patient data and clinical knowledge to determine if the patient fits a pattern that calls for specific care actions. Does the problem list include diabetes? The patient may need specific attention to that during an office visit. Is the patient presenting to the hospital with a problem for which there is a care guideline, such as community-acquired pneumonia? CDS can help sense patterns and identify such situations. Relevant CDS intervention types to support these assessments are outlined next.

   - **Data-triggered alerts** are well-suited here. They can point out that this patient is at high risk for VTE; has community-acquired pneumonia and needs to have the appropriate guideline applied; needs a private room for contagion risk; and many more. These alerts

can also help guide the care plan by highlighting contraindications, such as warning about dangers associated with performing a computed tomography (CT) scan with intravenous contrast dye on a patient who takes metformin.

   - **Smart documentation forms** such as checklists and clinical score calculators (such as PORT score assessment forms for risk-stratifying patients with pneumonia, or a stroke score assessment form) can fit smoothly into the patient-assessment and data-gathering workflow, help ensure that data needed for proper management are captured completely, and provide conclusions that help clinicians recognize a particular condition suggested by the data.

   - **Relevant data summaries** represent another visual way to improve clinician pattern recognition, using similar logic but assembling care-related items that need to be addressed, perhaps in a facesheet display that can be examined during the encounter.

   - **Predictive analytics** is a more complex form of data processing that may use statistical models or multiple logic rules to identify patients at high risk for venous thromboembolism, pressure ulcers, or other conditions requiring clinical attention.

   - **Expert advisors** have a role to play here, taking patient data and additional user input and suggesting possible diagnoses or recommended workups.

2. **Formulate a specific plan.** Once clinicians recognize a pattern, how should they best address it? Usually, this involves choices: selecting the best diagnostic studies, medications, and other therapies to address an issue that they already know needs attention. Relevant CDS intervention types include:

   - **Filtered reference information** and knowledge resources are of primary importance here, particularly for unfamiliar presentations, patients with comorbidities, or other situations that can affect the therapy choice. Appropriate tables, figures and management guides can make the difference between choosing an effective therapy and an ineffective one.

- Some of the interventions that are directed toward plan execution, such as situation-focused **order sets and care plans**, can also contain explicit reference information to help clinicians make choices as they are ordering or documenting; they also contain implicit advice by featuring options most appropriate for the situation.

- **Expert workup advisors** that are tuned to a specific part of the plan, such as a computerized antibiotic advisor, can help you select the best option given a number of pertinent parameters.

3. **Execute the plan.** Once clinicians decide how to address a particular clinical issue, CDS tools can help ensure that the plan is executed correctly, safely and completely.

- **Parameter-guidance tools**—with or without full order sets—can help clinicians appropriately order interventions when the patient has additional constraints (such as renal failure) that affect therapy. For example, parameter guidance tools can suggest necessary medication dosing adjustments in patients with abnormal kidney function.

- **Order sets and care plan tools** help ensure that the correct medications are ordered and administered in the correct doses and frequencies; similarly, they can help clinicians put into play complex plans for respiratory therapy, intravenous fluids, and other tests and treatments. Order sets are unique in that their list of recommended orders helps to formulate a plan, serving as a filtered reference, while their dose suggestions act as parameter guidance tools; thus they are applicable to both the planning and execution phase.

- **Critiques and warnings** help catch many potential errors that humans can easily forget, such as drug-allergy or drug-drug interactions, inappropriate or duplicate tests, or failure to order drug levels appropriately.

- Some **smart documentation forms**, especially those which encourage complete process execution such as **checklists**, ensure that clinicians address every item in the care plan.

- **Filtered reference information** such as procedure guides and medication dosing information tools can support correct care plan execution by providing information as needed. For example, reference material can address questions that nurses may have as they administer specific medications or that clinicians may have as they perform specific procedures.

4. **Monitor, detect and handle new events.** Once a care plan is in place and running, it is critical to ensure that the plan remains appropriate for the patient's clinical status and to respond appropriately as this status changes. For example, the patient may improve as expected or there may be new findings that arise—such as a high fever, an unexpected abnormal lab result, or a significant new arrhythmia. In any case, these events may trigger transitioning to new plan phases, or adapting the plan. This Core Action includes detecting and handling events in both a proactive way—such as using displays and other tools to continually present the status of one or more patients—and in a reactive way—such as by alerting clinicians specifically about unusual events, so that they can respond. Keep in mind that this Core Action, as well as others such as recognizing patterns, may involve patient populations and not just individual patients.

- **Multi-patient monitors** (for watching an entire service at once) and **relevant data display and summaries** (for single patients) concentrate, filter and present large amounts of information in a human-friendly, workflow-friendly way. This helps clinicians see what is most important, new or unusual about one or more patients.

- **Event-driven and time-driven alerts** are important ways to spot unusual and uncommon events that may indicate a need to change the care plan. In the ambulatory setting, alerts and reminders can be especially important to make sure that an ordered test has taken place and to make sure that abnormal results are noticed and managed.

- **Retrospective analytics** help clinicians monitor performance over a longer period of time and can detect patterns of adverse events, unsuccessful therapies, "bouncebacks" (unexpected repeat hospital admissions) and other variances from expected outcomes.

5. **Facilitate communication.** Good communication among care team members (including and especially the patient) is critical to ensure that all the other Core Actions are accomplished successfully and result in optimal outcomes. Communication gaps, however, are common and have many adverse effects—but CDS can help prevent them. For example, CDS interventions can help ensure that an ambulatory consultation is not wasted because the consultant doesn't have all the needed information.

- **Smart documentation forms** can contain embedded links that send messages to others connected with the patient—such as notifying the primary care physician that his or her patient has had an emergency department visit. When making referrals, smart documentation forms can also capture the relevant information that the consultant will need, such as the results of recent exercise tolerance tests and electrocardiograms in the case of a cardiology referral.

- **Filtered reference information** in the form of infobuttons and patient instruction links at discharge, tuned to the patient's actual conditions or therapies, streamline and partially automate the process of getting information to the patient, making it much more likely that the patient will actually receive that information from the provider. This information also serves as a foundation for shared decision making between the patient and their clinicians during and after an inpatient or outpatient encounter.

CDS in the Clinical Workflow

You must understand clinician and patient workflow in order to determine *when* are the most effective times to deliver CDS interventions. Different objectives are best addressed with CDS interventions at different points in this workflow. The best opportunity to favorably influence workflow is usually when:

- Key care delivery decisions and actions are ripe for support;
- Important clinical data become available;
- Pertinent persons can be reached with the intervention; and
- Those persons are prepared to act upon the information immediately.

These opportunities can be spread across healthcare system encounters, such as ambulatory or emergency department visits and inpatient admissions. The opportunities can arise at various points within an encounter, such as at pre-visit, patient intake and clinician documentation, ordering, and results review. Sometimes, the best opportunity occurs outside of any encounter, such as when test results are posted after an encounter or when a patient is performing self-care and home monitoring. For emerging care models, such as patient-centered medical homes and accountable care organizations, thinking across the care continuum is essential, and CDS—for both the patient and clinicians—can help ensure that the care plan remains on track between encounters.

The flowchart at the top of Figure 6-1 outlines basic process steps in many clinical encounters. This generalized workflow applies to both hospitalizations and ambulatory office visits (asterisks mark the two steps which would actually come after the encounter in the ambulatory setting). In full-care episodes for many conditions (such as coronary artery disease), the process often loops, with post-visit care for one encounter flowing into pre-visit activities for a subsequent encounter, whether planned or urgent.

The Core CDS Actions most closely associated with each workflow step are listed in the bottom of the figure; these sequential CDS Actions typically line up with the sequential workflow steps. The

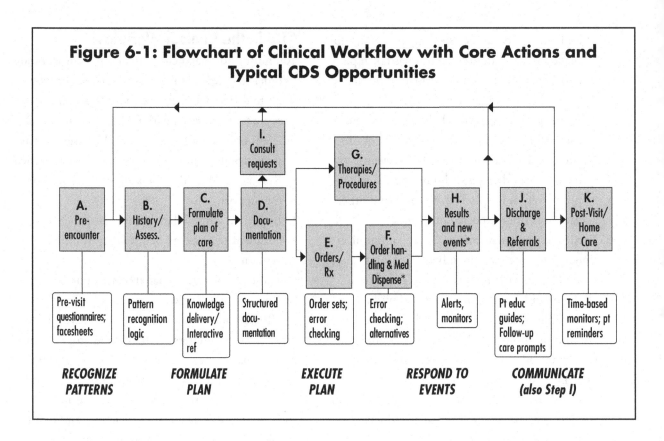

Figure 6-1: Flowchart of Clinical Workflow with Core Actions and Typical CDS Opportunities

middle of the figure illustrates CDS interventions appropriate to the Core Action and workflow step. Thus, when you consider the Core Actions needed for your particular objective, you will not only have insights into effective CDS intervention types, but also into promising points to deploy them into clinical workflow.

The care process analysis capabilities outlined in the workflow discussion in Chapter 3 become very important during intervention selection. As noted in Chapter 5, your CDS Team should analyze in detail all the care processes and workflows that determine whether or not you achieve your specific improvement objectives. That analysis should point you to places in workflow where breakdowns occur and where there are opportunities for process improvement. If you can identify where improvement is most needed, then corrective interventions at those particular steps might be particularly helpful and well received.

Say, for example, that increasing compliance with preventive care screening guidelines—such as periodic mammograms as indicated—is a prior-

ity objective in your organization due to a payer performance improvement program. If your process analysis determines that the sub-optimal testing rates result, in part, from clinicians having difficulty accessing information about the last time patients had the test, then an automated flowsheet with this information could be a useful intervention.

If you do not carefully analyze pertinent processes and simply assume where process breakdowns are occurring, you risk misdirecting your CDS efforts. For example, if you use order sets or alerts at the physician ordering stage to increase mammogram testing—when the problem is at the patient adherence stage—then your CDS interventions will likely have little impact on achieving the objective. In this case, CDS interventions directed toward the patient (such as providing information about the mammogram benefits, patient experience and logistics) would likely be much more useful. Again, when patients themselves are at the center of process breakdowns, it is important to work with them in advance to learn what support would be most valuable, and direct your efforts accordingly.

We next explore in more detail how to identify CDS intervention types (and their workflow insertion points) that will be appropriate for your objective, be desired (or at least accepted) by users, and favorably impact care processes and outcomes.

Questions for Determining Intervention Types for Specific Objectives

We have now related clinical objectives to CDS Core Actions, and related the Core Actions to typical workflow points and CDS intervention types particularly suited to those actions. These relationships can help you follow an orderly path from your objective to the most promising CDS intervention types and workflow points. The form in Figure 6-2 illustrates how to navigate this path.

Given an objective you want to achieve, use Figure 6-2 to go through the Core Actions and consider which of them apply to your situation by answering the questions in the first column. (This figure uses a specific sample objective; a blank version is presented as Worksheet 6-1.) If a particular Core Action is central to addressing your objective, jot down a few pertinent details in the second column. The third column indicates the workflow steps where that Core Action is commonly addressed. The fourth column suggests common CDS intervention types that support each Core Action; the first one or two at the top of each list are generally the most commonly used, but consider each and ask whether that intervention type could be applied to the details you entered in the second column. The point is for you and your CDS Team to broadly list interventions that could help you reach your objective.

We introduced Core Actions earlier in the chapter by considering care activities that apply to optimizing VTE prevention, which is a complex objective that includes many Core Actions and thus can be aided by several different CDS interventions. The example in Figure 6-2 deals with another complex objective: facilitating the best and fastest response to an acute myocardial infarction (MI). Here again, a package with three or four interventions working together provides a multi-pronged, powerful approach to strengthening care delivery activities. Other objectives may be simpler, involving only one or two Core Actions that might be addressed well with corresponding CDS packages that have only one or two interventions.

You will likely glean detailed insights into many specific and valuable CDS opportunities by engaging those responsible for care processes critical to achieving your objective in this exploration of support needs throughout pertinent workflows. To further help you generate and cross-check CDS intervention ideas, Figure 6-3 (page 192) lists several common objectives, along with Core Actions that have been used to address them, based our experience and in reports in the literature.[1, 2, 3]

Deciding among Several Available Intervention Types

A detailed analysis as just outlined will likely generate more potential CDS interventions than you should start with for a particular objective. Your available resources, workflow analysis and other intervention selection issues we cover in this section will help you determine how many and which interventions to tackle first. In general, you should aim for 'enough to get the job done' but not too many so that you have over-engineered the solution and created risks to success (from added complexity) that are not balanced by additional potential for significant benefit.

Your information system capabilities (as discussed in the Systems section in Chapter 3) play a major role in determining what interventions you can choose from, how easy it will be to work with these tools and how useful they will be to end users. Reviewing (or completing) the CIS inventory we recommended (see Worksheet 3-1) can be helpful in determining how best to select specific technical CDS intervention options from among the many theoretical support opportunities.

Some studies are beginning to explore the relative value of different types of CDS interventions for achieving specific objectives,[4] but this evidence base is very scant. Therefore, your intervention selections

Figure 6-2: Using Core Actions to Identify Suitable CDS Interventions to Achieve Objective

Objective: Provide prompt and full initial response to acute MI

Core Action Areas	Your Details	Likely Workflows	Likely CDS Types
RECOGNIZE PATTERNS: Is there need for help to recognize promptly that a particular situation, diagnosis, or presentation exists? What data are needed to recognize this?	*Yes — quickly recognize presentations that are managed differently* *Data: EKG, past medical history, symptoms (early); troponin markers (later)*	✸ A. Pre-encounter • B. RN & MD History/assessment	• Data-triggered alerts *Troponin* • Smart documentation forms, calculators, clinical scores *MI risk score* ✸ Relevant data summaries ✸ Predictive analytics ✸ Expert system
FORMULATE PLAN: Is there need for help in choosing the best therapies and/or diagnostic studies for this condition, symptom or diagnosis?	*Yes — advise re criteria for different primary treatment options (such as thrombolysis, percutaneous coronary intervention, glycoprotein IIb-IIIa inhibitors), and contraindications for each*	✸ B. RN & MD History/assessment • C. Formulate plan of care	• Filtered reference *Tables as per col. 2* • Reference info in order sets/care plans *Contain tabular info as in item directly above* ✸ Expert workup advisors
EXECUTE PLAN: Is there need for specific help: - to create orders or care plans correctly, completely and without errors? - in performing relevant procedures? - in carrying out orders or administering meds?	*Yes — dosing help for primary drug treatments; full therapy protocol including IV nitroglycerin, beta-blocker, ACE/ARB-inhibitor options* *Drug dilution guidance*	✸ D. Documentation • E. Orders/Rx ✸ F. Order handling/med dispensing ✸ G. Therapies/Procedures	• Order sets/care plans (suggested doses, protocols) *Anticoagulation and thrombolysis protocols* • Parameter guidance *Dosing help for thrombolysis, renal doses* • Critiques/warnings ("immediate alerts") *Maybe warfarin drug-drug* ✸ Smart documentation forms/checklists • Filtered reference info *Drug dilution calculator*

continued on next page

Figure 6-2 *continued*

Objective: Provide prompt and full initial response to acute MI			
Core Action Areas	**Your Details**	**Likely Workflows**	**Likely CDS Types**
MONITOR/DETECT/ HANDLE EVENTS: Is there need for help detecting new events that could be hazardous or require a change in plan: - on a single patient? - on an entire service? Is there need to monitor performance over time? Is there need to monitor patient self-care at home?	*Maybe—monitor antico-agulant effects (such as with PTT and INR tests if using unfractionated heparin or warfarin)* *Usual arrhythmia monitoring*	• H. Results and new events ✱ K. Post-visit/home care	• Event-driven alerts *PTT, INR panic-value alerts* ✱ Multi-patient monitors ✱ Time-driven reminders ✱ Retrospective analytics
COMMUNICATE: Is there need for help in: - deciding on need for consultation or referral? - notifying other caregivers about the patient's status? - providing proper information to the consultant? - engaging and informing the patient/family?	*Inform patient and family about diagnosis, and engage as appropriate in planning* *During later management phases:* *Possibly cardiac rehab programs* *Possibly patient lifestyle management*	✱ I. Consult requests • J. Discharge and referrals (from emergency depart-ment, and earlier too)	• Filtered reference information ✱ Smart documentation forms (with messaging links)

will be based largely on practical considerations such as those noted earlier, as well as how easy different intervention types are for you to implement, how acceptable they are likely to be to end users, and how much impact they are likely to have.

In Figure 6-4, we provide notes about ease of development, acceptability, impact, and special considerations for the 10 intervention types in Figure 5-5. These assessments are largely based on expert opinion rather than extensive science, but those who have used earlier versions of this material in the first edition of this guidebook have found it helpful. More research is beginning to appear on selection and acceptance factors for clinical decision support,[5,6,7] and you should follow these developments as well.

Figure 6-3: Typical Clinical Objectives and Associated Core Actions and Intervention Types

General Case	Examples	Core Actions	Suggestions
Determine which patients are at risk for an adverse event, and prevent it	• VTE prevention • Pressure ulcer prevention • Post-op infection prevention • Headache evaluation	**Recognize** **Plan** **Execute**	• Risk calculation and display (data-triggered alert) • Predictive analytics for more complex cases • Filtered reference (to identify the plan) • Order set/care plan
Order/perform applicable general health maintenance tests and interventions	• Perform regular cholesterol/LDL testing, and breast and colorectal cancer screening; give flu shots; measure hemoglobin A1c in diabetic patients	**Recognize** **Plan** **Execute**	• Relevant data summary to determine and present needed tests • Filtered reference for complex cases • Smart documentation form
Improve treatment promptness	• Prompt therapy for community-acquired pneumonia, meningitis	**Recognize** **Plan**	• Data-triggered alert • Filtered reference to guide treatment (possibly triggered by the alert)
Use optimal clinical and cost-effective tests and treatments for a given situation	• Determine most appropriate diagnostic study for acute stroke • Determine best medications for community-acquired pneumonia	**Plan**	• Filtered reference, specific to the patient's data • Same reference explicitly/implicitly included in order set
Streamline a complex operation	• TPN ordering assistant • ICU status and orders tool	**Execute**	• Specialized smart documentation forms, with reference links • Order set
Manage the sequence of a multi-step inpatient clinical pathway	• Cholecystitis clinical pathway • Chemotherapy admission • Bone-marrow transplant admission	**Monitor/react** **Execute**	• Monitor tools to track patient status • "Flowchart" protocol follower with reminders • Series of order sets grouped as a protocol • Complete care plan • Expert management advisor
Manage a chronic condition over time	• Chronic management of diabetes, hyperlipidemia, asthma — including response to therapy	**Plan** **Execute** **Monitor/react**	• Stepped-care reference, tuned to patient's current and past steps • Time-driven reminders • Expert management advisor • Data-triggered alerts, perhaps coupled to orders • Patient status flowchart • Order sets and protocols

continued on next page

Figure 6-3 *continued*

General Case	Examples	Core Actions	Suggestions
Avoid medication ordering and administration errors	• Prevent dangerous drug interactions, dosing errors, inadequate monitoring, duplication, formulary violations	**Execute**	• Parameter guidance • Critiques and warnings • Filtered reference
Detect and respond to acute events	• Respond to panic lab values, abnormal imaging results	**Monitor/react**	• Data-triggered alerts, perhaps coupled to remedial orders
Efficiently manage a group of similar patients	• OR tracking and scheduling • Emergency department tracking system • Service-wide warfarin monitoring	**Monitor/react**	• Unit monitor and status display • Data- and time-triggered alerts • Relevant data summaries
Assure appropriate communication between providers	• Automatic sign-out and visit notices • Proper information included in a referral	**Communicate**	• Data-driven initiation of communication • Smart documentation tools to cover proper information
Promote patient engagement, follow-up, understanding, self-care	• Promote for CHF patient understanding of their condition and management plan, and effective self-care • Improve communication to patients about upcoming procedures	**Communicate**	• Filtered reference • Data-driven communication • Event-driven alerts and reminders • Smart documentation forms for the patient to use
Assess key performance indicators for a large group	• Assess recent performance in early door-to-balloon time for acute MI patients	**Monitor/react**	• Retrospective analytics

Definition for Terms Used in Figure 6-4	
Ease of Development*	How much time will it take to develop the structure and content of the intervention? How much special skill is needed to produce it?
High:	No programming knowledge necessary; requisite data are clear-cut and easily available
Medium:	Low-level programming knowledge; moderately complex to integrate into the system; weeks to months to build and test
Low:	Complex programming or database knowledge typically needed; logic, presentation, or actions may be complex or nonstandard
Acceptability	How likely is your user community to adopt this intervention?
High:	Highly acceptable: knowledge is non-controversial, easy to use, doesn't slow user down
Medium:	Knowledge is more difficult to accept or user may be slowed slightly
Low:	Knowledge is difficult to accept or user will be significantly slowed
Impact	Assuming the intervention is accepted by users, how likely is the intervention to create the intended effect?
High:	Very good chance of creating the intended effect; usually interventions that provide easy access to direct, straightforward action
Medium:	Moderate chance of creating the intended effect
Low:	Lower chance of creating the intended effect

Figure 6-4: Intervention Selection Factors

1. Smart Documentation and Workup Forms
- *Ease of development (MEDIUM):*
  - Specifications are often easy to come by because of pre-existing paper documentation forms used in many hospitals and clinics.
  - Specialized forms, such as checklists and flowsheets, may be more difficult to envision and to execute.
  - If you seek structured, machine-usable output from the form (e.g., evaluation and management codes for billing), then the form elements must be mapped to standard dictionaries, which can be difficult.
- *Acceptability (LOW):*
  - Making the form easy to use can be difficult, particularly for large forms. However, acceptability increases dramatically if the form is responsive to a user-identified need for more efficient documentation, and it actually saves them time.
  - Clinical users often resist structured documentation forms, especially when the work required to fill them out is perceived as an administrative burden.
  - More acceptable forms are those used for specific activities that are very repeatable, such as a normal pregnancy visit or focused eye exam.
- *Impact (MEDIUM):*
  - If properly developed and accepted, such forms capture readable, usable data (often coded) to assist with decision making and serve as input to other CDS interventions.

continued on next page

---

* There ratings assume that your EHR and other HIT systems actually provide this intervention type and tools for you to develop/configure specific instances of it.

Figure 6-4 *continued*

- *Special considerations:*
  - Be sure to plan an organized method for naming and numbering elements on your documentation forms. This will make it easier for users to find them in your system and to use the data when you create reports and other decision support interventions such as alerts.
  - Personal (unvetted) forms are controversial, as they can lead to a large amount of difficult-to-control content.

2. **Order Sets, Care Plans and Multi-step Protocols**
[Information below primarily focuses on order sets but is applicable to the other subtypes.]
  - *Ease of development (LOW-MEDIUM):*
    - Content is easy if copying from an existing paper order form. Building new order sets or care plans, whether for computer or for paper use, is easy for the "broad-brush" content elements, but consensus on finer details can be difficult if the order set or care plan is to be widely applicable or if there are different providers that have different entrenched approaches. Keeping order sets current with evolving literature can be difficult.
    - They can often be built in modular fashion, with boilerplate admission orders kept in one proto-set, and orders specific to the current diagnosis kept in another; these can be sequenced or combined on demand.
    - There aren't currently widely used and successful approaches for handling comorbidities in a single patient that cause details in two pertinent order sets to conflict.
    - Order sets are typically created using two methods:
      - *Running a mock order session (entering orders in sequence, just as if one were doing it for an individual patient) is fast and easy to understand but leaves little room for varying parameters.*
      - *Tools that create order sets (templates) by placing individual orders on a form make for slower development, but the orders can be better organized and presented, and parameters (such as dose) can be varied through the use of drop-down list controls or text boxes.*
  - *Acceptability (MEDIUM-HIGH):*
    - If the pertinent order set is easy to find and use, they can greatly increase speed and efficiency. Order sets account for 30–40% of all orders in CPOE systems. Highly specific or rarely used order sets may be less acceptable simply because users may not remember that they exist.
    - Even with a commercially-produced order set collection, many providers find that they need to or wish to customize many of the sets for local circumstances.
  - *Impact (HIGH):*
    - Since they directly specify the care actions that are executed.
  - *Special considerations:*
    - Order sets can be helpful with internal care transitions—unit transfers, post-op care, and pre-admission orders. The workflow is tricky though, because the orders are entered now but are to be acted upon only after a specific future event has occurred. These are difficult to implement and require considerable testing, especially because of the possible delays in actual transfer of care.
    - As with documentation forms, personal order sets are highly controversial. They can improve individual efficiency, clinician buy-in and convenience—and are highly acceptable—but are increasingly seen as safety hazards because personal order sets are typically not maintained as carefully nor updated as frequently as departmental or organizational order sets that are reviewed by a regular process. Personal order sets introduce variations in care, which is in contradiction to current efforts toward standardizing care processes around best clinical evidence. In addition, if

continued on next page

Figure 6-4 *continued*

the personal set is derived from an organizational-level order set plus a few variations, the personal set may not be updated when the parent set is changed in other important ways.

— Remember that order sets can be used in ambulatory care, as well as in inpatient care. Order sets (used at the end of an office visit, or to place initial condition-specific orders in emergency medicine) can be powerful tools to improve consistency and optimal care in a rushed environment.

— It is sometimes suggested that order sets lead to excess ordering because the user can easily checkmark a whole string of orders. This potential should be considered in developing, launching and monitoring order sets.

— When an order set is used and approved, dozens of orders are submitted in rapid succession. Other CDS interventions should be considered and carefully constructed to handle potential order conflicts within the set and to efficiently perform checking and reactive alerting on individual orders within the set.

3. Parameter Guidance

- *Ease of development (LOW-MEDIUM):*
  - Highly dependent on the system interface's ability to provide these displays during order entry. If they are available, then inserting the specific data presentation may be straightforward.
  - For drug dosing, parameter guidance typically comes from the (usually commercial) drug dictionary. Some systems will permit you to modify these lists, but regular updates from the dictionary supplier will likely contain the original information. It takes effort to customize the many individual medications that you may need.
- *Acceptability (HIGH):*
  - Like most interventions which provide important information and which enhance the speed of a process — in this case, by eliminating the need to look up and calculate these parameters yourself — parameter guides are generally highly acceptable.
  - Entering sliding scales (such as for insulin dosing) and steroid tapers can be very difficult without a CDS tool to facilitate the process.
- *Impact (HIGH):*
  - The intervention happens right at the point of ordering or documentation, and this proximity increases overall impact.
- *Special considerations:*
  - May require at least 0.5 FTE pharmacist to maintain local drug information database versions (drug-drug, drug-allergy, and drug-condition alerts).
  - Impact is somewhat less for interventions that try to reduce ordering costs[8,9,10] (i.e., on the order of 5–15% reductions in overall charges for the target items[11]).
  - Guided-dose algorithms for renal failure, age, hepatic failure, pediatric dosing, etc., from commercial companies are relatively basic, although they are actively developing and improving this feature.
  - Displaying cost data for medications can be challenging. For example, some medications are less expensive at the pill level but may require a longer treatment course, which may result in overall higher costs. Also, in hospitals, costs vary based on current contracts and are often not reflected in charges.

4. Critiques and Warnings ("Immediate alerts" responding to user entry)

- *Ease of development (MEDIUM):*
  - Highly dependent on the tools provided for the purpose by the CIS application. Generally, tools supplied with your EHR will make it feasible for you to customize simple cases, such as responding to one piece of newly entered data,

continued on next page

Figure 6-4 *continued*

combined with no more than two pieces of existing data. Some systems may require you to work with the vendor for any custom warnings. Certification requirements may speak to this issue increasingly over time.

 – It is critical—and sometimes difficult—to configure warnings with sufficient specificity and sensitivity so as to avoid both nuisance alerting *and* safety hazards.

• *Acceptability (LOW-MEDIUM):*

 – Highly dependent on alert specificity (how often a change in management is actually indicated when the alert appears) and its conciseness. However, impact is dependent on sensitivity (how often an alert appears when a change in management is indicated) as well (see Impact, next).

 – Drug-drug interactions based on commercial databases are notorious for producing alert fatigue. They can have very low acceptability if the database is configured to show all possible interactions.[12] Most commercial drug-drug interaction products allow users to block presentation of alerts meeting specific criteria (e.g., low severity) or to filter presentation based on role (i.e., medical student vs. attending physician vs. pharmacist).

 – A general rule about alerts is that alerting for true error conditions is often more accepted than alerting for "advice." Be careful to make the advice universally applicable and very well directed at the condition of interest.

 – Highly dependent on the alert being well vetted with users and others before implementation.

• *Impact (MEDIUM-HIGH):*

 – Alerts are overridden frequently—sometimes inappropriately. This can create user frustration (from many false positive alerts) and care hazards (when true positive alerts are overridden due to alert fatigue). Chapter 7 provides guidance on configuring alerts for optimal acceptability and impact.

 – Alert fatigue effect: Impact for individual alerts is higher if alerts fire only infrequently and only for serious conditions.

 – Impact is higher for alerts that correct errors or offer basic alternatives without changing the fundamental plan of care.

• *Special considerations:*

 – All alerts should be carefully vetted for local appropriateness and value before implementation and reviewed at periodic intervals.

 – Testing and content validation is critical, especially when the alert is linked to a high-stakes action. You should be sure that if users are relying on it (for example, as a safety net), that its use and consequences are appropriate. Be sure clinicians understand that not all hazards will be caught by the system, and they are still responsible for bringing judgment to their clinical actions.

5. **Relevant Data Summaries:**

• *Ease of development (MEDIUM):*

 – Retrieving the correct patient information and displaying it at the appropriate moment (e.g., on an ordering form) can require additional programming.

 – Difficulty is increased when the relevant data elements can come from multiple source systems that may use different coding schemes.

 – Testing to make sure that the display is correct in various use cases is very important.

• *Acceptability (HIGH):*

 – High, as expected for an intervention that requires no additional user work, assuming data presentation doesn't interfere with other user tasks.

continued on next page

Figure 6-4 *continued*

- *Impact (MEDIUM):*
  - Typically high viewing levels, when properly deployed. Where a data display intervention points out a hazard, impact can be strong. Flowsheets and facesheets can also be very effective if they are routinely display users' expected workflow. However, if the summary shows too many data elements, a form of alert fatigue can result and lead to important information being ignored. Make sure presented data are truly "relevant" (for example, by using logic to show or highlight the most important data).
  - Strong impact by organizing all relevant data needed for a given scenario (for example, displaying completed and due immunizations).
- *Special considerations:*
  - Incorrect, missing or superfluous data can be displayed if underlying codes change (such as if the laboratory changes the method for a given test and assigns it a new code).
  - Test to make sure that the system responds appropriately if data are requested, but the source system for the data is unavailable (for example, by notifying the user).

6. Multi-patient Monitors
- *Ease of development (LOW):*
  - Real-time monitors are usually supplied by the system vendors and may be difficult to customize without their substantial input.
- *Acceptability (HIGH):*
  - Clinicians in units with well-designed status monitors refer to them constantly to get an overview of current needs and task priorities. As with other interventions that do not require much user input, there is little annoyance factor. Also, these displays are often continuously shown on screens in the department, so there is no effort at all to use them — not even extra effort to bring up the monitor in the first place.
- *Impact (MEDIUM):*
  - Impact can be high for its designed purpose, which is conveying relative urgency among the patients on a service and imminent task needs for any and all of them. Monitors can show alerts and pending tasks on each patient and ensure that those are constantly noticed by the staff; however, if you cannot take action directly from the monitor screen, then extra steps are involved, which can blunt the impact.
- *Special considerations:*
  - Pertinent to the note under Impact, some monitors are also interactive, containing controls, buttons and links that allow you to take action on the items that are displayed. Examples include an emergency department display that has buttons that let clinicians access modules for results review, order entry, admission request or other functions on any patient; and an operating room status display that shows a room about to become available and lets users rearrange room assignments for upcoming cases.
  - Be careful about overusing color to draw attention to particular events or data. If a display relies on more than three colors to have meaning, users may get confused or fatigued.

7. Predictive and Retrospective Analytics
- *Ease of development (LOW for predictive, HIGH for retrospective):*
  - Predictive tools rely on custom benchmarking and factor analysis; generally, they will be supplied by the analytics vendor. Retrospective tools usually provide many easy-to-use customization tools that generate reports for different purposes based on many different data combinations.

continued on next page

Figure 6-4 *continued*

- *Acceptability (MEDIUM-HIGH):*
  - Predictive tools present information without requiring much additional user entry, and this increases acceptability; however, users must trust the data and predictions presented—that is, believing that they are accurate, complete and reliable. Retrospective analytics are generally highly accepted because they are directly addressing a high-priority quality strategy, and because their primary users are highly motivated practice managers and quality leaders.
- *Impact (MEDIUM):*
  - These tools show important information, but they generally do not contain tools for directly acting on the information. Sustained effort by multiple individuals is typically required to turn the information into action and improved results.
- *Special considerations:*
  - Great way to present data on patient populations. Important tool to spot practice trends, perform control-chart analysis and address practice-wide pay-for-performance criteria.
  - Predictive analytics sometimes take some getting used to because their calculations may be complex and not transparent to users. However, they can predict hazards and actionable situations that no other intervention type can, so successful use can build loyalty among users.
  - We have emphasized that CDS efforts should involve close collaboration between the CDS Team and other performance improvement stakeholders. Since analytics tools are important for, and used in, these respective efforts, they represent a potential focal point for such collaborations.

8. Filtered Reference Information and Knowledge Resources
- *Ease of development (MEDIUM-HIGH):*
  - The content sources themselves (such as online clinical references) may be difficult to customize, but tools for delivering this content into workflow (such as portals and infobuttons) may have flexible configuration options. In addition, these delivery tools permit local content to be used.
  - You need to be responsible for ensuring content quality and currency, and this will be easier with commercially acquired references (see Chapter 4).
  - The HL7 infobutton standard provides a straightforward mechanism to deliver context-sensitive reference information into clinical information systems, and some content and CIS vendors are using it.
- *Acceptability (MEDIUM-HIGH):*
  - For user-requested reference, acceptability is high (assuming users accept the underlying reference information and navigation is straightforward) because it only appears when requested and does not require substantial user data entry.
  - For reference information tied to other displays or interventions that automatically appears when those interventions appear, acceptability is high unless the amount of content displayed is too long and too difficult to navigate or dismiss.
  - However, accessing and using reference information may not fit smoothly into busy clinical workflows. For example, early studies examining infobutton use often found that the reference information was accessed much less frequently than expected given how frequently clinical information needs arise.
- *Impact (LOW-MEDIUM):*
  - Impact is relatively low because the reference information itself does not directly translate into action. However, impact is higher when the reference display gives specific information necessary for the current management decision. There are care delivery 'sweet spots,' such as the Formulating the Care Plan Core Action, where a concise,

continued on next page

Figure 6-4 *continued*

focused, action-oriented reference content display can make a large difference in the care plan *if* users pursue the available information.

- *Special considerations:*
  - This intervention type also includes clinical calculators that may appear at appropriate times (e.g., drug-mixing calculators and compatibility charts that appear whenever a relevant drug is chosen in the medication administration record).
  - Reference information can be embedded in virtually all other intervention types. It can be linked to an alert, order set or clinical pathway, and displayed on ordering forms and various other screens throughout your information systems.
  - An optimally designed Alert, Critique or Warning always includes some reference material for justification and to help guide the user in considering the proper response to the alert. See Chapter 7 for more details.

9. Expert Workup and Management Advisors
- *Ease of development (LOW):*
  - These systems—ranging from diagnostic decision support systems to antibiotic advisors—are generally complex programs developed by a commercial supplier. The supplier will normally help you connect the system to necessary internal data sources, such as local antibiotic susceptibility and resistance tables. Nonetheless, it may take significant effort to tune these systems to local information and workflows.
- *Acceptability (LOW-MEDIUM):*
  - Diagnostic expert systems have been shown to add value, and they are theoretically attractive to help trainees build their knowledge base and to help more experienced clinicians with difficult cases. However, these tools have historically not been widely used. Increasing attention to the prevalence and costs associated with diagnostic errors, together with efforts to integrate diagnostic decision support tools better into workflow and clinical systems, may increase their acceptability and use.
  - Patients sometimes make use of diagnostic expert programs (or less rigorously developed differential-diagnosis guides on the Web).
  - Focused programs such as antibiotic advisors can have much higher acceptance when installed in the EHR and integrated smoothly into the workflow. Other similar programs, such as interactive dermatology, radiology or pathology atlases have medium penetration into niche audiences.
- *Impact: (LOW-MEDIUM):*
  - Expert advisors typically processed information needed to inform care decisions or actions, such as suggested diagnoses, antibiotics or radiologic findings. As with filtered reference information, it falls to the user to translate this information into action. Some expert programs not only suggest diagnoses but also the next test or procedure to do in order to further narrow the diagnosis; these can have a more direct impact on immediate action.
- *Special considerations:*
  - Expert advisor programs are available in various devices and formats, such as smart phones and independent websites; users' perceived needs for these systems are a major factor in their dissemination and use.
  - The underlying logical structures and potential to simulate intelligent information processing have intrigued informaticists for many years, and emerging technology advances could conceivably yield more powerful and widely used expert advisors.

continued on next page

Figure 6-4 *continued*

10. Event-driven Alerts and Reminders
- *Ease of development (MEDIUM-HIGH):*
  - Driven by certification requirements and other drivers, EHR producers are increasingly supplying tools for implementers to deliver and customize alerts and reminders, as well as simple critiques and warnings.
  - This intervention type is typically a 'CDS workhorse' and specifying triggers, data needs and outputs is theoretically straightforward. However, configuring the intervention for optimal acceptability and impact can be very challenging (see Chapter 7).
- *Acceptability (LOW-MEDIUM):*
  - The logical approach underlying alerts and reminders is straightforward and compelling ("if [this is true], then [this should happen]"), which makes them theoretically desirable performance improvement tools.
  - However, as we emphasize, alerts are frequently over-used and not specific and useful enough, which leads to end user alert fatigue and pushback. In addition, this intervention type is among the most intrusive—presenting as unexpected interruptions such as dialog boxes, text messages and pages—which heightens the necessity to make them helpful.
- *Impact (HIGH):*
  - A well-designed alert or reminder addresses a specific focused problem, provides enough information for the clinician user to make a decision, and often allows the clinician to take corrective action immediately and directly.
- *Special considerations:*
  - There is currently a young but growing industry to produce third-party, service-oriented critiques and alerts, which accept patient data through an interface to clinical information systems, and return guidance based on analyzing that data. Although paradigms for integrating this feedback into user workflows and information systems are relatively early in development, they could mature rapidly in the near future.
  - Presentation design considerations are important (see Chapter 7), including making sure that the intervention provides enough information to allow the clinician to confidently make a decision, while still being concise so that the workflow intrusion doesn't take up much time.

Don't Underutilize Patient-focused CDS Interventions

Evolving healthcare delivery and payment models—and secular trends toward more empowered consumers in general—are making it essential for patients to be active participants in their care. Far from some historic norms where doctors held unquestioned knowledge and authority in the therapeutic relationship, patients are now advised to "Ask questions. Understand your condition. Evaluate your options."[13]—and many are already demanding and stepping up to such engagement.

This can be good news for your CDS efforts, because among participants on the care team, patients arguably have the greatest incentive and time available to ensure that *their* care quality and safety is optimized. It is important to keep this (often untapped) potential in mind as you select CDS intervention types and workflow insertion points. For example, reviewing the Core Actions in Figure 6-2 reinforces that in every broad case—as well as for many of the specific details—patients play key roles. Even in cases where clinicians are primary decision makers (such as in emergent care situations in an emergency department or ICU), it remains important to engage others (such as the patient's family, and hopefully the patient at some point) in understanding decisions and actions being taken and their implications.

Figures 6-1 through 6-4 emphasize provider-centric workflows, decision support needs and CDS interventions, and these are certainly critical to improving care processes and outcomes. However, as you conduct process analyses, and use the information in this chapter to select interventions, you should devote careful attention to patient-centric workflows and corresponding decision support needs and opportunities. For example, you can use patient reminders to encourage them to obtain indicated preventive care screening or immunizations, or tools to help them understand and manage their conditions and treatments—including tracking and optimizing critical disease parameters.

You can deliver interventions to patients by technological means (such as via alerts in their PHR, secure messaging and text messages) or low-tech means (such as postal letters), depending on their computer use and comfort with technology. Multi-pronged interventions working toward the same objective that are delivered both to clinicians/staff and to patients can be particularly effective. For example, consider how interventions focused on both patients and clinicians can work in concert to ensure that women get indicated mammograms, or that diabetic patients have their HbA1c levels checked regularly and keep these levels in the normal range.

Liberally applying interventions that engage and empower patients can help ensure that you are leveraging a patient's full power to help you achieve CDS objectives—many of which require optimizing *their* health and well-being.

CONSIDERATIONS FOR HOSPITALS/HEALTH SYSTEMS
People (Stakeholders and Governance)

- Understand processes and individuals in your organization responsible for analyses and inter-vention selection activities described in this chapter (and the additional intervention configuration work described in Chapter 7). These individuals could include a chief medical information officer and/or chief nursing information officer, or the work could be based in the quality committee or IS department. Consider and discuss with these individuals and groups whether frameworks and approaches outlined in this chapter can support intervention selection efforts.

- Consider how your organization's CDS governance (see Chapter 2) influences intervention selection. For example, we have described an approach to selecting interventions that flows from objectives, through core actions and work-flow, to support opportunities. In many organizations, however, the CDS Committee has historically functioned in a more reactive mode, devoting substantial energy triaging requests from various departments in the form of, "We need an *alert* for …"

- Make sure that your governance model addresses issues such as who can initiate a request for a new *intervention* (as opposed to a CDS *objective*) and how such requests are triaged and approved. To optimize performance improvements, your CDS intervention selection process should generally be driven more by improvement objectives than by specific intervention requests. However, in some cases (such as Meaningful Use Stage 1 require-ments) specific interventions—rather than specific outcomes—*are* required.

- Make sure that potential intervention users—or their representatives or champions—*are* involved in considering which interventions would be most useful and valuable. This dialog should be an outgrowth of your care process analysis work. Use clinical champions to help align CDS Team intervention selection work with needs and expectations of those who will be using the tools. We have advocated involving champions early in CDS program development work, and it is like-wise important to engage them early in assessing and addressing improvement targets.

- Leverage your organization's various patient contact points to help engage patients in efforts to address their needs and support their workflows in ways that address shared objectives.

Planning (Resources and Work Processes)

- Keep in mind as you select interventions that each may have ripple effects on various workflows and other interventions. For example, interventions aimed at increasing test or medication use will affect workflows that supply these resources (this will be discussed more in the next chapter). Engaging all potentially affected stakeholders early in selecting and configuring interventions can optimize cooperation and head off problems that could crop up downstream without such collaboration.

- If you have a limited pipeline for developing CDS interventions—as almost all organizations will once the value of CDS becomes apparent—try to rotate resources and effort so as to support all requesting departments or strategic entities as appropriate. Sometimes a request to address a particular objective will need to jump the queue, such as after a sentinel event or when a new hospital's strategic priorities are established. Well-run CDS governance mechanisms should deal smoothly with dynamically allocating resources across intervention efforts.

- For care delivery networks, there may be different clinical approaches used in different settings. Even within a single clinical department there could be differences among senior physicians (such as different postoperative order sets for the same procedure from different surgeons). Your CDS Team and its performance improvement partners will need to judiciously establish balance between minimizing variation to improve safety and efficiency and supporting some process variations to meet end-user preferences.

- If different parts of your organization are using different EHRs, multiple challenges arise. You need to consider design and data-structure dif-

ferences if you wish to place the same clinical intervention into different systems. In addition, some practices may have, and others will not have, EHRs that support any specific intervention type—and you need to have strong knowledge management and governance processes to keep everything in sync. We discuss these issues further in the following chapters.

CONSIDERATIONS FOR SMALL PRACTICES
People (Stakeholder Involvement)

- Ensure that all practice members have participated as appropriate in examining workflows, performance and needs related to the improvement target and have helped determine which interventions will be used to address this objective. Because there are fewer people, departments and decision processes, this is easier for small practices compared to large practices or hospitals, but you must nonetheless handle this step carefully and completely. Doing so will help ensure that your interventions reflect the practice's collective best thinking and support stakeholder engagement in ensuring the interventions yield anticipated results.

- Although smaller practices may have fewer resources or channels to engage patients than larger organizations, you should leverage the relatively smaller total patient population size to learn, as best you can, about opportunities to select patient-focused interventions that can add significant value to your objective improvement efforts.

Focusing/Refining

- HIT software suppliers and user groups, state and national medical societies, local RECs, and other colleagues and groups (see Epilogue) might be able to supply you with case examples of successful target-focused intervention packages. These examples can help expand your thinking about useful interventions for similar targets in your practice and support consensus building around those choices.

- Know your practice's CDS experience level. Start small, and address clinical objectives important to your practice. Focus on easy-to-implement, highly acceptable, and high-impact interventions during initial phases in your CDS efforts to help ensure early successes. As your practice gains more experience and successes applying CDS strategies to improvement goals, try interventions that may be more difficult but promise high impact. Consider whether and how the details provided under implementation selection factors in Figure 6-4 should be adapted for your practice specifics.
- Avoid the trap of assuming that an interruptive alert is the most appropriate approach to every improvement target.

Capabilities

- As of this writing, there is preliminary work directed toward the possibility of providing public or commercial resources supplying well designed, tested, successful interventions. These developments may lead to an easier path for your practice to implement helpful interventions more rapidly with limited resources (see, for example, discussion and references in Chapter 4 under Using Sharing Services and Sources).

CONSIDERATIONS FOR HEALTH IT SOFTWARE PROVIDERS
Capabilities

- Consider supplying toolkits and templates for implementing your CDS interventions pertinent to common clinical objectives; for example, through your user groups, content supplier

partners or by other means. Become aware of, and consider joining, national efforts to make well-formed CDS interventions widely available.
- Provide tools that address national improvement priorities via a broad but pertinent selection of CDS intervention types, both for individual patients and groups of patients. This chapter shows that different intervention types may be preferable for different objectives; work to supply tools so your customers can use many intervention types described here. Participate in standards efforts to make these intervention types more 'plug-and-play' across clinical information systems.
- In particular, look for opportunities to use a range of intervention types to address more complex information needs and Core Actions. Simple "if-then" logic addresses some problems, particularly in patient safety, but more robust and interoperable CDS approaches are needed to address more complex quality guidelines and other important targets.
- Smart documentation prompts are an important CDS intervention subtype that is particularly helpful in serving the *measurable* component of delivering *measurably improved* care processes and outcomes. For example, they can help gather, in a manner friendly to clinical workflow, the data needed to report quality metrics. You work with clients to provide more robust and workflow friendly tools for this documentation, since providers will increasingly rely on these tools for workflow-integrated performance measurement to meet requirements under Meaningful Use, value-based purchasing and related initiatives.

WORKSHEETS

Worksheet 6-1

Determining the Best CDS Type for Your Objective

Worksheet 6-1 is a blank version of the table shown as Figure 6-2 in the text. You can use it to map your clinical objective to the CDS Core Actions, and from those Actions, to common CDS intervention types that can address that objective.

Given an objective you want to achieve, use this worksheet to go through the Core Actions and ask yourself which of them apply to your situation. Considering each question in the first column—drawing on what you learned from stakeholder interactions in performing a workflow analysis pertinent to your target objective—will likely trigger many ideas about interventions that are likely to be helpful. If a particular Core Action applies to your objective, jot down a few pertinent details in the second column.

The third column indicates workflow steps in which that Core Action is commonly addressed; check those that are pertinent, and add others as needed. The fourth column, in turn, points to common CDS intervention types that support that Core Action. The first one or two at the top of each list are generally the most commonly used, but consider all of the types listed there and ask whether the intervention type could be applied to the details you entered in the second column. Check intervention types that look promising for your needs, adding any others (see Figure 5-5) that might be appropriate to your needs based on this analysis. In this way, you will compile a robust list of interventions that could help you reach your objective. As discussed in the chapter, don't overlook promising opportunities to address important patient-centered support needs and opportunities.

Objective: _____

Core Action Areas	Your Details	Likely Workflows	Likely CDS Types
RECOGNIZE PATTERNS: Is there need for help to recognize promptly that a particular situation, diagnosis or presentation exists? What data are needed to recognize this?		✳ A. Pre-encounter ✳ B. RN & MD History/assessment	✳ Data-triggered alerts ✳ Smart documentation forms, calculators, clinical scores ✳ Relevant data summaries ✳ Predictive analytics ✳ Expert system
FORMULATE PLAN: Is there need for help in choosing the best therapies and/or diagnostic studies for this condition, symptom or diagnosis?		✳ B. RN & MD History/assessment ✳ C. Formulate plan of care	✳ Filtered reference ✳ Reference info in order sets/care plans ✳ Expert workup advisors

continued on next page

Worksheet 6-1 *continued*

Objective: _____

Core Action Areas	Your Details	Likely Workflows	Likely CDS Types
EXECUTE PLAN: Is there need for specific help: - to create orders or care plans correctly, completely and without errors? - in performing relevant procedures? - in carrying out orders or administering meds?		✳ D. Documentation ✳ E. Orders/Rx ✳ F. Order handling/med dispensing ✳ G. Therapies/procedures	✳ Order sets/care plans (suggested doses, protocols) ✳ Parameter guidance ✳ Critiques/warnings ("immediate alerts") ✳ Smart documentation forms/checklists ✳ Filtered reference info
MONITOR/DETECT/HANDLE EVENTS: Is there need for help detecting new events that could be hazardous or require a change in plan: - on a single patient? - on an entire service? Is there need for help to monitor performance over time? Is there need for help to monitor patient self-care at home?		✳ H. Results and new events ✳ K. Post-visit/home care	✳ Event-driven alerts ✳ Multi-patient monitors ✳ Time-driven reminders ✳ Retrospective analytics
COMMUNICATE: Is there need for help in: - deciding on need for consultation or referral? - notifying other caregivers about the patient's status? - providing proper information to the consultant? - engaging and informing the patient/family?		✳ I. Consult requests ✳ J. Discharge and referrals	✳ Filtered reference information ✳ Smart documentation forms (with messaging links)

Documenting CDS Intervention Packages

As discussed in the chapter text, multiple CDS interventions acting in concert (a CDS package) will have a greater impact than any single intervention. This is particularly true when dealing with multi-component quality initiatives and related objectives. Typically, these interventions will be directed to different persons at different clinical workflow steps. After using Worksheet 6-1 to identify likely successful interventions and workflows, you can use Worksheet 6-2 and/or 6-3 to document the planned intervention package, showing how they function throughout the care process. This documentation can help you and your team spot missed opportunities and optimize your overall CDS approach to the objective. The forms can also be used to communicate the high-level CDS approach to pertinent stakeholders within your organization. You can use these individually or together.

Worksheet 6-2 provides a documentation method based on the Core Actions and Workflows diagram (Figure 6-1), while Worksheet 6-3 adds more detail in a table view.

The hospital and small practice case scenarios in the Introduction to Part II illustrate what these forms look like when they are used to capture details of CDS intervention packages focused on venous thromboembolism prophylaxis and diabetes management, respectively.

Note: Figure 6-1, presented earlier in the chapter, is designed to show the steps before, during and just after an inpatient hospitalization or an ambulatory encounter. In situations where there is accountability across the care continuum, such as reducing hospital readmissions, both workflows may be needed to address pertinent targets. In such cases, you may wish to use the worksheets twice, once for inpatient care and once for ambulatory care.

Worksheet 6-2

CDS Package Configuration, Workflow Diagram View

At the top of the Worksheet 6-2, list the current performance on the specific objective to be improved. Below this, list the targeted intervention package-supported performance. Gather the candidate CDS interventions you have identified based on results from Worksheet 6-1 (or which you have determined in other ways, including those you are already using). Enter these into the blank boxes at the bottom of the form at the appropriate workflow point to create a graphic overview of how your CDS package uses interventions at several workflow stages to address your target. If applicable, you can modify the workflow backbone as needed for your circumstances. As discussed in the chapter, consider also patient-focused workflow activities, support opportunities and specific interventions.

The grayed out intervention types below the workflow steps are sample intervention types pertinent to the workflow step carried forward from Figure 6-1 to help trigger and cross-check your thinking about promising intervention types.

Current Performance:

Target Performance:
[In the two lines above, record available performance data about current and desired care processes and outcomes that are pertinent to your improvement objective.]

continued on next page

Worksheet 6-2 *continued*

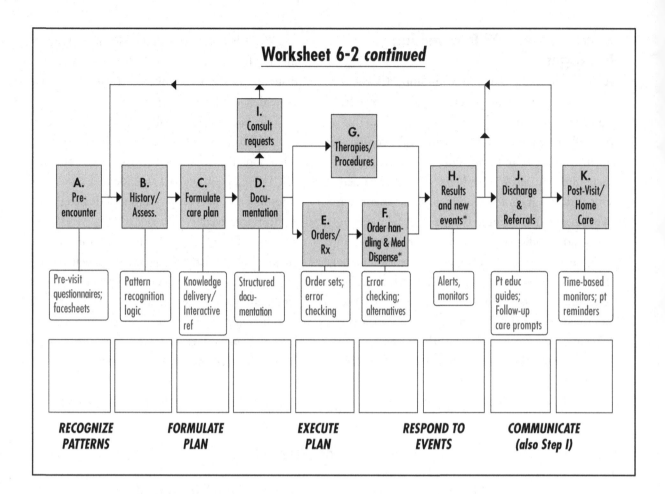

Worksheet 6-3

CDS Intervention Package Configuration, Table View

This form builds on the Workflow Diagram View just presented by documenting additional details about the various interventions in your CDS package, particularly details that fill out the CDS Five Rights dimensions for each intervention. As with the Workflow Diagram View, it is organized around the Core Actions and Workflow steps, which are captured in the table's second and third columns. This more detailed tabular documentation complements the 'at a glance' intervention package view in Worksheet 6-2.

Record the current and target performance information at the top of this form, as you did for the previous one. Each row in the form represents one intervention in your package, applied at one workflow step. For each intervention you will document, add a new row to the form below the appropriate workflow step listed in column 3, then fill in the row as follows:

- *List any specific information delivery objectives for a particular workflow step in the first column of that row—otherwise, form users should assume that the improvement target for the workflow step is the target noted at the top of the form.*
- *In the "What" and "How" row columns, list the information content—and its intervention format—you will provide (or are already providing) to drive improvements toward that target performance.*
- *In the "Who" and "Where" columns, document the other logistics for information delivery at this workflow step. That is, the information recipient, and channel through which that individual receives the information.*

The information pre-loaded into this table are presented only to help trigger and cross-check your thinking about promising interventions for your objective. They are not well vetted or specifically recommended approaches.

Current Performance:

Target Performance:
[In the two lines above, record available performance data about current and desired care processes and outcomes that are pertinent to your improvement objective.]

Objective	Core Action	Workflow	Content Delivery		Delivery Logistics	
			CDS Five Rights Dimensions			
		When[1] (Workflow Step)	**What** (Information)	**How**[2] (Intervention Type)	**Who**[3] (Person)	**Where**[4] (Channel)
	Recognize patterns	Pre-encounter **A**	Demographics, conditions, care gaps, self-progress	Per Worksheet 6-1	Patient, admin, case manager	PHR/registry/ EHR

continued on next page

Worksheet 6-3 *continued*

Objective	Core Action	Workflow	Content Delivery		Delivery Logistics	
			CDS Five Rights Dimensions			
		When[1] (Workflow Step)	**What** (Information)	**How[2]** (Intervention Type)	**Who[3]** (Person)	**Where[4]** (Channel)
	Recognize patterns / formulate plan of care	RN & MD History/assess. **B**	History/physical data, medications, prior data review, inferred conditions		Nurse/ physician	EHR, flowsheets, data facesheets
	Formulate plan of care	Formulate care plan **C**	Guidance on best-practice approach to workup and management		Nurse/ physician/ patient	EHR, smart reference, shared decision making
	Execute plan	Documentation **D**	Appropriate and complete documentation of observations, assessment, plan		Physician/ nurse	EHR (clinical docu. tools)
	Execute plan	Orders/Rx **E**	Appropriate, correct, and complete orders for evaluation and therapy		Physician/ prescriber	CPOE e-prescribing
	Execute plan	Order handling and med dispensing **F**	Safety and appropriateness checks on medications and other diagnostic and therapeutic interventions		Physician/ nurse/ pharmacist/ other clinicians/ patient	EHR/CPOE/ pharmacy system/ medication dispensing and admin systems
	Execute plan	Therapies/ procedures **G**	Reference information and relevant data pertinent to safe and effective procedures and techniques		Physician/ nurse/ other clinicians	Reference tools, EHR modules
	Respond to events	Results and new events **H**	Inferred hazards and improvement opportunities from lab and imaging results		Physician/ nurse/ patient	EHR/PHR, HIE, alerting devices

continued on next page

Worksheet 6-3 *continued*

Objective	Core Action	Workflow	Content Delivery			Delivery Logistics	
			CDS Five Rights Dimensions				
		When[1] (Workflow Step)	**What** (Information)	**How[2]** (Intervention Type)	**Who[3]** (Person)	**Where[4]** (Channel)	
	Communicate	Consult requests I	Guidance on appropriate use of consultation and best exchange of information to/from consultant		Physician	EHR, HIE, reference tools (referral guidance)	
	Communicate	Discharge & referrals J	Discharge instructions, medication instructions, home care and continuing care information		Physician/ nurse/ patient	Discharge modules, medication reconciliation apps	
	Respond to Events	Post-visit/ home care K	Patient guidance on self-care, data gathering for condition monitoring; abnormal conditions requiring attention		Patient/caregiver, case manager, visiting nurse	PHR, online portal, smart pillbox, home data monitors	

Notes:

1. If appropriate, you may substitute other applicable workflows. Additionally, for objectives that stretch across inpatient and ambulatory care in an expanded episode, you may wish to have two tables, one for the inpatient hospitalization and one for an ambulatory care encounter.
2. Consider the full spectrum of CDS intervention types; see Figure 5-5, Taxonomy of CDS Intervention Types.
3. Consider the full spectrum of potential CDS recipients, including clinicians, administrative staff and others on the care delivery team. Carefully consider options to support patients and their family caregivers as well.
4. See Figure 3-2, CIS Applications Pertinent to CDS Interventions, for additional pertinent channels, such as financial and administrative systems. Consider also other channels outside of clinical information systems, such as text messages to mobile telephones (such as for automated appointment reminders for patients, automated notices of critical test results to providers), secure health applications on smart phones, and patient support devices, such as smart pillboxes that track and notify about patient medication use.

REFERENCES

1   Hunt DL, Haynes RB, Hanna SE, et al. Effects of computer-based clinical decision support systems on physician performance and patient outcomes. *JAMA.* 1998 Oct 21; 280(15):1339-1346.

2   Amarasingham R, Plantinga L, Diener-West M, et al. Clinical information technologies and inpatient outcomes: A multiple hospital study. *Arch Intern Med.* 2009 Jan 26;1 69(2):108-114.

3   Jaspers MW, Smeulers M, Vermeulen H, et al. Effects of clinical decision-support systems on practitioner performance and patient outcomes: A synthesis of high-quality systematic review findings. *J Am Med Inform Assoc.* 2011 May 1; 18(3):327-334.

4   Dexter PR, Perkins SM, et al. Inpatient computer-based standing orders vs physician reminders to increase influenza and pneumococcal vaccination rates: a randomized trial. *JAMA.* 2004; 292:2366-2371.

5   Shah NR, Seger AC, Seger DL, et al. Improving acceptance of computerized prescribing alerts in ambulatory care. *J Am Med Inform Assoc.* 2006 Jan-Feb; 13(1):5-11

6   Seidling HM, Phansalkar S, Seger DL, et al. Factors influencing alert acceptance: a novel approach for predicting the success of clinical decision support. *J Am Med Inform Assoc.* 2011 Jul-Aug; 18(4):479-484.

7   Kilsdonk E, Peute LW, Knijnenburg SL, et al. Factors known to influence acceptance of clinical decision support systems. *Stud Health Technol Inform.* 2011; 169:150-4.

8   Sittig DF, Teich JM, Osheroff JA, et al. Improving clinical quality indicators through electronic health records: It takes more than just a reminder. *Pediatrics.* 2009 Jul; 124(1):375-377.

9   Fischer MA, Solomon DH, Teich JM, Avorn J. Conversion from intravenous to oral medications: assessment of a computerized intervention for hospitalized patients. *Arch Intern Med.* 2003; 163(21):2585-2589.

10 Tierney WM, Miller ME, McDonald CJ. The effect on test ordering of informing physicians of the charges for outpatient diagnostic tests. *N Engl J Med.* 1990; 322:1499-1504.

11 Bates DW, Kuperman GJ, Jha A, et al. Does the computerized display of charges affect inpatient ancillary test utilization? *Arch Intern Med.* 1997; 157:2501-2508.

12 Classen DC, Phansalkar S, Bates DW. Critical drug-drug interactions for use in electronic health records systems with computerized physician order entry: review of leading approaches. *J Patient Saf.* 2011 Jun; 7(2):61-65.

13 See AHRQ website for its "Questions are the answer" campaign: http://www.ahrq.gov/questionsaretheanswer/. Accessed August 23, 2011.

Chapter 7
Configuring the Interventions

Tasks

- Define the core components, parameters and logistical details for each chosen intervention to optimize stakeholder acceptance, ease and cost of implementation, workflow effects, and benefits. Document these specifications. (Worksheet 7-1)
- Ensure that critical elements are present to permit the user to fully understand the information presented and to take appropriate action.
- Run through likely intervention use cases to ensure that the intervention configurations will perform as intended.
- Validate the proposed CDS interventions with appropriate stakeholders and obtain necessary approvals; maintain continuous and effective communication with stakeholders throughout the process to increase chances that the intervention design will deliver desired results. (Worksheets 7-2 and 7-3)
- Provide mechanisms to make sure that the interventions continue to work as expected in a complex and dynamic environment. This includes procedures to detect and handle changed circumstances, such as a modified code for a laboratory test or medication in a CDS or CIS database. (See Chapters 4 and 9 for more on maintaining interventions.) Consider backup and fail-safe contingencies in case information system components that inform or deliver the intervention fail.

KEY LESSONS

- There are many logistical details about an intervention that need to be carefully established to ensure that it leads to the desired benefit.
- There are core structural parameters for each intervention type, including triggering, logic, supporting data, notification (including acknowledgment and escalation), presentation and action items. You must optimize these to make your interventions easy to use, specific and helpful for the issue at hand, and effective in achieving objectives.
- Workflow issues are again central in configuring interventions, as they were in selecting them. In particular, strive to improve user workflow (or at least avoid introducing significant new work) and provide all the information and tools that users need to take action.

KEY LESSONS

- Make sure that CDS users and clinicians—not the computer—control care processes. The intervention should not introduce any new policies without prior stakeholder consensus, and likewise should not totally restrict any clinical behavior except when there are definite and severe patient risks.
- Intervention configuration doesn't end with launch. Robust plans for gathering and responding to feedback from those receiving or affected by the interventions are needed to keep the material relevant, accurate and valuable. Continue rich stakeholder dialog about the intervention details all the way through the intervention lifecycle—before, during and after implementation until it is retired (see Chapters 4 and 9).

GENERAL APPROACH

The previous chapter offered guidance on selecting interventions likely to be helpful for achieving priority objectives. The next steps are to fully specify the details for each selected intervention, ensure that stakeholders validate and approve the specifications, and prepare the interventions for launch.

Typically, your EHR or other HIT vendors will supply tools corresponding to some or many intervention types described in Chapters 5 and 6. For example, there may be an order set capability, an alert engine, or a documentation template builder that you can use to configure your specific desired interventions. In some cases, actual content (i.e., fully built CDS interventions) corresponding to one or more clinical objectives may be supplied with the system. Even with such pre-supplied content, significant local customization and vetting are needed to harmonize the material with specific local workflows, administrative details and procedures, and care practices (see Chapter 4). Thus, you can expect to be building some interventions and configuring or customizing others. The details that follow are intended to assist with either case.

Specifying Intervention Parameters and Details

Simply stated, there are well executed interventions and poorly executed interventions. There are pre-cise, helpful alerts and annoying, non-specific alerts. There are highly usable and understandable order sets and confusing order sets that are difficult to follow and use. There are flowsheets and data-monitoring displays that make a complex process simpler and displays that do just the opposite. How you specify, implement and communicate an intervention's configuration details has a great effect on how well it is received and used to achieve the targeted objective.

Because CDS interventions are tightly coupled with clinical workflow, a central intervention configuration goal is to ensure successful workflow integration. Nothing will make an intervention more effective than user perception that it is convenient and helpful; nothing will make it less effective than the perception that it is distracting and difficult. When you are about to release an intervention into active use, consider what your users will think about these questions when the intervention appears:

- Am I glad to see this information presented right now? Is this the right time to affect a plan, or to make a course change? Does it help me without distracting me?
- Do I have enough information and data right in front of me to take action quickly and confidently?
- Is it easy for me to make my chosen action happen, right from the intervention?

Creating intervention content and mechanics based on these design specifications may require some combination of configuring parameters in installed information systems, developing new CDS content and integrating external CDS knowledge sources. When important functionality is required but not available in your systems, it may also require you or your vendor to write a small amount of new system software. For most organizations, time and expertise limitations will make extensive programming impractical. Developing substantial amounts of new CDS content internally will be similarly impractical for many organizations, though it is critical to provide some degree of internal review and approval for *all* CDS content that is deployed.

In many cases, then, intervention development from the implementer's standpoint mainly involves using CDS features provided by your CIS and CDS content vendors and adding/customizing/reviewing content as needed (such as for documentation forms, order sets and alerts). Whether you are developing interventions fully from the ground up—perhaps as a vendor, or as a user/developer with a particularly flexible system—or are specifying and customizing the interventions you need from a provided toolkit, the following considerations should be helpful in maximizing usability, acceptance and impact.

CDS interventions contain several core components.[1,2,3,4] Figure 7-1 illustrates these components, along with their inter-relationships and sequence in intervention execution. Note that EHR data may be utilized, or modified, in several steps. Each component has critical design issues that will affect usability and impact.

Although these components generally apply to all intervention types, different intervention types (such as alerts, order sets, documentation templates and reference information) each have unique logistical issues to consider when configuring specific interventions in that category. We emphasize computer-based interventions here, but some of these considerations are also important when paper-based delivery channels are used.

Triggering

Some interventions are automatically present in user workflow. These include multi-patient monitoring displays on a hospital unit and documentation forms that always appear on an EHR screen used in a particular care process. When interventions are only supposed to be available under specific circumstances, there needs to be some mechanism to trigger this appearance. That is, some event must tell the system to check to see if a particular condition exists that should cause an intervention to be activated and appear to the user. For example, a check for drug-drug interactions is triggered when a new drug is selected during CPOE or e-prescribing system use. Similarly, entering a new diagnosis for an admitted patient may trigger a process to see if there are any diagnosis-specific order sets available. A trigger event doesn't mean that something will automatically appear to the user; rather, it is background logic used to determine if any specific CDS-worthy conditions exist.

Triggering is usually *data-driven, absolute-time-driven, relative-time-driven,* or *user-driven.*

- *Data-driven triggers* typically occur after entry (automatic or manual) of a new order or order parameter (such as increased drug dose), a new problem or diagnosis, a new admission or discharge event, or a new test result. It is important that the EHR or other information software you are using has CDS trigger points (sometimes called insertion points) available for all these data entry events.

- *Absolute-time-driven triggers* occur at fixed times; a common example is a trigger every night at midnight to run logic checks on patients with physician office visits for the next day. An absolute-time trigger may also involve a "daemon" that runs every few minutes to check for new data when other triggers are not available.

- *Relative-time-driven triggers* are used to check on an event that should follow another event. For example, when a statin drug is prescribed to treat elevated cholesterol, a time trigger may be set to make sure that appropriate monitoring tests are

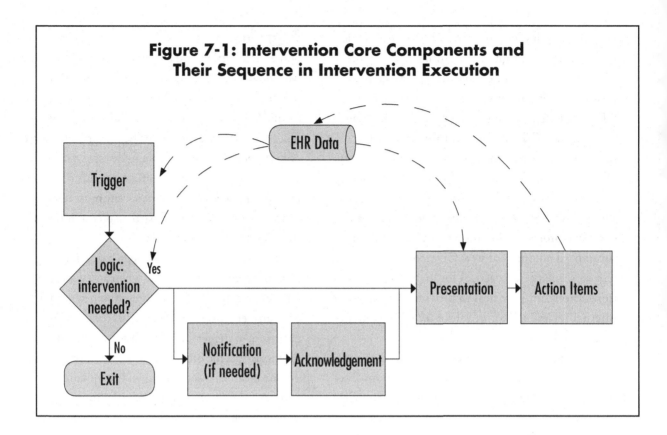

Figure 7-1: Intervention Core Components and Their Sequence in Intervention Execution

performed in the next month. When unfractionated heparin is ordered in the hospital, a trigger may be set four to six hours ahead to make sure that a partial thromboplastin time test is performed to monitor the drug's effects.

- *User-driven interventions* include information delivered in response to a user request, for example, clicking an infobutton to obtain reference information about a specific drug or clinical problem or calling up a particular calculator, order set or flowsheet.

Logic

Once a trigger occurs, logic is executed to determine whether a condition exists that requires CDS information to be presented to someone. Logic statements typically take the form, "IF [certain conditions are true], THEN [take some action or provide specific notification]." As we will emphasize in a moment, it is very important in the logic statements within an alert to also address in the "IF" section specific circumstances (called exclusion criteria) when the "THEN" actions should *not* happen.

Drug-drug interaction interventions are classic examples of how logic comes into play. The interaction-checking logic is triggered every time a new medication is ordered, but an intervention display will be delivered to a user only if the logic concludes that a significant drug interaction is present. The conditions driving this conclusion are the new drug ordered, existing patient data about other active medications, and the intervention's knowledge base. As another example, dosing-guidance logic can also be triggered when the medication is ordered, and the logic will check to see if the patient has an important condition such as renal failure, which should result in a different recommended-dose list being presented to the user.

This logic step is also where seeds for *alert fatigue* are planted with the alert and reminder intervention type. Whereas logic within other CDS interventions may modify what the user sees within a particular workflow (for example, smart documentation templates may hide or show certain documentation fields based on the patient's condition), logic within interruptive alerts forcefully draws users' attention to new information that otherwise wouldn't appear at all. If the alert logic isn't tuned carefully so that the new information only appears when it is pertinent and needed, then this nonspecific logic will produce many unexpected and unhelpful interruptions. This can slow down care processes and distract users from important tasks. When this happens repeatedly, users can become annoyed, often rapidly dismissing all alerts—without absorbing their contents—the moment they appear. This fatigue-induced desensitization leads to both superfluous *and* truly important alerts being dismissed—the latter creating potentially important patient safety risks.[5] Distractions caused by superfluous alerts can also introduce hazards by drawing attention from other critical patient care tasks.

When using alerts and reminders, therefore, you must very carefully configure the logic to avoid excessive alerting. This requires the logic to accurately identify the patients and situations where notification is required. For example, you might write exclusions into the logic to suppress alert firing when the test or medication the alert recommends is contraindicated for the particular patient or has already been administered or refused. In addition, you might elect to use overarching logic to suppress less critical alerts if individual logic statements call for several different alerts for a single patient to be delivered all at once. Addressing all these nuances adds complexity to specifying alert logic. This further reinforces the guidance emphasized in Chapter 6 about using the right CDS intervention for the job—and not overusing interruptive alerts.[6]

Data

Where will the patient data come from that are required by the intervention logic? For example, reminding clinicians when diabetic patients are overdue for a foot examination requires a reliable mechanism for determining when the last foot examination was performed. This determination can be difficult if the information is not recorded and readily accessible to the intervention logic as a coded data element. Your logic should check not only that

data are present but also that it is sufficiently recent to be relevant. Since data for the same event can come in different forms, it is important for the logic to have several options for obtaining the data. For example, you could capture the fact that a flu shot was administered through a CPT procedure code, an ICD-9 procedure code, or even through a visit code.

Coded data are the most useful triggers and inputs for CDS interventions. However, clinicians typically record subjective patient observations—such as foot examinations—as uncoded free text, which is difficult to use in CDS interventions. Systems that can capture observations in coded form, perhaps using standard vocabularies such as SNOMED CT, make CDS logic more specific and accurate. A particular 'hot spot' for data needed in CDS intervention logic is the patient problem list. These lists are maintained as coded data in some EHRs and as free text in others; some systems look for coded equivalents to what the user types in but allow free text to be chosen if a suitable match isn't found. The drug allergy list is another data type that is vital for many CDS logic statements but not always kept in coded form. Because a patient's problems and allergies are often very important data elements in CDS logic, your CDS governance should work to establish policies and mechanisms for clinicians to document these and other key data types in coded form.[7,8]

In some circumstances, automated text processing algorithms can assign terms from a structured vocabulary to free text[9] to facilitate processing by the intervention, although these are not yet common in production systems.

Notification

If the intervention is a direct response to user-entered data, such as an immediate critique of a new order, then it will appear on screen just after the data are entered (ideally without any delay noticed by the user). If the trigger is asynchronous—that is, it occurs while the target user is not necessarily working with the computer or even thinking about that patient—then there must be a more proactive mechanism to *notify* the user about the CDS information. For example, an asynchronous notification situation may occur when a CDS intervention detects that a newly posted serum drug level result indicates that the dose of that drug needs to be changed.

Notifications can be delivered through many different channels including a direct page or text message; a monitor screen (such as a unit monitor or tracking system); or through email. Notification messages can also be stored within an EHR or other information system and revealed when the user next accesses the patient record or other application during routine care activities.[3] Naturally, you should reserve the more intrusive notifications, such as an immediate page or text message, for very urgent and fairly infrequent circumstances. Keep in mind that automated notifications directed toward specific individuals or roles (such as a nurse or physician responsible for a patient at a particular time) require that the correct recipient be identified by some automatic process,[10,11,12] taking into account shift changes and physician sign-outs that occur.

In many situations, the notification should be formally *acknowledged* to ensure that it has been received. Most commonly, this acknowledgment is recorded when the user accesses the notifying application and acts on the intervention. If an intervention is delivering urgent information, it may be important to configure it to check if an acknowledgment is received within a specified time, If there is none, then the intervention should trigger *escalation*—that is, delivering a separate notification to another user, continuing this process until the notification has been acknowledged.

Presentation

How is the information delivered to the user? Presentation is different for different intervention types, and this user interface affects intervention acceptability and effectiveness. For example, a tracking display or monitor is usually a continuously-running, full-screen display that allows some drill-down through clicking on various screen areas. An order set lists orders and order parameters that the user can select by checking or unchecking items and editing small fields. An alert may appear in a separate pop-up window or may be integral to the EHR interface, using color, boldface or other visual cues to direct user focus to important data or evidence-based recommendations.

When you configure CDS information presentation, remember that the objective is to facilitate decision making and related actions—to "make the right thing to do the easy thing to do." Users typically interact with any given CDS intervention for a minute or two at most, so it is important to give them all the information they need; make it clear and convenient for them to understand, trust, and apply. Ensure that the critical CDS presentation elements are present in your intervention information displays, keeping in mind that these will vary somewhat depending on the intervention type. Figure 7-2 lists some considerations that apply to alerts as well other intervention types.

Usability Elements

How your users interact with the presentation design is an important factor in whether they accept the interventions and use them effectively. The following are additional usability and configuration issues to consider within and across interventions. Some are inherent to the EHR design, but others can be modified during intervention configuration.

- *Modal vs. non-modal interaction model.* A CDS intervention presentation is *modal* if the user cannot proceed with anything else on the display screen until the message is addressed in some way; it is *non-modal* if the user can proceed in their other work without dealing with the alert—for example, if it is presented as a notification somewhere on the screen, where the user can click on it or not as desired. Modal alerts obviously get more attention but must not be overused for reasons outlined in the previous alert fatigue discussion. Non-modal alerts are preferred for low-to-medium urgency issues, such as drug-drug interactions that produce relatively minor risks. Some EHR systems allow you to

---

Figure 7-2: Key Elements to Consider in Presenting a CDS Intervention

1. A clear, brief statement indicating the reason for the intervention;
2. Supporting data necessary to make a decision;
3. Information (including links for further details as appropriate) that explain the options;
4. Easy access to action items;
5. Mechanisms to document exceptions, if applicable; and
6. Ability to give feedback to the clinical intervention owners.

---

choose modal or non-modal alerting for different alert types.

- *Scrolling.* What is on the screen is what is noticed. Vertical scrolling, such as for a long list of orders in an order set, is sometimes necessary, but should be minimized if possible. It is important for busy clinicians to complete their orders and move on to the next patient care task, so it is common for them to scroll rapidly through a long list of orders without fully considering each one. Although there is debate on this, some argue that paging interfaces ("Next page" buttons, as can be seen in general search result and other displays) are friendlier than long scrolling lists. In any case, the total pages should be minimized. Horizontal scrolling is unfamiliar and uncomfortable for most users, and you should avoid including it in your CDS presentations.

- *Consistent, simple user interface (UI).* If your system has a variety of CDS interventions, try to keep them consistent with respect to color, font and other general appearance features. Using too many different colors, icons and other indicators is almost always confusing—and potentially dangerous if this confusion increases user error.

- *Speed, speed, speed.* Few things annoy computer users as much as having to click multiple times or go through multiple screens to get the information they seek. All the necessary information to act on the CDS intervention should be present on the main screen, or at most one click away.

- *Data privacy and security.* Ensure that Health Insurance Portability and Accountability Act (HIPAA) and related implications are considered, if applicable, particularly with respect to information presented in open patient care areas or on mobile devices.

Action Items

CDS information is often presented to support a possible change in decisions or actions. Thus, it should be possible for the user to take action directly from the CDS screens—usually through new orders or new documentation. For order sets, the actions are apparent in the ability to select or deselect order item check boxes, and edit the orders themselves. As noted previously, alerts should make it easy for the user to take the action (such as ordering, changing or cancelling a medication or test) recommended by the alert. For reference information displays, there may be no direct actions, but you can explore ways to tie the information to anticipated new orders or documentation, such as through proximity or direct links to tools for these functions.

Exceptions

Although effective and user-friendly interventions should make it very easy for the user to order or document what the intervention recommends, they shouldn't force the user into a particular action. Even when there are strong clinical guideline or safety issues (such as prescribing a drug to which the patient is allergic) underpinning the intervention, there may be other circumstances not factored into the computer logic.[13] For example, a particular medication may be required for life-saving reasons and therefore acceptable to administer despite a documented allergy. Similarly, not ordering a mammogram in response to a reminder is appropriate if the patient has had bilateral mastectomies. For situations in which users may take an action other than the one the intervention recommends, you can consider building into the intervention the capacity to elicit and document the reason for this deviation. This can be useful for clinical documentation, quality improvement and medico-legal purposes and can be accomplished by providing a list of standard exceptions that the user can select, as well as an "Other" text box for unusual exceptions.[2]

Override reasons might include items such as: clinician disagrees with recommendation; recommendation already implemented; alert fired inappropriately; patient ineligible for recommended intervention; patient refuses recommended intervention; and the like. Different intervention focus areas may require somewhat different exceptions, depending on how detailed the reasons are. Studies have examined allergy alert overrides and made specific recommendations for improving these alerts.[14] A predecessor to this book that addressed CDS specifically to improve medication use and outcomes[15] provided a detailed list of potential override reasons for medication-related orders. These exceptions (listed next) can be adapted to other situations as well, and are worth considering not only for exception documentation lists but also for other intervention design elements such as logic and action items.

- Patient is allergic or otherwise sensitive to the drug recommended by the intervention.
- Patient does not actually have the condition that triggered the alert.
- New patient data are available that indicate the CDS intervention's information is no longer valid (for example, an alert indicating that according to clinical guidelines the patient is not eligible for a transfusion, may not "be aware" that the patient is actively bleeding).

- New scientific evidence is available that invalidates the alert (for example, a new clinical guideline is available that contradicts the previous guideline that formed the basis for the alert).
- Alert is incorrect (for reasons encompassing or other than those previously listed).
- Decline suggestion. Reasons might include other comorbidities, treatment cost, patient refusal, or other reason (option for user to enter free text information here).
- Defer alert for: Specify or allow user to enter period, such as days, weeks or months, depending on alert type and IT capabilities.
- I acknowledge the risk and am planning/monitoring accordingly.
- Other: please enter text below. (This option can be problematic. If inputting text is not required, the request can easily be ignored. If it is required, users may simply enter a nonsensical response; for example, space, period or any character, and move on. Either way, evaluating these disparate free text reasons can be difficult and time consuming.)

In the specific case of an intervention or alert advising against the use of a drug, such as an allergy, drug-drug interaction or drug-duplication warning:

- Patient is not allergic or otherwise sensitive to the drug listed in an allergy warning. (When possible, the alert should display the reported allergic reaction and data source. This will help clinicians differentiate between a patient-reported intolerance to penicillin that caused abdominal discomfort from an anaphylactic reaction reported by an intensive care unit nurse).
- Patient is currently taking and tolerating the medication.
- Patient has taken and tolerated the medication in the past.
- Benefit of medication outweighs the risk to the patient.
- The dose has been adjusted accordingly (for example, a physician may intentionally and carefully order two medications in the same class for a particular clinical purpose, so a duplicate therapy warning would not need to be heeded).

- In the case of a drug-drug interaction the other interacting drug will be discontinued or its dose modified (this should usually be one of the available action items, rather than an exception).

Chapter 9 further discusses strategies for evaluating alert overrides. See, for example, the Sidebar, "A Deeper Dive into Alerting and Overrides."

Other Considerations in Configuring Interventions

In addition to the core intervention design elements just discussed, there are other considerations to keep in mind as you configure the interventions you chose to address specific targets. Several are listed next.

- **Link interventions to each other when appropriate.** Consider opportunities to join interventions in a manner that will increase their effect. For example, orders in order sets can be linked to reference material via infobuttons to facilitate correct ordering and user learning. When possible, use logic to avoid suggesting something in one intervention that will then generate a warning. For example, avoid providing an order set option that recommends a drug to which the patient is allergic. Such conditional presentation capabilities might not be present in all your information systems, but they should be considered to improve CDS effectiveness and acceptability when they are available.

- **Consider the effect of intervention-induced changes.** You should make sure that your organization is prepared for any new care processes that the intervention is designed to facilitate. For example, when an intervention is designed to increase use of underutilized screening tests such as mammograms or preventive therapies such as flu shots, the volume of tests or therapies may rise significantly if the intervention is successful. Preparing affected units for intervention success with adequate capacity and supplies will help you ensure that the CDS intervention achieves its overall intended result.

- **Consider unintended negative consequences.** You should respect and carefully explore the pos-

sibility that your intervention might, under some circumstances, result in actions that negatively affect care processes and outcomes.[16,17,18] There is increasing attention to these adverse HIT effects, and your sensitivity and attention to these issues early during design will reduce the chances for problems after launch.

- **Consider communication factors for interventions directed to patients.** These factors include the patient's native language, level of formal education, and culture and personal beliefs about health and illness. Clearly, interventions intended to inform and enhance patient decisions will be effective only to the extent that the patient understands the information and also to the extent that it doesn't conflict with his/her core beliefs. Consider also information delivery channels and tools through which you can deliver CDS interventions to patients in their home, such as websites, PHRs and other patient-oriented monitoring and communication applications. The better your interventions accommodate available communication capabilities and limitations, the more likely they are to be effective.

- **Consider site-specific factors.** Although many of your interventions will be based on national care guidelines, there are many local details that influence intervention configuration. Incorporating these can make the information more specific and valuable to the recipient and clinical circumstances. For example, incorporating local antibiotic resistance patterns and formularies when making antibiotic selection recommendations, providing site-specific referral lists when recommending consultations, offering practice-specific "favorites" lists (e.g., for drug and test orders), and others can all improve intervention acceptability and effectiveness.

- **Provide appropriate customization.** Building on the point just discussed, you should consider tailoring the intervention, when possible, for different departments, settings and situations within your organization. This should usually be done at the organization level; it is controversial whether *individual* users should be able to configure some specific interventions since, as we have mentioned, this can introduce hazards even though it increases user acceptance. For example, many organizations do not permit individuals to customize order sets for their own use. Although users consider these personalized order sets better for their workflow and practice style, they can introduce deviations from evidence-based care and produce errors resulting from non-standard care practices. In addition, having multiple individual variations on the same order set can dramatically increase or compromise maintenance efforts. The work to achieve consensus from clinicians and other stakeholders about clinical details before releasing an intervention can be a significant challenge for intervention configuration. However, when this work is successful, the chances that the intervention will achieve its ultimate objectives increase substantially.

- **Support and enhance user workflow.** An intervention is likely to be successful if (and only if) it supports and enhances workflow; this has been expressed as "make something better and nothing worse." Strive to avoid adding new work in the name of supporting decisions, since users will often ignore interventions or find workarounds when this happens. Likewise, avoid suggesting a change to an overall plan once it has been made; instead, intervene earlier so proper plans are established to begin with. We made this same recommendation regarding intervention selection in Chapter 6, but it pertains as well to configuring individual interventions. Finally, consider expressing a long clinical guideline as several short steps in one or more CDS interventions instead of one large change that has to be digested and addressed by the user all at once.

- **Don't use interventions to *establish* policy.** In configuring interventions, make sure that the stakeholders/users, not the computer, control patient management. Remember that "the computer doesn't make policy." In other words, any modifications to care practices should be fully dis-

cussed, vetted and approved through appropriate governance channels before they are implemented in a CDS intervention. Because information systems are so deeply involved in day-to-day clinical work operations, they already have substantial implied power. For example, CPOE systems literally control how prescribers' intentions can be carried out; the last thing clinicians want is to feel is that the computer is now simultaneously declaring and enforcing policy changes. As we have emphasized, stakeholder communication and inclusion are vital for successful CDS-related change efforts—and configuring intervention details related to clinical policy depend critically on this engagement. For example, a clinician who is urged by policy to use a new order set or protocol will feel much less resistant if he or she had input into—or was at least informed about—processes that led to the new underlying clinical policy.

- **Develop a fail-safe plan.** When configuring interventions, you should plan for situations where part or all of the underlying EHR, and/or the CDS intervention itself, becomes temporarily unavailable. Reasons for unavailability might include scheduled system maintenance or an unanticipated malfunction. Results to consider might be missing key data (affecting the data gathering required for intervention logic), no 'safety net' for high-risk care activities, and gaps in access to quality and efficiency tools (such as order sets). The broader information system failsafe plan in your organization should address such issues, and you should also anticipate and attempt to mitigate any more specific issues as you configure new interventions—especially those that are associated with high patient stakes and risks. Trend monitoring is one way to address this—if you can monitor the process change brought on by an intervention, such as the number of allergy alerts or the number of uses of a given order set, you can detect when the intervention is no longer working as designed.

- **Minimize intervention overload.** This is especially a concern with alerts as previously described, but is applicable to all intervention configuration decisions; CDS brings about many process changes and can have a profound impact on workload. You should consider the balance of costs (such as time and cognitive burden) and benefits (such as greater efficiency and confidence) to the user. While individual interventions might be quite valuable, overloading users with more information than they can easily handle can actually increase distractions and decrease safety.

- **Optimize incentives for use.** As noted earlier, each user who receives interventions you provide will experience workflow-related costs and benefits associated with its use. Because the interventions, by definition, affect workflow in some way, you should carefully consider approaches to optimize their overall value to users. As discussed in Chapters 1 and 2, pay-for-performance programs may represent a powerful driver for *organizational* CDS use, though a particular intervention user may only receive direct financial benefit in special cases, such as receiving a quality bonus related to the intervention's target. Consider other extrinsic rewards, such as providing continuing education credit opportunities, when appropriate, for clinicians who use CDS content. Intervention configuration details offer other ways to deliver important value to users—such as saving time, not having to leave a particular task to look up needed information, or otherwise making the task faster or easier to accomplish. Well-designed order sets and monitoring displays are particularly well-known as ways to save time, and the use of order sets often mitigates the initial increase in work surrounding a new CPOE implementation. As we have emphasized repeatedly, cultivating these benefits requires close collaboration with users on intervention details.

- **Build in feedback mechanisms.** As you configure intervention *delivery* details, you also need to consider user *feedback* and other *assessment* mechanisms so you can 'close the loop' on intervention effects on users and processes. This is particularly important for intrusive or high-stakes interventions, such as

unsolicited alerts about major safety hazards, but the ability to elicit user feedback in any circumstance provides an enhanced opportunity for you to improve the intervention, while also releasing temporary user frustration with an intervention that is causing problems. You might include mechanisms that enable recipients to provide their own comments and feedback about specific interventions when they occur, as well as auditing mechanisms that track how frequently a specific intervention is used and how the users respond to it. Collecting data about alert overrides, as discussed earlier, is a case example. These mechanisms are vitally important in CDS maintenance and in preventing CDS failures that may arise due to database changes or changes in clinical management strategies. Of course, you should also provide reliable mechanisms for prompt CDS Team response to the feedback and audits. Intervention effects monitoring are discussed in more detail in Chapters 8 and 9.

Putting It All Together

All the considerations just discussed inform decisions about to how configure interventions that, individually and collectively, fit smoothly into workflow and improve targeted outcomes. You should involve end users, champions and other stakeholders throughout the design process. As discussed in the following section, the next step will be to formally validate the design and obtain approval for development. Before doing this, you can review this guidance in this section and look for places where each intervention can be fine-tuned to make it more usable, concise, workflow-friendly and tailored to your end-user and organizational needs. Worksheet 7-1 can help you collect and review necessary details as you begin your design and can be continually updated as you refine your configuration.

CDS rules that underpin alerts and reminders are fraught with implementation challenges, as we have discussed. The sidebar on the next page complements the guidance discussed so far in this chapter by presenting rule implementation considerations that need to be addressed during rule design.

CDS Rule Implementation Considerations*

How will you make sure the rule aligns with your local clinical workflow, user privileges and local policy (e.g., corresponds to specific thresholds and constraints used locally)?
- Allowable range of test value limits; allowable range of medication dose limits; allowable range of time limits
- Mechanisms to ensure rule content is monitored for ongoing appropriateness

How will rule triggering be handled? [See also NQF CDS taxonomy: p 10-12.*]
How will the rule be triggered?
- **Patient-specific:** on chart open, on select order, on sign order, on sign document, on add problem or diagnosis, on test result post, on provider login, patient access to PHR...
- **Batch:** registry, periodic panel search, patient list for day
- **Timing Considerations:** is rule firing in advance of deadline for a specific indicated care intervention (e.g., notifying users about deadline) pertinent to a clinical event occurring now (e.g., triggered by inappropriate/missing order during order entry session), or indicating that indicated intervention is past due?

How will data be provided to trigger the rule?
- **By a specific system** (e.g., CPOE, EHR, PHR): are these data reliably available in coded format? What if it turns out not to be available in a specific circumstance – how does this affect rule behavior?
- **By a person** (who provides those data [patient, clinician, etc.], how the system enables them to provide it [e.g., where/how does data entry form appear to minimize workflow disruption?])

How will you make sure the rule triggers for the right patients? [See NQF CDS taxonomy p 13-15.]*
- **Additional inclusions/exclusions:** greater patient specificity to minimize false positives that might result from only following inclusions/exclusions explicitly mentioned in a guideline or eMeasure (e.g., excluding patients with bilateral mastectomy from breast cancer screening rule)
- **Exclude exceptions already documented in the system** [see next]: patient refusal, lost to follow-up...

How will the rule results affect the care delivery process? [Consider CDS Five Rights; NQF CDS taxonomy p 16-17.*]
Setting where notification is delivered, rule output recipient, and delivery channel
- **Where:** ED, hospital care unit, ICU, OR, physician office, wherever recipient is (e.g., via mobile device)
- **Who:** patient, nurse, pharmacist, physician, other member of care team; internal to system (e.g., when rule triggers another rule or action by the system)

continued on next page

- **How** (delivery channel): EHR (specific module, e.g., results review, CPOE, etc.), PHR, mobile device
- **When** (specific point in workflow): e.g., associated with a specific information system-based task; other

User interaction with rule output, including rule actions and notifications (What)
- Interactive vs. background (i.e., synchronous vs. asynchronous with care delivery processes)
- Elements for rule acceptance by users: rule rationale explicit, additional key data needed to make a decision presented, ability to easily take action on rule recommendation. Rule actions/notifications can include:
  - Message, pop-up, to-do list, order, notation in chart
  - Automatic scheduling, e.g., a follow-up visit or test
  - Execute another rule
  - Escalation, alternate recipient...
  - Will output be structured/documented, e.g., for internal QA and regulatory purposes?

Rule results disposition (e.g., processing user response)
- Facilitate specific user action (e.g., ordering an intervention, documenting)
- Enabling user documentation that patient is an exception to the rule

How will rule behavior and effects be monitored? [See NQF IT Utilization report: p 10-18.*]
- Rule availability in system, rule firing, recipient response (e.g., accept, reject, defer – perceived user value), workflow impact, effects on outcome; intended and unintended effects

---

*This CDS rule implementation considerations list was compiled as part of the AHRQ eRecommendation project.[19] The list references the CDS taxonomy from the National Quality Forum CDS Expert Panel report,[2] and the NQF Health Information Technology Utilization Expert Panel report.[20] Page numbers noted refer to these original documents.

Intervention Use Cases

Finalizing intervention design before approval and development includes ensuring that the intervention will function as envisioned once it is built and launched. This requires anticipating 'unusual circumstances' that arise during complex care delivery processes and that make the actual events surrounding a particular intervention quite different from the 'normal' expected events for which the intervention was designed. For example:

- An intervention designed to screen inpatients for venous thromboembolism risk on admission worked fine, except that every patient who arrived to deliver a baby fell into the high-risk group, and the intervention recommended that compression stockings be applied to all of them—a recommendation that was not very acceptable to the patients and their caregivers.

- An intervention promoting the conversion of intravenous to oral medications in a timely fashion did not consider patients who were intubated.
- The logic underlying an intervention that screened for tuberculosis risk went awry when the laboratory changed the code for a relevant microbiology test, resulting in a tenfold increase in patients directed to isolation rooms.

While you cannot predict all circumstances surrounding how interventions will function once released, you can avoid many problematic or embarrassing post-launch situations by contemplating—and preparing for—a wide range of typical and atypical scenarios.

At some point between the time you decide to use a particular intervention to address an objective and the time when you finalize its configuration, you should develop and apply intervention use cases. This involves envisioning, describing and validating several scenarios—involving different care settings, patient types, workflows and user types—for how the intervention will function in these circumstances. End users and other key stakeholders should be involved throughout this process; the use cases provide a formal mechanism to reconcile their needs and expectations with the CDS Team's configuration efforts.

You should subject interventions associated with higher clinical stakes, intrusiveness and potential hazards to more intensive use case development. This includes vetting the use cases themselves more carefully, as well as using the validated use cases in turn to vet the interventions. You can use the intervention component model outlined in Figure 7-1 (and related text) to inform use case development. As you create diverse use cases to design and evaluate your intervention's behavior, consider:

Trigger: Does the intervention need to trigger in an unusual care setting or in two or more care settings for different patient populations or workflows?

Logic and data: What if data needed by the intervention aren't available in the information system where the intervention expects to obtain it? What if the most recent relevant data item is too old to provide appropriate results? Could data be specified in a different way by different providers and therefore affect intervention output? Would the logic work differently for patients on different services? Do different venues have different ways of capturing and coding data? And even if these issues are checked, always ask the "alert fatigue" question: are there circumstances that could cause the intervention to appear excessively?

Presentation: Will the reasons and evidence backing for the intervention be clear to the user? Will there be a problem when presenting the intervention to one particular class of users? For example, do these users have different experience levels or access to different clinical services? Will users be able to understand the intervention and be authorized to take action?

Action items: Are reasonable action items easy for users to activate? Are the listed actions available in all venues? Do users need to leave the main application and go to a different process in order to respond? Are reasonable exceptions easy to declare? Will users ever be prevented from performing the action they desire after considering the presented information?

In addition to anticipating unusual or problematic situations, the use cases should also document details about how the interventions will function in more routine circumstances. Again, this helps ensure that designers and users have the same expectations about typical intervention behavior.

If your software permits, it can be very valuable to run the proposed intervention in a test environment, or if that is not available, to test it in a live environment in such a way that the intervention does not actually appear to users but still performs in a similar manner. This will help you get a sense of how often it will appear, whether it appears appropriately, and whether it will present incorrect or unwanted information in some circumstances. We'll say more about testing before launch in the next chapter. For example, Worksheet 8-4 helps you anticipate and address intervention 'failure modes' before launch, and you can look ahead at that now to reinforce these considerations during intervention design.

Intervention Validation and Approval

There are two major checkpoints between the time your CDS Team decides to use a particular intervention and when that intervention is released into workflow: when finalizing the intervention design and then when approving the intervention 'build' for launch. More complex interventions and related workflows will require more—and more detailed—iterations between the CDS Team, users (and other stakeholders), and use cases to reach each checkpoint. For example, an order set focused on a common condition, and containing embedded rules and documentation tools, may require extensive workflow analysis, use case development and application and user dialog. Less complex interventions, such as new infobutton links to reference information, require much less effort to design, build and validate.

The investments you made to identify stakeholders and cultivate champions earlier in your CDS efforts will pay off during these development and approval stages. Those who will be affected in some way by the CDS interventions are in a great position to help filter all the considerations discussed so far in this chapter into the intervention specifications, and subsequent build, testing and approval. You can refer back to the discussion about stakeholders in Chapter 2; Figures 2-4 through 2-6 identify key individuals, positions and committees and their roles. Remember to consider stakeholders with formal leadership positions, those who are respected opinion leaders, and those whose jobs will be affected by the intervention, as well as those workers who capture data necessary for the intervention.

Broad input into the intervention specification (and the development process, as needed) can lead to a more effective end product due to improved design, fewer objections, and a greater sense of intervention ownership among all stakeholders. While

these considerations are especially true in large care delivery organizations, stakeholder engagement with interventions that will affect them is also critical, even in small practice settings.

After you have addressed all the intervention design and configuration steps outlined in this chapter, you should conduct final reviews with stakeholders to ensure your design will perform as desired in both routine and atypical situations. Your CDS governance mechanisms should then formally approve the intervention design and its subsequent production. Similar vetting and approval steps are needed after the intervention is developed; these are discussed in detail in the next chapter. We now discuss tools that can support intervention design validation and approval.

When validating interventions with stakeholders, one of the most important first steps is to communicate the work that you have done and the thought you have put in up to that point about how the intervention will work and how it will affect operations. This provides stakeholders with a frame of reference and gives them a chance to start thinking about the intervention before they need to discuss and approve it, rather than coming in 'cold' to a demonstration and being expected to appreciate all the ramifications the intervention will have.

Worksheet 7-2 is a sample intervention communication form that summarizes intervention objectives, clinical and workflow implications, operation, and basic design. You can use a form like this to document key intervention details with clinical proponents and designers. This documentation can then support stakeholder communications prior to design approval, and then the actual approval and subsequent build. If you used intervention configuration forms (such as those in Worksheets 6-2 and 6-3) in selecting multiple interventions for a particular objective, they can likewise be very useful during the vetting, approval and build process. Worksheet 7-3 can be used to document discussions and decisions when the CDS intervention is presented to CDS governance for approval to proceed with the build.

CONSIDERATIONS FOR HOSPITALS/HEALTH SYSTEMS
People (Stakeholder Involvement)

- Consider the full range of settings within the organization—and pertinent roles and individuals in each. Configuration details will be numerous and complex depending on variations (such as in personnel, workflows, policies and cultures) in different departments and venues.

- Optimizing stakeholder acceptance requires that the CDS Team engage many end users throughout the configuration process. The more people who will ultimately be affected by the intervention that you can connect to the intervention configuration process, the less likely it will be that unexpected user resistance or other problems will arise after launch. The Considerations for Hospitals/Health Systems section in Chapter 2 can help ensure that you identify all pertinent stakeholders.

- Clinical champions can be particularly helpful, because they greatly amplify your ability to engage, communicate with, and reassure many stakeholders affected by the new intervention. As emphasized in Chapter 2, champions should be carefully selected to be credible, knowledgeable and highly trusted by their colleagues.

- During these stakeholder communications during intervention configuration, your CDS Team should ensure that the workflow analysis results are correct and applicable across settings where the intervention will be used.

Design

- Leverage your information system vendors' tools and insights to support intervention configuration. The size, customer footprint and resources that your hospital or health system has may create opportunities for you to work with your EHR and other vendors to obtain increased services or product accommodations to optimize your intervention development efforts.

- We have emphasized interplay between your new interventions and clinical workflow, and it is equally important to consider interplay between your CDS interventions and your organization's information systems (as discussed in Chapter 3). Your IT department should be significantly involved in your intervention design and configuration activities. Engaging both IT leadership and staff can help ensure that IT capabilities are fully leveraged (and pitfalls avoided) in your intervention design and that resources need to successfully build your intervention will be available when needed.

CONSIDERATIONS FOR SMALL PRACTICES
People (Stakeholder Involvement)

- Although there are typically fewer people affected by a particular CDS intervention in a small practice than a hospital, it is perhaps even more important in the more close-knit setting to ensure that everyone in the office affected by an intervention has a say in its development. These individuals should have been involved to at least some degree from the earliest stages of target selection and should remain connected through intervention configuration, vetting and approval.

- If interventions are being deployed in a network of small practices, clinician champions should travel to meet one-on-one with physicians in the local settings. These champions should be users of the CDS interventions, so they understand and can respond effectively to their colleagues' questions and concerns. They should be able to provide practical strategies—and compelling use cases and benefit examples—for using the forthcoming interventions to improve personal efficiencies (such as saving time) and patient outcomes. The earlier in the design process that this dialog begins, the better.

Capabilities

- Small practices typically have limited ability to alter much core intervention functionality, so your configuration efforts will largely be limited to adjusting parameters in vendor-supplied tools. For example, you may be able to set inclusion and exclusion criteria and actions for CDS rules, but not adjust information presentation, workflow insertion points or other design features.

- In some cases, information system suppliers may build rich flexibility into intervention configuration capabilities. If your practice has the expertise and time, you can then apply more fully the configuration guidance offered earlier in this chapter.

- Your system suppliers and their user groups, your local medical society or regional extension center, and other colleagues can be useful resources in ensuring that intervention configurations take full advantage of system capabilities.

- Services and structures for sharing fully-formed CDS *interventions* are currently in their infancy. As they become more mature and widespread, such services will be a boon to the small practice, allowing you to leverage a much larger intervention bank in a shorter time than you could generate yourself. As noted in the Epilogue, broad collaborations for sharing more general intervention *configuration approaches* are now getting underway.

Design

- For CDS interventions that depend on complete and accurate data (such as patient weight, smoking status, current medications or other clinical details), make sure there are workflows in place that ensure this information is entered appropriately and reliably. Vendors may provide multiple pathways for entering data (free text, drop-down menu, radio buttons and others); use an efficient, standardized data entry approach to ensure your CDS intervention has ready access to the data (usually structured and coded) it needs.

- Since small practices typically must rely on their system suppliers to provide largely pre-configured interventions, it is particularly important that the practice leader serve as a champion, validating that the intervention is clinically appropriate and helpful before further vetting with others in the practice.

Workflow

- Think ahead about possible changes to care processes in the office—such as new staff or different staff roles, new services offered by the practice, and the like—that might affect the planned intervention. Make sure that you will be able to deal with the possibility of increased visits, tests or therapies that may be brought about by CDS interventions, keeping in mind that eliminating an 'omission error' means that there is something new to be done. Develop a proactive approach to sensing and responding to these changes. Don't implement CDS interventions that result in process changes your practice can't handle.

- Seek EHR vendors and other HIT suppliers who provide interventions that enhance, and do not hamper, practice workflows. Their tools should support collaboration by all clinicians, such as having corresponding tools and displays for nurses and physicians that enhance communication and inter-related patient responsibilities. These related interventions should draw from the same underlying patient data and clinical knowledge and optimize this for specific user needs to maximize efficiency and minimize error. A small practice will often have single individuals filling multiple functional roles, so the CDS capabilities should be flexible enough to account for this in determining how interventions are directed to users.

- Consider the workflow implications for the practice if the CDS intervention becomes unavailable through a failure in the intervention itself or the underlying information system. If the intervention is critical for patient safety or efficiency, develop a backup plan.

Measurement

- Make sure that each CDS intervention—or related system functionality—enables you to measure the intervention use and impact, and generate data needed to continuously improve its value. You will typically depend heavily on your system supplier(s) for these capabilities, but you should explore these issues starting early on in your efforts to configure the intervention to deliver *measurable* value.

CONSIDERATIONS FOR HIT SOFTWARE PROVIDERS
Capabilities

- Provide support for many, if not all, of the CDS intervention types discussed in this chapter—especially those of the highest value and demand for implementers. Provide tools and support to enable implementers to configure these interventions in accordance with the guidance outlined in this chapter.

- For example, ensure that your interventions provide the vital elements (as outlined in Figures 7-1 and 7-2 and related discussion) so that users have all the information they need to make a decision and take appropriate action.

- Consider opportunities to foster and engage in collaborations between CIS and CDS suppliers, CDS implementers and others to develop more standardized approaches to key intervention components as outlined in Figure 7-1. For example:
  - Standards characterizing events that cause a decision support rule to be invoked;
  - Standard intervention routing mechanisms, such as sending a message to a clinician, showing a guideline, displaying an alert, or simply logging that an event took place;
  - Standard "Offered Choices" (action items) such as allowing the clinician to cancel a new order, choose a safer alternative drug, or override the alert and keep the order as written but provide an explanation;
  - Standard input data such as laboratory test results, patient demographics, and the patient's problem list.

- The CDS rules engine should support basic mathematical (such as MAX and MIN values), temporal (such as FIRST—earliest time a data element was stored in the patient's record, and LAST—most recent time a data element was stored in the patient's record), and logical (such as AND, OR, NOT, XOR) operators. These functions make it easier to include and exclude patient groups from rule-triggered recommendations as appropriate.

- In all places where CDS interventions provide clinical recommendations, enable users to act on the recommendation directly from the intervention screen. This includes permitting users to immediately add or cancel an order as recommended in an alert window.

- CDS content providers should accelerate efforts to deliver CDS interventions that healthcare organizations can easily configure and customize, incorporate into EHRs, and maintain. Service-oriented approaches are also of increasing interest to providers and may be worth investigating for your product line.

Design

- Ensure that your CDS content adheres to existing national data, quality/performance, and other pertinent standards, so that data needed to trigger or drive CDS rule logic can be processed in a standardized fashion and so that the interventions support improved performance against national targets. Make sure that any CDS intervention (a) supports measurements related to its use and impact, (b) is mapped to recognized CDS-related terminologies where applicable, and (c) can be used to generate data for quality measurement and reporting (such as Meaningful Use and value-based purchasing measures) as appropriate.

- CDS content should be evidence-based when possible and should track closely with the rapidly evolving clinical knowledge base. CDS content providers should provide transparency into your evidence-based process including editorial process, ongoing writer/editor training, literature surveillance and analysis, and update methodologies (see Chapter 4).

- Adhere to the good design principles for each intervention type, such as ensuring that intervention core elements are present. For example, alerts should include: brief précis of the concern; detailed explanation with supporting patient data, recommendation rationale to support user action (with links to deeper support if needed), and ability to easily execute action items.

- Note the usability suggestions provided in this chapter; implementers' ability to optimize intervention acceptability and usability depends critically on how well designed and robust your CDS tools and configuration options are. Provide interventions that don't hamper any user's work and that streamline that work if at all possible. The recommendations for implementers on using rich workflow analysis and stakeholder engagement apply equally to CDS tool suppliers.

- Consider workflows for different user types, and where possible, provide support for their collaboration; for example, having corresponding and mutually supportive tools and displays for nurses, doctors and pharmacists around common and important objectives such as decreasing drug dosing errors and interactions.

- The workflow for using interventions must align with corresponding clinical workflows and pertinent clinical roles. For example, a pharmacist and nurse have very different workflows and information needs. The underlying CDS content should be the same so that everyone is working from a common knowledge base. However, information delivered to pharmacists should address their needs (such as order validation, drug dispensing and laboratory monitoring) as should information delivered to nurses (who may need to focus more on drug administration, education, and symptom monitoring). Forcing everyone into a uniform workflow—not optimized by role—for interacting with CDS interventions can result in lost efficiencies and mistakes.

WORKSHEETS

Completed versions of the intervention specification forms in Worksheets 7-1 and 7-2, for all your planned and deployed CDS interventions (together with all your Worksheets 6-2 and 6-3), collectively document the configurations for CDS interventions within your organization's CDS program. This portfolio reflects the high-level CDS and clinical goals addressed by the program and the corresponding

clinical objectives that the interventions are designed to address. As such, this material is a foundation for your CDS knowledge management efforts (see Chapters 4 and 9). Worksheet 7-3 documents formal approval by your CDS governance processes to build specific interventions based on well vetted specifications; it too is pertinent to knowledge management efforts to document and coordinate CDS-related decisions.

Worksheet 7-1

Specification Form for Intervention Design

You can use Worksheet 7-1 to ensure that you have considered the core intervention components during design and to help make sure that all clinical and IT team members are aware of these key elements. This worksheet can become a living document, fostering discussion about various issues and evolving in response to those discussions. Consider using Worksheets 6-2 and 6-3 together with this one, especially when multiple interventions are developed together to address a particular objective.

Date:

CDS intervention name	Heparin in post-op orders
Description:	When post-op order sets are displayed, an item to order heparin (for thrombosis prophylaxis) will always be included
Clinical leader	Dr. Howard Klott, vascular medicine
Technical leader	Jennifer Rose, IT
EHR application affected	CPOE
Intervention type	Order set modification
Workflow step	Order set initiation (at post-op time)
Specifically triggered by	Order set user — that is, ordering clinician
Logic (in plain English) to determine if intervention is presented	Order set type = post-op *except:* patients already on any form of heparin, warfarin or dabigatran *except:* patient with history of gastrointestinal (GI) tract bleed, intracranial hemorrhage, subarachnoid hemorrhage or hemophilia
Data items needed / where found in the system	Order set type Problem list Medication list
Notification type, if any	None (synchronous display)
Presentation type	Order set item

continued on next page

Worksheet 7-1 *continued*

CDS intervention name	Heparin in post-op orders
Who is the primary user of intervention?	Ordering clinician
Summary précis or statement	THROMBOEMBOLISM PROPHYLAXIS:
Supporting data and knowledge to be presented	Postoperative thrombosis prophylaxis, for all patients not on anticoagulation and without significant bleeding risk, has been shown to reduce overall net vascular complications by 32%
Evidence source	Anderson and Wilkins' review of post-op clotting complications ACS recommendations on post-op anticoagulation
Offered action items	Order unfractionated heparin 5,000 units subcutaneously twice a day Order enoxaparin 1 mg/kg subcutaneously twice a day Order warfarin, start at 5 mg/day Order PTT Order INR
Feedback channels and plan	Contact information for responsible department already exists on order set

Intervention Communication Form for Validation

Worksheet 7-2 provides a vehicle to communicate higher clinical and operational intervention elements with stakeholders during the validation discussion. This includes not only the intervention content and mechanics but also the associated feedback channels, workflow, and organizational changes necessary to ensure intervention success in meeting objectives.

Think carefully about how each planned intervention will affect workflow, including that of clinicians, support staff, patients and others. The interventions almost inevitably will require at least some alterations in typical routines. The goal is to have targeted individuals perceive the changes as positive to the greatest extent possible. Identify ways to ensure that information is delivered in a format and at a time that will be most conducive to its being acted upon appropriately. Answering the questions and addressing the issues discussed in this chapter can help you with these specifications and stakeholder discussions. Again, Worksheets 6-2 and 6-3 can be helpful here.

The first several items in this worksheet carry over data from earlier worksheets, such as Worksheet 5-2. This information provides context for reviewers. The performance improvement targets may have evolved in the vetting process up to this point, but now is the time when key stakeholders will sign off on delivering against these targets. It might not be practical to assign hard quantitative targets for every single intervention. Nonetheless, the more aggressive you are about defining and cultivating measurable benefits, the more likely you are to reap tangible and meaningful improvements from your efforts.

If you have more than one intervention focused on achieving the target (a CDS package), these interdependencies can be noted in item 5 in the worksheet. A CDS package may have several specification forms covering the individual interventions in the package. Worksheets 6-2 and 6-3 illustrate this interplay in detail.

The remaining items on this validation form reflect the various specifications that result from your stakeholder dialogue, analysis, and vetting focused on issues and questions outlined in this chapter.

Worksheet 7-2

Intervention Communication Form for Validation[21]

Intervention Name: Flu shot (influenza vaccination) reminder system*

1. **Clinical objective:** Increase the number of eligible patients who get flu shots in our outpatient practices.

2. **Desired action:** Identify eligible patients who have visits each day; put reminders to give flu shots on the standard printed schedule sheet in effort to increase flu shot ordering and administration.

3. **Baseline performance:** Currently less than half of all high-risk patients are receiving flu shots. In addition, less than 20% of the general population receives flu shots.

4. **Desired outcome:** Reduction in outpatient visits related to the flu and hospitalizations of high-risk patients.

5. **Associated interventions focused on objective:** Radio and television ads reminding high-risk patients to get flu shots; postcard reminders sent to all high-risk patients.

---

* This example is intended only to illustrate communication form structure, not a preferred approach for addressing a particular clinical objective.

continued on next page

Worksheet 7-2 *continued*

6. **Workflow step:** Printing and distribution of daily schedules with reminders attached, pre-visit check-in for patients.

7. **Specific CDS intervention and pertinent CIS application(s):** Use the scheduling application along with clinical data warehouse to identify patients eligible for flu shot reminders; import list of eligible patients into application responsible for printing daily schedules.

8. **Approach:** Determine eligible patients who have visits today; put reminders to give flu shots on the standard printed schedule sheet.

9. **Clinical background:** Flu shots should be offered to eligible patients. In the past, mailings to patients have not been effective at increasing flu shot use. Many patients have not received flu shots even though they had a regular visit with their provider.

10. **Selection criteria:** Use Centers for Disease Control and Prevention (CDC) guidelines to determine which patients are eligible for flu shots and the duration of season in which to offer them.

11. **Exclusion criteria:** Patients whose health record data show a flu shot for the current flu season, or who have an egg allergy.

12. **Target population for intervention:** Primary care physicians and nurses in outpatient practices.

13. **User interface:** Printed suggestion to offer flu shot, if appropriate, at bottom of schedule sheet.

14. **Monitoring:** Assess whether patients who meet eligibility criteria get printed reminders; monitor proportion of patients getting flu shots.

15. **Evaluation:** Analyze proportion of eligible patients in practice who receive flu shots.

16. **Primary stakeholders:** Directors of ambulatory practices.

17. **Clinical champion for this project:** Dr. Phyllis Smith.

18. **Urgency/required delivery time:** Before September 1.

19. **Whose jobs do you expect to be affected by this project?** Practice managers or secretaries who print schedules; providers; nurses or assistants who administer flu shots.

20. **What are possible adverse consequences of implementing this project?** What if the reminder is given on a patient who had a flu shot already (elsewhere, or here but after reminder was queued or printed)? Will implement mechanisms to prevent extra flu shots.

Worksheet 7-3

Intervention Specification Approval Form

For interventions that have a substantial impact on your organization, it is important to formally present your intervention design to an appropriate governance body and receive approval for proceeding to the build stage. Worksheet 7-3 can be used to document these discussions and actions regarding your intervention specification forms. If there are relatively few objectives and interventions you are validating, you can put them all on one form; otherwise, it might be better to have a separate form for each objective or even each intervention.

You can use this form to document all your validation discussions with the many different stakeholders to help keep track of the various comments, or use it only to document final sign-off by the approvers. Similarly, you can record discussions and comments from individuals, committees or both.

Clinical Objective	Intervention Name	Reviewer (role)	Date Presented	Comments	Date Approved
Improve post-op heparin prophylaxis	Heparin post-op order set	Jim J. (Chief resident [graduate medical trainee] in surgery)	3 Jan	Need to make text clear that neuro-surgical patients should not receive this therapy	5 Jan
Improve PTT monitoring in heparin patients	PTT Alert	Mary K. (nurse manager, post anesthesia care unit)	3 Jan	Need to educate nurses on the prophylaxis policy, so that they will comply with the alert; approval withheld pending training plan	
	PTT Order Set	Jim L. (Surgery)	3 Jan	None	5 Jan
Improve compliance with care guideline for heparin and low molecular weight heparin	Heparin guideline reference link	George D. (division chief of cardiology)	3 Jan	Need to clarify that link will fire for both inpatient and outpatient locations	5 Jan

REFERENCES

1   Wright A, Sittig DF, Ash JS, et al. Development and evaluation of a comprehensive clinical decision support taxonomy: Comparison of front-end tools in commercial and internally developed electronic health record systems. *J Am Med Inform Assoc.* 2011 May 1; 18(3):232-242.

2   National Quality Forum. Driving quality and performance measurement—a foundation for clinical decision support. Washington, DC: National Quality Forum, 2010. Available online at: http://www.qualityforum.org/Publications/2010/12/Driving_Quality_and_Performance_Measurement_-_A_Foundation_for_Clinical_Decision_Support.aspx. Accessed September 15, 2011.

3   Kuperman GJ, Teich JM, Bates DW, et al. Detecting alerts, notifying the physician, and offering action items: a comprehensive alerting system. *J Am Med Inform Assoc.* 1996; 3(suppl):704-708.

4   Kuperman GJ, Teich JM, Tanasijevic MJ, et al. Improving response to critical laboratory results with automation: Results of a randomized controlled trial. *JAMIA.* 1999; 6(6):512-522.

5   Among many examples is this one in which many users in a health system missed a very important alert: Hamill SD. Entire UPMC transplant team missed hepatitis alert. Sunday, July 10, 2011. Available online at: http://www.post-gazette.com/pg/11191/1159219-455-0.stm. Accessed September 15, 2011.

6   Sittig DF, Teich JM, Osheroff JA, et al. Improving clinical quality indicators through electronic health records: It takes more than just a reminder. *Pediatrics.* 2009 Jul; 124(1):375-377.

7   Wang SJ, Bates DW, Chueh HC, et al. Automated coded ambulatory problem lists: Evaluation of a vocabulary and a data entry tool. *Int J Med Inform.* 2003 Dec; 72(1-3):17-28.

8   Rothschild AS, Lehmann HP, Hripcsak G. Inter-rater agreement in physician-coded problem lists. AMIA Annu Symp Proc. 2005:644-648.

9   Meystre S, Haug PJ. Automation of a problem list using natural language processing. *BMC Med Inform Decis Mak.* 2005 Aug 31; 5:30.

10 Petersen LA, Orav EJ, Teich JM, et al. Using a computerized sign-out program to improve continuity of inpatient care and prevent adverse events. *Jt Comm J Qual Improv.* 1998 Feb; 24(2):77-87.

11 Nabors C, Peterson SJ, Aronow WS, et al. Physician reporting of clinically significant events through a computerized patient sign-out system. *J Patient Saf.* 2011 Sep; 7(3):154-160.

12 Hiltz FL, Teich JM. Coverage List: A provider-patient database supporting advanced hospital information services. Proc Annu Symp Comput Appl Med Care. 1994: 809-813.

13 Weingart SN, Toth M, Sands DZ, et al. Physicians' decisions to override computerized drug alerts in primary care. *Arch Intern Med.* 2003; 163:2625-2631.

14 Hsieh TC, Kuperman GJ, Jaggi T, et al. Characteristics and consequences of drug allergy alert overrides in a computerized physician order entry system. *JAMIA.* 2004; 11(6):482-491.

15 Osheroff JA, ed. *Improving Medication Use and Outcomes with Clinical Decision Support: A Step-by-Step Guide.* Chicago:HIMSS; 2009.

16 Ash JS, Sittig DF, Campbell EM, et al.Some unintended consequences of clinical decision support systems. AMIA Annu Symp Proc. 2007 Oct 11:26-30.

17 Ash, JS, Berg M, Coiera E. Some unintended consequences of information technology in health care: The nature of patient care information system-related errors. *JAMIA.* 2004; 11:104-112. DOI.

18 Koppel R, Metlay JP, Cohen A, et al. Role of computerized physician order entry systems in facilitating medication errors. *JAMA.* 2005; 293:1197-1203.

19 See eRecommendation project page on AHRQ website: http://healthit.ahrq.gov/structuring_care_recommendations_for_CDS. Accessed August 26, 2011.

20 See web page for NQF NQF HIT Utilization Expert Panel report entitled "Driving Quality—A Health IT Assessment Framework for Measurement": http://www.qualityforum.org/Publications/2010/12/Driving_Quality_-_A_Health_IT_Assessment_Framework_for_Measurement.aspx. Accessed August 26, 2011.

21 Adapted from Abookire SA, Teich JM, Bates DW. An institution-based process to ensure clinical software quality. Proc AMIA Symp 1999; (1-2):461–465.

Chapter 8

Putting Interventions into Action

Tasks

- Develop and implement an intervention rollout plan that addresses user communications, training and feedback, as well as responsibility for monitoring implementation status. (Worksheets 8-1 and 8-2)
- Confirm that you have anticipated and prepared for altered workflows and care delivery needs related to the interventions; for example, increasing capacity to provide more procedures, testing or medications that may result from successful CDS interventions.
- Before launch, test the planned CDS intervention content, mechanics and logistics (Worksheet 8-3); consider ways the intervention could fail, and plan remedial actions. (Worksheet 8-4)
- Consider how you will phase CDS intervention releases. (Worksheet 8-5)
- Gather, document and address user feedback before, during and after intervention rollout (Worksheet 8-6); make sure your CDS Team has adequate capacity to obtain and respond to this feedback.

KEY LESSONS

- It is essential to carefully and completely test all new CDS functionality—as well as other affected CDS and CIS systems and workflows—to ensure that the planned interventions perform as expected. Testing details depend on the CDS intervention type, the nature of the clinical content and the underlying technology used to create the CDS intervention.
- Everyone who will use, or might be affected by, the new CDS functionality must be well-informed about project status and upcoming events to minimize unintended consequences and optimize their constructive participation.
- Anticipate users' training needs and provide training opportunities that fulfill them as conveniently as possible for the users.
- Consider the nature of both the CDS intervention and the clinical and technical environment when determining the speed, scope and order (that is, which interventions or units go first) for rolling out new CDS interventions.

GENERAL APPROACH

After you have designed and built specific CDS interventions, your next step is to ensure that they perform as expected in a testing environment (if one is available) and in the production information system(s). Once you have validated their performance, the interventions are ready for your CDS Team to introduce them—using a carefully considered and vetted plan—into the patient care process.

This preparatory work ensures that the interventions you specified in Chapter 6 and configured in Chapter 7 will be delivered successfully to the intended recipients and achieve the desired results smoothly and efficiently. As noted previously, successful interventions will have a significant effect on clinical decision making and workflow, so it is critical to carefully manage this change.

The processes and workflow routines that CDS interventions alter are complex; they may involve many different individuals and roles, be stressful, have high stakes and be multifaceted. Your efforts to support these processes with CDS interventions should be based on very detailed workflow analysis and stakeholder interactions, as discussed in Chapters 3, 6, and 7. This analytical and collaborative approach provides a solid foundation for success and must continue through intervention rollout planning, testing and launch to ensure that intended recipients embrace the decision support and use it effectively.

Your CDS program's approaches to decision making and stakeholder interaction (see Chapter 2) will determine who is responsible for and oversees CDS intervention launch activities. Depending on the breadth and complexity of interventions to be launched, and your organizational resources, there might be several individuals or teams responsible for the different testing, communication and support tasks at this stage.

Launching CDS interventions—particularly those with significant impact on workflow—can be challenging for both implementers and end users, regardless of the implementation setting. Close collaboration among these groups focused around

CDS purpose and methods, as outlined in previous chapters, can help you manage tension and risk and increase your chances for success. Key tasks and considerations associated with three major rollout activities are addressed in this chapter: change management, prelaunch testing and rollout logistics (such as phasing, training and communication). Before diving into those details, we next reinforce a benefits-oriented framework for approaching intervention launch.

Implement with Anticipated Benefits in Mind

Hopefully, you have laid a strong foundation for your intervention launch by carefully assessing your organization's priority opportunities for improving care delivery, selecting realistic improvement goals based on local conditions and national benchmarks, and preparing CDS interventions that will help achieve those goals. The fundamental challenge for intervention rollout is to ensure that when the CDS is available to users, it produces the anticipated benefits and desired outcomes.

A benefits sentence that succinctly and quantitatively captures what the implementation effort is all about can help keep all stakeholders working synergistically toward the goal. This assumes, of course, that they've all committed to the objective, and the stakeholder engagement approaches outlined earlier in Parts I and II can help make sure this is the case. Depending on implementation scope, benefits may be high-level, such as "We will reduce over the following 12 months the rate of preventable harm from inappropriate medication ordering by 20%, from Y% to X%; the specific harms include ..." Or they could be more granular, such as substituting "medication use" with "avoidable allergic reactions." In practice, the higher-level statement will often consist of several more specific targets and statements.

While it may be difficult for you to gather all the quantifiable data needed to make such a detailed benefits statement, it's an important goal. Worksheets in Chapters 5, 6, and 7 speak to current performance and desired actions and outcomes, so hopefully your intervention development work has been based to at least some degree on measurable indicators. Quantitative benefits statements can serve as guideposts for all the various launch activities outlined later in this chapter. For example, you can emphasize them in rollout communications to help keep the objective top-of-mind for all stakeholders. A clear, consensus-driven picture of a priority target can help keep everyone attuned to the key question underlying success in rollout and beyond, which is "What can we do to help ensure that we achieve the desired outcome [that we all agree is important]?" Although this may seem (and be) an overly optimistic expectation for typical end users, the closer you can realize this ideal, the more likely your ultimate success.

As we discuss in detail in the next chapter, tracking progress in an accurate and meaningful way may be challenging due to problems with data availability, formats and interchange across systems. Although difficult, quantifying progress toward stated goals is one of your most powerful tools for supporting positive change. Because a benefits statement makes explicit where your organization is, and where it is trying to go, with respect to a priority objective it can therefore not only help drive improvement, but also guide and motivate efforts to measure results from your CDS intervention efforts.

The following is an overview of key benefits-driven system implementation components.[1] This work is deeply rooted in the key tasks outlined in earlier chapters and "meets the road" during intervention launch.

- The *benefits framework* drives everything else—it outlines the strategic outcome(s) anticipated from the CDS interventions and typically does not include the tactical details. The framework uses "benefit sentences," previously mentioned, to ensure that everyone is clear on specific goals addressed by one or more interventions.
- *Forecasts* are developed for each item on the benefits framework to serve as targets and motivation. The process of developing the targets adds to a shared understanding about how the benefits are realized with the CDS tools.

- *Metrics*, based on each forecast, measure whether the forecast has been met; monthly or quarterly operational reports are produced to monitor progress and guide quick interventions when desired results are not realized (see Chapter 9).
- *Benefit requirements* are developed for each expected benefit. These are detailed technical "specs" that describe process, technology and cultural changes required for the benefit to be realized. Intervention specification worksheets, along with workflow analyses, use cases and other tools described earlier in Part II outline these requirements. The benefit requirements will evolve as interventions are developed and vetted, for example, if requirements reveal shortcomings in the existing tools that will lead to benefits *not* being realized. Forecasts and metrics may likewise change as the process unfolds. Once finalized and approved, benefit requirements inform the implementation work plan—which we will discuss later in this chapter—to ensure that the benefit requirements are achieved.

Change Management

Because it involves altering work processes and decision-flows, deploying CDS interventions in clinical practice is, in essence, a change management exercise. Many CDS implementers find it invaluable to consult resources on how to effectively lead organizational change. John Kotter and other change management thought leaders have written excellent general guides on this topic,[2] which has also been addressed from a CDS-specific perspective in other sources.[3]

We next provide guidance on some specific change management activities surrounding intervention launch.

Do CDS with Affected Stakeholders, Not to Them

A central theme that will be emphasized throughout this chapter (building on recommendations made previously in this guide) is that launching CDS interventions shouldn't be the first time that your

CDS Team reaches out to end users and related stakeholders. Rather, the launch phase should be a transition from joint planning to joint execution, with extensive collaborative work already done, as outlined in previous chapters. This foundational work includes building a shared appreciation among stakeholders for the critical challenges affecting care delivery, conducting a detailed analysis of pertinent end-user workflows, and preparing potential CDS interventions that address targeted improvement opportunities.

Ideally, those affected by new CDS interventions should enthusiastically anticipate (and help prepare for) their launch, as an opportunity to test the shared hypothesis that the new processes will drive enhancements mutually desired by all parties. By researching and documenting modified workflows throughout the design process (for example, using use case scenarios), you can help instill confidence in a positive outcome by answering questions such as: How will the new intervention(s) change tasks, data and knowledge flow, and how will these changes drive desired outcomes?

Addressing these questions may uncover conflicts between the needs and constraints of the various stakeholders—for example, some clinicians may have to take on significant extra work to achieve the desired CDS-enabled objective. In these situations, cultivating shared commitment toward important targets, and other personal incentives for intervention adoption as mentioned in Chapter 7, can help ensure productive engagement from everyone. In any case, the more you can generate stakeholder commitment and shared vision about the CDS intervention use and goals you can generate before launch, the more likely that the launch will be successful and achieve desired results.

As you prepare to roll out new CDS interventions, keep in mind the various roles and processes that might be affected. These include all the links in the chain required to deliver the intervention's targeted end result. As discussed in Chapter 7, your workflow analysis should have uncovered these important linkages. For example, if the goal is to substantially increase the proportion of patients who receive a particular immunization as indicated, will an adequate vaccine supply be available to accommodate this goal? Is there adequate storage in the pertinent settings? Will the added time required to deliver the immunization (and perform related documentation tasks) adversely affect workflow and staffing needs? When we refer to "intervention stakeholders" in the remainder of this chapter, keep in mind not only the CDS recipients directly affected but also all these other links in the chain to the desired outcome.

Assess the "Change" Environment

To the extent that there has been prior dialog with the intervention stakeholders, your CDS Team will appreciate the obstacles and facilitators for the workflow and cultural changes that the new interventions will require. In order to understand exactly where these stakeholders are currently on the path to this change, you should consider conducting a formal or informal readiness assessment before launch—especially for proposed interventions that are very important or disruptive. This might involve the following activities (all of which are rooted in work outlined in previous chapters):

- Determine the extent to which end users are committed to achieving the targets on which the CDS interventions are focused.
- Assess their preconceived perceptions and experiences with the CDS types you will be using (for example, alerts, documentation tools or infobuttons) and for the underlying CISs (such as EHR applications and CPOE functions) that will be delivering the CDS.
- Identify end-user expectations about the specific interventions that will be launched (response times, length/components of information delivered, etc.) and potential obstacles to information use and value.
- Expose a wider spectrum of users to the new intervention(s) prelaunch than might have been engaged at earlier stages (see Testing section later in this chapter); listen carefully to their feedback

and its implications for the workflow and other changes that will be needed after launch.

- Consider how well intervention stakeholders other than recipients—and the key related processes these stakeholders perform—are prepared to provide a strong link in the chain to success.

As we have repeatedly emphasized, it is ideal to have all stakeholders' interests aligned behind the CDS intervention by launch time. These stakeholders include all care delivery team members (including clinicians and the patient, and especially intervention recipients and enablers), organizational leadership, and others with a role or stake in achieving targeted objectives. To the extent that interests are not aligned, you may encounter problems at rollout or soon thereafter. For example, if a hospital or practice deploys an alert to change physician ordering behavior and the physician doesn't agree with the recommended practice, then the desired change is unlikely to occur. This disconnect may be due to the physician's informed disagreement or to an educational gap. In either case, you should assess and address organizational culture issues such as general receptivity to CDS interventions prior to launch (see discussions in Chapter 2).

After launch you will need resources for various key tasks—including assessing intervention effectiveness and addressing subsequent enhancements to the CDS interventions or CIS infrastructure—that are required to monitor and further improve intervention effectiveness. Assessing and reaffirming strong leadership and other support prior to launch (and ideally before requesting formal sign-off for launch) can help identify problems and corrective approaches early. Intervening early (that is, before formal intervention approval and certainly before launch) when there is insufficient support or other problems is generally most effective.

End-user satisfaction is a critical metric that the CDS interventions should either preserve or enhance; degrading user satisfaction is a key factor in deployment failure. The readiness assessment should establish a baseline for this satisfaction with the pertinent systems, workflows and other intervention-related factors. Both quantitative and qualitative data are useful, but resources and organizational support may limit what you can gather. When satisfaction with deployed information systems is high prior to launching interventions, you should take care to ensure that the new processes add perceived value and do not undermine satisfaction. If there are already problems with pertinent workflows, or user interactions with underlying information systems, or prior CDS interventions, it is unlikely that new CDS interventions layered on top will be optimally successful until these are addressed. Hopefully by this point, you will have built into your new interventions the capability to enhance workflow; for example, by making it more convenient to access needed information (such as via relevant data displays or patient data flow sheets) or complete specific tasks (through order sets or documentation tools).

End-user expectations and receptivity regarding CDS in general, and the planned CDS interventions in particular, are important factors for you to consider. They help determine the practice's or hospital's capacity for absorbing the changes that may be required to workflows, policies and responsibilities. What do the targeted clinicians (or patients) see as the value from CDS in addressing their priorities? To what extent do they consider interruptive alerts in general to be helpful versus inappropriate, disruptive or a nuisance? What is their tolerance for perceived false positives in specific types of alerts (for example, related to drug allergies or interactions)?

Alignment around goals and a collaborative climate developed early in the intervention development process can help you minimize conflict during the launch phase. For example, physicians may tolerate some false-positive alerting when they are fully committed to the objective that the alert is supporting and have had input into optimizing its deployment and value.

Your prelaunch assessment process and results can further deepen collaboration between the implementation team and end users. For example, the CDS Team can gain insights into acceptable alerting thresholds, and clinicians can gain an appreciation for the factors required to optimize intervention value, such as any need for specific clinician-entered data to support more relevant alerting. This collaborative work should track all through intervention development, and during the prelaunch phase, you need to determine whether these efforts have been successful in producing an intervention likely to be helpful (we'll further discuss formal testing shortly).

Many seasoned CDS implementers recommend a "start low and go slow" approach. This strategy focuses initially on launching interventions that address the highest priority outcomes and for which organizational receptivity and success are likely (that is, beginning with the "low-hanging fruit"). Subsequent deployment efforts can advance the program incrementally by building on early wins, thereby fostering stakeholder engagement and goodwill. Proceeding at a pace that overwhelms individual and organizational capacity to absorb change decreases the chance for success and can trigger negative stakeholder sentiment toward not only the specific intervention but potentially toward the entire improvement effort and CDS Team. You should consider examining pertinent attitudes as part of a readiness assessment, and use what you find to guide rollout sequencing and pace (we discuss this further later in this chapter).

If you have a newly implemented EHR or CPOE, ensure there is some user comfort and satisfaction with these systems before introducing too many interruptive CDS elements. Determine the extent to which clinicians are using the existing clinical system as intended and designed, and find ways to optimize use of the components most critically needed for CDS intervention success.

It can be very helpful for you to encourage users to actually see the intervention in action (for example, in test systems) prior to implementation (testing is discussed shortly). If they haven't seen the system, then the anticipated alterations in workflow, value from the delivered information and other parameters remain theoretical—they might sound good but in reality may prove impractical. Having end users (especially champions) directly observe CDS capabil-

ities and limitations will help bring into sharp focus critical issues that may affect rollout success—at a time when they may be addressed before creating more difficult problems. Conversely, to the extent that the CDS implementation team has "gotten it right" based on a thorough and systematic approach to the development process, your end-user preview can drive the enthusiasm and support that will help ensure success.

Involve the Right People

Your CDS governance and management processes (see Chapter 2), including the CDS program charter, provide the framework for intervention launch; that is, they define the "who, what, where, when, why and how." As you get closer to rollout, different stakeholders in the processes and outcomes related to the interventions will assume specific roles in ensuring success. The readiness assessment helps prepare these stakeholders for this step—and ensures that your interventions are ready for their task.

"Support from above" is very important—that is, organizational leadership must fully back the improvement objectives and CDS plans for achieving them. At least as important, however, is strong engagement and modeling of desired end-user responses by champions, who are peers of targeted users.[4] As discussed in Chapter 2 and other previous chapters, champions are CDS program stakeholders who play a critical role in its success. These individuals are respected members of the constituencies that will be receiving the CDS (for example, nurses, pharmacists, patients and physicians), who fully understand and support the CDS efforts, goals and strategies and can serve as ambassadors for successful use by their peers.

Ideally you will have strongly engaged these champions throughout the CDS intervention lifecycle, and they will already be serving as a rich communication channel between their peers and the CDS Team. At launch then, they should model enthusiastic and effective intervention use, and generously share these strategies and results in a manner that fosters similar successes by their colleagues.

The more specific that champions can be about the intervention's role in saving time, avoiding errors, increasing professional satisfaction (such as through better access to information for answering questions and guiding decisions), and other personal benefits, the better.

Last but not least, the CDS Team responsible for deploying the interventions has a critical role in managing *all* the tasks outlined in this chapter. This team should be highly multidisciplinary, with input from appropriate stakeholders. For example, the CDS Team should carefully monitor, along with intervention results during the period surrounding launch, the needs and concerns experienced by all key intervention stakeholders. These include end users from pertinent clinical areas, subject matter experts, and other links in the outcome chain. This broad focus is important even when an intervention is seen as only directly affecting one user type, because the care team's interdependent nature will likely result in some intervention effects for other stakeholders. Hopefully these interconnections will have been made explicit through your workflow mapping. If not, your implementation team can create or modify these maps as new insights emerge for use in subsequent enhancement rounds.

Move to Consensus and Support

An important tool in successful change management is to show stakeholders exactly what things are changing, so that they can feel excited about the change and more committed to helping it move forward.[5] In the launch communication section later in this chapter, we suggest you use tools such as conversations or brochures that emphasize the rationale behind new interventions and present intervention screen shots and user-specific benefits. Such material is a good step in the right direction. As noted earlier, champions, in particular, are important agents for generating consensus and excitement about interventions.

Before you launch your interventions, they need to be tested in several different ways. We discuss these next.

CDS Intervention Testing

The details of your testing approach will vary somewhat depending on the CDS intervention type and scope, the nature of the content, the implementation setting, and the underlying CDS intervention technology. For example, simple links to reference material on an intranet site would not require as much testing as a new patient-specific alert. If you have modified or expanded the CDS functionality in an existing clinical information system (such as how rules are handled), then you (and/or your system vendor) need to test both the new functionality and any underlying functions that might have been modified or affected. On the other hand, if the CDS interventions only involve adding specific rules or other content to an existing and well-functioning CDS application, then testing can focus primarily on the new components.

The basic steps in a standard quality assurance (QA) approach are outlined next. Although you should consider the following steps for each intervention, smaller practices and hospitals with fewer resources may not have the bandwidth to complete these tasks. A vendor or consultant may provide the resources needed to account for these recommendations in your implementation. Nonetheless, it's important you understand the concepts outlined next, since they will help you ensure proper communication with consultants or vendors.

You can adapt these steps as needed to address the specific implementation needs. Various resources are available with additional details on QA procedures if you need more information on this topic.[6] Prelaunch CDS testing considerations that apply across delivery settings are outlined next.

Does the Intervention Function as Designed?
USE CASES AND TESTING SCENARIOS

Use cases (discussed in Chapter 7) that you develop to evaluate typical and atypical intervention use scenarios are now applied to testing your completed interventions. If significant time elapses between when the scenarios were vetted and this testing stage, you should ensure that they remain valid and appropriate according to clinical users and subject matter experts—including those users who were not necessarily involved in their development. All validated use cases should be included in the final software requirements documentation.

Typically, you will have developed at least one or two basic use cases that relate to the intervention's primary objective. For example, the use case for a drug-allergy alert might include the user placing a drug order for a patient with a documented allergy to the drug. With further thought, you can envision many special cases and unusual situations. For example, these scenarios might include the following: when a drug is ordered from a drug family that is cross-allergenic to the patient's documented allergy; a drug is ordered to which patient is allergic, but the alert has been overridden in the past; the person viewing the alert is not authorized to make a final decision on whether it is safe to give the drug; and other variations.

You should derive basic use cases from business needs, such as eliminating preventable allergic reactions to drugs. The more sophisticated variants result from taking a careful look at the basic case and filtering in rich clinical knowledge and practice experience from your CDS Team and their collaborators. Use case variants are an important way to catch needed design changes before launch and deserve careful consideration. The more thought your team puts into identifying these issues during the intervention design stage, the better; making changes after the intervention has already been configured will be more costly than addressing them earlier in the process.

Develop the narrative use cases into formal testing scenarios that describe exactly how the user will interact with the intervention and the results from that interaction. Any changes necessitated by testing, and made to either the scenarios or the system design, should be reflected in the corresponding documentation. These testing scenarios will be used both by intervention developers and end users in the testing steps outlined next. Also, once the use case and testing scenarios are formalized, you can modify them for

future use as needed—such as in making additional enhancements to the intervention after launch.

UNIT TESTING

Software developers perform this testing to ensure that the pertinent application will deliver the CDS intervention as it has been built and that it functions as designed, independent of other CIS components. It involves applying the testing scenarios to ensure that valid inputs produce valid and appropriate outputs. Various invalid inputs that might occur in practice should also be tested to ensure that they are handled appropriately.

For technically straightforward interventions, such as links to reference material or documentation templates, this testing will be relatively simple. For more complex interventions, such as alerts that process a lot of patient-specific data, all logical branches and internal program flow should be validated. Unit testing for these more complex applications may involve special software for debugging and testing. This testing is typically handled by application developers/vendors, not the software QA staff in a hospital or the CDS Team in a practice. If possible, developers should use staff to do unit testing who were not directly involved in creating the intervention. Consider opportunities for clinicians on the CDS Team to examine testing results at this stage and the next to help ensure that clinically inappropriate performance hasn't crept into the intervention.

Bear in mind that most CIS vendors will test the programming that underlies CDS interventions they support (such as rules engines for alerting), but if your organization has locally customized the application, you may need additional testing to verify that these changes haven't introduced unexpected intervention behavior. Similarly, verify that any processing done to incorporate clinical knowledge into the CDS intervention has not changed its clinical meaning or effect.

INTEGRATION TESTING

Once each individual intervention component is working as designed, the next step is integration (functional) testing. Here, system developers and local staff ensure that every individually developed system component works appropriately (for example, as called for in the use cases) when integrated with the existing CIS environment. For example, integration testing verifies that the CIS response time is adequate at both peak and steady-state use levels after the new interventions have been added. Regression (verification) testing might also be necessary when the new intervention involves significant modification to the underlying CIS. This selective testing ensures that all new software is working as expected and that no new bugs have been introduced that might impact system performance.

Does the Intervention Work for the Clinical Users?
USER ACCEPTANCE TESTING

This final prelaunch testing involves having clinical end users ensure that the system works for them as intended and meets all planned business and clinical requirements. If possible, set up user accounts in a non-production environment to allow physicians, pharmacists, nurses and other end users—together with IT staff—to simulate receiving and responding to CDS interventions during patient care activities. This helps identify possible glitches in system design both from a workflow and an IS perspective, without potentially harming real patients.

This user evaluation often begins with testing scenarios that have been developed from the use cases, as previously discussed. After the system has been shown to handle these successfully, you can ask users to go through several "real-life" situations or other scenarios that they provide. Carefully selecting end users to perform this testing is critical to ensure that the results accurately reflect the broader user experience with the intervention that may occur after launch. You should include representatives from all the pertinent user groups, as we emphasized in discussions about working with intervention stakeholders in previous chapters.

Be particularly attentive to user testing results; they can help you assess widespread user readiness

for the interventions and identify the need for additional education, support or incentives to ensure successful adoption. It is important in this context that you develop and use standard forms or templates to document testing results. This testing also can uncover difficulties, such as unexpected or counterproductive side effects, workflow implications, or costs associated with the intervention. Potential remedies that can be instituted before launch may emerge from these evaluations. However, the careful analysis and validation steps already accomplished should significantly reduce surprises at this late stage.

If you have not done so already, test the user feedback channels. Make sure that e-mail links, calls to help desk and pager numbers, and the like are routed and responded to appropriately.

BETA TESTING/PILOT LAUNCH

After your CDS intervention has successfully passed all the testing phases discussed, it is ready to be moved to the live CIS and the patient care environment. When a new intervention does not disrupt workflow very much and is not controversial (such as straightforward links to reference material), it is often appropriate to release the intervention to all clinical users at the same time. For very complex or intrusive interventions (such as multistep protocols or workflow-interrupting alerts), it might be helpful for you to release the intervention initially to a few selected clinical pilot users, such as a single clinician, practice or inpatient unit, when feasible.

During this pilot or beta-testing period, it's important that you supply an easy and convenient method for users to provide feedback to the intervention deployment and development teams. You should make sure you have adequate staff to seek out and respond to this input to help ensure success during the subsequent full-scale rollout. (See discussion on rollout communications later in this chapter.)

As a double-check on intrusive alert behavior, consider configuring these alerts to fire in the background in the production environment prior to go-live, when this is feasible. In other words, allow alerts to be triggered by clinical events in the production system but do not display the resulting messages to clinical users during testing. This approach is particularly important with CISs that do not allow robust simulation of "real-world use" in preproduction environments. Your CDS Team can review a log of the alerts, in collaboration with pertinent experts and users, to assess their appropriateness. You can then fine-tune alerting criteria and other details as needed prior to "turning on" the alert for clinical end users. Keep in mind the following points about this testing strategy:

- It can sometimes provide an estimate of how frequently alerts might fire, and this information can be used in preparing users through communications as outlined later in this chapter.

- Some manual chart review may still be needed to validate that triggers are correct.

- Monitoring alert background firing could reveal possible incorrect triggers (false positives) but will not identify those patients for whom an alert should have been triggered but was not (false negatives). Identifying false negative behavior will require supplementary analysis besides reviewing alert firing logs.

- You should develop a timeline that allows alerts to be added gradually, over a defined period. Adding alerts just for the sake of alerts, of course, is not advisable, but you should have a mechanism to prioritize alert deployments based on need. You may build into your timeline a several-week period to evaluate new alerts, followed by an additional few weeks to make needed revisions. In any case, have a plan for when you will take alerts live after testing to ensure they move smoothly toward production (intervention rollout phasing is discussed further later in this chapter).

- For alerts that fire in the background during this testing, consider the clinical implications of important alerts that may fire (for example, if an actual patient danger is identified) and provide mechanisms for making sure appropriate actions can be taken.

FULL-LIVE EVALUATION

Once the intervention has proven successful during limited use, you can release it to all intended users. Your CDS Team should use proactive monitoring, together with intervention-related feedback channels you have developed along with the intervention, to assess effects and user response over time. We will discuss ongoing evaluation in greater detail in Chapter 9.

Not all CDS interventions will require extensive testing. Nonetheless, a thoughtful testing approach can help prevent surprises from derailing the positive results your careful intervention planning and development should deliver. It can also help you engender confidence in the program and in individual interventions from both leadership and end users. You can use a form such as Worksheet 8-3 to document prelaunch testing for each intervention.

Substantial user input and iterative assessments should prevent major surprises during full intervention launch. Nonetheless, you should remain alert for unexpected showstoppers that may appear. Ideally, you can focus your attention after launch on validating that the interventions perform as designed and are on track to deliver expected results. You should also seek implementation nuances that can be addressed to ensure optimal user satisfaction and intervention success. These could include more tweaks to the intervention itself or further communications or training to further enhance user workflow and value from the intervention. Worksheet 8-4 can help you consider where things can go wrong—even when an intervention performs as designed—and proactively address these pitfalls, ideally before launch.

A question may arise at this point about how you get busy clinicians to devote significant time for the evaluation and feedback activities outlined in this section (and earlier chapters). We believe the answer ties back to the governance and prioritization tasks outlined in Chapter 2. You should have used key committees and other pertinent management structures to create a shared purpose and goals among pertinent stakeholders about the targeted performance improvements, and should have developed a collaborative approach to driving this change. Difficulty getting clinicians' attention around new intervention testing and launch may be a warning sign about user receptivity to the intervention. If this happens, consider whether you need more work on the foundational issues—that is, doing CDS *with* key stakeholders not *to* them as discussed previously (especially in Chapters 2 and 7).

Rollout Logistics: Phasing, Communication, Training, and Other Tasks

Next we consider several key steps associated with releasing your tested interventions to the intended end users.

Communicate Launch Details

Users and others who will be affected by CDS interventions about to be launched should be well informed about forthcoming rollout events to minimize surprises (for both them and for your CDS Team) and optimize their constructive participation in intervention success. During the prelaunch phase, gaining widespread CDS recipient buy-in on the interventions (particularly interruptive ones such as alerts) and their delivery details can help you ensure that these individuals will handle the delivered content appropriately after launch. Communications about the launch set the tone for this acceptance.

It is helpful if you frame these implementation details with the broader goals, strategies and vision for the CDS program. Sharing (and getting feedback on) this context can help your organization "see the big picture," which can help drive appreciation and adoption of the forthcoming interventions. It can also help pave the way for more successful development and launch of subsequent interventions as the CDS program unfolds. For example, if you are launching specific interventions to improve VTE prophylaxis rates or diabetes patient management (as illustrated in the case studies in the Part I and Part II Introductions), then you should tie these deploy-

ments back to both these particular objectives, as well as broader organizational goals related to care safety and quality.

You can also discuss your broader CDS strategies (such as using the CDS Five Rights approach) when communicating about the specific intervention details. This broader context can help support follow-on discussions about additional interventions to address these and other targets—which may require increasing user workflow adaptations.

Hopefully, your CDS Team has established rich communications channels and used them to appropriately involve intervention users and other stakeholders in all the steps from target selection to intervention configuration and testing. If so, it is much more likely that you will avoid many common causes of problematic and failed CIS and CDS implementations. It is still imperative that you design and execute a well thought-out plan to communicate pertinent information about new or significantly modified interventions to *all* stakeholders around launch time. This messaging helps reinforce everyone's understanding and enthusiasm about the goals that are being addressed, the changes to workflow and processes that will be taking place, the benefits different stakeholders can expect, the channels that are available for feedback, and the like.

When all the preliminary steps leading up to launch have been carefully addressed, these communications solidify the foundational work. To the extent that the environment hasn't been fully prepared, the information may be new to some stakeholders, so conveying it thoroughly and carefully is especially critical. Insufficient communication is an important contributor to failed CIS and CDS implementations.[7,8]

You should fully leverage all available communication channels and resources as appropriate in your outreach efforts. It is likely that prior IT implementations at your facility—for example, EHR components or CPOE—have spawned formal communication tools and channels with the various stakeholders and groups that you can use for the CDS intervention rollout. Be sure to include these in your planning, keeping in mind that inadequate communication presents a much greater risk than communicating too much.

One approach to handling communications about forthcoming CDS interventions is the "8 x 8 communication strategy." It involves conveying key information eight different times in eight ways to ensure that stakeholders are aware of important system and workflow changes. See Worksheet 8-2 for an example of what this might look like for the hospital setting. Small practices might not need such an elaborate approach to communication, but the underlying theme remains the same: it's critical to have very rich communication with end users and other stakeholders to ensure a successful launch. Again, launch should be the transition from joint planning to joint execution, so many instances of these communications should ideally happen well before rollout.

You should address any last major concerns that surface during these rollout exchanges through subsequent communications using the appropriate channels and through changes to the intervention and rollout as well, if possible. The CDS Team must be careful to avoid appearing defensive about any identified intervention or communication shortcomings and remain open to improvement opportunities. Even when you cannot address major concerns right away, reassurances that the CDS Team is listening and taking issues seriously can help build trust in the CDS program and team.

An important issue to keep in mind for communication and planning purposes is how potential CIS/CDS/computer system outages might impact interventions and users. Your organization may already have experience addressing these 'downtime' issues with CISs already deployed. In any case, you should consider the impact such downtime may have on the CDS interventions you are launching, such as reference tools, alerts, order sets, documentation tools and the like. In many cases, there may be potentially straightforward workarounds, such as using alternative channels (paper, Internet) for providing users with the needed information that the

intervention normally delivers. You should consider, though, implications from key safety net interventions (such as certain critical, interruptive alerts) not being available. Planning during intervention development and/or testing should address these issues, which can be included as appropriate in user communications.

Ideally, clinical intervention proponents who are thought leaders should provide early communications to all other affected users before launch. This—along with other guidance outlined in Chapter 7 about stakeholder engagement in intervention configuration—can help avoid strong negative reactions that can occur when a clinician suddenly feels that "the computer has changed the plan" without prior warning.

Be creative and think broadly about opportunities and forums to get the word out about the new CDS intervention(s). You can consider both informal exchanges and more formal presentations. Workflow problems or other negative intervention side effects that you missed in the design phase can often be caught here. It is important that intervention proponents—such as those on and working with the CDS Team, especially champions—be well-informed about the interventions so they convey accurate information. They too should keep an open mind for constructive input and not be defensive about "protecting" the planned intervention.

Other channels to let users know about the launch of new CDS interventions include formal advertising campaigns, e-mail notices or printed brochures, bulletin boards, and the like. These may have been set up earlier in the process for major new CIS initiatives, as outlined in Chapter 3. If not, they can be utilized now during launch, as appropriate.

Since CDS interventions and programs evolve over time, maintaining and using effective communication channels is an ongoing process. As with the earlier project phases, you should be alert to any generalized negative response to intervention components, as well as individual detractors. Unless you address these people and issues thoughtfully and directly, such problems are unlikely to go away after launch. A collaborative approach to moving forward with the CDS plan based on shared goals (such as optimizing care processes and outcomes), stakeholder needs, and organizational constraints is generally the best strategy for these potentially difficult situations.

Establish Rollout Phasing

Since organizations have limited capacity to develop interventions and absorb the resulting change, your CDS interventions will be rolled out incrementally. Factors driving this phasing include the relative benefits expected from the interventions, resource availability, end users' receptivity toward the interventions, ease with which they can be deployed, and related variables.

One common example to consider might include how medication alerts could be implemented when introducing or enhancing a CPOE system. Without a clear strategy, all available medication alerts might be turned out at once, leading rapidly to alert fatigue and user frustration with the CPOE system and CDS. As discussed in Chapter 7, this can introduce patient safety hazards and undermine user engagement with CDS efforts. In contrast, a thoughtfully staged approach to implementing these medication alerts might allow easier adaptation and less workflow disruption for the end user—and ultimately better drug alert acceptance and value. Such a staged approach should include a plan for user feedback and data analysis to ensure that the target recipients can successfully accept new interventions.

The lesson illustrated by such examples is that carefully planned, incremental rollouts allow users to accept each successive CDS layer and permit the CDS Team time needed for appropriate design, testing and early aggressive monitoring for each new intervention. By prioritizing rollout sequence and managing the pace of releases, you can better accommodate your organization's and end users' ability to absorb change.

Training

Having raised awareness among those targeted by a CDS intervention, your next step is to ensure that these users will interact with the intervention in a manner that leads to the intended benefits.

View communication and training/education as two distinct activities. The education/training activities themselves have two components: training about the intervention itself and ensuring that clinicians have the appropriate framework to understand and apply the clinical guidance conveyed through the intervention.

For example, notification via multiple avenues may be sufficient "communication" to inform users that drug-allergy alerts will be activated in the system, *if* they are in agreement with the alert recommendations. However, an intervention designed to change clinician behavior for an area in which they may have important knowledge gaps (such as concerning a new test or treatment) should be more successful when coupled with "education or training."[9] A case in point: a study performed at Northwestern Memorial Hospital to increase gastroprotection among non-steroidal anti-inflammatory drug (NSAID) users showed that the combination of an alert with education was superior to either education or alert alone.[10]

Depending on the intervention type, you may need varying degrees of training to ensure that users appropriately respond to the intervention mechanics. Normally, formal training is required when new CIS applications are implemented (such as CPOE or electronic clinical documentation), but not when relatively straightforward CDS interventions are launched. For example, intuitive interventions such as infobuttons may require little or no training. In this case, hyperlinks—a well accepted interface paradigm—implicitly conveys to users "click here to get more information."

Interventions that are more complex or that involve more nuanced user action may require formal training. This might include ensuring that physicians understand the opportunities and steps to properly access and complete order sets in an electronic environment, such as within a CPOE application. Of course, deeply involving end users throughout all the earlier development and testing stages should help make the interventions as intuitive as possible and therefore minimize training needs.

Consider also whether your CDS intervention will require specific skills such as typing, in which all end users may not be proficient. Strategies such as advanced training on these skills, alternative data entry or other workaround might be helpful.

Strategies to enhance your training efforts include the following:

- Explore pertinent training resources available from your CIS and CDS vendors; ask about printed materials, websites and other computer-based offerings, as well as live training programs.
- Tailor training duration and intensity to user needs and constraints; make training resources available prior to formal training sessions to optimize use of training time.
- Pay very careful attention to expressed concerns and non-verbal communication during training, especially from those who were not "friends of the project" during earlier stages. These can provide clues to potential problems that may arise after launch.
- Remember that most "training" will occur on the job after launch, so make sure there is adequate CDS staff (or others they have trained) available to support end users. This may include staff potentially "at their shoulder" during early launch phases with more intrusive or complex interventions, and readily available via phone or e-mail as needed, in all cases.

Formalize and Execute the Launch Plan

Details about how your CDS program will address the communication, training, feedback and other rollout elements should be documented in a formal launch plan. This will help you ensure that all stakeholders (such as the CDS Team and its sponsors, as well as other interested stakeholders) can all have a shared picture of the path to a successful launch. This explicit documentation and sharing can also make it easier to gain broader input into plan details and thereby help anticipate and address potential challenges and opportunities.

You can use Worksheet 8-1 as a model to develop your own tool for documenting the plan to notify the affected community about the upcoming launch, train them on effectively using the intervention, gather their feedback after implementation, and assign responsibility and timetables for intervention maintenance.

Similarly, you can use Worksheet 8-5 to track in detail how the rollout phasing is progressing. It is especially useful when more than a few interventions will be launched in this cycle or when individual interventions will be launched in several stages. Besides overall project tracking, it can serve other specific needs, including planning and allocating personnel for intervention testing, training and support. Worksheet 8-6 is a model for logging user feedback about interventions, and their disposition.

Closing the Performance Improvement Loop

This launch phase marks both an end and a beginning. The complex planning and configuration stages culminate in delivering knowledge interventions to clinicians and patients. This in turn begins the process of (hopefully) enhancing decisions and actions to measurably improve care processes and outcomes.

Once again, this process presents you with more of a change-management challenge than a technological one. Success will depend on the extent to which you have anticipated and addressed barriers in the earlier phases. Similarly, a launch that smoothly and effectively addresses communication, training and rollout phasing creates the foundation that will help lead to realizing expected benefits. Creating short-term wins with CDS interventions in areas that are important to key stakeholders will help you demonstrate the CDS program value, diffuse skepticism and build momentum.

Even before any CDS intervention delivers knowledge to an end user, it is likely that your organization will have reaped significant benefits from intensified focus on optimizing critical workflows, and CDS opportunities, as outlined so far in this

Guide. For example, work to identify and prioritize ways to improve care processes with CDS will likely have beneficial effects on related process- and outcome-improvement activities beyond the specific interventions now being launched. Hopefully, these CDS interventions themselves also will generate substantial returns, but it is worth considering these related side effects so you can cultivate these additional benefits.

Your next step in the performance improvement cycle is to ensure that the launched interventions achieve their desired results and that you continually maintain this material and enhance and expand its value. Chapter 9 covers these tasks in detail.

CONSIDERATIONS FOR HOSPITALS/HEALTH SYSTEMS
People (Stakeholder Involvement)

- Even if key stakeholders throughout the organization have been involved throughout the process, there will usually be many users who have not been as deeply connected to the details as they unfold. They too will need to be engaged on each intervention's why, what and how (in addition to the broader CDS program context) so that they respond in a manner that helps achieve the desired organizational outcomes. Sharing details about how broad stakeholder input was gathered and used in earlier stages can help reassure these users that their needs were carefully considered during the design and development. You should strive to ensure that each person affected by a new intervention sees some personal value from it; champions and other liaisons between the CDS Team and end users can help with this.

- It is very helpful for administrative and clinical leadership to visibly reinforce understanding and meaningful commitment to the high-level goals (for example "we strive to eliminate preventable harm from medication use") and to the corresponding CDS as a means to these ends (such as "we are investing heavily in systems and processes to achieve this goal in concert with our CDS strategy"). More detailed objectives and tactics related to the interventions should likewise be supported by clinical managers (such as heads of nursing, pharmacy, clinical departments and medical staff) and informatics team leads (such as the CMIO). You should ideally line up this support for interventions and their intended outcomes well before launch. If these stakeholders aren't well engaged, then it is less likely that resources will be available to ensure intervention success.

- In assessing end-user population readiness, consider both the "typical" intervention users, as well as other key constituencies that may not have opportunity to use the intervention as often or in the same way. These might include pediatric, perioperative, ED, and outpatient surgery areas. Your CDS Team should have ensured that their particular needs and constraints have been addressed throughout the intervention development process, and you should continue the dialog during the rollout phase and beyond. Successful CDS implementation across diverse settings involves a balance between addressing local needs (which can become unmanageable in the extreme) and having a one-size-fits-all approach (which can impede acceptance and value). To the extent possible, you should strongly encourage standardization based on a consensus-building model. The readiness assessment can help you determine an optimal balance.

Planning (Rollout and Training)

- It is even more important to consider the appropriate roll-out sequencing when rolling out interventions across facilities in a multihospital system. Some organizations prefer to focus on a single facility and "get all the kinks worked out" before moving to other sites. Other organizations prefer what some call a "big bang" approach in which CDS functionality is launched simultaneously (perhaps along with major CIS components, such as CPOE) across multiple facilities. There are examples of these big bang rollouts working successfully, but clearly, tremendous preparation and attention to all the user and organizational issues and impact emphasized throughout this book are critical.

- Additional considerations for training approaches beyond those mentioned earlier include:
  - Adopt "train the trainer" approaches that include cultivating local super users who understand the intervention logic and mechanics well and can serve as a resource to their colleagues.
  - Ensure that key representatives from the various departments (especially those expected to include heavy intervention users) are trained and engaged early to minimize bumps after rollout. Offer training at times convenient to users or on-demand to ensure ample opportunity for affected users.
  - Leverage existing formal training mechanisms and venues that may be available for nursing, pharmacy and other clinical staff, and layer intervention-related training on top of these other activities.
  - Provide shorter, more focused training as necessary; for example, physicians often require a more informal and ad hoc process. Web-based training and cultivating super users may be very helpful here as well.
- For both training and support, use outreach by the CDS project's clinical informatics leadership (for example, CMIO) directly to physicians and other influential clinicians to ensure that these groups' needs and concerns are adequately addressed for interventions in which they play a central role (such as intrusive alerts in CPOE). These clinicians typically fit into different categories, each of which may benefit from a tailored approach:
  - Early technology adopters—those who are likely to explore the intervention soon after launch, or who might be early users of the underlying CIS through which the CDS will be delivered (for example, CPOE);
  - Clinical thought leaders—for example, clinicians whose patient care expertise is respected by colleagues and whose response to the CDS will be particularly noteworthy to peers;
  - Clinicians closely connected to management— for example, chief quality/safety officer, who may play influential roles in CDS governance and may, therefore, be particularly sensitive to how the interventions work;
  - Super users—who understand intervention mechanics well and can help other users solve problems;
  - Champions—who can model successful intervention use and how this use can drive value for their peers and patients.

Communication

- It may be difficult to have all users eager to receive each specific new intervention due to limited time and other resources necessary for building such engagement. These receptivity issues may be particularly essential for physicians affiliated with hospitals, but not employed by them. If these physicians feel burdened or annoyed by CDS interventions, it can not only threaten the intervention success but also can potentially add strain to the delicate symbiotic relationship with the hospital. Alignment around shared CDS program goals and specific intervention objectives—developed within a collaborative climate and beginning early in the process—will minimize conflict during the launch phase. Here again, champions from among affiliated physicians can help engage and communicate with their peers during intervention rollout.
- An innovative step to help you achieve support for a CDS intervention is to use digital video to graphically demonstrate what the "future state" might look like and the benefits it will bring. You can develop such material in-house with an inexpensive video camera and local staff doing the production. The video can depict the new work-flows throughout the processes affected by the intervention, as well as real benefits that accrue to specific stakeholders (for example, efficiency gains for clinicians and care safety and quality for

the patient). To the extent that the appropriate groundwork for the intervention has been laid, scripting such a video should be straightforward. We have heard anecdotal reports that this demonstration technique worked effectively to solidify consensus and support around needed change. Although an illustration this elaborate won't be practical for most interventions, and possibly not at all, it is worth keeping in mind as a model for the see-feel-change paradigm for process improvement and may stimulate similar creative approaches in your organization.

- As we have emphasized, you should "bake" thorough monitoring for CDS intervention benefits and unintended consequences into your program and individual interventions from the outset; this is critical during intervention launch to ensure that these channels are in place and functioning well. You should leverage whatever mechanisms are in place for feedback from your broader CIS efforts—including helpdesk capabilities, e-mail and telephone feedback channels, and the like.
- Your CMIO (or equivalent) and other CDS Team members should be highly visible and accessible through various channels during major CDS intervention launches. These individuals should not only be open to spontaneous feedback during the launch period but also should proactively seek input. Consider formal and informal meetings with champions and end users, CDS Team ward walk rounds, and other face-to-face communication approaches. Consider also various paper and electronic channels (such as surveys, bulletin boards, mailboxes for the support team and others). During the critical launch period, it is particularly important that the CMIO—and clinical, quality and other leaders—can reinforce for end users that CDS interventions are elements in a broader collaborative performance improvement effort.
- Confirm that the CDS Team (and its IS and other collaborators) has the capacity to provide timely responses to user feedback—especially regarding critical issues that may arise. If your organization

doesn't already have good processes for handling such feedback, you should devote extra attention to this issue when launching major new CDS interventions. This may include revisiting launch phasing, deepening collaborations with IS staff, clinical experts and others, and related approaches. If you can't respond quickly and efficiently to major post-launch issues, you could undermine credibility in your CDS interventions and program.

CONSIDERATIONS FOR SMALL PRACTICES
People (Stakeholder Involvement)

- By the time an intervention is ready to launch, each practice clinician and staff member should be invested in its success and be clear on their role in this success. This readiness flows directly from all the preparatory collaborative work to understand the improvement need, analyze related workflows and configure helpful interventions. If there isn't a strong foundation by launch time, you should take time to reinforce it before releasing the intervention. For example, make sure everyone is clear about—and supports—the intervention objectives and logistics and what this means for their activities.

Planning (Rollout and Training)

- Make sure that interventions are thoroughly tested for usability and safety before deployment and formally approved for launch.
  - Anticipate that upgrades and modifications to the EHR and other systems—including new CDS functionality—might have unexpected effects on key features such as usability, workflow and system response times. Evaluating and addressing these issues with end users prior to launch are important to avoid glitches that might frustrate or alienate them.
  - New or enhanced interventions will likely be tested within the 'live' system, so make sure with the vendor that there are backup and failsafe measures in place to ensure that the new

intervention testing and subsequent release do not disrupt the system or other clinical processes. Anticipate possible changes to the intervention arising during testing (such as adjusting the threshold or display properties of an alert) and prepare for them prior to implementation. If users in the practice have been engaged throughout the intervention configuration processes, there shouldn't be any major surprises or rework.

- Although it doesn't need to be elaborate, it is ideal to at least sketch out an explicit deployment plan for the intervention (see Worksheet 8-1). You can use this documentation to help ensure that everyone knows what's happening, when and how. This documentation not only helps everyone in the practice participate optimally in getting the intervention off the ground, it also provides a more solid baseline for further refining intervention launches in subsequent deployment rounds.

• Concerns about workflow or the intervention itself may arise during intervention testing or rollout. For example, new CDS-enabled clinical documentation or ordering functionality may have glitches not anticipated or identified during earlier intervention preparation. Of course, the more detailed your earlier intervention preparations, the less likely these surprises will be. In some cases, you might address these challenges with policy or workflow changes; in others you may have to tweak the intervention—perhaps with support from the vendor. In any case, consider in advance and prepare for how you will address such situations.

• Consider also cultural issues the intervention may raise, such as altered responsibility (and power) balance between physicians and nurses; for example, based on shifts such as nurses administering interventions (such as flu shots) by protocol rather than individual physician order. Addressing these issues before rollout will be easier than dealing with them during busy clinical activities.

• Check with your intervention-related HIT providers to see what training resources and other support they offer for successful CDS intervention rollout. HIT providers and RECs may be able to offer materials and other support to ensure that practice members know what is expected with these new interventions, how workflows will change, and how to get the most out of the new tools. This is especially valuable when internal training resources are limited.

• Consider also intervention rollout support you might be able to get from peers farther along in the journey (for example, as identified through professional societies in which practice clinicians participate). In addition to training on technical intervention features, consider also any clinical training that will be needed to ensure that practice clinicians fully understand and can effectively use the CDS intervention's content.

• Consider and address how an intervention may alter interactions with patients. It may be helpful to give clinicians an intervention-specific script or talking points list as background for how they can explain interventions (such as new patient education tools) to a patient. Informal internal discussions, at least, can be helpful in preparing for this outreach to patients.

Workflow

• Make sure the practice is well prepared for altered workflows and care delivery needs that the intervention will cause. For example, if the intervention will increase nursing workload (by gathering more data, doing more tests or administering more flu shots), make sure this extra work can be accommodated. Your use cases and other preparatory work should have laid a solid foundation for this, but follow this closely around launch time.

Communication

• Make sure everyone in the practice affected by the intervention understands the details—why, when, how, who, where, etc. Fully leverage whatever communication channels the practice has—such as bulletin boards in break rooms, formal practice meetings, informal gatherings among practice staff, and the like—to get out the word and make sure everyone is 'on board' for intervention launch. Just because there will be relatively few people involved and general information flow may be pretty good, don't assume that everyone fully understands all the key details—especially their personal responsibilities. Verify this, so balls don't get dropped after launch.

Measurement

- Make sure you have the capacity in place to obtain user feedback and to deal rapidly with immediate concerns after launch. Although in a small, single office practice it may not be hard to know when something is going wrong with a CDS intervention, you should still proactively develop plans for documenting, triaging and addressing issues that arise with CDS interventions—especially around the critical launch period (see Worksheet 8-6). If your practice has multiple clinicians or locations, then an explicit plan for proactively and reactively gathering user feedback will be important. These are discussed further in Chapter 9.

CONSIDERATIONS FOR HIT SOFTWARE PROVIDERS
Planning (Rollout and Training)

- Consider mechanisms to support your clients in sharing replicable implementation success models—and pitfalls to avoid—in deploying your CDS interventions. This might occur through a client user group (perhaps through an exchange focused specifically on CDS tools) or directly through your staff.
- Consider providing training resources and other support needed for successful intervention rollout. When feasible, offer mechanisms (such as written tests or intervention simulations) to ensure that users understood the training and are

competent to use important and complex interventions effectively.

Capabilities

- Provide functionality for intervention testing in a simulation or non-production environment to help implementers strengthen and streamline the intervention design, build and test cycle.
- Dashboard-type functionality is desirable to enable implementers to turn various interventions on and off based on various criteria in order to optimize how they apply the CDS Five Rights. These criteria include variables such as user training level, computer location, condition severity underlying an alert, specific practices, physicians, specialties, clinical situations (such as bone-marrow transplant patients, terminally ill or comfort measures–only patients, pregnant women), patient types (such as day surgery or outpatients), time of day, physician performance patterns, or locations within a practice or hospital setting. Ideally, implementers should be able to track (in close to real time) intervention use and results by these different criteria, to help them improve the intervention and accelerate clinical performance improvement.
- You should be available to respond quickly and efficiently with the appropriate intensity (within days for critical issues, within weeks for improvement suggestions) to address questions and needs pertinent to system/intervention rollout. Actual fixes may take longer, but, as with the relationship between your implementer clients and their end users, there should ideally be an effective and responsive collaborative relationship.

Measurement

- Provide mechanisms for collecting user feedback within workflow (and then managing this feedback); for example, a 'feedback button' on CDS-related pages that feeds into appropriate CDS Team users and a summary report form.

WORKSHEETS

Worksheet 8-1

Intervention Launch Plan

Worksheet 8-1 can be used to document your plan to notify the affected community about the upcoming launch, train them on effectively using the intervention, gather their feedback after implementation, and assign responsibility and timetables for intervention maintenance. Documenting this information can be used to build a clear and shared picture about plan details for the implementation team and also to gather input from selected stakeholders to help optimize the plan.

This sample worksheet is organized by the individual CDS interventions (followed by the corresponding objective) listed in the first and second columns and brought forward from earlier worksheets (such as Worksheet 7-2). You might want to organize this worksheet differently—for example, by the clinical objective you are addressing—depending on how many interventions you are launching at this stage and how they interrelate. Similarly, if there are several major components to your launch (such as different intervention packages for different objectives), you might want to create a separate worksheet for each component.

In the third column, list the individual responsible for the intervention, and in the fourth the information system that will be used to deliver it. These first four columns provide context for the details in the next three columns regarding the communication, training and launch monitoring plans. You might want to break one or more of these columns out into a separate table. For example, you might create a table as in Worksheet 8-2 to document your communication plan. You can use the last column to document notes for the project team or plan reviewers.

Intervention Name	Clinical Decision Support Objective	Owner	Clinical IS	Communication Plan	Training Plan	Launch Monitoring Plan	Notes
Prescription allergy alert window	Reduce preventable ADEs	James E. CQO	Better care CPOE	E-mail, clinical IT advisory committee	Individual training on site	CDS Committee members will monitor intervention use directly through walk rounds, frequent checks to feedback inbox, and phone line	We will watch response to this very closely, as it is first interruptive alert in CPOE

Communication Plan

This chapter emphasizes conveying messages in multiple ways at different times through several channels to ensure that all stakeholders are well-prepared for intervention launch. Worksheet 8-2 illustrates an '8X8' communication plan that uses eight different channels to convey important information about the forthcoming launch of an intrusive, high-stakes CDS intervention. You can use this worksheet as a template for documenting your own communication approaches for major CDS intervention launches and updates.

This example mainly focuses on outgoing communications from the CDS Team to other stakeholders. As emphasized in this and other chapters, bi-direction dialog is important throughout the CDS intervention lifecycle, so consider documenting more completely in your own communication plan the return channels whereby the CDS Team will receive input from, and engage in conversations with, intervention stakeholders. In other words, how you will receive the feedback documented in Worksheet 8-6.

Worksheet 8-2

8 x 8 Communication Plan Example

Event to Be Communicated	Method	Message	Start Date	End Date	Responsible Party
Launch of new interruptive alerting about dangerous drug-drug interactions in CPOE system	E-mail — 2 instances	An updated CPOE version with new alerting for the most high-risk drug interactions will be in production on 1 June. Extensive work with end users and the CIS/CDS vendors has taken place to minimize nuisance alerting. It won't be perfect at launch, and the CDS Team is committed to continually optimizing the value of these alerts. Several channels for feedback are available and will be monitored closely. [Click here to send message to CDS Team]	1 April	15 May	Kerry F.
	Notices on launch day — via various electronic and paper channels	Same as above	Same as above	1 June	Same as above
	Brochures — distributed in workplaces of each intervention stakeholder and electronically on intranet	See mock-up — includes summary of interactions to be targeted, rationale for selection, benefits expected, highlights from e-mail message	Same as above	Until supplies run out after launch	Luke S.

continued on next page

Worksheet 8-2 *continued*

Event to Be Communicated	Method	Message	Start Date	End Date	Responsible Party
	Bulletin boards in pertinent gathering places (such as medical staff lounge)	Same as above	Same as above	1 July	Luke S.
	EHR notice	New high-risk drug interactions will be in production on June 1; click here for details [link to brochure on intranet]	1 May	31 May	Jim W.
	Web notice to departmental intranet sites (such as nursing, pharmacy, radiology, etc.)	Same as brochure	Same as above	Same as above	Rhonda J.—intranet; John F.—conference
	Presentation at medical and other staff meetings, prior to launch	Combination of all the above and below; will take time to gather feedback, questions, concerns from stakeholders	15 May	15 May	David W., MD, CMIO
	Positive buzz created by physician and pharmacy champions with colleagues	"There is close collaboration between the medical staff, pharmacy staff, CDS implementation team and others on these alerts; they're not perfect but they work well. In realistic testing scenarios, we've seen how they really will make a significant difference in patient safety."	1 May	Ongoing	Julie P., MD, medical staff, Sam K., RPh, clinical pharmacist

Worksheet 8-3

Prelaunch Testing

Worksheet 8-3 can be used to document your prelaunch testing and results. For some intervention types, professionals in your information services division or a consulting company assisting with intervention development may complete this worksheet. It is organized by intervention, since that is generally how the testing will be conducted. In the second column, list the clinical decision support objective targeted by the intervention; this can help reinforce this key connection for those completing and reviewing this worksheet.

In the third column, identify the owner, or champion, for this intervention. Columns four and five document the test type and scenario. Testing type includes unit testing, user verification testing, integration testing, and pilot testing. The last three columns are used to document when the testing was done, who did it, the results, and other pertinent notes that the testers wish to convey back to the implementation team.

Intervention Name	Clinical Decision Support Objective	Owner	Test Type	Test Scenario	Date/Tester	Results	Note
Prescription allergy alert window	Reduce preventable ADEs	James E. CQO	User-simulation	Prescriber given medication orders to enter, with some triggering alerts — user timed and surveyed	4-10/ Dr. Tai	User interface intuitive; ordering process minimally perturbed	

Worksheet 8-4

Simplified FMEA Drill Down

Anticipating Intervention Failure Opportunities: FMEA Drill Down

Worksheet 8-4 is intended to help you anticipate potential problem areas for the proposed CDS intervention(s) so they can be addressed prior to launch. The example presented takes you through a modified Failure Mode and Effects Analysis (FMEA)[11] that spans the medication management process. You should conduct the FMEA analysis well before intervention launch—ideally, in some cases, before intervention specifications are finalized (as in Worksheet 7-2), so that the build plans address potential intervention failure modes.

Traditionally, the severity score used in an FMEA analysis is a numerical value from 1–10, with 10 being the most frequent, less detectable, and harmful, respectively. A simplified version uses a three-point scale (1–3).

For severity, 1 = no patient harm, not a quality issue; 2 = potential patient harm; 3 = significant patient safety issue/harm.

Full FMEA analyses also score occurrence frequency and detection; for this simplified analysis, we only rate occurrence and do so on a 3-point scale (1–3).

For occurrence, 1 = few patients, 2= moderate # of patients, 3 = many patients; these numbers are relative to other occurrences in the FMEA analysis for the particular intervention.

Typically, the scores are subjectively determined. Since in the sample intervention, "prescription allergy alert window" happens during ordering in the medication management cycle, we will focus on five scenarios that would cause this intervention to fail (for example, when the medication that the patient is allergic to is ordered). The failure mode(s) with the highest result from multiplying severity times occurrence is likely to give the best return if the failure mode can be remedied. The scores and prioritization can be revised once data are collected (for example, regarding actual alert override rates), providing a dynamic picture of priority opportunities to address potential intervention problems.

Clinical Decision Support Objective: Prevent prescription of medications to allergic patients

Intervention Name and ID: Prescription allergy alert window (Ordering Workflow Step)

Failure Mode	Causes	Effects	Occurrence Score	Severity Score	Occurrence X Severity	Work Process Action	Technical Action
Wrong patient selected and alert window not triggered	Mis-clicked	Medication ordered	1	3	3	Verify correct patient identifier	Insert patient ID validation screen

continued on next page

Worksheet 8-4 *continued*

Failure Mode	Causes	Effects	Occurrence Score	Severity Score	Occurrence X Severity	Work Process Action	Technical Action
Alert window not triggered	Penicillin allergy not known	Medication ordered	3	3	9	Ensure accurate updating of patient allergy list	Require allergy update prior to order entry
Alert window not triggered	Trigger rules not specific	Medication ordered	2	3	6	Revise trigger rules	
Physician 'clicked through' alert	Physician in a hurry to order	Medication ordered	2	3	6	Place hard stops in ordering process that require override signatures	
Physician override alert	Physician with inaccurate allergy information	Medication ordered	2	3	6	Ensure accurate updating of allergy list for patient	Track alert overrides per physician

Worksheet 8-5

Implementation Status

Worksheet 8-5 is a dynamic document that provides a snapshot of the interventions you are rolling out, individually and collectively. Once again, the interventions being rolled out can be organized in various ways; in this sample, for example, it is organized by individual intervention. The first four columns can be brought forward from earlier worksheets, such as Worksheet 8-1. Documenting intervention users in the fifth column can help with tracking intervention types that are deployed for different end-user types.

The testing completed date in the sixth column identifies when the intervention has completed the pre-rollout evaluation. This information can help alert you to interventions that might be stuck at this stage. The seventh column specifies the target date for initially launching each intervention. Seeing all these dates together can be helpful for sequencing and appropriately spacing out the individual intervention launches and modifying the schedule as needed. The actual launch dates and locations in the eighth and ninth columns track your rollout progress. This can be helpful both for reporting progress to other stakeholders and for tracking the pace at which the organization can successfully deliver and absorb new interventions.

Intervention Name and ID	Objective	Owner	Clinical IS System	Implementation Clinical Users	Date Testing Completed	Planned Launch Date	Actual Launch Date	Launch Location	Notes
Prescription allergy alert window	Reduce preventable ADEs	James E. CQO	Better Care CPOE	Physicians	4/2	4/6	4/7	5south	Anticipate proceeding to DDI alerts after allergy alerts have stabilized

Worksheet 8-6

Feedback and Resolution

Each intervention you are launching can be listed in Worksheet 8-6; again, the first two columns can be carried forward from others in this chapter. In the third column, list the feedback strategy details, such as the use of online feedback, surveys, polls, etc. As discussed earlier in this chapter, these should include feedback mechanisms that are both user-initiated (such as e-mail links within interventions) and implementation-team initiated (such as surveys and interviews), as appropriate. Record all the substantive feedback you receive for each intervention through the various channels in the fifth column, indicating the date and source for the feedback in the fourth column.

Although the details might not be immediately apparent, a plan for addressing each substantive issue should be documented at some point in the sixth column. When the issue is resolved, that can be noted in this column as well; the seventh column can be used to indicate the target or actual date for resolution, as appropriate. Use the last column to indicate the priority for addressing the issue (for example, low, medium, high), ideally based on criteria established by the CDS governance mechanisms. These criteria might include how many patients are affected and the how serious the consequences are, how the 'fix' will affect other CDS program resources and priorities, and the like.

Intervention Name and ID	Clinical Decision Support Objective	Feedback Strategy	Feedback Date and User	Feedback	Plan/Resolution	Target Date/ Actual Date	Priority
Prescription allergy alert window	Reduce prevent-able ADEs	Survey	4-21/ Dr. B.	Took too much time to override alerts	Analyze/improve override process	5-15	High

REFERENCES

1 These items are based on: Thompson D, Johnston P. A benefits-driven approach to system implementation. *Hospital and Health Networks Magazine.* Spring 2008. Available online at: http://www.hhnmag.com/hhnmag_app/jsp/articledisplay.jsp?dcrpath=HHNMOSTWIRED/Article/data/Spring2008/080709MW_Online_Thompson&domain=HHNMOSTWIRED. 02 July 2008, Accessed June 17, 2011.

2 See, for example, John Kotter's website: www.kotterinternational.com, which has detailed information about the 8 steps he recommends for leading change, as well as information about his widely used and recommended books on the subject (such as *Leading Change* and *The Heart of Change*). Accessed August 29, 2011.

3 See, for example, Ash JS. Organizational and cultural change considerations in Greenes RA, ed. *Clinical Decision Support: The Road Ahead.* London: Elsevier; 2007: 385-402.

4 Krall MA. Clinician champions and leaders for electronic medical record innovations. *The Permanente Journal.* 2001; 5(1):40-45. Available online at: http://xnet.kp.org/permanentejournal/winter01/HSchamp.html. Accessed June 17, 2011.

5 For example, as outlined in the See-Feel-Change approach outlined in Kotter JP, Cohen DS. *The Heart of Change.* Boston: Harvard Business School Press; 2002.

6 See, for example, Galin D. *Software Quality Assurance: From Theory to Implementation.* Boston: Addison –Wesley; 2003.

7 Wadhwa R, Fridsma DB, Saul MI, et al. Analysis of a failed clinical decision support system for management of congestive heart failure. AMIA Annual Symposium Proceedings. 2008:773-777. Available online at: http://www.ncbi.nlm.nih.gov/pmc/articles/PMC2655961. Accessed June 15, 2011.

8 Dykstra R. Computerized physician order entry and communication: reciprocal impacts. AMIA Annual Symposium Proceedings. 2002; 230-34.

9 See talk on "Education and Clinical Decision Support: Reuniting Twins Separated at Birth" by JA Osheroff at the MedBiquitous Annual Conference 2007. Available online at: https://docs.google.com/viewer?url=http://www.medbiq.org/events/conferences/2007/presentations/OsheroffJ_Plenary.pps&pli=1. Accessed August 30, 2011.

10 Coté GA, Rice JP, Bulsiewicz W, et al. Use of physician education and computer alert to improve targeted use of gastroprotection among NSAID users. *Am J Gastroenterol,* 2008; 103(5):1097-1103.

11 See, for example, FMEA information and tools on the IHI website: *Institute for Healthcare Improvement. Failure Mode and Effects Analysis Tool.* http://www.ihi.org/knowledge/Pages/Tools/FailureModesandEffectsAnalysisTool.aspx, Accessed August 30, 2011.

Chapter 9

Measuring Results and Continuously Refining the Program

Tasks

- Develop for each intervention a plan for identifying, tracking and addressing on an ongoing basis: availability, use, and usability; unintended behavior and effects; and outcomes. (Worksheets 9-1 through 9-3)
- Develop a plan for reporting intervention effects to pertinent stakeholders and supporting continuous monitoring and improvement. (Worksheet 9-3)
- Track victories and exceptional efforts, frequently communicating and leveraging them to sustain performance and set up enthusiasm for future CDS interventions.
- Identify owners or responsible parties for all your CDS interventions and their content, and implement tools and processes to maintain and update intervention periodically and as needs arise. (Worksheets 4-1 and 9-4)
- Apply what you learn from evaluation to continually enhance your CDS program's interventions and increase their value to users and their impact on organizational goals and objectives. (Worksheet 9-5)

KEY LESSONS

- Stakeholders and organizational leadership can help establish reasonable measurement intervals and expectations for improvement. Evaluating intervention effectiveness requires both quantitative and qualitative approaches.
- Log files and other approaches to tracking intervention use can be helpful for monitoring intervention effects. Details of interest include when and how the intervention was invoked, where the user and patient were at the time, when in the workflow it happened, and how the information delivered was handled and applied.
- It is critical to iteratively refine interventions to improve their use and benefits. Improvement opportunities emerge from evaluation efforts, in concert with evolving capabilities in your CIS infrastructure and available CDS tools, new clinical knowledge, and the changing healthcare delivery environment.

GENERAL APPROACH

Throughout this Guide, we have emphasized that measuring CDS intervention effects is an ongoing process that must be considered from the earliest intervention development stages. This chapter delves deeply into the "what, how and when" measurement dimensions for CDS interventions and intervention packages that your CDS program has deployed and also covers what to do with your evaluation results. It may be helpful to review the Measurement discussion in Chapter 3, especially the sections on "Why Measure" and "Who Will Measure." We also revisit key CDS knowledge management points from Chapter 4 and apply them to maintaining specific CDS interventions.

What to Measure
Measurement Philosophy

You should examine in some way the results from every CDS alert or other intervention type you implement. An acronym can serve as a helpful guidepost for your evaluation effort: METRIC—Measure Everything That Really Impacts Customers.[1] For our purposes, "customers" includes all CDS intervention stakeholders—for example, the organization's leadership, front-line clinicians, other key ancillary and clinical support roles, and patients. Although this ideal may not always be attainable, the acronym helps focus attention on measurement priorities.

In determining what to measure, avoid selecting measurements in a vacuum; make sure the proposed measurements (just as the interventions) align with the existing and planned organizational improvement initiatives. You should consider how the CDS intervention objectives relate to other pertinent organizational activities for which measurement targets and processes may be in place. For example, if the interventions address targets that are the focus of reporting or reimbursement requirements (such as core measures from The Joint Commission and CMS), you may already have the commitment and processes necessary for capturing key data related to CDS interventions addressing these targets. Similarly, your organization may be capturing care process and outcome data needed for various purposes related to Meaningful Use (such as CPOE utilization and specific clinical measures) or other performance improvement initiatives (perhaps related to diabetes care management or healthcare-associated complications), so you should seek and nurture synergies between your CDS measurement needs and these efforts.

Especially in larger organizations, clashes often occur between evidence-based, research purists, and the more practical clinical and business process owners regarding the required scientific rigor for evaluation methods. Purists argue that a randomized clinical trial (RCT) is required for firm conclusions about intervention effects,[2] while business process owners often argue that they do not have enough time or the ability to randomize EHR/CDS access or features. They may also note that it is unethical to withhold potentially life-saving CDS interventions from patients. On the other hand, researchers have also argued that different types of evaluations are necessary to fully understand what is working and what is not.[3]

Whatever your CDS Team's philosophy, collecting adequate baseline data for targeted measures prior to implementing new CDS interventions is always a good idea for several reasons. First, even if you are planning an RCT, it is often the case that baseline differences in individual or group performance can overwhelm changes due to the intervention. Second, while correlation does not prove causation, it is very likely that the CDS intervention did not have the desired effect if the targeted parameter worsens following the intervention.

With these caveats in mind, you should attempt to collect baseline data for a long enough time to make sure that you have accounted for seasonal or other sources of cyclic variation. For example, if you are attempting to measure the effect from a new influenza vaccine reminder, you should make sure that the measurements account for the expected increase in influenza prophylaxis during the fall and winter in the northern hemisphere. Also, you should attempt to collect data to help control for as many potentially confounding variables as possible that might affect how you interpret intervention effects. For example, consider potential organizational changes (such as modified nursing availability to carry out tasks required for intervention success), financial changes (such as discount generic drug prescription pricing in retail pharmacies that may affect patient and clinician drug preferences), or clinical changes (such as the FDA adding a new black box warning regarding the medication targeted by the CDS intervention). Again, look for baseline data that are already being collected as part of ongoing quality, safety or administrative projects.

Having emphasized how important it is to carefully evaluate any and all interventions, and to do so in light of related organizational activities, we now turn to specific metrics. Chapter 3 introduced four metric types, and we now consider these in more detail. A growing literature also examines evaluation targets for CIS and CDS applications, as indicated by the many evaluation studies cited throughout this Guide (especially Chapter 1). In the discussion that follows, additional studies are cited as well. Regardless of your organization's size, this literature is a helpful method for learning about what parameters investigators have measured and how they assessed these intervention effects. Some of the approaches may be adaptable to your setting.

Four Types of Metrics

In planning to evaluate the desirable and other effects of individual interventions and interventions packages you are launching (such as in Worksheet 9-1), there are four types of metrics you should consider. These are outlined next.

System Response Time Measures

You should keep system response times at a minimum because users typically consider waiting for an intervention more than one or two seconds as "taking forever" and therefore an unwelcome workflow intrusion. In Chapter 8 we discussed prelaunch testing and noted that it is important to consider system response times. We now provide some additional

details about this measure, which can be periodically reassessed in ongoing evaluation of users' experiences with the deployed CDS portfolio.

When examining system response times, you should explicitly consider the start and stop events that surround the measurement and whether these events are system or user initiated. For example, when a clinician enters a drug name into a CPOE system (the start event), how long does it take for the system to display a pertinent alert (the stop event), such as a warning about a potential DDI or patient allergy? The user experience and workflow intrusion will be influenced by both the *system response time* and the time it takes for users to access, process and address the CDS information presented—that is, the *user response time*. We consider user response times later under process metrics.

Some CDS and CISs can automatically assess and report certain system and user response times. Keep in mind there are many potential reasons (and solutions) for increases in system response time other than simply adding new CDS interventions. In small practices, the CDS implementer will have a sense of intervention impacts on end users from informal interactions, so aggregate reporting is less critical. Nonetheless, close monitoring to ensure that new interventions don't slow down users—and quick resolution if they do, with support from the system vendor and others as needed—is important.

Structure Measures

To appropriately interpret the effects that your CDS interventions are having, you must develop a clear picture of how these interventions are deployed. Structure measures characterize this infrastructure and the forces that are helping drive observed changes. For example, structure indicators for a DDI alert might indicate any differences in how these alerts are configured to fire between nursing floors or between different physician and patient types. This difference might be pertinent if otherwise dangerous combinations are permissible in the alert logic on certain clinical services, such as cardiology or oncology. As we discussed in earlier chapters, your underlying system capabilities will determine what situation-specific functionality is available for your CDS interventions; the question for CDS-related structure measurement is how these capabilities are configured to achieve the desired CDS objective.

Specific structure measures that relate to CDS interventions themselves include (among many others):

- Number and nature of interruptive alerts deployed, including systems in which these are displayed, such as CPOE, EHR, automatic dispensing cabinets, and smart pumps;
- Number and nature of non-interruptive notices/alerts deployed, such as information about patient allergies or decreased kidney function that may be available on various user displays within CISs, such as pharmacy systems or CPOE;
- Number of alerts deployed by recipient role (nurse, provider, pharmacist, patient, other) and whether specific alerts are configured to not fire for certain roles, locations, patients and the like;
- Whether and how end users can override alerts and document override reasons; how individual override reasons are handled—for example, as free text or coded data;
- Number of order sets deployed and the topics they cover;
- Where and how infobuttons, documentation tools, relevant data displays and the like are deployed;
- Number and nature of CDS intervention packages deployed in the practice, including all the specific patient conditions addressed.

Related factors for you to consider are whether the CDS components are working as expected and usage data are available. For example, are alerts firing when and where you expect them to and being presented to appropriate end users at the correct point in their workflow? The monitoring and feedback mechanisms you established to help answer these and related questions (as discussed in Chapters 7 and 8) are an important infrastructure component that should be assessed through structure measures as well (for example, see Worksheet 7-1, the Feedback

Channels and Plan row in which such information may have been documented).

Besides characterizing the deployed CDS interventions themselves, you need to understand how use of underlying CISs will affect opportunities for CDS (see Chapter 4). For example:

- Is the CIS environment "mixed" in that some clinicians are using a particular application such as CPOE, while others are not?
- Are prescribing providers using CPOE to place orders themselves, or are they relying heavily upon verbal or telephone orders?
- If verbal and telephone orders are used, are the providers staying on the phone for complete verbal read back, and are those taking the orders reviewing and discussing each alert?
- Are end users entering information as codified options rather than as free text options (such as allergies and medication orders)?

All these structural considerations provide the foundation for understanding how the deployed CDS interventions affect processes and outcomes, which we discuss in the following two sections.

PROCESS MEASURES

Process measures answer questions such as, *How are the CDS interventions affecting end users—and their decisions and work activities—at each workflow step?* By characterizing whether and how CDS interventions are actually affecting care processes and flow, these metrics help you determine how well users accept and value these interventions. There are many important process indicators; in the following sections, we highlight some considerations around assessing intervention use, their effects on workflow, and on users' time and satisfaction.

Intervention Use

CDS interventions such as infobuttons, order sets and the like are often used less in practice than implementers expect. Your careful attention to the prelaunch details can help minimize this mismatch, but in any case, it is important to determine how often interventions are actually being used. Some pertinent use dimensions to assess include:

- How many order sets or order sentences are utilized[4] (as opposed to deployed)? (See Process Indicator Report sidebar on the next page for an example of how one organization answers questions such as this one.) Are these interventions being accepted and adopted as expected?
- When, how, where and why are interventions such as infobuttons,[5] flowsheets or documentation tools being used?[6] What can be gleaned about missed opportunities for effective use from these patterns?
- How often do various alerts actually fire across all systems, and how do end users respond?[7] Process measures related to alerting and overrides are considered in more detail in a sidebar later in this section.
- Who is using the interventions, and what does the adoption curve look like? Pertinent adoption characteristics include:
  - *Adoption Rate.* How many total users are accessing the interventions over time?[8] A shallow adoption rate, indicating low usage and slow growth, can delay the time until full intervention value is realized and can decrease momentum on progress toward improvement goals.
  - *Adoption Audience Demographics.* What characteristics differentiate users with different adoption rates? You may want to review how both provider and patient characteristics can influence how well users accept and respond appropriately to CDS alerts and other interventions.[9] These nuances can help you refine interventions, as well as your training and communication process, to support more effective uptake. For example, you might tailor CDS training to emphasize how different clinician types can optimally use the intervention. Pertinent clinician characteristics include age, gender, training, experience with computers, clinical role and experience, relationship to the hospital (employed or affiliated), exposure

time to pertinent IS per day, and comments and opinions regarding the system expressed during feedback sessions.[10] Pertinent patient characteristics include age, gender, diagnosis and comorbidities.

- More specifically for prescribers, does role (such as physician, nurse practitioner, physician assistant, resident or fellow) affect use? You might track and record, for example, information about prescriber role (accessible via CPOE sign-on information and logs) and relate this information to alerts triggered and resulting action. This can potentially help with fine-tuning alert triggers and suggesting the need for modified role-based training.
- Likewise for medication administration, information about the intervention recipient (such as the nurse administering the drug) can be retrieved from the pertinent system—such as the electronic medication administration record (eMAR), bar-code point-of-care system, or smart pump—and used in similar ways.
  - *CDS Use in CPOE.* Pertinent statistics to consider over time include:
    - Percent medication orders entered into computer by physicians—sometimes referred to as "percent CPOE" for medication orders;
    - Number of clicks on infobuttons in CPOE linking out to reference information;
    - Number of alerts in CPOE that are fired, accepted and overridden (see sidebar, next, on alerting and overrides);
    - Time saved by using automated weight-based dosing instead of manual dose calculation;[11]
    - Turn-around time from order entry to medication administration.[12]

Effects on Workflow

In Chapter 3, we discussed core CDS program capabilities around workflow analysis and mapping, and in earlier chapters in Part II we discussed apply-

Process Indicator Report Example from Memorial Hermann Healthcare System

Figure 9-1 is a snapshot illustrating how often specific CDS interventions, in this case care plans and order sets, are used in two different healthcare facilities at Memorial Hermann over a one-week period. Although presented here for hospitals, this approach can be relevant for smaller settings as well.

This report can help your CDS Team understand how use varies among interventions over time and between different facilities. Such reports should ideally be automated to run on a regular basis and monitored closely to identify any gaps or trends in how often specific CDS interventions are used. Such changes might indicate some problem with the intervention itself or changing care delivery circumstances that might alter intervention use or usefulness.

Figure 9-1: Use of Specific Care Plans and Order Sets in Two Facilities over One Week

Person Location - Facility (From)	Plan Name	# care plans
Hospital #1	OB/GYN Vaginal Delivery Multiphase MPP	70
	Admission Common Orders - Adult (Direct Admit) MPP	37
	Admission Common Orders (Post EC) MPP	29
	Pain, Acute	28
	Respiratory, Impaired Gas Exchange	27
	ESP, Anxiety/Fear/Hopelessness	19
	OB/GYN Cesarean Delivery Multiphase MPP	18
	Admission Common Orders - Adult ICU MPP	10
	Neonatal Admission Common Orders Nursery Level 1 MPP	10
	Cardiac, Chest Pain	9
Person Location - Facility (From)	Plan Name	# care plans
Hospital #2	Pain, Acute	54
	Cardiac, Tissue Perfusion	23
	Cardiac, Chest Pain	18
	Infection, Actual	16
	Neuro/Muscular/Safety, Impaired Physical Mobility	15
	Cardiac, Fluid Volume Deficit	12
	Respiratory, Impaired Gas Exchange	10
	PT, Ambulation Deficits	9
	Neuro/Muscular/Safety, Risk for Injury	8
	Respiratory, Ineffective Breathing Pattern	8

Source: Memorial Hermann Healthcare System, Houston, TX. Used with permission.

ing these capabilities to selecting and configuring interventions to address particular objectives. After launching these interventions, it is critical to revisit your earlier hypotheses about opportunities to support workflow and thereby enhance care processes, decisions and outcomes.

Any workflow maps your CDS Team created—such as for key care processes in general, or for the 'current state' and 'desired state' in relation to specific CDS interventions and objectives—document the 'before' picture pertinent to your new interventions. Once interventions are launched, you should revisit the process analysis to clearly understand the 'after' picture. As we discussed in Chapters 3 and 8, what you *expected* to happen might not be what is *actually* happening, and you need to apply the same multifaceted approach (combining direct observation, data review, stakeholder conversations and the like) to accurately understand post-intervention workflows.

Even with all the careful planning and stakeholder engagement we have advocated, don't be surprised if interventions don't affect workflow in exactly the fashion you anticipated. These deviations can be important joint learning opportunities between the CDS Team and intervention users and provide helpful input to ongoing efforts to refine and add CDS interventions to support clinical workflow.

Effects on Users' Time and Satisfaction

An important use and usability process measure—also related to workflow—is how long it takes users to interact with the intervention once it has been presented to them. The user experience with the intervention will include both this *user* response time, as well as the *system* response time discussed earlier. Time pressures that force non-essential care processes—or those that consume excessive time—to be overlooked are a major reason why clinicians (physicians especially) may not use certain CDS interventions. As a result, you should carefully assess user-response times to make sure that unacceptable delays aren't adversely affecting intervention use.

Some specific issues to consider, among others, are the following:

- Is the speed and ease with which users can complete a specific task after the CDS has been added better or worse? In some cases, processes may take longer (for example, CDS-enabled electronic prescribing in some studies),[13] and you must determine if this delay is acceptable. Answering this acceptability question requires that both the evaluator and end user consider the broader intervention effects, such as prescriber time saved in avoiding pharmacy calls and having to correct medication orders.

- For interruptive alerting, how long does it take from the time the alert is displayed until the end user acts on it? This is the time, for example, from the point at which a duplicate therapy or drug interaction alert fires, to when the triggering condition is addressed by the user (such as by changing the prescription) or the alert is dismissed.

- For non-interruptive alerting (such as displaying a patient's allergies in an ordering screen header, or pertinent patient lab values in the order detail for certain medications), what is the length of time taken until this information is recognized and acted on? For example, how much time elapses from when information about impaired kidney function is available onscreen until appropriate manual dosage adjustment is entered (or at least until the user notices the pertinent information)?[14]

- Similarly, for other interventions, how much time elapses from when the intervention is displayed to when the user notices it and completes the interaction? For example, do users notice that order sets might be available for a given condition (in paper or electronic environments)? How long does it take them to find the pertinent order set or determine that none is available? How long does it take to complete an order set once it has been accessed? For infobutton links to Internet/intranet information sources, how long do users spend reviewing retrieved information? Likewise for data flowsheets or data entry forms?

Pertinent end-user workflows and time constraints—together with intervention "user friendliness"—influence these user response times and users' impressions about these times.[15] The post-intervention process analysis mentioned earlier provides a foundation for evaluating this dimension. Some information systems may be able to automatically report some time details though you will need to augment this with manual onsite workflow assessments. Small practices may need to rely on outside assistance, for example, from their REC or system vendors, for help with needed measurements.

This manual analysis might include the evaluator documenting factors related to task completion. For example, whether the user experienced difficulty or delays dealing with (or noticing) the intervention, or was also doing other things at the same time he or she was interacting with the intervention (that is, multitasking). These observations can augment and help you interpret system-generated response time data, for example, by answering, "What was taking so long? Directly observing intervention use can also suggest intervention enhancements, such as improved support for important multitasking activities that users may typically do in association with the intervention. Remember to consider both the system and user response time components (as applicable) to fully appreciate the workflow delays that users may experience with various interventions.

Keep in mind that specific process effects on users, such as time required to interact with interventions, workflow changes, usefulness of information provided and others, combine to influence users' satisfaction with specific CDS interventions, and with your CDS program more broadly. You should assess this satisfaction level because it is often an important factor in building the collaborative relationship that is key to program success. More recommendations about assessing user satisfaction—which can apply to clinicians, patients and others—are presented in the "How to Measure" section later in this chapter. (See sidebar on the next page for alert process indicator considerations.)

OUTCOME MEASURES

The metrics we have considered so far (system performance, structural measures characterizing deployed interventions, and process measures indicating how they affect users and workflows) illuminate key features of your deployed CDS portfolio. It is essential to track and improve these measures in order to optimize CDS intervention use and usability. Keep in mind though, that an ultimate purpose for launching the interventions is to influence important care delivery results. These include safer and more effective care and resulting increases in patient health and decreases in preventable mortality and harm. Patient and clinician satisfaction with the care delivery process are also important results. Outcome measures demonstrate the extent to which these and related objectives are being achieved.

Properly interpreting outcome measures depends on results from the other measure categories. For example, if you see a change in outcomes (length of hospital stay, drug utilization, patient disease parameters and the like) but have no data to demonstrate that clinicians are using as anticipated the CDS interventions that are focused on these targets, then it may be difficult to convince stakeholders that the interventions are driving the changes.

Questions that CDS outcome measures are designed to answer include:

- Did an order get changed as the result of an alert and thereby help avoid patient harm, such as a specific adverse drug event?
  - If it was not changed, did an ADE develop because the alert was ignored?
  - Were there any unplanned medical or surgical interventions that were required to address the resulting preventable ADE?
- Has there been a measurable positive effect from an order set (or other CDS interventions) on patient care outcomes?
  - Is there a reduction in average length of stay (ALOS) or mortality for conditions in which order sets are being used?[22]

A Deeper Dive into Alerting and Overrides

Since intrusive alerts and how users respond to them are such an important and often problematic issue in CDS deployment, we provide more detailed considerations on pertinent process indicators for this intervention type.

To continually improve the alerts' value and the clinical practices alerts are intended to support, you should carefully monitor how these interventions affect work processes. Because intrusions into clinical workflow can be both irritating and potentially dangerous for patients, it is important to evaluate which alerts are being overridden, by whom, from which locations, and why.[16,17]

Many organizations are shocked by the surprisingly high alert override rate (which may be greater than 99%) when they first turn on a new alert for important situations such as medication safety concerns. Often implementers will respond by inserting a pop-up form requiring that clinicians enter the reason they are overriding the alert before they can continue using the system. This form may contain both a coded list of likely override reasons (such as "Patient currently on medications and tolerating well" or "Will monitor patient closely") along with a free text field in which the user can enter unstructured comments.

In managing excessive alert overrides, your goal is not necessarily to eliminate all alert overrides but rather to reduce them to a reasonable level. CDS developers hypothesize that if they understood why clinicians were overriding the alerts, they could refine their alert logic and reduce many false-positive events.[18] Be careful when introducing mandatory pop-up forms to collect this information. For one thing, clinicians may already be annoyed that they received the alert, and become more displeased that you're now asking them to enter one more piece of data that provides them with no direct value. Therefore, they may be inclined to select the first item from the list as the reason, just to get past the pop-up and move on. Obviously, such spurious override data are of little or no use your CDS Team.[19] In addition, a report[20] found that in a small, but clinically significant number of instances, clinicians tried to use the free text override field to "communicate" important information to other clinicians. Since these alert override reasons are processed by the CDS Team and not routinely displayed to any other users on the patient's care team, it can be problematic when CDS recipients use this communication strategy.

If you experience high alert override rates, use mandatory override reason forms judiciously. In this situation, you might turn on these forms for a short time (such as a few weeks), review the override data, and make any appropriate changes to the alert logic. You can then test, implement the changes, and review the new override rate and reasons. Some tips can help increase clinician acceptance of override reason documentation screens. For example, if prescribers override an allergy alert and give "Not a true allergy" as a reason, you should consider offering the capability to easily modify the allergy documentation to reflect this information. In any case, once the high false-positive alerting problem has been resolved, consider removing the mandatory override reason

continued on next page

A Deeper Dive into Alerting and Overrides *continued*

screen. If the problem has not been solved, then consider removing the alert until you develop a suitable plan to reduce false-positive alerting.

To the extent that you approach CDS deployment (including intrusive alerting) as a joint effort among stakeholders, your end users may better appreciate why it is important to document reasons for not accepting an alert's recommendation. Responsiveness from your CDS Team, as reflected by alert refinements based on feedback from override reasons, can further enlist user support in supplying this information when it is most needed.

The following are detailed alert-related indicators to assess, along with how this information can be used:

- Alert-related process measures as noted earlier. For example, what alerts are *actually firing* for various users at each step in workflow, and in various ISs? These metrics indicate how programmed alert triggers are translated into delivered messages. Is this actual information delivery appropriate (within the CDS Five Rights framework) for addressing the objective that the alert is designed to support? The frequency with which the alert triggers occur can be useful in subsequent efforts to decrease false-positive alerting by fine-tuning the triggers and logic (see Chapter 7). Keep in mind that rules and alerts designed to prevent very rare events that should never occur may rarely fire or never fire yet can still be useful.

- How often is each alert overridden? Can you measure—by specific end user—to determine whether there is a pattern by individuals or whether there is a more global issue with the intervention? Override data provide feedback to the CDS Team about how helpful users (individually and collectively) find the alert to be. If users are overriding alerts that demand attention, then appropriate action should be taken to address the cause. For example, when disagreement exists about the alert recommendations (which will hopefully be infrequent if the earlier steps in this guide are followed), then end-user education/dialog about the underlying clinical issues—through pertinent clinical oversight bodies—might be helpful. When there is agreement with the recommendations, and "alert fatigue" caused by excessive false-positive alerting is the culprit, then you should undertake efforts to increase overall alert appropriateness. For example, your CDS Team should explore potential refinements to specific triggering data, alerting logic, and other approaches (such as revisiting the CDS Five Rights for the objective) that could be used to reduce these nuisance alerts.

- Which coded reasons offered by the CIS are users selecting for each override? This information will help you determine, when supplemented with further investigation as needed, whether coded override reasons are only chosen based on their placement on the list (for example, when the first choice is the most often selected choice whether or not it is pertinent) or if they accurately reflect a thoughtful user response. This metric and investigation also help you determine if the override reasons available for the user to select are appropriate and sufficiently specific—for example, if they are considered clinically relevant.

continued on next page

A Deeper Dive into Alerting and Overrides *continued*

- Is there a specific physical location or provider type—such as surgery suite or oncology unit, or individual provider in a small practice—that is experiencing an abnormally high override rate? Again, this could indicate a specific type of false-positive alerting that might potentially be addressed by refining alert triggers or display rules. A study examining DDI alert overrides found that, although many recipients want to turn off specific DDI alerts, recipients agreed that no frequently overridden alert could be safely turned off hospital-wide.[21] These results reinforce the premise that tuning alerts to recipients might be a fruitful avenue to explore.

Although we have recommended care in using mandatory forms for documenting override reasons, these forms do serve useful purposes, such as in diagnosing excessive alerting. Close collaboration with end users and thoughtful deployment can help you decrease the nuisance caused by this tool. For example, presenting users with pre-defined/coded override reasons in a drop-down list (as opposed to requesting free text entry) is one useful approach for speeding the process for users and gathering data that are easier to analyze and act on.

As previously noted, you may have to perform some careful further investigation when interpreting the override reason data, since users may simply select the first choice on the list for expediency. If the list is so long that a vertical scroll bar is necessary, it's unlikely that users will ever select reasons at the end of the list. We recommend you keep the list of reasons short, simple and relevant to the specific alert that has been displayed; when possible, make the first item on the list the most likely reason in most cases.

The Chapter 7 section on Exceptions provides detailed override reasons that have been used for different alert types within several leading organizations. Hopefully, when you configure alerts, you are carefully considering whether and how to use such override reasons; for example, providing a customized list for each different alert type (such as DDI warnings or preventive care reminders).

Note that some CISs do not allow implementers to provide different override reasons for different alert types. This can lead to inappropriate override reasons appearing for some alerts if you don't determine the options globally with this constraint in mind. Also, you should filter the considerations mentioned earlier in this sidebar into determining whether to make it voluntary (if your systems provide this functionality) for users to enter an alert override reason.

- Have medication costs decreased because prescribers are selecting less expensive, equally efficacious drugs?
- Are drug-resistant organisms less prevalent as a result of more appropriate antibiotic selection and therapy duration?
- Is there a decrease in inappropriate laboratory testing and imaging studies (and resulting improvements in efficiencies, costs and patient safety) due to workup guidance provided by the order set?

As these examples illustrate, CDS may influence various patient and organizational outcomes, including care efficiency, safety, quality and cost. Because the factors that determine these results are often numerous and complex, it may be difficult for you to definitively sort out the specific contribution from the CDS intervention(s). The following are approaches for teasing out CDS effects and considerations for using each, with references to studies that demonstrate those approaches in action:

- Comparing variables before CDS intervention versus after intervention.[23]
  - Before/after studies can be difficult to interpret because introducing certain interventions (for example, when potentially harmful conditions trigger alerting) often sheds light on previously unrecognized medication use problems, which can make it falsely appear that the new system is causing more errors.
  - Before/after conditions can also be affected by other initiatives the organization may have simultaneously undertaken, such as performance improvement initiatives not involving the CDS interventions being evaluated.
  - CDS results can be affected by periodic environmental variations, and these must be accounted for when assessing intervention effects over time. For example, a new resident and intern class may alter background care processes and results related to the CDS intervention due to a rapid shift in user training level. Seasonal changes in condition and CDS activity should likewise be considered, for example,

in assessing CDS for influenza immunization during flu season.

- Prospective, randomized trial in which some clinicians, units or patients have the intervention and some do not.[24]
  - These studies can be expensive, and difficult to carry out. It may be hard to get administrators to allow you to "withhold" CDS from some patients or clinicians on ethical grounds, even though there isn't proof that the intervention is effective.[25] As mentioned in Chapter 3, you should consider the need for institutional review board (IRB) approval before conducting such research studies.
  - It may be difficult to keep all other conditions constant during the trial. For example, nursing may institute a new policy that requires additional staff training, and this training can have a greater impact on specific outcomes than the CDS intervention.[26] Often many CIS infrastructure elements are changing in significant ways that aren't anticipated at the trial outset, and this too affects what the results mean.
  - It may be technically difficult to provide some clinicians with the interventions while others do not receive the interventions, since this may require additional EHR or CDS intervention configuration. For example, it may be necessary to add to the alert logic's "IF" clause a list of clinicians randomized to receive the alert. It must be clear to the technical team whether and how this should be done.
- Rolling or staggered implementation with repeated measures in which different parts of the organization (such as nursing units within a hospital) are sequentially implemented.[27]
  - This allows units on which the intervention is deployed to later serve as controls for the initial units implemented.
  - If you observe similar changes (such as in magnitude and direction) on multiple units, then it is more likely that the observed changes are related to the intervention and are not merely artifacts.

– Although these methods are more susceptible to selection bias and other limitations than prospective randomized, controlled trials, they can be very helpful in identifying and isolating program-wide effects.

Other issues to keep in mind when developing and applying metrics to assess outcomes include:

• Are the needed data generally available in a consistent, codified form appropriate for analysis, and if so, will they be reliably available in each patient-specific instance?

• Can the outcome "numerator" and "denominator" be determined in a widely accepted and unambiguous way? For example, if the outcome of interest is reducing drug overdoses, does consensus exist on a clear, computable definition for what is meant by "drug overdose" (the measure numerator), as well on what comprises the population in which this outcome will be assessed (the denominator)?

• Are the data submitted voluntarily or are they automatically captured from ISs? Since voluntary submission typically underestimates occurrence significantly,[28] you should seek automated means for quantifying objective outcomes when possible. Information submitted voluntarily about important outcomes, however, can provide useful details and identify issues and opportunities missed by automated methods. When submitted and collected appropriately, these data can supplement data collected through automated means. Consider approaches that balance the strengths and limitations of various outcome detection methods.[29]

Even though it can be difficult to create an indisputable cause and effect link between a CDS intervention and a clinical outcome, it is important that you thoughtfully gather and interpret data to get a sense of what, if any, relationship exists. Based on this analysis, together with guidance provided by easier-to-measure process indicators, you can strengthen the actual and perceived CDS value in improving outcomes in a data-driven manner.

We now outline in more detail several key clinical outcome types that you should carefully consider in setting up and evaluating outcome metrics for your CDS interventions. They cover clinical, operational and financial dimensions. Keep in mind that in research studies, as well as in your own efforts, these outcome types can be considered together within a single evaluation initiative.

Safety

A central goal in incorporating CDS interventions into care delivery processes is to reduce preventable patient harm. As discussed earlier in this guide, there are increasing financial motivations for eliminating adverse patient events, in addition to all the clinical and ethical ones. For example, Figure 1-5 lists several hospital-acquired conditions for which CMS does not provide additional reimbursement and for which CDS approaches can be helpful. You should evaluate effects from your CDS interventions on safety targets covered by public reporting, reimbursement, accreditation and other drivers in close collaboration with those in your organization responsible for addressing these drivers. This includes selecting the specific safety-related metrics you will examine, as well as conducting the evaluation and using the results to drive further improvements.

Problems with medication use are an important patient safety hazard and have been a primary target for CDS intervention. A previous book in this series provides guidance on implementing and assessing medication-focused CDS interventions,[30] and an article entitled "Clarifying Adverse Drug Events: A Clinician's Guide to Terminology, Documentation, and Reporting" provides a helpful overview of ADE terms and their implications for clinicians.[31] You can assess ADE rates, both before and after applying targeted CDS, by looking in CISs for signals suggesting possible drug-related incidents, such as sudden medication stop orders, antidote ordering and certain abnormal laboratory values.[32]

The Institute for Healthcare Improvement (IHI) built on earlier research in developing a broadly applicable tool for estimating ADE rates. This Trigger Tool for Measuring ADEs consists of "triggers" that suggest a possible ADE. Triggers include administration of diphenhydramine (commonly used to treat allergic reactions to medications) or naloxone (used to reverse narcotic overdoses). Figure 9-2 provides a detailed trigger list and the ADE-related process that may be associated with each.[33] The triggers do not confirm an ADE, but they suggest situations that may warrant further investigation to determine whether an ADE has occurred. In addition to a trigger list, IHI also provides a Web-based tool for tracking and investigating trigger events and tools for estimating event rates per admission and per 1,000 drug administrations.[34]

IHI also provides trigger tools for identifying adverse events in other situations, such as for peri-operative, outpatient, pediatric and intensive care unit settings.[35] Others in your organization might be using such trigger tools in safety-related efforts, and you can explore whether and how these tools might be useful in assessing safety outcomes related to your CDS efforts.

As noted in the process metrics discussion, you should look for adverse events (such as drug-drug interactions, missed health maintenance testing, missed laboratory monitoring, etc.) that result when the recipient overrides an alert that could have prevented the error if it was addressed appropriately. When you find these, you should investigate causes for the missed CDS opportunities (for example, alert

---

Figure 9-2: Trigger Tool: List of Triggers Suggesting Possible ADEs

Trigger	Process identified
T1: Diphenhydramine	Hypersensitivity reaction or drug effect
T2: Vitamin K	Over-anticoagulation with warfarin
T3: Flumazenil	Oversedation with benzodiazepine
T4: Droperidol	Nausea/emesis related to drug use
T5: Naloxone	Oversedation with narcotic
T6: Antidiarrheals	Adverse drug event
T7: Sodium polystryene	Hyperkalemia related to renal impairment or drug effect
T8: PTT > 100 seconds	Over-anticoagulation with heparin
T9: INR > 6	Over-anticoagulation with warfarin
T10: WBC < 3000 x 10⁶/µl	Neutropenia related to drug or disease
T11: Serum glucose < 50 mg/dl	Hypoglycemia related to insulin use
T12: Rising serum creatinine	Renal insufficiency related to drug use
T13: *Clostridium difficile* positive stool	Exposure to antibiotics
T14: Digoxin level > 2 ng/ml	Toxic digoxin level
T15: Lidocaine level > 5 ng/ml	Toxic lidocaine level
T16: Gentamicin or tobramycin levels peak > 10 µg/ml, trough > 2 ug/ml	Toxic levels of antibiotics
T17: Amikacin levels peak > 30 µg/ml, trough > 10 µg/ml	Toxic levels of antibiotics
T18: Vancomycin level > 26 µg/ml	Toxic levels of antibiotics
T19: Theophylline level > 20 µg/ml	Toxic levels of drug
T20: Oversedation, lethargy, falls	Related to overuse of medication
T21: Rash	Drug related/adverse drug event
T22: Abrupt medication stop	Adverse drug event
T23: Transfer to higher level of care	Adverse event
T24: Customized to individual institution	Adverse event

PTT = prothrombin time; INR = international normalized ratio; WBC = white blood cells.

Source: Rozich JD, Haraden CR, Resar RK. Adverse drug event trigger tool: a practical methodology for measuring medication related harm. *Qual Saf Health Care.* 2003; 12(3):194-200. Used with permission.

fatigue as suggested by a high ratio of overrides/total number of alerts).

Another safety-related issue (tied to a process metric) to examine on a periodic basis is the number and percent of orders entered as free text in CPOE systems.[36] CDS interventions, such as order sets and order sentences, should minimize the orders entered in this fashion since they may be more prone to error and not subject to CDS safety checks. It is important to determine if such free text-related errors are occurring, and to take corrective steps as needed.

Keep in mind that while CDS can help reduce patient harm, it can also inadvertently cause it, or lead to other unintended consequences. e-Iatrogenesis is a term that refers to patient harm caused, at least in part, by HIT. It is therefore critical that you remain vigilant for these potential complications from your CDS efforts.[37] CDS-related e-Iatrogenesis can arise in various ways, including errors in logic or knowledge underlying the intervention, or in users' response to information presented, as well as other related problems that lead to inappropriate treatment.[38] You can minimize these complications through careful attention to development and testing as outlined in earlier chapters. As discussed earlier, excessive false-positive alerting can also distract clinicians from important care details and thus create problems. Real or imagined e-Iatrogenesis can undermine confidence and support for your CDS interventions, so you should look carefully for any hazards that the interventions create and address them appropriately.

Quality

The Institute of Medicine (IOM) has defined healthcare quality as: "The degree to which health services for individuals and populations increase the likelihood of desired health outcomes and are consistent with current professional knowledge."[39] Safety metrics, as just discussed, examine whether CDS is helping to avoid "undesirable health outcomes"; quality metrics look more broadly at whether CDS is supporting "desirable health outcomes" (such as patients living longer or being less burdened by disease).

As with safety, this link can be very difficult to firmly establish. Again, evaluating pertinent CDS structure and process metrics, together with outcomes more directly associated with care quality, can help assess the relationship between CDS interventions and corresponding quality measurements—and enhance it over time.

The quality outcomes supported by your CDS interventions may take a long time to manifest and may cross care settings. For example, CDS interventions targeted to increase appropriate inpatient medication use after a heart attack may not fully deliver outcome benefits until long after the patient is discharged. In these cases, proxy measures that examine processes (for example, the extent to which evidence-based services are ordered and delivered) and intermediate outcomes (such as length of hospitalization, disease-severity indicators such as HbA1c in diabetics, readmissions, and short-term mortality) can shed light on the role of CDS in supporting desirable quality outcomes.

As emphasized earlier, your specific metrics and measurement efforts should be connected to the greatest extent possible with broader organizational improvement and reporting initiatives. For your CDS intervention quality targets, there often—if not always—should be broader improvement efforts beyond the specific CDS approach. Your CDS interventions and measurement approach should have been developed in concert with these efforts, and CDS-related measurement activities should likewise occur collaboratively.

Guides are available for calculating some statistics pertinent to healthcare quality measurement, such as ALOS, mortality and morbidities.[40] Your organization should use, to the greatest extent possible, industry standard metrics that are most appropriate to the issue at hand. This helps establish credibility for evaluation results; as with any measurement effort, there is a tendency for those who disagree with the results to argue with methods.

To illustrate important nuances in outcome metrics, consider two methods that can be used to calculate ALOS:

- Method 1: (total discharge days/total discharges) = ALOS (in days);
- Method 2: (total inpatient days of care/total admissions) = ALOS (in days).

Because different data items are used in these calculations, they may produce different results in some circumstances. For example, if there is a large percentage of long-stay patients that are in the facility for longer than the measurement interval, Method 2 will not fully account for those inpatient days.[41] This example illustrates the importance of carefully choosing the metric most appropriate for the circumstance and doing so in coordination with related measurement and reporting efforts.

Because medication orders are an important component of "health services likely to increase desired health outcomes," you should consider measuring medication-related CDS effects on the number, class and type of medications ordered and the situations in which they are used. The literature sampling on outcomes—and related CDS to help improve them—outlined in the following bullets may help augment your approach to quality-related outcome measures for CDS to improve medication use:

- Percent of patients treated with recommended drugs for specific conditions.[42]
  - CDS in the form of guidelines and recommended options delivered via CPOE improve appropriate prescribing.
- Percent of patients requiring VTE prophylaxis that actually received it and effects on VTE events.[43]
  - Alerts increased prophylaxis rates and markedly reduced VTE events (deep vein thrombosis and pulmonary embolism) in high-risk hospitalized patients.
- Percent appropriate antimicrobial prescribing and effects on mortality and drug resistance.[44]
  - Local clinician-driven guidelines embedded in a decision support system reduced mortality, ADEs and cost per treated patient with no increase in antimicrobial resistance.

- Improvement in symptoms and quality of life for patients in primary care practice with upper GI complaints.[45]
  - Evaluation with (cases) and without (control) intervention using CDS tool for complaint diagnosis/treatment; tool improved symptom severity and quality of life. Physician visits, medication costs and diagnostics tests were all significantly reduced among cases. The average cost for six months' treatment and follow-up was $199 for cases, compared with an average of $336 in the control group.

Financial

As noted in the CDS literature overview in Chapter 1, there is no current robust evidence base documenting strongly favorable CDS effects on financial outcomes, though some studies show positive effects.[46,47] As financial pressures on health systems, providers and consumers escalate, it will become increasingly important for you to quantify and optimize these effects. There are many potential financial metrics to consider, along with related quality and safety effects. Keep in mind that financial implications are pertinent for all stakeholders (for example, hospital or practice, patient and others). The following small sampling of categories will hopefully help stimulate ideas for specific financial metrics to track for CDS interventions and intervention packages within your CDS program.

- Cost savings to patients and providers from appropriate laboratory and radiologic test usage;
- Percent of all medication orders for preferred formulary drugs; CDS intervention (for example, order sets, alerts, automatic generic substitutions of P&T committee-approved medications, etc.) effects on this number; financial implications from resulting increased formulary compliance;
- Number of medication orders switched from an IV to oral (PO) route (for example, triggered by order sets or alerts)[48] and resulting effects on inpatient ALOS and costs;
- Financial implications of CDS targeted toward increasing quality and safety (for example, from

decreasing additional costs and ALOS related to ADEs or VTEs); see report from AHRQ, *Reducing and Preventing Adverse Drug Events to Decrease Hospital Costs;*[49]

- Costs and returns associated with CDS itself (for example, for use in cost/benefit analysis[50] and optimization);
  - Did automating specific processes with CDS (for example, replacing manual chart reviews to identify condition improvement opportunities with surveillance based on CDS rules) free up staff resources that can be deployed in other ways? Can the amount and value of this additional resource availability be quantified? This will be increasingly important as organizations apply CDS to address value-based purchasing programs (discussed in Chapters 1 and 2);
  - What are the costs associated with deploying the CDS interventions, and can they be optimized further? For example, excessive false-positive alerting or poor user acceptance of CDS interventions may require additional technical and clinical personnel time to remedy and address user concerns. What are the costs associated with this, and how can these be minimized (for example, through alert trigger tuning, user education, etc.) for this intervention? Can the learning from this experience be applied to increase the cost-effectiveness of subsequent intervention efforts?

External Standardized CDS Evaluation Tools

As healthcare payers exert increasing pressure on providers to ensure that they are buying safe and effective care, they are turning greater attention to the role that CDS plays in supporting these outcomes. A good example is the Leapfrog CPOE Evaluation Tool,[51] which was developed to encourage hospitals to successfully deploy CDS functionality targeted on improving specific patient safety and clinical quality indicators. Acute care hospitals can use the Leapfrog CPOE Evaluation Tool for credit toward the Leapfrog Group's CPOE standard, and to increase value from their CPOE/CDS efforts.

The Leapfrog CPOE Evaluation Tool works by simulating several different clinical scenarios that should evoke CDS responses. Organizations taking the test create mock patients based on the scenarios within their production CPOE system.* The evaluation examines how the system responds when the user enters various unsafe or otherwise problematic medication orders from the scenarios for these test patients. Figure 9-3 describes the various CDS categories that are evaluated by the Leapfrog tool. Individual organizations have described their experience using the tool, and such reports may be useful in optimizing how your organization approaches such tools. A study analyzing results from 62 hospitals that voluntarily used the Leapfrog CPOE test demonstrated substantial opportunities for improving their CDS performance.[52] An updated version of an outpatient-focused CPOE evaluation tool should be released by 2013 (through a mechanism other than the Leapfrog Group).[53]

EHR and CDS certification pressure may lead to increased development and use of such standardized CDS evaluations over the next several years as the Meaningful Use requirements become more stringent. Your CDS Team should consider whether and how such CDS assessment tools could accelerate your CDS and performance improvement efforts. Many organizations using standardized evaluation tools—and comparing results and lessons learned— could help widely accelerate CDS-mediated healthcare improvements.[54]

How to Measure

As the previous discussion suggests, there are somewhat different considerations for evaluating each metric type.

---

* Some healthcare organizations resist adding "test" patients within their production system. We discourage this position, since, for example, experience with the Leapfrog test has found many errors in organizations that had not activated all CDS interventions developed in the "test" system into their "live" system. Thoroughly testing a "live" EHR—including CDS interventions— is critical for safe and effective EHR operation.

Figure 9-3: CDS Categories Assessed by the Leapfrog CPOE Evaluation Tool

Category	Description
Therapeutic duplication	Therapeutic overlap with another new or active order; may be same drug; same drug class, or components of combination products
Single and cumulative dose limits	Specified dose that exceeds recommended dose ranges; will result in a cumulative dose that exceeds recommended ranges; can also include dose limits for each component of a combination product
Allergies and cross allergies	Allergy has been documented or allergy to other drug in same category exists
Contraindicated route of administration	Order specifying a route of administration that is not appropriate for the identified medication
Drug-drug and drug-food interactions	Results in known dangerous interaction when administered together with a different medication or results in an interaction in combination with a drug or food group
Contraindications/dose limits based on patient diagnosis	Contraindication based on patient diagnosis or diagnosis affects recommended dosing
Contraindications/dose limits based on patient age or weight	Contraindication based on age or weight
Contraindications/dose limits based laboratory studies	Contraindication based on laboratory studies or for which laboratory studies must be considered for dosing
Contraindications/dose limits based radiology studies	Contraindication for this patient based on interaction with contrast medium (in ordered radiology study)
Corollary	Intervention that requires an associated or secondary order to meet the standard of care (prompt to order drug levels during medication ordering)
Cost of care	Test that duplicates a service within a time frame in which there is typically minimal benefits from repeating the test
Nuisance	Order with such a slight or inconsequential interaction that clinicians typically ignore the advice/prompt

Source: Kilbridge PM, Welebob EM, Classen DC. Development of the Leapfrog methodology for evaluating hospital implemented inpatient computerized physician order entry systems. *Qual Saf Health Care.* 2006; 15(2):81-84. Used with permission.

This section provides additional details on gathering needed data and managing the measurement process.

By the time you launch target-focused CDS interventions, your CDS Team should have developed and vetted a formal intervention evaluation plan—ideally beginning early in your efforts to assess improvement opportunities and develop the interventions. This plan can evolve as needed and should consider each pertinent metric type. The following discussion outlines tasks that you should keep in mind in formulating and executing your intervention evaluation approach. Worksheets 9-1 through

9-5 can help your team think through and document these tasks.

Develop a Generic Protocol for Intervention Assessment

Your organization's response to certification, regulatory, payment and accreditation requirements likely include at least some mechanisms in place that are useful for evaluating CDS effects pertinent to these drivers. As with selecting the metrics themselves, you should likewise leverage these inter-relationships in gathering and addressing data pertinent to your chosen CDS metrics. For example, nearly all acute care facilities are reporting to CMS "core measure" performance information, such as the percentage of patients receiving specific drugs indicated for particular diseases. Infrastructure currently used for measuring, reporting and improving performance might also serve related CDS program evaluation needs.

Your framework for leveraging available infrastructure to address CDS evaluation needs might contain the following elements:

- Document how you are capturing pertinent evaluation information today. For example, time and resources required, collection method, impact on end users (if any), and timing (during or pre/post clinical encounter).
- Review measurement options for each intervention.
  - Does the new CDS intervention enable enhanced means for gathering needed evaluation information?
  - Can a report be created to automatically capture the desired information from available ISs? Determine when that report will run and confirm that information will be captured in the system, preferably in a codified manner.
  - Do you need to augment the information capture with other methods, such as chart review or end-user shadowing?
- Finalize method for capturing information (see next section).
- Educate end users on their role (such as expectations, communications, follow-up plans).

- Begin measurement process and apply to each intervention deployed.

Keep the following considerations in mind when collecting, analyzing and applying CDS performance data:

- Be careful that the data you collect mean what you think they mean. Always check with some end users to make sure that you are collecting data that reflect what is really going on in the clinical setting.
- Strive for data that are practical to gather, relevant, actionable, credible, valid, accurate and reliable. Data that are not believable or are inaccurate may not be useful—or worse (for example, if they direct attention and resources toward nonproductive activities).
- Consider practical significance in addition to statistical significance.
- Use highly readable scorecards to organize data for analysis and presentation. For example, summary graphs and red/yellow/green "stoplight" analyses, with drilldown to fuller details, can be more useful for many purposes than massive spreadsheets packed with numbers.
- Remember that you may need to cleanse the information (that is, delete irrelevant data) and use risk adjustment to facilitate appropriate comparisons.
- Remember, "Not everything that counts can be counted (for example, specific end-user concerns about intervention usefulness), and not everything that can be counted, counts."[55]

In the sections that follow, we outline more specific approaches for fleshing out the generic assessment protocol.

Consider and Select Data Collection Methods

Two important—and sometimes difficult—tasks in evaluating CDS interventions are determining where data needed for analysis reside and how you will obtain them. Reports from the systems serving up the CDS interventions (such as CPOE, EHR and other CIS/CDS applications) will be core information sources about how these interventions are performing. Most CIS/CDS vendor systems come with some standard reports, but in many cases, you will want to develop custom reports to address your specific needs. You should think about this early to maximize the reports' value and better shape how the intervention—and associated measurement capabilities—are built.

You should explore whether you can extract CDS-related error data from your facility's EHR safety reporting mechanisms.[56] Ideally these will include electronic sources, such as homegrown or commercial tools that look at administrative and/or clinical data. This information can be augmented with data from online or paper forms for clinician error reporting, if available and needed. Consider using a structured scheme for documenting patient safety events pertinent to your CDS interventions, such as the 'Common Formats' specified by AHRQ (which include HIT devices),[57] or the National Coordinating Council for Medication Error Reporting and Prevention (NCC-MERP) medication error taxonomy[58] that allows for merging and comparing medication error information across facilities *in your organization*. Note that the Institute for Safe Medication Practices (ISMP) and NCC-MERP have expressed that "Use of medication error rates to compare health care organizations is of no value."[59] This is due to differences across organizations in factors such as culture, error definitions and reporting systems, and patient populations that affect reporting and underlying error incidence. You should consider these issues carefully if you plan to compare facilities within your organization as well.[60]

Keep in mind that the data available for analysis in voluntary reporting systems will reflect actual errors only to the extent that these errors are recognized and entered into the system. Culture comes into play here, and voluntary error reporting generally isn't as rich in healthcare as in other high-risk activities such as aviation. In addition to actual errors, near-misses can be important sources for improvement pearls. If your organizational culture encourages clinicians to be open about, document and learn from all these events,

then you can leverage this information in evaluating and improving CDS interventions.

You can acquire CDS *usage* data from various sources, including CIS/CDS system-generated log files (see Figure 9-4 for an example); electronic surveys deployed close to the time interventions are used; and direct observation by, or in-person feedback sessions to, the evaluation team members.

Figure 9-5, shown on page 288, illustrates an example of how these sources facilitate data gathering to assess CDS use and effects for an order set intervention; you can use this to trigger ideas about evaluation methods for your specific interventions. For each data collection method, consider the available and desirable balance between free text versus structured information. Free text can be more expressive, while structured information is generally much easier to aggregate and analyze. Some methods such as incident reports, documentation forms completed during user shadowing, and surveys can have both free text and structured elements; you can adapt the data format to best address specific needs and constraints. Though this example is inpatient focused, you can use similar approaches to develop and document CDS evaluation data in outpatient settings. You can also glean ideas on strategies to gather outcome information from the discussion and literature references in the earlier section under *What to Measure*.

Once you're informed about data-collection methods available in your organization and ISs generally, you can begin to develop more detailed protocols for evaluating use and effects for each deployed CDS intervention—and for applying this information to drive continuous improvements.

Assess Intervention Use

We presented the foundations for this evaluation in the sections on response time, structure and process metrics. You can use the data-collection methods and other elements presented in Figure 9-5 as a starting point for a plan to answer key questions about intervention use. For example, who is using the intervention? Why (or why not)? When? Where? How?

Figure 9-4: Sample Alert Log File

Alert ID	Provider ID	Patient ID	Physical Location	Date/ Time	Alert Accepted, Rejected (or Simply Closed)	Override Reason
1234 (Heparin_physician _post-op)	1234 (Dr. C)	1243 (J., Mary)	4 West (Post-surgical care)	2 Feb 1:00 PM	Accept	
1234 (Heparin_physician _post-op)	1243 (Dr. Y)	1253 (J., Roberta)	4 West (Post-surgical care)	2 Feb 12:06 PM	Accept	
1234 (Heparin_physician _post-op)	1234 (Dr. C)	1278 (L., Rebecca)	4 West (Post-surgical care)	3 Feb 2:07 PM	Reject	Aware/Will monitor
1234 (Heparin_physician _ post-op)	1543 (Dr. M)	1987 (Q., Mary)	4 West (Post-surgical care)	3 Feb 12:19 PM	Closed	
1234 (Heparin_physician _post-op)	1090 (Dr. S)	1009 (C., Victoria)	4 West (Post-surgical care)	29 Jan 12:54 PM	Accept	
1234 (Heparin_physician _post-op)	9834 (Dr. K)	1009 (C., Victoria)	3 South (Med-surg)	15 Jan 1:45 PM	Reject	Patient not eligible
1234 (Heparin_physician _post-op)	3457 (Dr. H)	0456 (C., Douglas)	3 South (Med-surg)	4 Feb 2:00 PM	Accept	

In general, you should use basic usage measurement (such as for each question just mentioned, except for "why") as much as possible via automated or custom reports whose output is objective. Some data gathering may still require patient chart review and/or end-user interaction in person or electronically, for example, to answer "why" an intervention is being used.

Figure 9-6 is a sample protocol for evaluating order set use, both in paper-based and CPOE environments, and applying the results.

Assess End-User Impact, Satisfaction and Workflow

Again, foundations for how to conduct and interpret these measurements are presented in the earlier discussion on response time, structure and process

metrics. Some effects on users are suggested by response time data (how much time do users spend waiting for CDS or responding to the intervention?) and process data (what can be inferred about user frustration based on alert override data?).

These objective clues are supplemented by more subjective measurements based on eliciting feedback from each end-user group. You can determine their satisfaction with CDS intervention value and usability with data-collection methods such as those outlined in Figure 9-5. Also consider the following approaches:

- Survey assessments pre- and post-intervention launch and periodically thereafter;
- End-user interviews, as well as ad hoc interactions with evaluation team members to elicit feedback;
- An online forum for user feedback, including specific e-mail channels or an intranet blog.

Figure 9-5: Methods for Gathering CDS Use and Effects Data as Applied to Inpatient Order Sets

Data Collection Method	Assessments/Goals	Timing	Data Gathering Resources (to Supplement Evaluation Team)
Chart review (electronic [semi-automated vs. manual] vs. paper)	Review appropriateness and outcomes related to medication ordering for specific diseases	Post-discharge	Clinicians
End-user shadowing	Reasons for using/not using order sets Workflow impact End-user satisfaction/issues	Real time	Qualitative researchers
System-generated reports (CPOE)	Overall utilization by diagnosis and physician Specific medication utilization for each order set Modifications to default medication selections	During hospitalization	Data analysts to extract data or run reports
Incident reporting	Identify specific CDS-related problem areas; self-reported, ad hoc	During hospitalization or post-discharge	Clinicians involved in patient care
Qualitative end-user surveys	End-user satisfaction	Post-discharge	Individuals experienced in data interpretation

Intervention effects on workflow are important factors in user satisfaction, productivity and efficiency. Key questions here include:

- How many steps and how much time is needed to use an intervention (for example, order set, documentation tool, infobutton), and how does this compare with alternative approaches for users to perform the underlying tasks?
- For alerts, how many steps and how much time is needed to accept an alert and its suggestions, or to override it?
- How much variation is there from the "accepted" workflow? Many times, individuals don't use recommended workflows because they are following prior habits or because they have found an easier or better way than the recommended approach to accomplish the same task.

As with user satisfaction, you can glean some of this workflow information from system reports on response times, but subjective information is useful to flesh out user perceptions. You can obtain more objective data by shadowing users on a periodic basis and documenting a brief time and motion study.[61]

Assess Patient Impact

We considered approaches for evaluating CDS effects that are particularly important to patients (such as improvements in care safety and quality) earlier in the discussion on outcomes. These effects may include:

- Avoiding harmful clinical errors;
- Appropriately using prophylactic medications to prevent avoidable complications and conditions (such as VTE and vaccine-preventable illness);

Figure 9-6: Measuring Order Set Utilization

Paper Order Sets

- Method – chart review, user feedback
- Steps
  - Choose a manageable number of priority order sets for initial evaluation (such as those that address conditions covered by core measures).
  - Make sure all order sets are available in all areas in which ordering takes place (for example, ED, all units, ambulatory offices, online).
  - After discharge, run a report for all patients discharged with same diagnoses (for example, those pertinent to the core measures under study).
  - Perform chart pulls (for a random subset of discharges covering all pertinent physicians/specialties and locations), and determine whether order set was utilized.
  - Review key order set subsections, such as medications or tests covered by the measure.
    - Capture which items (medications/tests) were used.
    - When a specific key item (such as aspirin for heart attack) was not used, determine if reason was captured in chart and catalog it.
  - Interview/survey a subset of physicians (especially those who did not use the order set at all or did not use the key items as called for by core measures) to assess reasons for non-compliance, or (in those who did respond as desired) feedback on order set use.
- Reports
  - Create order set utilization report by physician, and determine if there is a difference by:
    - Specialty
    - Ordering location (ED, floor, office, other)
  - Create report of which key items were:
    - Ordered (including user feedback on the intervention)
    - Not ordered when expected (catalog reasons documented in chart and conveyed personally by prescriber)
- Goals
  - These reports should be used to drive enhancements, such as:
    - Increased ease with which order sets are accessed
    - Continual refinement of the order sets, the medications on them and how they are presented (for example, explanatory text, default order selections)
    - Updated communications to the end users, for example, about order set value

Electronic Order Sets with CPOE

- Method – electronic reporting with chart review as necessary; user feedback
- Steps
  - Choose a manageable number of priority order sets for initial evaluation (such as those that address conditions covered by core measures).
  - Make sure all order sets under study are available online through the system.
  - Run a report by diagnosis and physician to determine how often pertinent order set was utilized (many CPOE systems provide this functionality).

continued on next page

Figure 9-6 continued

○ Create a report to show whether key items (such as medications or tests) indicated by core measure were ordered (you may need to perform chart reviews to determine this).

○ Create a report to show reason documented by prescriber for not ordering indicated key item (for example, if alerts/reminders are fired and include opportunity for prescriber to document override reason). Ideally, you will have set up the CPOE system to accept coded reasons and deployed it in such a way that users are properly documenting reasons; some manual review (ideally through an electronic system) may be needed to determine why an indicated item was not ordered.

— Interview/survey a subset of physicians (especially those who did not use the order set at all or did not use key items as called for by core measures) to assess reasons for non-compliance, or (in those who did respond as desired) feedback on order set use.

• Reports and Goals (same as previously outlined for paper order sets, plus the following item)

— Improve end-user training, as needed, on underlying CPOE system and order set "tips and tricks" to increase use and usefulness.

• Appropriately using therapies that minimize morbidity and mortality from acute and chronic disease;

• Patients understanding their conditions and treatments better, resulting in their increased satisfaction, engagement, adherence and health status;

• Patient financial benefits resulting from prescribers selecting cost-effective diagnostic and treatment approaches;

• Patient satisfaction with their care experience, for example, as assessed through survey tools.[62]

Once again, this information can be collected by automated reports and manual queries in information systems, formal and informal patient interviews, surveys, and other means.

Although clinicians typically have been the primary recipients for CDS interventions, patients themselves are increasingly important CDS intervention users. More widespread use of PHRs and related tools is accelerating this trend. As a result, the "end user" assessments presented earlier regarding utilization, workflow and satisfaction will apply to patients, as well, when they are the end users.

Assess Financial Impact to the Organization

You can use the metric types discussed earlier under "Financial" in the "Outcome Measures" section to quantify the effects that one or more interventions have on departmental and organizational finances. Data for these assessments will typically come from a combination of chart review (ideally electronic and semi-automated) and system-generated reports (for example, from administrative and financial systems).

For metrics such as formulary adherence, ALOS, and cost per case, available ISs can typically produce needed reports. In cases for which it is necessary to correlate data from disparate clinical and financial systems, the analysis can be problematic because these systems may use different coding schemes and definitions for key terms. You may need patience, perseverance and close collaboration with pertinent individuals in finance, IT, and your system vendors, and other departments to appropriately assess financial effects from CDS interventions. This effort can be very worthwhile, especially in organizations such ROI data influences resource allocation to projects. As cited earlier in the section on financial metrics, there are examples of well-executed ROI studies that might trigger ideas for your evaluations.

Emerging financial drivers in healthcare—such as value-based purchasing and Meaningful Use initiatives—will trigger major changes in how your organization delivers care and manages related business functions. For example, your CDS interventions will increasingly be tied to metrics that have financial implications. You should undertake CDS financial evaluation activities in the context of—and leveraging tools from—your organization's broader response to these financial imperatives.

When to Measure

Measurement takes place throughout the intervention lifecycle—from needs assessment through design, testing, launch and maintenance. After launch, the appropriate measurement frequency is driven by what you are measuring, how quickly the underlying outcomes and processes are likely to change, and how you will use the evaluation results. For example, the measurements may drive intervention enhancement, public reporting, and/or incentive-based staff compensation—each of which may have implications for assessment timing. Ideally, you should only release interventions if you can devote at least some attention to evaluating effects, so *every* deployed intervention should be subject to at least *some* periodic analysis.

Early after initially deploying CDS interventions, you should evaluate response time, as well as structural and process metrics to ensure proper functioning and look for negative unanticipated consequences. Outcome measures (such as clinical, operational, and financial) should be assessed at the earliest time you would expect to see a change; sooner if the other metrics suggest that something about the CDS interventions might be moving things in the wrong direction. Once the evaluation reveals how much and how fast key post-launch metrics are changing, you can adjust the measurement scope, detail and frequency accordingly.

The reality is that most organizations do not have enough resources or time to measure every

intervention with the detail just described, and as often as they would like. Therefore, you must prioritize measurement activities, focusing at least on ensuring that there are no major problems with any intervention and getting at least a gross sense of their value and any unintended consequences. Beyond that, you should use governance mechanisms (as discussed in Chapter 2) to prioritize and schedule measurement efforts across interventions in a manner that optimally supports your CDS program goals.

What to Do with the Results

Your overall evaluation goals should include determining the extent to which the deployed CDS interventions are achieving the targeted objectives, the nature of any unintended consequences, and lessons that can be applied to continually enhancing the value that the CDS interventions bring to improving care delivery and outcomes. Key activities related to these goals include communicating the evaluation results and their implications to stakeholders and using the results as input to subsequent performance improvement cycles.

Many organizations devote substantial resources to deploying CISs and associated CDS functionality, yet underplay evaluation and, therefore, fail to fully engage in effective PI. Those who heed the guidance to plan for measurement beginning in early project phases, and execute a thoughtful evaluation approach throughout the intervention lifecycle, are well-positioned to use this feedback loop to close the gap between desired and actual clinical and CDS performance.

If the data about CDS results are accurate, pertinent and credible, they will provide a strong foundation for action. Your task then is to convey this information to other stakeholders (especially organizational leadership) so they can respond appropriately, including supporting subsequent improvement rounds.

As discussed under "Who Will Measure" in Chapter 3, one or more individuals responsible for your CDS evaluation should clearly and credibly articulate the intervention evaluation results and implications to others. Your objective is to have the recipients understand and believe the information, and to prepare and motivate them to take action appropriate for their role (for example, as outlined in Figures in 2-1 and 2-6).

The following are some considerations for this critical communication function:

- Why should evaluation results be communicated?
  - To the extent that senior organizational or practice leadership drives CDS-supported goals, the evaluation results will be very important to them and others. For example, when compensation plans and other powerful drivers are tied to results, then scrutiny over the accuracy of results (particularly if unfavorable) may be intense. Methodologic rigor, transparency and close stakeholder engagement throughout the evaluation process can be helpful here.
  - Each stakeholder can help enhance the CDS intervention value, and you should consider what information each person and role needs in order to do this. Tasks associated with these roles may include revising targets and priorities and allocating resources (leadership); designing and launching enhanced CDS interventions to address current or revised targets (the CDS Team and collaborators); and helping make interventions practical and useful and successfully adopting them (end users). Information about what has been done so far (that is, from structure measurements) and the result (from process and outcomes measures) is key to addressing these tasks.
- Who should receive this information? (See Figure 2-5 for potential stakeholders.)
  - Consider assessing each "customer type" who needs communication about the evaluation results; create a strategy and tracking tool to determine what communication they need, how often they need it, and who will deliver it. The following identifies several such "customers" who will likely appear on your list, depending on your care setting.
    - Project and organizational leadership;

- End users (in larger organizations, usually at a department level at a minimum and, in many cases, at an individual level);
- Others besides intervention end users, whose care-related activities are required for ultimate intervention success (such as those who provide tests or services called for by the intervention);
- Patients and community (care quality improvements can be a differentiator in the healthcare marketplace);
- CIS and CDS vendors (to continually improve the systems and their capabilities);
- In hospitals and large practices, quality and PI teams, as well as the pertinent CIS team (such as EHR, CPOE, PHR).
- How can the information be conveyed? (See also communication discussions in Chapter 8.)
  - Dashboards
    - Focus on organizing and presenting data. Many analytical and business intelligence applications can create dashboards for review and presentation. Consider different dashboards for different audiences to address specific perspectives and needs for this overview information.
  - Scorecards
    - Convey information about performance relative to specific targets. Like dashboards, scorecards can be created via automated systems or manually from available data and generic applications such as spreadsheets; often used with departments and individual clinicians for feedback on performance.[63]
  - Department or practice meetings
    - Representatives from the CDS, quality, or PI team present evaluation results at regular department meetings with a focus on continual performance improvement. Over time, representatives from the specific functions should present the data and manage the communication to their peers. It is also important to consider adding informal communication among physician leadership.

Both anecdotes and data can be powerful 'story tellers' to build support for the CDS interventions and program.

– Marketing (formal or informal)

   ○ In collaboration with the marketing function and others within the organization, develop and execute a communication plan to convey pertinent messages about the program results, as appropriate, to the community, other internal stakeholders, and other organizations (for example, via journal publications and conference presentations). Recall the caution noted earlier about obtaining IRB approval if you are considering publishing evaluation results.

• When should evaluation results be presented?

   – Develop a schedule that is appropriate for each stakeholder group and each intervention type. Keep in mind the pace at which metrics are likely to change and the role that each stakeholder plays in responding to the results.

If you have conducted your evaluation thoughtfully and paid careful attention to communicating about it, then the analysis results should speak clearly to recipients about what the results mean and what should be done about them. When powered by these data, subsequent iterations through the steps outlined in this guide should become more efficient and effective.

Managing Interventions and Related Processes Over Time

As detailed in Chapter 4, knowledge management is a crucial CDS program activity that applies to the overall CDS asset portfolio, as well as to individual interventions. Monitoring and maintaining the portfolio's currency and appropriateness over time should occur in conjunction with your efforts to assess and improve individual intervention use and usefulness. For example, stakeholders receiving CDS intervention evaluation results include those responsible for maintaining that intervention's content. In a small practice, this might be a single individual (in consultation with partners), while in a large hospital

or health system, it may be a formal CDS or departmental subcommittee (perhaps directed by a subject matter expert). In any case, the evaluation results are one input into decisions about potential refinements to the intervention content.

At this point, you might review Chapter 4 on knowledge management, focusing on recommendations there for maintaining deployed interventions. For example, Figure 4-1: Key Attributes to Track for Deployed CDS Interventions; the section on Maintaining your CDS Assets; and Worksheet 4-1 might be particularly useful.

CONSIDERATIONS FOR HOSPITALS/HEALTH SYSTEMS
Measurement (Outcomes)

• For interventions that may cause system-generated delays for uses (such as alerts that require time-consuming calculations), consider generating a system response time report similar to that shown in Figure 9-7. These data should be monitored on a regular basis and any increases in response time addressed ASAP. For example, new interventions that require complex processing, overall processing load on hardware systems, and many other factors, can affect processing time—and these effects aren't rare. Corrective actions might include fixing any bugs that creep into the intervention and adding system memory and processing capability. These issues illustrate the importance of close collaboration between the CDS Team and IT staff in monitoring and addressing system performance related to deployed interventions.

• Your organization may be using dashboards more frequently to address various performance improvement imperatives—including those that are the focus for your CDS interventions—and you can explore collaboration opportunities with pertinent departments and users. This might include the CDS Team helping to enhance other dashboards with useful information gathered from CDS evaluations and those other users contributing data and dashboard functionality helpful for tracking performance of specific interventions.

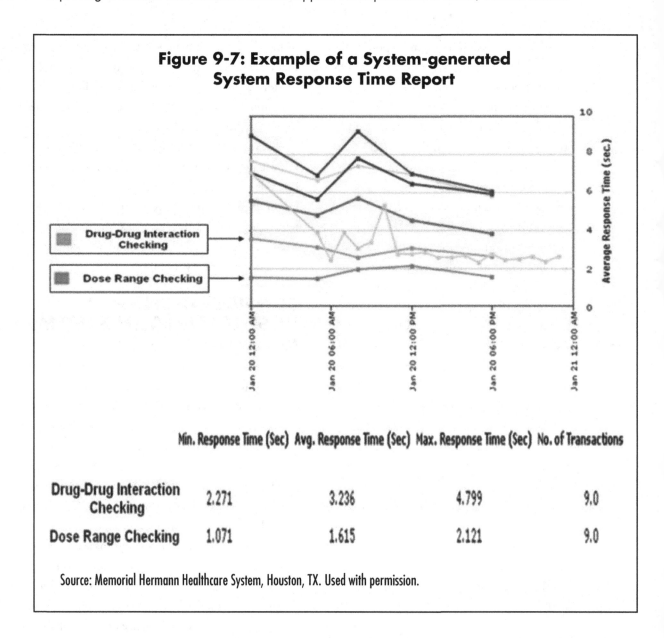

Figure 9-7: Example of a System-generated System Response Time Report

	Min. Response Time (Sec)	Avg. Response Time (Sec)	Max. Response Time (Sec)	No. of Transactions
Drug-Drug Interaction Checking	2.271	3.236	4.799	9.0
Dose Range Checking	1.071	1.615	2.121	9.0

Source: Memorial Hermann Healthcare System, Houston, TX. Used with permission.

- Consider publicizing your evaluation strategies and results via articles, presentations at local and national healthcare meetings, collaborative initiatives (such those your vendor may provide or the effort mentioned in the Epilogue). Such sharing will be important for delivering CDS-enabled performance improvements at the speed and global scale that are now required.

Measurement (Processes)

- Interact directly as much as possible with end users and other stakeholders, especially regarding high-stakes CDS interventions you have launched. There's no substitute for face-to-face interactions to really learn what's going on. Schedule interviews and focus groups, as well as ad hoc interactions from evaluation team walk rounds to elicit feedback. The CMIO, physician champion(s), other leaders and CDS Team members should be highly visible—especially during early post-launch evaluations for major interventions.

Maintenance (See also Chapter 4)

- Make sure you have a multidisciplinary team with adequate expertise and clear leadership responsible to monitor and maintain the clinical content in new interventions. Balance the team's clinical perspectives on the content—including generalist and specialty physicians, nursing, pharmacy, patients and others as appropriate.

- Consider working toward a clinical content repository—external to clinical applications and with a Web-based viewer that allows anyone in the organization to review the clinical content—to foster maintenance. When all knowledge artifacts cannot reside in a single knowledge base, the repository can be a virtual one, pointing to the various places and applications in the overall health information system where the knowledge resides and can be viewed.

- Keep any eye on emerging local and broader-based tools for CDS content management. Explore options to purchase, develop or collaborate on such tools. Purchase or develop an enterprise-wide tool to maintain the controlled clinical terminology concepts required to trigger your CDS interventions.

CONSIDERATIONS FOR SMALL PRACTICES
Measurement

- Execute your plan for identifying, tracking and addressing intended and unintended intervention behavior and effects, as outlined in this and the preceding two chapters. Hopefully, you will have worked with your CIS/CDS suppliers to apply their system capabilities to collect, store and make available the data required to measure and monitor CDS intervention performance. Use these data to understand:
  - Whether the intervention is functioning as expected (for example, ensuring that it does not adversely affect system response time and that it appears in the proper fashion at the correct time);
  - Whether and how the intervention affects clinician behavior (for example, if it leads to improved documentation in targeted areas);

Whether the intervention affects care process measures (such as whether it is improving a specific PQRS measure); and
  - How the intervention affects patient outcomes (for example, whether HbA1c levels in diabetic patients—and associated morbidities—are improving).

- If there's only one physician and one nurse in the practice, than reviewing the intervention results and planning next steps might not require extensive discussion—though even then, feedback from others such as peer practices, the CIS/CDS supplier and REC can be useful. In general, at least some internal discussion about the CDS intervention results and follow-up will be necessary and valuable.

Communication

- Make and use an intervention effects communication plan for reporting intervention results to pertinent stakeholders and for supporting continuous monitoring and improvement (the launch communication discussion in Chapter 8 provides additional ideas and tools to support this work). The plan should address who will gather and share the results, to whom will they be communicated and how often, and how decisions will be made about next steps.

- This communication and planning should be scaled to the intervention and practice size—that is, it should be robust for major new CDS intervention configurations tied to central practice drivers (such as pay for performance targets), but much less involved for more minor CDS enhancements (such as a specific new problem-specific documentation form). Likewise, small practices with several clinicians will need more formal communication approaches than one with just a physician and nurse.

- Use available communication channels—such as formal practice meetings, informal gatherings and conversations, and paper/electronic bulletin boards—to share and celebrate successes from each round of applying CDS to achieving practice improvement goals. A growing sense of shared potency within the practice around leveraging CDS will provide the foundation needed to tackle increasingly challenging and important improvement goals.

Maintenance

- Execute your plan for reviewing and updating deployed interventions, periodically and as needs arise (see Chapter 4). Although your CIS/CDS providers may largely handle actual content updating, there should be a person in the practice responsible for monitoring each intervention's currency and appropriateness.

- Make sure that the EHR and any related CDS content suppliers have processes in place to ensure that your interventions are evidence-based and current. Ideally, you should be able to engage in detailed discussions about their editorial process, ongoing training of editors, literature surveillance and analysis, content update methodologies and tools, and ensure that these are in sync with your practice needs and expectations.

- Determine—with input from these suppliers—whether, when and how practice personnel (such as CDS champion/content owner or practice manager) can and should customize CDS logic and/or content; for example, drug-drug interaction checking, drug-allergy checking, quality measure reminders, order sets and documentation templates. Work with these suppliers to make it as easy as possible to validate and incorporate updates, monitor appropriateness, and ensure critical changes as needed to the CDS intervention content. This can include securing appropriate training for practice staff that will make these changes and providing feedback that helps the vendors enhance tool user-friendliness and needed functionality.

- If your small practice has a collaborative culture that has embraced CDS, informal e-mail communication can stand-in for formal knowledge management procedures in select situations. For example, an asynchronous conversation via e-mail about a non-controversial change to an intervention parameter might be adequate to achieve consensus about the change, rather than a more formal meeting and decision process. In any case, significant changes should be documented for future reference and medico-legal purposes.

CONSIDERATIONS FOR HEALTH IT SOFTWARE PROVIDERS
Capabilities

- CIS/CDS system suppliers should provide mechanisms that enable their provider clients to collect, store and make available the data required to measure and monitor the CDS intervention metrics discussed throughout this chapter.

- Ideally, all measurements should be stored in an easily accessible location and include information that will help users understand and apply the information; for example, time/date stamp, patient and intervention user identity, and intervention delivery/access location. Aggregating and sharing information about intervention use and effects—at least among intervention vendor clients—could accelerate advancement and widespread adoption of CDS best practices (see, for example, initiative referenced in the Epilogue).

- User-friendly CDS dashboards for presenting these measurements would be very helpful to provider organizations. For example, by displaying summary statistics (with graphs as appropriate) for each CDS intervention including, for example, the firing and override rate for all alerts, the number of times each order set was used, and how often users accessed online reference information.

- The dashboard should allow CDS implementers to drill down to see for example, how specific clinicians responded to particular alerts, which order sets were used the most, or which type of clinical users were using the reference information the most.

- Ready access to this dashboard information—and how the metrics change over time—can be helpful to CDS implementers in an analogous fashion to how organized patient data presentation helps clinicians and patients make informed clinical decisions.

Maintenance

- It is an increasing challenge for provider organizations to ensure that all their deployed CDS interventions remain current and appropriate. Consider ways that you can enhance your support for this critical task, for example, through closer CIS and CDS supplier collaborations on making CDS interventions more 'plug-and-play' across clinical information systems. These collaborations should be informed by national HIT policy and aim toward more efficient tools for CDS implementation teams to monitor and maintain this more standardized logic and content.

WORKSHEETS
Make Sure You Have Appropriate Metrics to Assess Intervention Performance

This chapter explores in detail important metrics that covey what results your CDS interventions are producing. For each intervention, you should select specific measurements that will help your CDS Team understand how successful the intervention is in achieving the desired objective, as well as its related effects on care participants and processes.

Selecting these metrics should begin early in the needs assessment and intervention development process—certainly well before intervention launch. The selection process should involve discussions with key stakeholders, as well as your information system suppliers and others as appropriate. Worksheet 9-1 is a sample tool you can use to facilitate and document this work.

Worksheet 9-1

Metric Selection and Use

This worksheet is intended to help your CDS Team brainstorm and make explicit how you will select and use metrics to assess your intervention effects. It contains sample clinical, operational and financial metrics that are arranged into four outcome categories: efficiency, quality, safety and cost. For each intervention, complete a separate checklist. At the top of the worksheet record the CDS objective targeted by the intervention and, below that, list the intervention name. Note that interventions may address more than one clinical objective, and clinical objectives may be targeted by more than one intervention; you can modify this worksheet's structure accordingly. Consider what specific metrics might be appropriate for assessing the intervention's role in addressing its corresponding objective, and place an X in the first column for rows where the metric seems pertinent. The last three columns are a scratchpad for thinking through the "who," "when" and "how" for using each metric that you select for the intervention.

Clinical Decision Support Objective: Prevent Prescription of Medication to Allergic Patients				
Intervention Name: Prescription Allergy Alert Window				
Check Those That Apply	**Metric Type**	**Metric Owner**	**Measurement Schedule**	**Collection Method**
	Quality			
X	Mortality rate	PI coordinator	Monthly	Existing adverse event reporting process
X	Morbidity rate (including adverse drug events and reactions)	PI coordinator	Monthly	Existing adverse event reporting process
X	Length of stay changed?	Sam D. (medical records)	Monthly	Chart review— semi-automated
X	NCC-MERP outcome metrics	Jean S. (pharmacist)	Monthly	Chart review
X	Effects of CDS on number, class, and type of medications ordered	Jean S. (pharmacist)	Monthly	Existing pharmacy database

continued on next page

Worksheet 9-1 *continued*

Clinical Decision Support Objective: Prevent Prescription of Medication to Allergic Patients				
Intervention Name: Prescription Allergy Alert Window				
Check Those That Apply	**Metric Type**	**Metric Owner**	**Measurement Schedule**	**Collection Method**
	Safety			
	Are number of errors reduced at each of the following medication management nodes:			
X	Prescribing	PI coordinator	Monthly	Existing adverse event reporting process
0	Transcribing			
X	Dispensing	PI coordinator	Monthly	Existing adverse event reporting process
X	Administering	PI coordinator	Monthly	Existing adverse event reporting process
X	Are number of errors reduced at each NCC-MERP category (B to I)?	Jean S. (pharmacist)	Monthly	Existing adverse event reporting process
X	Are there unintentional adverse effects?	James V. (CDS Team/ evaluation)	Monthly X 6	Walk rounds, focus groups with clinicians to assess qualitative alert responses
	Efficiency			
X	By how much has time taken to use system increased or decreased?	PI coordinator	Weekly X 4	Silent observer, system logs
	How has efficiency been affected at the following medication manage-ment process nodes:			
X	Prescribing	PI coordinator	Weekly X 4	Silent observer, system logs
0	Transcribing			
0	Dispensing			
0	Administering			
	Cost			
X	Resource management changes due to CDS implementation — cost/benefit ratios	Joan R. (billing)	Monthly	Query current billing system
X	Change in prescribed medication costs pertinent to CDS interventions	Joan R. (billing)	Monthly	Query current billing system

Evaluate Intervention Use and Usefulness

Accurately interpreting data about CDS intervention effects—whether or not these results are favorable—requires an accurate picture of how the interventions are being used and received; for example, who is and is not accessing each CDS intervention, and what do they like and dislike about them. In addition, it is important to plan and track the CDS Team's response to any concerns raised by intervention users. Tools such as Worksheet 9-2 can help provide this picture of intervention use and issues.

Worksheet 9-2

Use and Usability Issues Log

In the first column of Worksheet 9-2, list the interventions you are monitoring. In the second column, synthesize data from all the various intervention use quantification and feedback channels as discussed in this chapter. Include both quantitative information about how often users interact with the intervention and their qualitative comments about its use and impact. Including the source for the feedback can be useful if additional details about the issue are needed from the person(s) who raised it. Documenting the feedback channel can be helpful in checking on the use and usefulness of the various feedback channels in place. For example, remediation plans can be directed as needed by the implementation team toward overuse or underuse of specific channels.

The third column logs the date that the issue first surfaced or the usage data was gathered. These dates can be helpful in assessing the rate at which the implementation team is addressing the various issues and in documenting usage trends over time (e.g., through multiple rows for the intervention, each with usage statistics and corresponding observation date). In some cases, it can be helpful to plot these data on a graph to show changes in intervention usage over time, perhaps overlaying communications and training events to demonstrate their effect.

A remediation plan for each major issue should be developed and documented in the fourth column. In the last column, you can assign relative priorities for addressing the issue, using a scale developed by the CDS Team with input from other stakeholders. This prioritization can help guide resource allocation and the remediation schedule and is driven by various factors. These include the risk to patient care from not correcting the problem, the number of users affected, the resources and time required for the fix, and the like. These relative priorities can change over time as resources such as personnel change and other interventions develop new usage issues.

This is a working document. Successfully resolved issues can be removed (ideally archived elsewhere with the date they were resolved), and new issues can be added as they occur.

continued on next page

Worksheet 9-2 *continued*

Intervention Name	Usage and Usability Issues (source/channel)	Date Noted	Remediation Plan (responsible party, date resolved)	Priority
Heparin post-op alert	Avg. 20 firings/day (EHR); 97% rejection rate. High user dissatisfaction (Anne M – intervention owner).	1 Mar	Analysis in progress to add in better data on contraindications for heparin therapy. Alert removed from production awaiting resolution (5 Mar 2005)	Medium
PTT order set	Avg. 16 uses/day (CPOE); No issues noted; good user satisfaction (Robert V – intervention owner).	1 Apr	NA	NA
PTT alert	Avg. 50 firings/day (EHR); 80% rejection rate. Nurses do not feel that it is accurate and don't have time to contact physicians after it fires (George F -CNO).	1 Apr	Consider removing the intervention.	High
Heparin post-op order set	Avg. 13 uses/day (CPOE); no issues noted (Glenda J – intervention owner).	1 Apr	NA	NA

Evaluate Intervention Impact on Target Objectives

In some respects, this is the bottom line for this whole Guide and your entire CDS program. The substantial efforts in both instances are directed toward realizing measurable and important improvements in targeted healthcare processes and outcomes through well-received and helpful CDS interventions. Preceding chapters covered selecting, configuring and launching target-focused CDS interventions. Worksheet 9-3 is the reckoning: How well have investments in the CDS intervention(s) paid the anticipated dividends? The answer should consider all the potential benefit types—and unanticipated consequences—discussed in this chapter.

To the greatest extent possible, your assessments should be quantitative and compared to baseline measurements. Ideally, you have an individual or team in place focused on realizing CDS benefits that is charged with gathering and analyzing the needed evaluation data and reporting the results. Getting the needed quantitative information can be difficult for some improvements and may require a combination of strategies. These can include extracting data through various reporting mechanisms from your organization's clinical, administrative and financial databases. These systems often produce standard reports or have query tools, though some data might still need to be processed manually.

Keep in mind that key definitions might vary across these systems, making it difficult to create a unified picture of intervention effects. For example, if medical conditions are defined differently in financial and clinical systems, it might be problematic to assess the financial implications of specific clinical changes. Healthcare data analysis vendors and consultants have experience with such complexities and can also help generate the needed measurement information.

Often, multiple interventions are focused on a single clinical objective, so it is important to clarify whether the targets and performance measures pertain to the objective or to a specific intervention. For example, a clinical objective might be to improve monitoring for patients receiving IV heparin, so that 95% of patients on this therapy receive the indicated monitoring.* A physician order set that makes it easier to include this testing with other orders might be one useful CDS intervention to accomplish this. However, the compliance target for this intervention might be less than 100% (e.g., if only a fraction of physicians are using CPOE). Thus, targets and baselines for objectives and the corresponding interventions need to be considered and evaluated separately. Improved compliance with the intervention is expected to improve performance toward the clinical objective. However, this should not be taken for granted because a variety of factors can decouple these changes.

Enhancements assessed qualitatively are also important and should be documented as well. For example, user-perceived improvements in workflow, confidence in decision making, and appreciation for the "clinical safety net" are all desirable intervention effects worth noting.

Be aware that careful benefits measurement is often time-consuming and costly, and relatively few organizations currently do it very well. Considering these measurement issues early in working with your CIS infrastructure and developing the CDS interventions hopefully helped optimize your access to needed measurement data. As CIS and CDS systems evolve further, especially in light of pay-for-performance trends, these data should become easier to obtain.

Do not necessarily expect to fully achieve your objectives on the first measurement round. Progress will depend on various factors, including time between measurements. Establish reasonable measurement intervals and expectations for improvement speed based on input from key stakeholders. If formal accountability for realizing CDS benefits has been assigned (for example, with implications for job performance assessment or departmental budgeting), then care and collaboration in setting and measuring these benefits becomes particularly critical.

---

* 100% might not be a reasonable target for many objectives (e.g., because there are often extenuating circumstances for a small percent of patients that would preclude them from being managed according to the objective).

Worksheet 9-3

Performance against Objectives

This worksheet is anchored in the first column with the clinical objectives for which you are tracking deployed interventions. In the second column, record the organizational priority that the intervention addresses—this helps further anchor intervention monitoring in organizational imperatives. Include the broad organizational priority category (Efficiency, Quality, Safety, Cost) and the specific clinical goal (for example, from the top of Worksheet 5-2). Data for the following four columns can be brought forward from other worksheets where you have recorded this information (such as Worksheet 7-2). Note that a single clinical objective might be followed by several rows of interventions if an intervention package was implemented to address the objective. When documenting baseline performance and desired and actual improvement, make sure you are clear on whether these pertain to the specific desired action targeted by the intervention, or to the broader objective.

In the sixth column, record the measured progress toward the key target of interest, and in the seventh column, record the related intervention effects—both positive and negative.

Clinical Objective	Organizational Priority	Desired Action	Intervention Name	Baseline Performance	Target Performance	Actual Performance	Other Effects
Improve heparin prophylaxis in post-op patients	Quality & Safety: reduction in VTE events	Increase orders for post-op heparin prophylaxis	Heparin post-op order set	62% compliance	98% for patients without contraindications	85% compliance in follow up (not yet able to reliably exclude patients with contraindications)	Users indicated intervention had a positive effect on workflow; complained when it was briefly unavailable
			Heparin post-op alert	71% compliance	95% compliance	90% compliance	Users dislike the alert so that many more have begun to use the order set

continued on next page

Worksheet 9-3 *continued*

Clinical Objective	Organizational Priority	Desired Action	Intervention Name	Baseline Performance	Target Performance	Actual Performance	Other Effects
Improve monitoring of heparin for patients on IV heparin	Safety and Efficiency: avoid ADEs, timely lab use (minimize STAT labs)	Increase routine PTT orders for patients prescribed IV heparin	PTT order set	88% compliance	100% compliance when indicated	92% compliance	None
		Increase timely PTT collection by nursing	PTT alert	66% compliance	95% of specimens collected wtihin 1 hour of specified time	84% compliance	Alert has been accompanied by training and workflow enhancements that have improved compliance

Continually Maintain Deployed Interventions, and Enhance Their Value to Users and Impact on CDS Goals and Objectives

Approaches to monitoring and maintaining CDS assets are presented in Chapter 4 and this chapter, and tools such as Worksheet 4-1 can support this work. As you perform these knowledge management activities—and address evaluation results such as outlined in Worksheets 9-2 and 9-3—your CDS Team will make decisions and take actions in collaboration with other stakeholders. While you probably couldn't and shouldn't capture them all in a single log, there will be certain circumstances in managing CDS interventions where you will want to record the process and outcomes for key decisions. Worksheet 9-4 is a sample tool for this purpose that you can adapt to your specific needs.

Worksheet 9-4

Decision Log

Depending on the situation, you might track decisions using different tools and formats. This worksheet is a sample to trigger your thinking about the situations in which you may want to track key decisions and how you might do so.

Clinical Decision Support Objective	Decision Name	Decision Description	Decision Date	Decision Owner	Critical Decision Factors	Impact	Follow-up/ Comments
Reduce preventable allergic reactions	Interruptive allergy alert override	Make coded alert override reason a mandatory field when prescriber overrides an allergy alert	4/25	CPOE alerts committee	Coded reasons necessary to rapidly process data; plan reviewed with end user champions and stakeholders, who agreed to trial this approach to enhance safety	May still get pushback from some physicians, but approach consistent with alerting plan. Will provide communications/support before/during go-live	Revisit user response and log data in 3 months and re-evaluate whether mandatory override reason still necessary

Worksheet 9-5 is, in some respects, a capstone to all the other worksheets presented in this Guide. Its purpose is to help your CDS Team look broadly at your target-focused CDS interventions and results and consider how you might better address your chosen objective—as well as related objectives and goals within your CDS program.

If you use a tool like this, you can revisit earlier worksheets to help you flesh out the enhancement plans. For example, Worksheet 2-1 can be used to update stakeholder goals and objectives, Worksheets 6-2 and 6-3 can help broaden your thinking about how to optimize CDS configuration dimensions, and Worksheets 9-2 and 9-3 can help focus your attention on important remaining clinical and intervention performance gaps.

True to the cyclic nature of CDS-enabled performance improvement, this ending is a beginning for subsequent CDS program enhancement rounds—and iteration through the steps in Parts I and II of this book.

Worksheet 9-5

CDS Program Enhancement Plans

In the first column of Worksheet 9-5, enter the high level goals that give rise to your specific CDS objectives and interventions; for example, as documented in Worksheets 2-1, 5-1, and others. In the second column, record objectives that flow from these goals, as documented on earlier worksheets and gleaned from stakeholder discussions. As you gather these CDS program goals and objectives, be on the lookout for other CDS goals or high-level clinical objectives that might be appropriate to address within your CDS program—after appropriate vetting. In fact, if and when your organization is ready to contemplate significant program enhancements, you can actually begin the next pass through all the steps outlined in this book.

In the third column, list all the interventions you have developed to address each objective; for example, as documented in Worksheet 9-3. For the effectiveness summary in the fourth column, enter the "Actual Performance" information from Worksheet 9-3, and any other pertinent notes from your evaluation. The Issues and Usability summary synthesizes the major issues and opportunities documented in the second column of Worksheet 9-2.

The last column is the punch line for this worksheet. It presents an overview of the next major steps in your approach to specific targeted objectives, and also the CDS program more broadly. It should outline a plan for improving intervention acceptance and use among recipients and effectiveness in achieving target objectives. You can also begin noting additional interventions that might help achieve objectives, as well as additional objectives and goals to tackle based on ongoing dialogue with other stakeholders and any capability enhancements to underlying CIS infrastructure.

As with other worksheets, this one too should be dynamic and reflect over time your evolving CDS program status and enhancement plans. As such, it can be useful for communicating with and engaging deeper support from organizational leadership, end users and other stakeholders.

continued on next page

Worksheet 9-5 *continued*

High-level Clinical Goal	Clinical Objective	Intervention Name	Effectiveness Summary	Issues and Usability Summary	Enhancement Plans
Improve anticoagulation use safety and effectiveness					Given success of initial interventions, will add better adherance to enoxaparin guidelines as objective for next round CDS
	Improve Heparin prophylaxis in post-op patients	Heparin post-op order set	Moderate — 9% improvement		None
		Heparin post-op alert	High — 19% improvement		Add the prophylaxis order to the alert; the action on the alert may improve user satisfaction
	Improve PTT monitoring in patients on IV heparin	PTT order set	Low — 4% but baseline was relatively high		Add header above the PTT order to make it easier to see
		PTT alert	Very high — 28% improvement		Improvements may have been related to increased awareness and in-services; remove alert for now, with careful monitoring of compliance

REFERENCES

1 We learned of this acronym from Mark Granville, Senior Vice President, Client Experience, Healthcare, Thomson Reuters.

2 Liu JLY, Wyatt JC. The case for randomized controlled trials to assess the impact of clinical information systems. *J Am Med Inform Assoc.* 2011 Mar-Apr; 18(2):173-180.

3 Kaplan B. Evaluating informatics applications--some alternative approaches: theory, social interactionism, and call for methodological pluralism. *Int J Med Inform.* 2001; 64:39e56.

4 Payne TH, Hoey PJ, Nichol P, Lovis C. Preparation and use of preconstructed orders, order sets, and order menus in a computerized provider order entry system. *J Am Med Inform Assoc.* 2003 Jul-Aug;1 0(4):322-329.

5 Del Fiol G, Haug PJ, Cimino JJ, Narus SP, Norlin C, Mitchell JA. Effectiveness of topic-specific infobuttons: a randomized controlled trial. *J Am Med Inform Assoc.* 2008 Nov-Dec; 15(6):752-759.

6 Bennett KJ, Steen C. Electronic medical record customization and the impact upon chart completion rates. *Fam Med.* 2010 May; 42(5):338-342.

7 Paterno MD, Maviglia SM, Gorman PN, Seger DL, Yoshida E, Seger AC, Bates DW, Gandhi TK. Tiering drug-drug interaction alerts by severity increases compliance rates. *J Am Med Inform Assoc.* 2009 Jan-Feb; 16(1):40-46.

8 Kaushal R, Kern LM, Barrón Y, Quaresimo J, Abramson EL. Electronic prescribing improves medication safety in community-based office practices. *J Gen Intern Med.* 2010 Jun; 25(6):530-536.

9 Sittig DF, Krall MA, Dykstra RH, et al. A survey of factors affecting clinician acceptance of clinical decision support. *BMC Med Inform Decis Mak.* 2006; 6:6.

10 Boonstra A, Broekhuis M. Barriers to the acceptance of electronic medical records by physicians from systematic review to taxonomy and interventions. *BMC Health Serv Res.* 2010 Aug 6; 10:231.

11 Menachemi N, Ettel DL, Brooks RG, et al. Charting the use of electronic health records and other information technologies among child health providers. *BMC Pediatr.* 2006; 6:21.

12 Jensen J. The effects of Computerized Provider Order Entry on medication turn-around time: a time-to-first dose study at the Providence Portland Medical Center. *AMIA Annu Symp Proc.* 2006: 384-388.

13 Overhage JM, Perkins S, Tierney WM, et al. Controlled trial of direct physician order entry: effects on physicians' time utilization in ambulatory primary care internal medicine practices. *J Am Med Inform Assoc.* 2001; 8(4):361-371.

14 McCoy AB, Waitman LR, Gadd CS, Danciu I, Smith JP, Lewis JB, Schildcrout JS, Peterson JF. A computerized provider order entry intervention for medication safety during acute kidney injury: a quality improvement report. *Am J Kidney Dis.* 2010 Nov; 56(5):832-41.

15 Feldstein AC, Smith DH, Robertson NR, Kovach CA, Soumerai SB, Simon SR, Sittig DF, Laferriere DS, Kalter M. In: Henriksen K, Battles JB, Marks ES, Lewin DI, editors. Decision Support System Design and Implementation for Outpatient Prescribing: The Safety in Prescribing Study. Advances in Patient Safety: From Research to Implementation (Volume 3: Implementation Issues). Rockville (MD): Agency for Healthcare Research and Quality (US); 2005 Feb.

16 Weingart SN, Toth M, Sands DZ, et al. Physicians' decisions to override computerized drug alerts in primary care. *Arch Intern Med.* 2003; 163(21):2625-2631.

17 Shah NR, Seger AC, Seger DL, et al. Improving acceptance of computerized prescribing alerts in ambulatory care. *J Am Med Inform Assoc.* 2006; 13(1):5-11.

18 East TD, Henderson S, Pace NL, et al. Knowledge engineering using retrospective review of data: a useful technique or merely data dredging? *Int J Clin Monit Comput.* 1991-1992; 8(4):259-262.

19 Lin CP, Payne TH, Nichol WP, et al. Evaluating clinical decision support systems: monitoring CPOE order check override rates in the Department of Veterans Affairs' computerized patient record system. *J Am Med Inform Assoc.* 2008; 15(5):620-626.

20 Chused A, Kuperman GJ, Stetson PD. Alert override reasons: A failure to communicate. *AMIA Annu Symp Proc.* 2008: 111-115.

21 van der Sijs H, Aarts J, van Gelder T, et al. Turning off frequently overridden drug alerts: limited opportunities for doing it safely. *J Am Med Inform Assoc.* 2008; 15:439-448.

22 Fleming NS, Ogola G, Ballard DJ. Implementing a standardized order set for community-acquired pneumonia: impact on mortality and cost. *Jt Comm J Qual Patient Saf.* 2009 Aug; 35(8):414-421.

23 Bates DW, Leape LL, Cullen DJ, et al. Effect of computerized physician order entry and a team intervention on prevention of serious medication errors. *JAMA*. 1998; 280(15):1311-1316.

24 Hicks LS, Sequist TD, Ayanian JZ, et al. Impact of computerized decision support on blood pressure management and control: a randomized controlled trial. *J Gen Intern Med*. 2008; 23(4):429-41.

25 Strom BL, Schinnar R, Aberra F, Bilker W, Hennessy S, Leonard CE, Pifer E. Unintended effects of a computerized physician order entry nearly hard-stop alert to prevent a drug interaction: a randomized controlled trial. *Arch Intern Med*. 2010 Sep 27;170(17):1578-1583.

26 Selvan MS, Sittig DF, Thomas EJ, Arnold CC, Murphy RE, Shabot MM. Improving erythropoietin-stimulating agent administration in a multihospital system through quality improvement initiatives: a pre-post comparison study. *J Patient Saf*. 2011 Sep; 7(3):127-31.

27 Agency for Healthcare Research and Quality. *Monitoring and Evaluating Medicaid Fee-for-Service Care Management Programs: A User's Guide*. AHRQ Publication No. 08-0012. 2007 Nov. http://www.ahrq.gov/qual/medicaidffs/, accessed September 9, 2011.

28 Nuckols TK, Bell DS, Liu H, et al. Rates and types of events reported to established incident reporting systems in two US hospitals. *Qual Saf Health Care*. 2007; 16(3):164-168.

29 Ferranti J, Horvath MM, Cozart H, et al. Reevaluating the safety profile of pediatrics: a comparison of computerized adverse drug event surveillance and voluntary reporting in the pediatric environment. *Pediatrics*. 2008; 121(5): e1201-1207.

30 Osheroff, JA, ed. Improving medication use and outcomes with CDS, a step by step guide. HIMSS. 2009.

31 Nebeker JR, Barach P, Samore MH. Clarifying adverse drug events: a clinician's guide to terminology, documentation, and reporting. *Ann Intern Med*. 2004; 140(10):795-801.

32 Classen DC, Pestotnik SL, Evans RS, et al. Computerized surveillance of adverse drug events in hospital patients. *JAMA*. 1991; 266(20):2847-2851.

33 Rozich JD, Haraden CR, Resar RK. Adverse drug event trigger tool: a practical methodology for measuring medication related harm. *Qual Saf Health Care*. 2003; 12(3):194-200.

34 Institute for Healthcare Improvement. *Trigger tool for Measuring Adverse Drug Events*. http://www.ihi.org/ knowledge/Pages/Tools/ TriggerToolforMeasuringAdverseDrugEvents.aspx . Accessed September 7, 2011.

35 Institute for Healthcare Improvement. *IHI Global Trigger Tool for Measuring Adverse Events*. http://www.ihi.org/ knowledge/Pages/Tools/ IHIGlobalTriggerToolforMeasuringAEs.aspx, accessed September 7, 2011.

36 Sittig DF, Campbell EM, Guappone K, et al. Recommendations for monitoring and evaluation of in-patient Computer-based Provider Order Entry systems: results of a Delphi survey. *AMIA Annu Symp Proc*. 2007: 671-675.

37 Campbell EM, Sittig DF, Ash JS, et al. Types of unintended consequences related to computerized provider order entry. *J Am Med Inform Assoc*. 2006 Sep-Oct; 13(5):547-56.

38 Sittig DF, Singh H. Defining health information technology-related errors: new developments since to err is human. *Arch Intern Med*. 2011 Jul 25;171(14):1281-1284.

39 Institute of Medicine. *Crossing the Quality Chasm: A New Health System for the 21st Century*. http://iom.edu/ Reports/2001/Crossing-the-Quality-Chasm-A-New-Health-System-for-the-21st-Century.aspx accessed 06/13/11.

40 See, for example, Horton LA. *Calculating and Reporting Healthcare Statistics*, 2nd Edition. Chicago: American Health Information Management Association; 2006.

41 See discussion in PA Department of Health's Health Statistics – Technical Assistance Tools of the Trade: http:// www.portal.state.pa.us/portal/server.pt?open=514&objID= 556449&mode=2, accessed June 23, 2011.

42 Teich JM, Merchia PR, Schmiz JL, et al. Effects of computerized physician order entry on prescribing practices. *Arch Intern Med*. 2000; 160(18):2741-2747.

43 Kucher N, Koo S, Quiroz R, et al. Electronic alerts to prevent venous thromboembolism among hospitalized patients. *N Engl J Med*. 2005; 352(10):969-977.

44 Pestotnik SL, Classen DC, Evans RS, et al. Implementing antibiotic practice guidelines through computer-assisted decision support: clinical and financial outcomes. *Ann Intern Med*. 1996 May 15; 124(10):884-890.

45 Horowitz N, Moshkowitz M, Leshno M, et al. Clinical trial: evaluation of a clinical decision-support model for upper abdominal complaints in primary-care practice. *Aliment Pharmacol Ther*. 2007; 26(9):1277-1283.

46 Kaushal R, Jha AK, Franz C, et al. Return on investment for a computerized physician order entry system. *J Am Med Inform Assoc*. 2006; 13(3);261-266.

47 Massachusetts Technology Collaborative. *Saving Lives Saving Money: The Imperative for Computerized Physician Order Entry in Massachusetts Hospitals*. 2008 Feb. http:// www.masstech.org/ehealth/cpoe/cpoe08release.html, Acessed June 17, 2011.

48 Teich JM, Petronzio AM, Gerner JR, Seger DL, Shek C, Fanikos J. An information system to promote intravenous-to-oral medication conversion. *Proc AMIA Symp.* 1999:415-419.

49 Agency for Healthcare Research and Quality. *Reducing and Preventing Adverse Drug Events to Decrease Hospital Costs.* http://www.ahrq.gov/qual/aderia/aderia.htm, Accessed June 17, 2011.

50 See reports cited in this chapter that outline cost benefit analyses, such as: Kaushal et. al. *Return on investment for a computerized physician order entry system*; and Massachusetts Technology Collaborative. *Saving Lives Saving Money: The Imperative for Computerized Physician Order Entry in Massachusetts Hospitals.*

51 The Leapfrog Group. *Leapfrog CPOE Evaluation Tool.* https://www.leapfroghospitalsurvey.org/cpoe/, accessed September 7, 2011.

52 Metzger J, Welebob E, Bates DW, Lipsitz S, Classen DC. Mixed results in the safety performance of computerized physician order entry. *Health Aff (Millwood).* 2010 Apr; 29(4):655-663.

53 Personal communication, David Classen to Jerome Osheroff, September 7, 2011.

54 Calls to systematically capture, analyze and apply results from CDS and HIT implementations include: Leonard KJ, Sittig DF. Improving information technology adoption and implementation through the identification of appropriate benefits: creating IMPROVE-IT. *J Med Internet Res.* 2007; 9(2):e9; and Osheroff JA, Teich JM, Middleton B, et al. A roadmap for national action on clinical decision support. *J Am Med Inform Assoc.* 2007; 14(2):141-145. – see Strategic Objective E on assessing and refining national experience with CDS.

55 For an example of the compliexities associated with presenting evaluation data, and an attribution for this quote, see: McKee M. Not everything that counts can be counted; not everything that can be counted counts. *BMJ.* 2004; 328(7432):153. http://www.bmj.com/cgi/content/short/328/7432/153, Accessed June 17, 2011.

56 For example, through your local patient safety organization (PSO). For information about PSOs, see the AHRQ PSO website: http://www.pso.ahrq.gov/. Accessed September 7, 2011.

57 See: Common Formats for Patient Safety Data Collection and Event Reporting. Federal Register; *A Notice by the Agency for Healthcare Research and Quality on 10/22/2010.* http://federalregister.gov/a/2010-26667. Accessed September 7, 2011.

58 See website for the National Coordinating Council for Medication Error Reporting and Prevention: http://www.nccmerp.org/, and the page on the medication error taxonomy: http://www.nccmerp.org/pdf/taxo2001-07-31.pdf. Both accessed September 7, 2011.

59 The Institute for Safe Medication Practices. *Frequently Asked Questions (FAQ).* http://www.ismp.org/faq.asp# Question_6, Accessed June 17, 2011.

60 Callen J, Braithwaite J, Westbrook JI. The importance of medical and nursing sub-cultures in the implementation of clinical information systems. *Methods Inf Med.* 2009;48(2):196-202.

61 For more information, see the AHRQ National Resource Center for Health IT's webpage: "Using Time and Motion Studies to Measure the Impact of Health IT on Clinical Workflow," http://healthit.ahrq.gov/portal/server.pt/ community/health_it_tools_and_resources/919/using_ time_and_motion_studies_to_measure_the_impact_of_ health_it_on_clinical_workflow/24072. Accessed September 8, 2011.

62 For example, surveys provided under AHRQ's Consumer Assessment of Healthcare Providers and Systems (CAHPS) program. https://www.cahps.ahrq.gov. Accessed September 8, 2011.

63 See, for example, the Southeast Texas Medical Associates (SETMA) webpage, "Public Reporting of Provider Performance on Quality Measures" (http://www.setma.com/ PublicReporting.cfm - accessed August 18, 2011), as well as links from the "Public Reporting" tab on this webpage to further details on SETMA physician performance on diabetes and other measures, and CDS interventions used in the SETMA practice to enhance performance on these measures.

Epilogue

A Call for Collaboration

Clinical decision support tools and approaches offer tremendous potential for accelerating the global movement toward better care quality, safety, cost and efficiency. The HIMSS CDS Guidebook Series[1] aims to help translate this promise into effective action and desirable results by providing practical guidance for CDS implementers and other stakeholders in CDS-enabled care improvements. Successive installments have enlarged the international pool contributing to—and benefiting from—these CDS best practice syntheses, and have served as launching pads for further collaboration toward advancing CDS approaches and deployments.

This book is the latest manifestation of this broadening community. The processes to develop it engaged over 100 individual contributors and organizational collaborators (many who had not contributed to prior guidebooks), and likewise is a springboard for further joint effort to accelerate CDS use, usefulness and value. For example, a follow-on initiative is focused on a strategic objective outlined in the ONC-commissioned Roadmap for National Action on Clinical Decision Support.[2]

More specifically, individuals and organizations that participated in developing this current Guide (along with others less directly involved) are coming together to address the CDS Roadmap Objective E calling for efforts to:

> "Assess and refine the national experience with CDS by systematically capturing, organizing, and examining existing deployments. Share lessons learned and

use them to continually enhance implementation best practices."

Scores of stakeholders—including workgroups within three co-publishers of this current guidebook (Society of Hospital Medicine, Scottsdale Institute, and HIMSS)—have formed a collaborative to create mechanisms for documenting and sharing target-focused CDS intervention configurations and their results. This work centers on high-profile improvement objectives—such as performance measures central to Meaningful Use and value-based purchasing—that are top priorities for many care delivery organizations. Importantly, collaborators include information system suppliers in addition to implementers; this is intended to foster the closer collaboration between these interdependent stakeholders that we advocate throughout this Guide.

The collaborative is leveraging models and content in this Guide (such as the CDS Five Rights framework and related intervention configuration Worksheets 6-2 and 6-3) to underpin its work. The hypothesis shared by participants is that this documentation process will advance local CDS efforts on improvement imperatives by highlighting areas where additional 'what, who, when, how and where' CDS options can be brought to bear. Similarly, examining CDS strategies that peers have tried (and results they have achieved) should enhance learning and accelerate local efforts toward the same objectives. More broadly, systematically analyzing many sets of strategies and results for the same targets could help extend the guidance in this Guide by providing more specific best practices for improving specific outcomes. You can learn more about this collaborative from an online description.[3]

We believe that for CDS, 'state of the art' should be a dynamic process driven by collaborative exploration, discovery, innovation, measurement and continuing refinement. Echoing the invitation offered in the Preface, we hope you will join this quest. You can do this by joining the initiative outlined above, sending us feedback about the book,* and participating in a conversation on Facebook[†] about how you and others are applying the guidance in this book and strategies for optimizing its practical value.

REFERENCES

1   See online site: www.himss.org/cdsguide for more information about this series. Accessed August 15, 2011.

2   Osheroff JA, Teich JM, Middleton B, et al. A roadmap for national action on clinical decision support. *J Am Med Inform Assoc.* 2007; 14(2):141-145. Available online at: http://www.ncbi.nlm.nih.gov/pmc/articles/PMC2213467/ Accessed June 24, 2011.

3   See the public description for the "CDS for PI Imperatives" Initiative. Available online at: https://sites.google.com/site/cdsforpiimperativespublic. Accessed August 15, 2011.

---

* Send email to cdsguide@himss.org

† Visit www.facebook.com/cdsguidebook to participate in this conversation.

Appendix

Medico-legal Considerations

Liability concerns are often cited as an important consideration in CDS implementation, and even as an outright barrier by some healthcare providers. Risk management and related liability issues surrounding CDS deployments are complex and in flux as CDS and CISs mature. Consultation with legal counsel, peers, the literature and other sources can be very important in avoiding missteps. In the following paragraphs, we outline a few issues that are raised elsewhere this Guide and point to further resources on the topic.

Commonly expressed legal concerns include the fear that a CDS intervention may increase liability exposure for clinicians and healthcare organizations. For example, could an allegation of malpractice be supported by evidence that a clinician ignored a pertinent alert? A review[1] on the topic noted that courts have treated CDS systems in the same way as a textbook that a clinician consults. Courts have permitted clinical practice guidelines to be used as evidence about the standard of care and likely will also admit adherence to clinical decision support systems as similar evidence—*if* an expert attests that the intervention reflected reasonable and customary care. A clinician's departure from the CDS protocols could then be offered as evidence of negligence. It is important to recognize, however, that clinical decision support systems have limitations and a practitioner's actions in exercising independent professional judgment in departing from the suggested protocols may be clinically appropriate in certain situations.

This same review suggests that organizations establish a policy on CDS tools that clarifies this intent to support rather than supplant clinical judgment; you could document this intent within your CDS charter (see Chapter 2) or related policy documents within your CDS program. The review also suggests adding language in contracts with CDS vendors to ensure that the knowledge bases are drawn from nationally recognized sources and regularly updated. Similar considerations presumably apply to organizational responsibility for modifications made to commercial knowledge sources that CDS implementers have acquired. A review on using commercial knowledge bases for CDS has recommended that, "To minimize risk, healthcare organizations create explicit policies and procedures regarding knowledge editing. Such policies should require that rule specifications be documented explicitly and that an identified individual or clinical committee be responsible for the content of the rule. The organization must assure that the edited knowledge is behaving as intended."[2] You can address these recommendations through a robust knowledge management program, as discussed in Chapter 4.

Other liability concerns include how organizations deliver alerts to clinicians and manage circumstances surrounding alert firing. These processes may include tracking how clinicians respond to the alert and whether and how they can indicate override reasons (see discussion in Chapter 9 about alerting and override reasons). For example, practitioners may intentionally or accidentally ignore recommendations provided via CDS alerts. If the alert is based on incomplete clinical data or outdated treatment protocols, the clinician may appropriately believe that the suggested action should be disregarded.

Alternatively, a clinician may become insensitive to frequent, unhelpful prompts (see discussion about alert fatigue in Chapter 7). Knowledge management and measurement approaches (discussed in Chapters 4 and 9) can help preserve the context in which a specific CDS intervention instance appears in workflow, including the CDS content state at the time an intervention about a specific patient was delivered. If questions are raised about a clinician's decision involving a CDS intervention, for example, in a malpractice allegation, these techniques may help establish the exact intervention context to help others understand why a particular decision was made.

A key issue is whether alert triggers, messages delivered, user response and the like become part of the legal medical record and/or are retained in an archive or log. This decision has implications for discovery in a medical malpractice action.

Organizations have addressed in various ways the fear that such detailed information about alert firing will be subject to discovery in a medical malpractice action and used *against* clinicians or the organization. Some healthcare providers inactivate CDS intervention logging, thus removing this documentation source that might be discoverable in a medical malpractice action. This approach potentially limits an organization's ability to learn from and improve CDS intervention use (as discussed in Chapter 9). Others keep such logs, but explicitly declare through policies that they are not part of the legal medical record (that is, to be used only for internal quality improvement initiatives) and thus, theoretically, not discoverable. However, it is questionable whether such information (which often is referred to as *metadata*) can be prevented from discovery. State law, which governs most malpractice litigation, varies as to the discoverability and permissibility of introducing metadata into litigation.

Keep in mind also that faulty CDS is itself a potential source of liability, and careful testing before and during the implementation period—using approaches such as outlined in Chapters 7 and 8—is a key to managing this risk.

Although legal discussions about CDS most commonly address liability questions related to *using* CDS tools, they also frequently raise the issue of potential liability for *not using* (or *not making available*) such tools.[3,4] In a malpractice action, a claimant needs to prove that there was a deviation from the standard of care—as practiced in a particular geographic area—that causes harm. Some commentators have suggested that the use of CDS in a given area may generally *increase* the clinical standard of care because evidence (outlined in Chapter 1) indicates that such systems can improve care quality and reduce medical errors. From this perspective, the availability—but failure to adopt and use—a CDS program may *increase* malpractice liability exposure because its absence might be cited in an action as evidence that an organization did not use available technology to prevent patient harm.

The sources just cited note that there is precedent for such negligence applying even in cases in which the technology is not yet widely adopted, as could be argued for some CDS intervention types such as alerts in computerized practitioner order entry (CPOE). Moreover, there is evidence in the scientific literature suggesting that physicians who have adopted electronic health records are less likely to have a paid malpractice liability claim than those who have not, although the study did not analyze the use of CDS within the electronic health records (EHRs).[5]

In summary, this book outlines a careful approach to selecting, configuring, testing, deploying, monitoring and maintaining CDS interventions to improve care processes and outcomes. Although not intended in any way to represent legal advice, this systematic approach hopefully will be a useful component of your organization's efforts to minimize CDS-related liability risks. As we noted earlier, legal issues around CDS are complex and in flux, so you should consult legal counsel specializing in health information and technology issues as appropriate.

Peers in other organizations can also be a useful source of input—through your personal network, as well as through informatics-related professional society listservs or communities (such as those provided by HIMSS, AMDIS, AMIA and the Scottsdale Institute). In addition to the references just cited, other literature sources may also provide useful background for legal considerations in CDS. A starting point for such exploration may include the following:

- American Health Information Management Association (AHIMA). *The New Electronic Discovery Civil Rule.* Available online at: http://library.ahima.org/xpedio/groups/public/documents/ahima/bok1_031860.hcsp?dDocName=bok1_031860. Accessed October 21, 2011.
- Berner ES. Ethical and legal issues in the use of clinical decision support systems. *J Healthc Inf Manag.* 2002; 16(4):34-37.
- Fox J, Thomson R. Clinical decision support systems: a discussion of quality, safety and legal liability issues. Proc AMIA Symp. 2002: 265-269.
- Greenberg M, Ridgely MS. Clinical decision support and malpractice risk. *JAMA.* 2011; 306(1):90-91.

- Hoffman S, Podgurski. E-Health hazards: provider liability and electronic health record systems. *Berkeley Technology Law Journal.* 2009; 24:4; 1523-1582. Available online at: http://www.btlj.org/data/articles/24_4/1523_Hoffman.pdf. Accessed October 21, 2011.
- Klein SR. Welcome to the digital age: New federal e-discovery rules require digital records management. *J Healthc Inf Manag.* 2007; 21:6-7. Available online at: http://www.jhimdigital.org/jhim/2007fall/?pg=8. Accessed October 21, 2011.
- Miller RA. Legal issues related to medical decision support systems. *Int J Clin Monit Comput.* 1989; 6(2):75-80.
- Miller RA, Gardner RM. Recommendations for responsible monitoring and regulation of clinical software systems. *J Am Med Inform Assoc.* 1997; 4(6):442-457.

Further reassurance regarding CDS intervention use is expected to come from the establishment of quality standards for software systems and knowledge bases, and health IT certification efforts based on such standards.[6]

REFERENCES

1 Klein SR, Jones JW. Clinical decision support programs can be risky business. *J Healthc Inf Manag.* 2007; 21(2):15-17.

2 Kuperman GJ, Reichley RM, Bailey TC. Using commercial knowledge bases for clinical decision support: opportunities, hurdles, and recommendations. *J Am Med Inform Assoc.* 2006; 13(4):369-371.

3 Annas GJ. The patient's right to safety – improving the quality of care through litigation against hospitals. *N Engl J Med.* 2006 May 11; 354(19):2063-2066.

4 Miller RA, Miller SM. Legal and Regulatory Issues Related to the User of Clinical Software in Health Care Delivery. Greenes RA, editor. *Clinical Decision Support: The Road Ahead.* London: Elsevier. 2007; 423-444; and Appendix B: Medico-legal considerations with CDS.

5 Virapongse A, Bates DW, Shi P, et al. Electronic health records and malpractice claims in office practice. *Annals Int Med.* 2008; 168(21):2362-2367.

6 For example, see discussion about the Health IT Standards Committee charge and activities on the ONC website: http://healthit.hhs.gov/portal/server.pt/community/healthit_hhs_gov__health_it_standards_committee/1271. Accessed September 15, 2011.

Index

"*f*" next to page number denotes a Figure

Printed in the United States
by Baker & Taylor Publisher Services